www.wadsworth.com

www.wadsworth.com is the World Wide Web site for Wadsworth and is your direct source to dozens of online resources.

At *www.wadsworth.com* you can find out about supplements, demonstration software, and student resources. You can also send email to many of our authors and preview new publications and exciting new technologies.

www.wadsworth.com
Changing the way the world learns®

Cases on Public Law
and Public Administration

PHILLIP J. COOPER
University of Vermont

THOMSON

WADSWORTH

Australia • Canada • Mexico • Singapore • Spain
United Kingdom • United States

Publisher: *Clark Baxter*
Executive Editor: *David Tatom*
Assistant Editor: *Amy McGaughey*
Technology Project Manager:
  Melinda Newfarmer
Editorial Assistant: *Reena Thomas*
Marketing Manager: *Janise Fry*
Marketing Assistant: *Mary Ho*
Advertising Project Manager: *Stacey Purviance*
Project Manager, Editorial Production:
  Rita Jaramillo

Print/Media Buyer: *Lisa Claudeanos*
Permissions Editor: *Joohee Lee*
Production Service: *Mary Deeg, Buuji, Inc.*
Copy Editor: *Alan DeNiro, Buuji, Inc.*
Cover Designer: *Brian Salisbury*
Cover Printer: *Webcom*
Compositor: *Buuji, Inc.*
Printer: *Webcom*

For more information about our products,
contact us at:
Thomson Learning Academic Resource Center
1-800-423-0563

For permission to use material from this text
or product, submit a request online at
http://www.thomsonrights.com.
Any additional questions about permissions
can be submitted by email to
thomsonrights@thomson.com.

Library of Congress Control Number:
  2003114336

ISBN 0-534-64321-3

Wadsworth/Thomson Learning
10 Davis Drive
Belmont, CA 94002-3098
USA

Asia
Thomson Learning
5 Shenton Way #01-01
UIC Building
Singapore 068808

Australia/New Zealand
Thomson Learning
102 Dodds Street
Southbank, Victoria 3006
Australia

Canada
Nelson
1120 Birchmount Road
Toronto, Ontario M1K 5G4
Canada

Europe/Middle East/Africa
Thomson Learning
High Holborn House
50/51 Bedford Row
London WC1R 4LR
United Kingdom

Latin America
Thomson Learning
Seneca, 53
Colonia Polanco
11560 Mexico D.F.
Mexico

Spain/Portugal
Paraninfo
Calle Magallanes, 25
28015 Madrid, Spain

Contents

Preface

*P*ublic Law and Public Administration is now in its third edition. Although those who have used the book have been most generous in their reception of it, many have asked about a small casebook to accompany the text. This is a difficult field in which to provide a casebook for a number of reasons that, although perhaps obvious to experienced people in the field, are worth noting.

First, there are so many types and levels of agencies with significantly varying policies and practices that it is difficult to choose how to provide a reasonable and appropriate sample of materials. In particular, the fact that these agencies operate on literally thousands of different statutes means that it is difficult to think in doctrinal terms unless one narrows the field, taking us backward to the days when the subject was only understood in terms of narrow procedural issues.

Second, because these agencies at the federal, state, and local levels operate in a very dynamic environment, it is difficult to keep pace with developments. The case law of public administration, although sometimes coming from the Supreme Court, more often emerges from the lower courts that are so numerous and diverse throughout the nation.

Third, this is not a field in which the neat disciplinary boundaries of the law school curriculum are very helpful. The public law of public administration consists of issues, legal authorities, and cases that some might consider constitutional, statutory interpretation, civil procedure, administrative procedure, torts, contracts, and so on. If we think of the law of public administration from the perspective of the public service professional and not just from the traditional assumptions of disciplines, the picture is more understandable, if not neat and simple.

Fourth, these cases are often lengthy and complex. That should come as no surprise. They often reach the courts after years of development within the agency or many interactions between a local government and an administrative agency. In fact, because these cases are part of what Louis Fisher so accurately calls a "constitutional dialogue," the cases have often been through an agency, through one or more court rulings, and back to an agency, perhaps with some legislative change in the interim and new executive direction as well before they move back again to the courts. Obviously, a volume such as this can only provide brief, hopefully clear and representative, excerpts of a portion of that conversation.

Finally, because there is so much in progress and since there is so much rapid change in the field, such a volume is most helpful if it can be regularly updated. Dick Welna of F.E. Peacock (since acquired by Wadsworth) encouraged the preparation of this volume with the idea that it could be kept updated on a reasonable schedule. This means that it is even more essential to limit what is included in this casebook.

All of that said, I hope this is a useful and helpful collection edited in a way that is as readable as it can be for students who will use it. The effort is to provide brief but adequate introductions to each section; but, for the most part, to let the opinions speak for themselves. This volume does not reproduce the materials provided as appendices in *Public Law and Public Administration* such as the Administrative Procedure Act.

Although this book is clearly designed to be used along with *Public Law and Public Administration*, it will offer additional information and, where appropriate, commentary. It can also be used as a stand-alone text.

In order to keep the book from becoming too lengthy, the decision was made to limit the cases to the core areas of administrative law plus law and public personnel and administrative responsibility. Hence the chapter numbering does not mirror *Public Law and Public Administration, Third Edition*.

A quick note on the methods of editing for the opinions is in order. The decision was made to present fewer opinions, but to provide more of the substance of those cases that have been included than one finds in many casebooks. These are often complex cases, sometimes involving more than one statute and in a number of instances constitutional provisions. They flow out of intricate policies and arise within contexts filled with technical as well as political arguments. The more complete discussion of the case helps to understand these complexities. In some situations, a concise edit of the opinion was used to provide the fact pattern in the introduction to a case rather than summarizing for the student. The introductions are also comments about the case or, in some instances, indications of what happened after the ruling in question. The editing of the opinions was in each case done to highlight the aspect of the case relevant to the particular purpose for its inclusion in the book. Deletions from the original text are not noted by ellipses but any additions are noted in brackets. Quotations in opinions retain their quotation marks, but the citations were removed unless they were particularly important. Interested readers can certainly go to the full opinions if desired. In general, few citations have been left in the opinions. Those cites that remain were included because of the connection they show among important opinions.

Some opinions were included primarily as a basis for discussion and not because they are controlling precedents. For example, the Alabama jails case and the Indian Trust Fund opinion provide excellent opportunities for discussions on the problems confronting judges in dealing with recalcitrant state or federal agencies. The North Miami prohibition on the hiring of smokers is a similar kind of opinion.

Finally, many of the cases were selected because they are quite contemporary and interesting cases, but the effort has been made to balance these with important opinions that reach back some years. However, at the suggestion of reviewers, I have included Chapter 6, which provides a small but important set of historical cases that can be used for students who lack background in fundamental concepts of American constitutional law or in order to compare or contrast with contemporary rulings.

ACKNOWLEDGMENTS

Needless to say, I've been encouraged by many colleagues in the field to prepare this volume. They have all been most kind and supportive notwithstanding the fact that each of them has listened to me repeat the challenges to the project as noted here. John Rohr, Robert Gilmour, and Rick Green have been particularly encouraging. I thank them for their confidence. The reviewers of this manuscript undertook the tedious business of assessing a casebook which requires both patience and knowledge of the case law that has been edited. I appreciate their thoroughness, as well as their appreciation of the fact that no two professors would edit an opinion the same way. These reviewers include Lawrence Becker, California State University at Northridge; Edwin Dover, Western Oregon University; Rick Green, University of Utah; and John Rohr, Virginia Polytechnic Institute. Dick Welna was the editor and publisher at F.E. Peacock when this project began and was encouraging and patient. Amy McGaughey picked up the project when Peacock was acquired by Wadsworth and has been most helpful. Thanks, too, to Mary Deeg on the production work.

1

⚖️

Agency Rulemaking*

O ne of the most complex areas of administrative law today is agency rulemaking. The primary complications have been political (as Chapters 4 and 5 of *Public Law and Public Administration, Third Edition* explain), but those political debates have produced a variety of opinions testing longstanding principles of law. One of the areas of boundary testing has concerned the authority and jurisdiction of agencies as they have been created and empowered by the legislature. After considering those important questions, the chapter will address the binding nature of an agency's rules. It will then turn to cases attempting to clarify the relationships among legislative rules, interpretive rules, and policy statements; as well as the significance of each. Finally, it will address congressional efforts to intervene in rulemaking, first through the legislative veto and later through a somewhat modified approach in the Congressional Review Act.

---

* Related Material in *Public Law and Public Administration, Third Edition*, Chapter 5.

DELEGATION, NONDELEGATION, AND JURISDICTION

The first requirement that an agency must meet in order to issue rules is to demonstrate that it has a proper delegation of authority from the legislature to take such an action. Traditionally, that obligation is met when an agency shows that: (1) it has the substantive authority to act as it has, (2) it has jurisdiction to apply that authority to the particular people or activities it has targeted, and (3) its delegation of authority does not violate the so-called nondelegation doctrine. Once fully established, a substantive rule and the delegation on which it is based are binding on the parties involved and continue until either the delegation or the rule is formally modified.

The Matter of Authority and Jurisdiction

For many years, it was tempting for observers of the regulatory scene to assume that it would be very difficult to constrain major federal agencies acting within their area of specialty, whether legislation clearly established their authority to act or not. However, the effort by the U.S. Food & Drug Administration to regulate tobacco sales and marketing to minors proved that challengers may sometimes prevail even on this basic point.

Food and Drug Administration v. Brown & Williamson Tobacco Corp., 529 U.S. 120 (2000).

INTRODUCTION: Few regulatory battles have raged longer or with greater intensity than the fight over the regulation of cigarettes and other tobacco products.[1] While there were many participants in the train of events that resulted in the assertion by the Food and Drug Administration of regulatory jurisdiction over cigarettes, the key decisionmaker was FDA Commissioner David Kessler. A dual qualified professional with both legal and medical credentials, Dr. Kessler developed the strategy for regulation. In so doing, he was challenging a longstanding political unwillingness to push too hard or directly against the tobacco industry.

There is no question that the FDA has a great deal of substantive regulatory authority under statute to regulate drugs and medical devices, including the power to ban those found to be life threatening. By the 1990s there was no question that the use of cigarettes and other tobacco products was life threatening in a variety of ways. The question then was whether cigarettes fall within

---

1. A. Lee Fritschler, *Smoking and Politics, 4th Ed.* (Englewood Cliffs, NJ: Prentice Hall, 1989).

the meaning of a drug or so-called combination device, a mechanism for administering a drug. If so, then there was a serious question whether the FDA would eventually have to ban cigarettes. Hence, the question of jurisdiction, the ability of an agency to apply its authority in a particular situation, was clearly crucial to the entire national debate over cigarette regulation.

The litigation that emerged challenging the FDA action was extremely basic in that it attacked the FDA claim of authority and jurisdiction over cigarettes and, more generally, tobacco and tobacco products. At the same time, it was extremely complex and sophisticated, much of it grounded in the very fact that the FDA had decided to change course and pursue a policy of direct regulation. In that sense, the tobacco industry was using its own political success at preventing serious policy action as a foundation for its legal case; and it was a successful strategy. In essence, the argument ran, the fact that Congress and the FDA would not take on tobacco earlier was evidence that FDA should not be permitted to do so later.

✷✷✷✷✷

JUSTICE O'CONNOR wrote the opinion for the Court.

This case involves one of the most troubling public health problems facing our Nation today: the thousands of premature deaths that occur each year because of tobacco use. In 1996, the Food and Drug Administration (FDA), after having expressly disavowed any such authority since its inception, asserted jurisdiction to regulate tobacco products. The FDA concluded that nicotine is a "drug" within the meaning of the Food, Drug, and Cosmetic Act (FDCA or Act) and that cigarettes and smokeless tobacco are "combination products" that deliver nicotine to the body. Pursuant to this authority, it promulgated regulations intended to reduce tobacco consumption among children and adolescents. The agency believed that, because most tobacco consumers begin their use before reaching the age of 18, curbing tobacco use by minors could substantially reduce the prevalence of addiction in future generations and thus the incidence of tobacco-related death and disease.

Regardless of how serious the problem an administrative agency seeks to address, however, it may not exercise its authority "in a manner that is inconsistent with the administrative structure that Congress enacted into law." And although agencies are generally entitled to deference in the interpretation of statutes that they administer, a reviewing "court, as well as the agency, must give effect to the unambiguously expressed intent of Congress." *Chevron U.S.A. Inc. v. Natural Resources Defense Council, Inc.,* 467 U.S. 837, 842–843 (1984). In this case, we believe that Congress has clearly precluded the FDA from asserting jurisdiction to regulate tobacco products. Such authority is inconsistent with the intent that Congress has expressed in the FDCA's overall regulatory scheme and in the tobacco-specific legislation that it has enacted subsequent to the FDCA. In light of this clear intent, the FDA's assertion of jurisdiction is impermissible.

I. The FDCA grants the FDA the authority to regulate, among other items, "drugs" and "devices." The Act defines "drug" to include "articles (other than food) intended to affect the structure or any function of the body." It defines "device," in part, as "an instrument, apparatus, implement, machine, contrivance, . . . or other similar or related article, including any component, part, or accessory, which is . . . intended to affect the structure or any function of the body." The Act also grants the FDA the authority to regulate so-called "combination products," which "constitute a combination of a drug, device, or biologic product." The FDA has construed this provision as giving it the discretion to regulate combination products as drugs, as devices, or as both.

On August 11, 1995, the FDA published a proposed rule concerning the sale of cigarettes and smokeless tobacco to children and adolescents. The rule, which included several restrictions on the sale, distribution, and advertisement of tobacco products, was designed to reduce the availability and attractiveness of tobacco products to young people. A public comment period followed, during which the FDA received over 700,000 submissions, more than "at any other time in its history on any other subject."

On August 28, 1996, the FDA issued a final rule entitled "Regulations Restricting the Sale and Distribution of Cigarettes and Smokeless Tobacco to Protect Children and Adolescents." The FDA determined that nicotine is a "drug" and that cigarettes and smokeless tobacco are "drug delivery devices," and therefore it had jurisdiction under the FDCA to regulate tobacco products as customarily marketed—that is, without manufacturer claims of therapeutic benefit. First, the FDA found that tobacco products "'affect the structure or any function of the body'" because nicotine "has significant pharmacological effects." Specifically, nicotine "exerts psychoactive, or mood-altering, effects on the brain" that cause and sustain addiction, have both tranquilizing and stimulating effects, and control weight. Second, the FDA determined that these effects were "intended" under the FDCA because they "are so widely known and foreseeable that [they] may be deemed to have been intended by the manufacturers;" consumers use tobacco products "predominantly or nearly exclusively" to obtain these effects; and the statements, research, and actions of manufacturers revealed that they "have 'designed' cigarettes to provide pharmacologically active doses of nicotine to consumers." Finally, the agency concluded that cigarettes and smokeless tobacco are "combination products" because, in addition to containing nicotine, they include device components that deliver a controlled amount of nicotine to the body.

Having resolved the jurisdictional question, the FDA next explained the policy justifications for its regulations, detailing the deleterious health effects associated with tobacco use. It found that tobacco consumption was "the single leading cause of preventable death in the United States." The FDA found that 82% of adult smokers had their first cigarette before the age of 18, and more than half had already become regular smokers by that age. The FDA accordingly concluded that if "the number of children and adolescents who begin tobacco use can be substantially diminished, tobacco-related illness can be correspondingly reduced because data suggest that anyone who does not begin smoking in childhood or adolescence is unlikely ever to begin."

II. The FDA's assertion of jurisdiction to regulate tobacco products is founded on its conclusions that nicotine is a "drug" and that cigarettes and smokeless tobacco are "drug delivery devices." Again, the FDA found that tobacco products are "intended" to deliver the pharmacological effects of satisfying addiction, stimulation and tranquilization, and weight control because those effects are foreseeable to any reasonable manufacturer, consumers use tobacco products to obtain those effects, and tobacco manufacturers have designed their products to produce those effects. As an initial matter, respondents take issue with the FDA's reading of "intended." We need not resolve this [arguments over the term "intended"], however, because the FDA's claim to jurisdiction contravenes the clear intent of Congress.

A threshold issue is the appropriate framework for analyzing the FDA's assertion of authority to regulate tobacco products. Because this case involves an administrative agency's construction of a statute that it administers, our analysis is governed by *Chevron U.S.A. Inc. v. Natural Resources Defense Council, Inc.*, 467 U.S. 837 (1984). Under *Chevron*, a reviewing court must first ask "whether Congress has directly spoken to the precise question at issue." If Congress has done so, the inquiry is at an end; the court "must give effect to the unambiguously expressed intent of Congress." But if Congress has not specifically addressed the question, a reviewing court must respect the agency's construction of the statute so long as it is permissible. Such deference is justified because "the responsibilities for assessing the wisdom of such policy choices and resolving the struggle between competing views of the public interest are not judicial ones" and because of the agency's greater familiarity with the ever-changing facts and circumstances surrounding the subjects regulated, see *Rust v. Sullivan,* 500 U.S. 173, 187 (1991).

In determining whether Congress has specifically addressed the question at issue, a reviewing court should not confine itself to examining a particular statutory provision in isolation. The meaning—or ambiguity—of certain words or phrases may only become evident when placed in context. It is a "fundamental canon of statutory construction that the words of a statute must be read in their context and with a view to their place in the overall statutory scheme." A court must therefore interpret the statute "as a symmetrical and coherent regulatory scheme," and "fit, if possible, all parts into an harmonious whole." Similarly, the meaning of one statute may be affected by other Acts, particularly where Congress has spoken subsequently and more specifically to the topic at hand. In addition, we must be guided to a degree by common sense as to the manner in which Congress is likely to delegate a policy decision of such economic and political magnitude to an administrative agency.

With these principles in mind, we find that Congress has directly spoken to the issue here and precluded the FDA's jurisdiction to regulate tobacco products. Viewing the FDCA as a whole, it is evident that one of the Act's core objectives is to ensure that any product regulated by the FDA is "safe" and "effective" for its intended use. In its rulemaking proceeding, the FDA quite exhaustively documented that "tobacco products are unsafe," "dangerous," and "cause great pain and suffering from illness." It stated that "more than 400,000 people die each year from tobacco-related illnesses, such as cancer, respiratory illnesses, and heart disease, often suffering long and painful deaths," and that "tobacco alone kills more people each year in the United States than acquired immunodeficiency syndrome (AIDS), car accidents, alcohol, homicides, illegal drugs, suicides, and fires, combined." Indeed, the FDA characterized smoking as "a pediatric disease" because "one out of every three young people who become regular smokers . . . will die prematurely as a result."

These findings logically imply that, if tobacco products were "devices" under the FDCA, the FDA would be required to remove them from the market. [W]ere tobacco products within the FDA's jurisdiction, the Act would deem them misbranded devices that could not be introduced into interstate commerce.

Second, the FDCA requires the FDA to place all devices that it regulates into one of three classifications. [T]he agency would have to place cigarettes and smokeless tobacco in Class III because, even after the application of the Act's available controls, they would "present a potential unreasonable risk of illness or injury." Under these provisions, the FDA would be prohibited from approving an application for premarket approval without "a showing of reasonable assurance that such device is safe under the conditions of use prescribed, recommended, or suggested on the labeling thereof."

The FDCA's misbranding and device classification provisions therefore make evident that were the FDA to regulate cigarettes and smokeless tobacco, the Act would require the agency to ban them. In fact, based on these provisions, the FDA itself has previously taken the position that if tobacco products were within its jurisdiction, "they would have to be removed from the market because it would be impossible to prove they were safe for their intended use."

Congress, however, has foreclosed the removal of tobacco products from the market. A provision of the United States Code currently in force states that "the marketing of tobacco constitutes one of the greatest basic industries of the United States with ramifying activities which directly affect interstate and foreign commerce at every point, and stable conditions therein are necessary to the general welfare." More importantly, Congress has directly addressed the problem of tobacco and health through legislation on six occasions since 1965. Nonetheless, Congress stopped well short of ordering a ban. Congress' decisions to regulate labeling and advertising and to adopt the express policy of protecting "commerce and the national economy . . . to the maximum extent" reveal its intent that tobacco products remain on the market. Indeed, the collective premise of these statutes is that cigarettes and smokeless tobacco will continue to be sold in the United States. A ban of tobacco products by the FDA would therefore plainly contradict congressional policy.

The FDA apparently recognized this dilemma and concluded, somewhat ironically, that tobacco products are actually "safe" within the meaning of the FDCA. In promulgating its regulations, the agency conceded that "tobacco products are unsafe, as that term is conventionally understood." Nonetheless, the FDA reasoned that, in determining whether a device is safe under the Act, it must consider "not only the risks presented by a product but also any of the countervailing effects of use of that product, including the consequences of not permitting the product to be marketed." Applying this standard, the FDA found that, because of the high level of addiction among tobacco users, a ban would likely be "dangerous."

It may well be, as the FDA asserts, that "these factors must be considered when developing a regulatory scheme that achieves the best public health result for these products." But the FDA's judgment that leaving tobacco products on the market "is more effective in achieving public health goals than a ban" is no substitute for the specific safety determinations required by the FDCA's various operative provisions.

A straightforward reading of this provision dictates that the FDA must weigh the probable therapeutic benefits of the device to the consumer against the probable risk of injury. Applied to tobacco products, the inquiry is whether their purported benefits—satisfying addiction, stimulation and sedation, and weight control—outweigh the risks to health from their use. To accommodate the FDA's conception of safety, however, one must read "any probable benefit to health" to include the benefit to public health stemming from adult consumers' continued use of tobacco products, even though the reduction of tobacco use is the raison d'etre of the regulations. In other words, the FDA is forced to contend that the very evil it seeks to combat is a "benefit to health." This is implausible.

The FDA's conception of safety is also incompatible with the FDCA's misbranding provision. Although banning a particular product might be detrimental to public health in aggregate, the product could still be "dangerous to health" when used as directed. Section 352(j) focuses on dangers to the consumer from use of the product, not those stemming from the agency's remedial measures.

Consequently, the analogy made by the FDA and the dissent to highly toxic drugs used in the treatment of various cancers is unpersuasive. Although "dangerous" in some sense, these drugs are safe within the meaning of the Act because, for certain patients, the therapeutic benefits outweigh the risk of harm. Accordingly, such drugs cannot properly be described as "dangerous to health" under 21 U.S.C. §352(j). The same is not true for tobacco products.

The FDA, consistent with the FDCA, may clearly regulate many "dangerous" products without banning them. Indeed, virtually every drug or device poses dangers under certain conditions. What the FDA may not do is conclude that a drug or device cannot be used safely for any therapeutic purpose and yet, at the same time, allow that product to remain on the market.

In determining whether Congress has spoken directly to the FDA's authority to regulate tobacco, we must also consider in greater detail the tobacco-specific legislation that Congress has enacted over the past 35 years. Congress has enacted six separate pieces of legislation since 1965 addressing the problem of tobacco use and human health. Those statutes, among other things, require that health warnings appear on all packaging and in all print and outdoor advertisements; prohibit the advertisement of tobacco products through "any medium of electronic communication" subject to regulation by the Federal Communications Commission (FCC); require the Secretary of Health and Human Services (HHS) to report every three years to Congress on research findings concerning "the addictive property of tobacco;" and make States' receipt of certain federal block grants contingent on their making it unlawful "for any manufacturer, retailer, or distributor of tobacco products to sell or distribute any such product to any individual under the age of 18."

In adopting each statute, Congress has acted against the backdrop of the FDA's consistent and repeated statements that it lacked authority under the FDCA to regulate tobacco absent claims of therapeutic benefit by the manufacturer. In fact, on several occasions over this period, and after the health consequences of tobacco use and nicotine's pharmacological effects had become well known, Congress considered and rejected bills that would have granted the FDA such jurisdiction. Congress has created a distinct regulatory scheme to address the problem of tobacco and health, and that scheme, as presently constructed, precludes any role for the FDA.

Not only did Congress reject the proposals to grant the FDA jurisdiction, but it explicitly preempted any other regulation of cigarette labeling: "No statement relating to smoking and health, other than the statement required by . . . this Act, shall be required on any cigarette package." Further, the Federal Cigarette Labeling and Advertising Act (FCLAA) evidences Congress' intent to preclude any administrative agency from exercising significant policymaking authority on the subject of smoking and health.

In 1977, ASH [Action on Smoking and Health] filed a citizen petition requesting that the FDA regulate cigarettes, citing many of the same grounds that motivated the FDA's rulemaking here. In denying ASH's petition, FDA Commissioner Kennedy stated that "the interpretation of the Act by FDA consistently has been that cigarettes are not a drug unless health claims are made by the vendors." After the matter proceeded to litigation, the FDA argued in its brief to the Court of Appeals that "cigarettes are not comprehended within the statutory definition of the term 'drug' absent objective evidence that vendors represent or intend that their products be used as a drug."

Taken together, these actions by Congress over the past 35 years preclude an interpretation of the FDCA that grants the FDA jurisdiction to regulate tobacco products. We do not rely on Congress' failure to act—its consideration and rejection of bills that would have given the FDA this authority—in reaching this conclusion. To the contrary, Congress has enacted several statutes addressing the particular subject of tobacco and health, creating a distinct regulatory scheme for cigarettes and smokeless tobacco. In doing so, Congress has persistently acted to preclude a meaningful role for any administrative agency in making policy on the subject of tobacco and health.

Finally, our inquiry into whether Congress has directly spoken to the precise question at issue is shaped, at least in some measure, by the nature of the question presented. Deference under *Chevron* [See Chapter 3] to an agency's construction of a statute that it administers is premised on the theory that a statute's ambiguity constitutes an implicit delegation from Congress to the agency to fill in the statutory gaps. In extraordinary cases, however, there may be reason to hesitate before concluding that Congress has intended such an implicit delegation.

Owing to its unique place in American history and society, tobacco has its own unique political history. Congress, for better or for worse, has created a distinct regulatory scheme for tobacco products, squarely rejected proposals to give the FDA jurisdiction over tobacco, and repeatedly acted to preclude any agency from exercising significant policymaking authority in the area. Given this history and the breadth of the authority that the FDA has asserted, we are obliged to defer not to the agency's expansive construction of the statute, but to Congress' consistent judgment to deny the FDA this power.

By no means do we question the seriousness of the problem that the FDA has sought to address. Nonetheless, no matter how "important, conspicuous, and controversial" the issue, and regardless of how likely the public is to hold the Executive Branch politically accountable, an administrative agency's power to regulate in the public interest must always be grounded in a valid grant of authority from Congress. [I]t is plain that Congress has not given the FDA the authority that it seeks to exercise here. For these reasons, the judgment of the Court of Appeals for the Fourth Circuit is affirmed.

JUSTICE BREYER wrote a dissent joined by STEVENS, SOUTER, and GINSBURG.

The Food and Drug Administration (FDA) has the authority to regulate "articles (other than food) intended to affect the structure or any function of the body. . . ." Unlike the majority, I believe that tobacco products fit within this statutory language.

In its own interpretation, the majority nowhere denies the following two salient points. First, tobacco products fall within the scope of this statutory definition, read literally. Cigarettes achieve their mood-stabilizing effects through the interaction of the chemical nicotine and the cells of the central nervous system. Both cigarette manufacturers and smokers alike know of, and desire, that chemically induced result. Hence, cigarettes are "intended to affect" the body's "structure" and "function," in the literal sense of these words. Second, the statute's basic purpose—the protection of public health—supports the inclusion of cigarettes within its scope. Unregulated tobacco use causes "more than 400,000 people [to] die each year from tobacco-related illnesses, such as cancer, respiratory illnesses, and heart disease." Indeed, tobacco products kill more people in this country every year "than . . . AIDS, car accidents, alcohol, homicides, illegal drugs, suicides, and fires, combined."

Despite the FDCA's literal language and general purpose, the majority nonetheless reads the statute as excluding tobacco products for two basic reasons: (1) the FDCA does not "fit" the case of tobacco because the statute requires the FDA to prohibit dangerous drugs or devices (like cigarettes) outright, and the agency concedes that simply banning the sale of cigarettes is not a proper remedy; and (2) Congress has enacted other statutes, which, when viewed in light of the FDA's long history of denying tobacco-related jurisdiction and considered together with Congress' failure explicitly to grant the agency tobacco-specific authority, demonstrate that Congress did not intend for the FDA to exercise jurisdiction over tobacco.

In my view, neither of these propositions is valid. Rather, the FDCA does not significantly limit the FDA's remedial alternatives. And the later statutes do not tell the FDA it cannot exercise jurisdiction, but simply leave FDA jurisdictional law where Congress found it.

In short, I believe that the most important indicia of statutory meaning—language and purpose—along with the FDCA's legislative history are sufficient to establish that the FDA has authority to regulate tobacco. The statute-specific arguments against jurisdiction that the tobacco companies and the majority rely upon are based on erroneous assumptions and, thus, do not defeat the jurisdiction-supporting thrust of the FDCA's language and purpose. The inferences that the majority draws from later legislative history are not persuasive, since one can just as easily infer from the later laws that Congress did not intend to affect the FDA's tobacco-related authority at all. And the fact that the FDA changed its mind about the scope of its own jurisdiction is legally insignificant because the agency's reasons for changing course are fully justified. Finally, the degree of accountability that likely will attach to the FDA's action in this case should alleviate any concern that Congress, rather than an administrative agency, ought to make this important regulatory decision.

After studying the FDCA's history, experts have written that the statute "is a purposefully broad delegation of discretionary powers by Congress," and that, in a sense, the FDCA "must be regarded as a constitution" that "establishes general principles" and "permits implementation within broad parameters" so that the FDA can "implement these objectives through the most effective and efficient controls that can be devised." This Court, too, has said that the "historical expansion of the definition of drug, and the creation of a parallel concept of devices, clearly show . . . that Congress fully intended that the Act's coverage be as broad as its literal language indicates—and equally clearly, broader than any strict medical definition might otherwise allow."

That Congress would grant the FDA such broad jurisdictional authority should surprise no one. In 1938, the President and much of Congress believed that federal administrative agencies needed broad authority and would exercise that authority wisely—a view embodied in much Second New Deal legislation. Nor is it surprising that such a statutory delegation of power could lead after many years to an assertion of jurisdiction that the 1938 legislators might not have expected. Such a possibility is inherent in the very nature of a broad delegation. In 1938, it may well have seemed unlikely that the FDA would ever bring cigarette manufacturers within the FDCA's statutory language by proving that cigarettes produce chemical changes in the body and that the makers "intended" their product chemically to affect the body's "structure" or "function."

But it should not have seemed unlikely that, assuming the FDA decided to regulate and proved the particular jurisdictional prerequisites, the courts would rule such a jurisdictional assertion fully authorized. After all, this Court has read more narrowly phrased statutes to grant what might have seemed even more unlikely assertions of agency jurisdiction.

II. The tobacco companies contend that the FDCA's words cannot possibly be read to mean what they literally say. The statute defines "device," for example, as "an instrument, apparatus, implement, machine, contrivance, implant, in vitro reagent, or other similar or related article . . . intended to affect the structure or any function of the body. . . ." Taken literally, this definition might include everything from room air conditioners to thermal pajamas. The companies argue that, to avoid such a result, the meaning of "drug" or "device" should be confined to medical or therapeutic products, narrowly defined.

The companies may well be right that the statute should not be read to cover room air conditioners and winter underwear. But I do not agree that we must accept their proposed limitation. For one thing, such a cramped reading contravenes the established purpose of the statutory language. For another, the companies' restriction would render the other two "drug" definitions superfluous.

Although I now oversimplify, the FDA has determined that once nicotine enters the body, the blood carries it almost immediately to the brain. Nicotine then binds to receptors on the surface of brain cells, setting off a series of chemical reactions that alter one's mood and produce feelings of sedation and stimulation. Nicotine also increases the number of nicotinic receptors on the brain's surface, and alters its normal electrical activity. And nicotine stimulates the transmission of a natural chemical that "rewards" the body with pleasurable sensations (dopamine), causing nicotine addiction. The upshot is that nicotine stabilizes mood, suppresses appetite, tranquilizes, and satisfies a physical craving that nicotine itself has helped to create—all through chemical action within the body after being metabolized.

The tobacco companies' principal definitional argument focuses upon the statutory word "intended." The companies say that "intended" in this context is a term of art. They assert that the statutory word "intended" means that the product's maker has made an express claim about the effect that its product will have on the body. The FDCA, however, does not use the word "claimed"; it uses the word "intended." And the FDA long ago issued regulations that say the relevant "intent" can be shown not only by a manufacturer's "expressions," but also "by the circumstances surrounding the distribution of the article." Thus, even in the absence of express claims, the FDA has regulated products that affect the body if the manufacturer wants, and knows, that consumers so use the product.

The companies also cannot deny that the evidence of their intent is sufficient to satisfy the statutory word "intended" as the FDA long has interpreted it. In the first place, there was once a time when they actually did make express advertising claims regarding tobacco's mood-stabilizing and weight-reducing properties—and historical representations can portend present expectations. In the late 1920's, for example, the American Tobacco Company urged weight-conscious smokers to "'Reach for a Lucky instead of a sweet.'" The advertisements of R J Reynolds (RJR) emphasized mood stability by depicting a pilot remarking that "'It Takes Steady Nerves To Fly the Mail At Night. . . . That's why I smoke Camels. And I smoke plenty!'" RJR also advertised the stimulating quality of cigarettes, stating in one instance that "'You get a Lift with a Camel,'" and, in another, that Camels are "'A Harmless Restoration of the Flow of Natural Body Energy.'" And claims of medical proof of mildness (and of other beneficial effects) once were commonplace. (Brown & Williamson advertised Kool-brand mentholated cigarettes as "a tonic to hot, tired throats);" Phillip Morris contended that "recognized laboratory tests have conclusively proven the advantage of Phillip Morris;" RJR proclaimed "'For Digestion's sake, smoke Camels. . . ! Camels make mealtime more pleasant—digestion is stimulated—alkalinity increased.'"

Second, even though the companies refused to acknowledge publicly (until only very recently) that the nicotine in cigarettes has chemically induced, and habit-forming, effects, the FDA recently has gained access to solid, documentary evidence proving that cigarette manufacturers have long known tobacco produces these effects within the body through the metabolizing of chemicals, and that they have long wanted their products to produce those effects in this way.

For example, in 1972, a tobacco-industry scientist explained that "'smoke is beyond question the most optimized vehicle of nicotine,'" and "'the cigarette is the most optimized dispenser of smoke.'" That same scientist urged company executives to "'think of the cigarette pack as a storage container for a day's supply of nicotine. . . . Think of the cigarette as a dispenser for a dose unit of nicotine [and] think of a puff of smoke as a vehicle of nicotine.'"

With such evidence, the FDA has more than sufficiently established that the companies "intend" their products to "affect" the body within the meaning of the FDCA.

The majority nonetheless reaches the "inescapable conclusion" that the language and structure of the FDCA as a whole "simply do not fit" the kind of public health problem that tobacco creates. That is because, in the majority's view, the FDCA requires the FDA to ban outright "dangerous" drugs or devices (such as cigarettes); yet, the FDA concedes that an immediate and total cigarette-sale ban is inappropriate.

First, the FDCA permits the FDA to regulate a "combination product"—i.e., a "device" (such as a cigarette) that contains a "drug" (such as nicotine)—under its "device" provisions. And the FDCA's "device" provisions explicitly grant the FDA wide remedial discretion.

The Court points to other statutory subsections which it believes require the FDA to ban a drug or device entirely, even where an outright ban risks more harm than other regulatory responses. But the cited provisions do no such thing. [T]he statute plainly allows the FDA to consider the relative, overall "safety" of a device in light of its regulatory alternatives, and where the FDA has chosen the least dangerous path, i.e., the safest path, then it can—and does—provide a "reasonable assurance" of "safety" within the meaning of the statute. A good football helmet provides a reasonable assurance of safety for the player even if the sport itself is still dangerous. And the safest regulatory choice by definition offers a "reasonable" assurance of safety in a world where the other alternatives are yet more dangerous.

In any event, it is not entirely clear from the statute's text that a Class III categorization would require the FDA affirmatively to withdraw from the market dangerous devices, such as cigarettes, which are already widely distributed.

[The] "misbranding" language [of the FDCA] is not determinative. [S]urely the agency can determine that a substance is comparatively "safe" whenever it would be less dangerous to make the product available than suddenly to withdraw it from the market. Indeed, the FDA already seems to have taken this position when permitting distribution of toxic drugs, such as poisons used for chemotherapy, that are dangerous for the user but are not deemed "dangerous to health" in the relevant sense.

The statute's language, then, permits the agency to choose remedies consistent with its basic purpose—the overall protection of public health.

[E]xperience counsels against an overly rigid interpretation of the FDCA that is divorced from the statute's overall health-protecting purposes. A different set of words, added to the FDCA in 1958 by the Delaney Amendment, provides that "no [food] additive shall be deemed to be safe if it is found [after appropriate tests] to induce cancer in man or animal." The FDA once interpreted this language as requiring it to ban any food additive, no matter how small the amount, that appeared in any food product if that additive was ever found to induce cancer in any animal, no matter how large a dose needed to induce the appearance of a single carcinogenic cell. This interpretation—which in principle could have required the ban of everything from herbal teas to mushrooms—actually led the FDA to ban saccharine, though this extremely controversial regulatory response never took effect because Congress enacted, and has continually renewed, a law postponing the ban.

In my view, where linguistically permissible, we should interpret the FDCA in light of Congress' overall desire to protect health. That purpose requires a flexible interpretation that both permits the FDA to take into account the realities of human behavior and allows it, in appropriate cases, to choose from its arsenal of statutory remedies. A statute so interpreted easily "fits" this, and other, drug- and device-related health problems.

III. In the majority's view, laws enacted since 1965 require us to deny jurisdiction, whatever the FDCA might mean in their absence. But why? Do those laws contain language barring FDA jurisdiction? The majority must concede that they do not. Do they contain provisions that are inconsistent with the FDA's exercise of jurisdiction? With one exception the majority points to no such provision. Do they somehow repeal the principles of law that otherwise would lead to the conclusion that the FDA has jurisdiction in this area? The companies themselves deny making any such claim. Perhaps the later laws "shape" and "focus" what the 1938 Congress meant a generation earlier. But this Court has warned against using the views of a later Congress to construe a statute enacted many years before. And, while the majority suggests that the subsequent history "controls our construction" of the FDCA, this Court expressly has held that such subsequent views are not "controlling."

The FCLAA has an express pre-emption provision which says that "no statement relating to smoking and health, other than the statement required by [this Act], shall be required on any cigarette package." This pre-emption clause plainly prohibits the FDA from requiring on "any cigarette package" any other "statement relating to smoking and health," but no one contends that the FDA has failed to abide by this prohibition. Rather, the question is whether the FCLAA's pre-emption provision does more. Does it forbid the FDA to regulate at all? This Court has already answered that question expressly and in the negative. See *Cipollone v. Liggett Group, Inc.,* 505 U.S. 504 (1992). *Cipollone* held that the FCLAA's pre-emption provision does not bar state or federal regulation outside the provision's literal scope.

When the FCLAA's narrow pre-emption provision is set aside, the majority's conclusion that Congress clearly intended for its tobacco-related statutes to be the exclusive "response" to "the problem of tobacco and health," is based on legislative silence.

IV. [Finally,] until the early 1990's, the FDA expressly maintained that the 1938 statute did not give it the power that it now seeks to assert. It then changed its mind. The majority agrees with me that the FDA's change of positions does not make a significant legal difference. Nevertheless, it labels those denials "important context" for drawing an inference about Congress' intent. In my view, the FDA's change of policy, like the subsequent statutes themselves, does nothing to advance the majority's position.

When it denied jurisdiction to regulate cigarettes, the FDA consistently stated why that was so. In 1963, for example, FDA administrators wrote that cigarettes did not satisfy the relevant FDCA definitions—in particular, the "intent" requirement—because cigarette makers did not sell their product with accompanying "therapeutic claims." And subsequent FDA Commissioners made roughly the same assertion.

What changed? For one thing, the FDA obtained evidence sufficient to prove the necessary "intent" despite the absence of specific "claims." This evidence, which first became available in the early 1990's, permitted the agency to demonstrate that the tobacco companies knew nicotine achieved appetite-suppressing, mood-stabilizing, and habituating effects through chemical (not psychological) means, even at a time when the companies were publicly denying such knowledge.

Finally, administration policy changed. Earlier administrations may have hesitated to assert jurisdiction for the reasons prior Commissioners expressed. Commissioners of the current administration simply took a different regulatory attitude.

Nothing in the law prevents the FDA from changing its policy for such reasons. By the mid-1990's, the evidence needed to prove objective intent—even without an express claim—had been found. The emerging scientific consensus about tobacco's adverse, chemically induced, health effects may have convinced the agency that it should spend its resources on this important regulatory effort. As for the change of administrations, I agree with then-Justice Rehnquist's statement: "A change in administration brought about by the people casting their votes is a perfectly reasonable basis for an executive agency's reappraisal of the costs and benefits of its programs and regulations. As long as the agency remains within the bounds established by Congress, it is entitled to assess administrative records and evaluate priorities in light of the philosophy of the administration." *Motor Vehicle Mfrs. Assn. of United States, Inc. v. State Farm Mut. Automobile Ins. Co.,* 463 U.S. 29, 59 (1983) (concurring in part and dissenting in part).

V. Insofar as the decision to regulate tobacco reflects the policy of an administration, it is a decision for which that administration, and those politically elected officials who support it, must (and will) take responsibility. Presidents, just like Members of Congress, are elected by the public. Indeed, the President and Vice President are the only public officials whom the entire Nation elects. I do not believe that an administrative agency decision of this magnitude—one that is important, conspicuous, and controversial—can escape the kind of public scrutiny that is essential in any democracy.

*****

The Nondelegation Doctrine

Although the challenge to the FDA was successful, efforts to block Environmental Protection Agency (EPA) rulemaking on the basis of the long-standing, but rarely used, nondelegation doctrine was not. As *Public Law and Public Administration, Third Edition* explains in Chapter 4, the nondelegation doctrine is based in the idea that one who possesses a delegated power cannot later delegate that authority away to someone else. The argument was that Congress has power to legislate delegated from the people through Article I of the Constitution. Standardless and excessively vague delegations of rule-making authority from Congress to administrative agencies were unconstitutional. This doctrine was only rarely invoked to block federal agency action [see the references in the *Whitman* opinion that follows to *Panama Refining Co. v. Ryan,* 293 U.S. 388 (1935) and *A. L. A. Schechter Poultry Corp. v. United States,* 295 U.S. 495 (1935)], though it has more commonly been used under the law of some states to constrain state agencies. If it were to be applied zealously, the doctrine could block much of what the legislature requires agencies to accomplish. However, a number of contemporary opponents of administrative authority, led by Chief Justice William Rehnquist, have argued that there has been an unacceptable lack of attention to the nondelegation doctrine and have tried to reinvigorate it.[2]

Whitman v. American Trucking Associations, 531 U.S. 457 (2001).

INTRODUCTION: This case began as a complex, but more or less routine, rule-making action for the purpose of updating environmental standards for ambient air quality by the U.S. Environmental Protection Agency under the Clean Air Act. However, some of the regulated groups calculated that perhaps it was time once again to test the constitutional boundaries of congressional authority to delegate broad regulatory authority to federal agencies. That strategy appeared to pay off when the United States Circuit Court of Appeals for the D.C. Circuit indeed concluded that Congress had violated the nondelegation doctrine.

From that moment on, administrative law scholars and practitioners watched closely to see if the increasingly conservative Supreme Court was ready to respond to Rehnquist's call for a reinvigoration of the nondelegation

---

2. *Industrial Union Department, AFL-CIO v. American Petroleum Inst.,* 448 U.S. 607 (1980), Rehnquist, J., concurring.

doctrine, possibly imposing dramatic limitations on federal regulation and the agencies that administer it.

This opinion has been edited to focus on the delegation issue, rather than on the substantive issues associated with the Clean Air Act and the EPA implementation of it.

*****

JUSTICE SCALIA wrote the opinion for the Court.

These cases present the following question: (1) Whether §109(b)(1) of the Clean Air Act (CAA) delegates legislative power to the Administrator of the Environmental Protection Agency (EPA). (2) Whether the Administrator may consider the costs of implementation in setting national ambient air quality standards (NAAQS) under § 109(b)(1). (3) Whether the Court of Appeals had jurisdiction to review the EPA's interpretation of Part D of Title I of the CAA, 42 U.S.C. §§ 7501-7515, with respect to implementing the revised ozone NAAQS. (4) If so, whether the EPA's interpretation of that part was permissible.

I. Section 109(a) of the CAA, requires the Administrator of the EPA to promulgate NAAQS [National Ambient Air Quality Standards] for each air pollutant for which "air quality criteria" have been issued. [T]he Administrator must [then] review the standard "at five-year intervals" and make "such revisions . . . as may be appropriate." These cases arose when, on July 18, 1997, the Administrator revised the NAAQS for particulate matter (PM) and ozone. American Trucking Associations, Inc., and its co-respondents, which include, in addition to other private companies, the States of Michigan, Ohio, and West Virginia—challenged the new standards in the Court of Appeals for the District of Columbia Circuit.

The District of Columbia Circuit accepted some of the challenges and rejected others. It agreed with the respondents that §109(b)(1) delegated legislative power to the Administrator in contravention of the United States Constitution, Art. I, §1, because it found that the EPA had interpreted the statute to provide no "intelligible principle" to guide the agency's exercise of authority. *American Trucking Assns., Inc. v. EPA,* 175 F.3d 1027, 1034 (D.C.Cir. 1999). The court thought, however, that the EPA could perhaps avoid the unconstitutional delegation by adopting a restrictive construction of §109(b)(1), so instead of declaring the section unconstitutional the court remanded the NAAQS to the agency. [And it rejected the respondents' challenges to the rule on the other three issues, though the EPA disagreed with the court's resolutions and interpretations with respect to the third and fourth issues noted above.]

II. In *Lead Industries Assn., Inc. v. EPA,* 647 F.2d 1130, 1148 (CADC 1980), the District of Columbia Circuit held that "economic considerations [may] play no part in the promulgation of ambient air quality standards under Section 109" of the CAA. In the present cases, the court adhered to that holding. Respondents argue that these decisions are incorrect. We disagree; and since the first step in assessing whether a statute delegates legislative power is to determine what authority the statute confers, we address that issue of interpretation first and reach respondents' constitutional arguments in Part III, infra.

Section 109(b)(1) instructs the EPA to set primary ambient air quality standards "the attainment and maintenance of which . . . are requisite to protect the public health" with "an adequate margin of safety." The EPA, "based on" the information about health effects contained in the technical "criteria" documents compiled under [the Act] is to identify the maximum airborne concentration of a pollutant that the public health can tolerate, decrease the concentration to provide an "adequate" margin of safety, and set the standard at that level. Nowhere are the costs of achieving such a standard made part of that initial calculation.

[T]o prevail in their present challenge, respondents must show a textual commitment of authority to the EPA to consider costs in setting NAAQS under §109(b)(1). And because §109(b)(1) and the NAAQS for which it provides are the engine that drives nearly all of Title I of the CAA, that textual commitment must be a clear one. Congress, we have held, does not alter the fundamental details of a regulatory scheme in vague terms or ancillary provisions—it does not, one might say, hide elephants in mouseholes. See *FDA v. Brown & Williamson Tobacco Corp.*, 529 U.S. 120, 159-160 (2000). Respondents' arguments ultimately founder upon this principle.

The text of §109(b), interpreted in its statutory and historical context and with appreciation for its importance to the CAA as a whole, unambiguously bars cost considerations from the NAAQS-setting process, and thus ends the matter for us as well as the EPA.

III. Section 109(b)(1) of the CAA instructs the EPA to set "ambient air quality standards the attainment and maintenance of which in the judgment of the Administrator, based on [the] criteria [documents of § 108] and allowing an adequate margin of safety, are requisite to protect the public health." The Court of Appeals held that this section as interpreted by the Administrator did not provide an "intelligible principle" to guide the EPA's exercise of authority in setting NAAQS. "[The] EPA," it said, "lacked any determinate criteria for drawing lines. It has failed to state intelligibly how much is too much." The court hence found that the EPA's interpretation (but not the statute itself) violated the nondelegation doctrine. We disagree.

In a delegation challenge, the constitutional question is whether the statute has delegated legislative power to the agency. Article I, §1, of the Constitution vests "all legislative Powers herein granted . . . in a Congress of the United States." This text permits no delegation of those powers and so we repeatedly have said that when Congress confers decisionmaking authority upon agencies Congress must "lay down by legislative act an intelligible principle to which the person or body authorized to [act] is directed to conform." *J. W. Hampton, Jr., & Co. v. United States,* 276 U.S. 394, 409 (1928). We have never suggested that an agency can cure an unlawful delegation of legislative power by adopting in its discretion a limiting construction of the statute. The idea that an agency can cure an unconstitutionally standardless delegation of power by declining to exercise some of that power seems to us internally contradictory. The very choice of which portion of the power to exercise—that is to say, the prescription of the standard that Congress had omitted—would itself be an exercise of the forbidden legislative authority. Whether the statute delegates legislative power is a question for the courts, and an agency's voluntary self-denial has no bearing upon the answer.

We agree with the Solicitor General that the text of §109(b)(1) of the CAA at a minimum requires that "for a discrete set of pollutants and based on published air quality criteria that reflect the latest scientific knowledge, [the] EPA must establish uniform national standards at a level that is requisite to protect public health from the adverse effects of the pollutant in the ambient air." Requisite, in turn, "means sufficient, but not more than necessary." These limits on the EPA's discretion are strikingly similar to the ones we approved in *Touby v. United States,* 500 U.S. 160 (1991), which permitted the Attorney General to designate a drug as a controlled substance for purposes of criminal drug enforcement if doing so was "'necessary to avoid an imminent hazard to the public safety.'" They also resemble the Occupational Safety and Health Act provision requiring the agency to "'set the standard which most adequately assures, to the extent feasible, on the basis of the best available evidence, that no employee will suffer any impairment of health'"—which the Court upheld in *Industrial Union Dept., AFL-CIO v. American Petroleum Institute,* 448 U.S. 607, 646 (1980), and which even then-Justice Rehnquist, who alone in that case thought the statute violated the nondelegation doctrine would have upheld if, like the statute here, it did not permit economic costs to be considered.

The scope of discretion §109(b)(1) allows is in fact well within the outer limits of our nondelegation precedents. In the history of the Court we have found the requisite "intelligible principle" lacking in only two statutes, one of which provided literally no guidance for the exercise of discretion, and the other of which conferred authority to regulate the entire economy on the basis of no more precise a standard than stimulating the economy by assuring "fair competition." See *Panama Refining Co. v. Ryan,* 293 U.S. 388 (1935); *A. L. A. Schechter Poultry Corp. v. United States,* 295 U.S. 495 (1935). We have, on the other hand, upheld the validity of the Public Utility Holding Company Act of 1935, which gave the Securities and Exchange Commission authority to modify the structure of holding company systems so as to ensure that they are not "unduly or unnecessarily complicated" and do not "unfairly or inequitably distribute voting power among security holders." We have approved the wartime conferral of agency power to fix the prices of commodities at a level that "'will be generally fair and equitable and will effectuate the [in some respects conflicting] purposes of the Act.'" *Yakus v. United States,* 321 U.S. 414, 420-426 (1944). And we have found an "intelligible principle" in various statutes authorizing regulation in the "public interest." In short, we have "almost never felt qualified to second-guess Congress regarding the permissible degree of policy judgment that can be left to those executing or applying the law."

It is true enough that the degree of agency discretion that is acceptable varies according to the scope of the power congressionally conferred. While Congress need not provide any direction to the EPA regarding [for example] the manner in which it is to define "country elevators," which are to be exempt from new-stationary-source regulations governing grain elevators, it must provide substantial guidance on setting air standards that affect the entire national economy. But even in sweeping regulatory schemes we have never demanded, as the Court of Appeals did here, that statutes provide a "determinate criterion" for saying "how much [of the regulated harm] is too much." In *Touby*, for example, we did not require the statute to decree how "imminent" was too imminent, or how "necessary" was necessary enough, or even—most relevant here—how "hazardous" was too haz-ardous. Similarly, the statute at issue in *Lichter v. United States,* 334 U.S. 742 (1948), authorized agencies to recoup "excess profits" paid under wartime Government contracts, yet we did not insist that Congress specify how much profit was too much. It is therefore not conclusive for delegation purposes that, as respondents argue, ozone and particulate matter are "nonthreshold" pollutants that inflict a continuum of adverse health effects at any airborne concentration greater than zero, and hence require the EPA to make judgments of degree. "[A] certain degree of discretion, and thus of lawmaking, inheres in most executive or judicial action." Section 109(b)(1) of the CAA fits comfortably within the scope of discretion permitted by our precedent.

To summarize our holdings in these unusually complex cases: (1) The EPA may not consider implementation costs in setting primary and secondary NAAQS under § 109(b) of the CAA. (2) Section 109(b)(1) does not delegate legislative power to the EPA in contravention of Art. I, §1, of the Constitution. (3) The Court of Appeals had jurisdiction to review the EPA's interpretation of Part D of Title I of the CAA, relating to the implementation of the revised ozone NAAQS. (4) The EPA's interpretation of that Part is unreasonable.

JUSTICE THOMAS wrote a concurring opinion.

I agree with the majority that §109's directive to the agency is no less an "intelligible principle" than a host of other directives that we have approved. I write separately, however, to express my concern that there may nevertheless be a genuine constitutional problem with §109, a problem which the parties did not address.

The parties to this case who briefed the constitutional issue wrangled over constitutional doctrine with barely a nod to the text of the Constitution. Although this Court since 1928 has treated the "intelligible principle" require-ment as the only constitutional limit on congressional grants of power to adminis-trative agencies, the Constitution does not speak of "intelligible principles." Rather, it speaks in much simpler terms: "All legislative Powers herein granted shall be vested in a Congress." U.S. Const., Art.1, §1. I am not convinced that the intelligible principle doctrine serves to prevent all cessions of legislative power. I believe that there are cases in which the principle is intelligible and yet the signifi-cance of the delegated decision is simply too great for the decision to be called anything other than "legislative."

As it is, none of the parties to this case has examined the text of the Constitution or asked us to reconsider our precedents on cessions of legislative power. On a future day, however, I would be willing to address the question whether our delegation jurisprudence has strayed too far from our Founders' understanding of separation of powers.

JUSTICE STEVENS wrote an opinion concurring in part and concurring in the judgment, joined by JUSTICE SOUTER.

The Court convincingly explains why the Court of Appeals erred when it concluded that §109 effected "an unconstitutional delegation of legislative power." I wholeheartedly endorse the Court's result and endorse its explanation of its reasons, albeit with the following caveat.

The Court has two choices. We could choose to articulate our ultimate disposition of this issue by frankly acknowledging that the power delegated to the EPA is "legislative" but nevertheless conclude that the delegation is constitutional because adequately limited by the terms of the authorizing statute. Alternatively, we could pretend, as the Court does, that the authority delegated to the EPA is somehow not "legislative power." Despite the fact that there is language in our opinions that supports the Court's articulation of our holding, I am persuaded that it would be both wiser and more faithful to what we have actually done in delegation cases to admit that agency rulemaking authority is "legislative power."[3]

The proper characterization of governmental power should generally depend on the nature of the power, not on the identity of the person exercising it. If the NAAQS that the EPA promulgated had been prescribed by Congress, everyone would agree that those rules would be the product of an exercise of "legislative power." The same characterization is appropriate when an agency exercises rulemaking authority pursuant to a permissible delegation from Congress.

My view is not only more faithful to normal English usage, but is also fully consistent with the text of the Constitution. In Article I, the Framers vested "All legislative Powers" in the Congress, Art. I., §1, just as in Article II they vested the "executive Power" in the President, Art. II, §1. Those provisions do not purport to limit the authority of either recipient of power to delegate authority to others. Surely the authority granted to members of the Cabinet and federal law enforcement agents is properly characterized as "Executive" even though not exercised by the President.

It seems clear that an executive agency's exercise of rulemaking authority pursuant to a valid delegation from Congress is "legislative." As long as the delegation provides a sufficiently intelligible principle, there is nothing inherently unconstitutional about it.[4]

*****

---

3. See *Mistretta v. United States,* 488 U.S. 361, 372, 102 L. Ed. 2d 714, 109 S. Ct. 647 (1989) ("Our jurisprudence has been driven by a practical understanding that in our increasingly complex society . . . Congress simply cannot do its job absent an ability to delegate power . . .").

4. Justice Breyer also wrote an opinion concurring in part and concurring the judgment, but his opinion was not concerned with the delegation holding of the Court.

Durable Delegations and Binding Rules

Courts generally allow administrators considerable discretion in the rulemaking process, including even the question of whether to undertake a rulemaking proceeding (unless there is a clear statutory mandate to do so). However, once it is clear that a valid delegation of authority exists and it has been used to issue a rule, things change. In a string of important cases, the federal courts, including the U.S. Supreme Court, have made clear that delegations remain in force and that rules are binding on the agencies that issued them until revoked or altered by a proper process.

Assuming that a delegation is valid, many political executives have wished that they could reach into an agency exercising a clearly delegated authority under statute that has been subdelegated by a cabinet officer or the president. In challenges to these attempts, the Court has indicated the limitations that valid delegations impose.

United States ex rel. Accardi v. Shaughnessy, 347 U.S. 260 (1954).

INTRODUCTION: This classic case involved a decision by the Attorney General to intervene in a decisionmaking process that he had delegated to the Immigration and Naturalization Service (INS). Accardi was facing deportation and had applied to the INS for a suspension of deportation. However, while his case was pending, the Attorney General sent a "confidential list of 'unsavory characters'" to the decisionmakers. The petitioner claimed that his case was thereby prejudiced.

*****

JUSTICE CLARK wrote the opinion for the Court.

Hearings on the deportation charge and the application for suspension of deportation were held before officers of the Immigration and Naturalization Service at various times from 1948 to 1952. A hearing officer ultimately found petitioner deportable and recommended a denial of discretionary relief. On July 7, 1952, the Acting Commissioner of Immigration adopted the officer's findings and recommendation. Almost nine months later, on April 3, 1953, the Board of Immigration Appeals affirmed the decision of the hearing officer. A warrant of deportation was issued the same day and arrangements were made for actual deportation to take place on April 24, 1953.

Regulations with the force and effect of law supplement the bare bones of §19(c). The regulations prescribe the procedure to be followed in processing an alien's application for suspension of deportation. The regulations pinpoint the decisive fact in this case: the Board was required, as it still is, to exercise its own

judgment when considering appeals. In unequivocal terms the regulations delegate to the Board discretionary authority as broad as the statute confers on the
Attorney General; the scope of the Attorney General's discretion became the
yardstick of the Board's. And if the word "discretion" means anything in a statutory or administrative grant of power, it means that the recipient must exercise his
authority according to his own understanding and conscience. This applies with
equal force to the Board and the Attorney General. In short, as long as the regulations remain operative, the Attorney General denies himself the right to sidestep
the Board or dictate its decision in any manner.

We think the petition for habeas corpus charges the Attorney General with
precisely what the regulations forbid him to do: dictating the Board's decision.
The petition alleges that the Attorney General included the name of petitioner in
a confidential list of "unsavory characters" whom he wanted deported; public
announcements clearly reveal that the Attorney General did not regard the listing
as a mere preliminary to investigation and deportation; to the contrary, those listed
were persons whom the Attorney General "planned to deport." And, it is alleged,
this intention was made quite clear to the Board when the list was circulated
among its members. In fact, the Assistant District Attorney characterized it as the
"Attorney General's proscribed list of alien deportees." To be sure, the petition
does not allege that the "Attorney General ordered the Board to deny discretionary relief to the listed aliens." It would be naive to expect such a heavy-
handed way of doing things. However, proof was offered and refused that the
Commissioner of Immigration told previous counsel of petitioner, "We can't do a
thing in your case because the Attorney General has his [petitioner's] name on
that list of a hundred." We believe the allegations are quite sufficient where the
body charged with the exercise of discretion is a nonstatutory board composed of
subordinates within a department headed by the individual who formulated,
announced, and circulated such views of the pending proceeding.

It is important to emphasize that we are not here reviewing and reversing the
manner in which discretion was exercised. If such were the case we would be discussing the evidence in the record supporting or undermining the alien's claim to
discretionary relief. Rather, we object to the Board's alleged failure to exercise its
own discretion, contrary to existing valid regulations.

If petitioner can prove the allegation, he should receive a new hearing before
the Board without the burden of previous proscription by the list. After the recall
or cancellation of the list, the Board must rule out any consideration thereof and
in arriving at its decision exercise its own independent discretion, after a fair hearing, which is nothing more than what the regulations accord petitioner as a right.[5]

*****

As the *Accardi* case demonstrates, the importance of a valid delegation of
authority is not limited to cases in which the delegation comes directly from

---

5. Justice Jackson dissented, joined by Justices Reed, Burton, and Minton, arguing that this
   kind of administrative decision should have been unreviewable.

legislation, but applies as well to delegations from executive officials. Indeed, President Nixon's famous Watergate tapes case turned in significant part on the question whether the administration could interfere in the delegation of authority given to the Watergate Special Prosecutor.

United States v. Nixon, **418 U.S. 683 (1974).**

INTRODUCTION: The Supreme Court ultimately recognized the existence of executive privilege in this famous case, but rejected the president's claim of absolute privilege. Indeed, the Court unanimously (Rehnquist not participating) concluded that Nixon's claim to privilege had to yield to a demand for evidence in an ongoing criminal case. However, the White House had argued that the Court should not even consider the case, since the dispute was an internal executive branch matter. The Court rejected that argument on the delegation grounds. The excerpt that follows is taken from that portion of the *Nixon* opinion.

✶✶✶✶✶

CHIEF JUSTICE BURGER wrote the opinion for the unanimous Court.

II. JUSTICIABILITY

In the District Court, the President's counsel argued that the court lacked jurisdiction to issue the subpoena because the matter was an intra-branch dispute between a subordinate and superior officer of the Executive Branch and hence not subject to judicial resolution. That argument has been renewed in this Court with emphasis on the contention that the dispute does not present a "case" or "controversy" which can be adjudicated in the federal courts. The President's counsel argues that the federal courts should not intrude into areas committed to the other branches of Government. He views the present dispute as essentially a "jurisdictional" dispute within the Executive Branch which he analogizes to a dispute between two congressional committees. Since the Executive Branch has exclusive authority and absolute discretion to decide whether to prosecute a case, it is contended that a President's decision is final in determining what evidence is to be used in a given criminal case. Although his counsel concedes that the President has delegated certain specific powers to the Special Prosecutor, he has not "waived nor delegated to the Special Prosecutor the President's duty to claim privilege as to all materials . . . which fall within the President's inherent authority to refuse to disclose to any executive officer." The Special Prosecutor's demand for the items therefore presents, in the view of the President's counsel, a political question under *Baker v. Carr,* 369 U.S. 186 (1962), since it involves a "textually demonstrable" grant of power under Art. II.

The mere assertion of a claim of an "intra-branch dispute," without more, has never operated to defeat federal jurisdiction; justiciability does not depend on such a surface inquiry. Our starting point is the nature of the proceeding for which the evidence is sought—here a pending criminal prosecution. It is a judicial proceeding in a federal court alleging violation of federal laws and is brought in the name of the United States as sovereign. Under the authority of Art. II, §2, Congress has vested in the Attorney General the power to conduct the criminal litigation of the United States Government. It has also vested in him the power to appoint subordinate officers to assist him in the discharge of his duties. Acting pursuant to those statutes, the Attorney General has delegated the authority to represent the United States in these particular matters to a Special Prosecutor with unique authority and tenure. The regulation gives the Special Prosecutor explicit power to contest the invocation of executive privilege in the process of seeking evidence deemed relevant to the performance of these specially delegated duties. So long as this regulation is extant it has the force of law. In *United States ex rel. Accardi v. Shaughnessy,* 347 U.S. 260 (1954), regulations of the Attorney General delegated certain of his discretionary powers to the Board of Immigration Appeals and required that Board to exercise its own discretion on appeals in deportation cases. The Court held that so long as the Attorney General's regulations remained operative, he denied himself the authority to exercise the discretion delegated to the Board even though the original authority was his and he could reassert it by amending the regulations. *Service v. Dulles,* 354 U.S. 363, 388 (1957), and *Vitarelli v. Seaton,* 359 U.S. 535 (1959), reaffirmed the basic holding of *Accardi.*

Here, as in *Accardi,* it is theoretically possible for the Attorney General to amend or revoke the regulation defining the Special Prosecutor's authority. But he has not done so. So long as this regulation remains in force the Executive Branch is bound by it, and indeed the United States as the sovereign composed of the three branches is bound to respect and to enforce it. Moreover, the delegation of authority to the Special Prosecutor in this case is not an ordinary delegation by the Attorney General to a subordinate officer: with the authorization of the President, the Acting Attorney General provided in the regulation that the Special Prosecutor was not to be removed without the "consensus" of eight designated leaders of Congress.

Here at issue is the production or nonproduction of specified evidence deemed by the Special Prosecutor to be relevant and admissible in a pending criminal case. It is sought by one official of the Executive Branch within the scope of his express authority; it is resisted by the Chief Executive on the ground of his duty to preserve the confidentiality of the communications of the President. Whatever the correct answer on the merits, these issues are "of a type which are traditionally justiciable." The independent Special Prosecutor with his asserted need for the subpoenaed material in the underlying criminal prosecution is opposed by the President with his steadfast assertion of privilege against disclosure of the material.

In light of the uniqueness of the setting in which the conflict arises, the fact that both parties are officers of the Executive Branch cannot be viewed as a barrier to justiciability. It would be inconsistent with the applicable law and regulation, and the unique facts of this case to conclude other than that the Special Prosecutor has standing to bring this action and that a justiciable controversy is presented for decision.

*****

The Court also addressed the attempt to intervene in a delegated authority when the Congress sought to step into the administrative rulemaking process with its legislative veto. See the excerpt from *Immigration and Naturalization Service v. Chadha,* 462 U.S. 919 (1983) later in this chapter.

AGENCY DUTY TO OBEY ITS OWN RULES

Assuming that an agency acts under a legitimate delegation of authority and within its proper jurisdiction, its rules are binding on the agency, as well as on those who have cases before it. This basic principle of administrative law is often ignored by many critics of rulemaking, who see rules as simply burdens on those outside government. A reading of the leading cases establishing this principle suggests that politicians who claim success by virtue of the number of the regulations they cause to be eliminated should perhaps be a bit careful about bragging about their success. After all, they are in many cases eliminating constraints on agency discretion and paving the way for the possibility of arbitrariness.

Vitarelli v. Seaton, 359 U.S. 535 (1959).

INTRODUCTION: Dr. Vitarelli was employed by the Department of the Interior as an Education and Training Specialist in the Pacific islands. The Department fired him during the Red Scare of the early 1950s, based on vague allegations that "because such associations and activities tended to show that petitioner was 'not reliable or trustworthy' his continued employment might be 'contrary to the best interests of national security.'" It happens that Vitarelli had no involvement with any sensitive information or work and, ironically, he was serving in an "at will" position, which means he could be fired at any time. However, the Secretary of the Interior had issued specific procedural rules to be followed where an employee was to be terminated as a security risk. After Vitarelli challenged his termination, the Secretary scrambled to cover the action, by firing him again, only this time without security allegations in order to avoid the problem that he had already created the first time. The Court, in an opinion by one of its best known conservative justices, rejected the sham and the attempt by the agency to disregard its own rules.

*****

JUSTICE HARLAN wrote the opinion for the Court.[6]

It is true that the Act of August 26, 1950, and the Executive Order did not alter the power of the Secretary to discharge summarily an employee in petitioner's status, without the giving of any reason. Nor did the Department's own regulations preclude such a course. Since, however, the Secretary gratuitously decided to give a reason, and that reason was national security, he was obligated to conform to the procedural standards he had formulated in Order No. 2738 for the dismissal of employees on security grounds. *Service v. Dulles,* 354 U.S. 363 [1957]. That Order on its face applies to all security discharges in the Department of the Interior, including such discharges of Schedule A employees. Having chosen to proceed against petitioner on security grounds, the Secretary here, as in *Service,* was bound by the regulations which he himself had promulgated for dealing with such cases, even though without such regulations he could have discharged petitioner summarily.

Preliminarily, it should be said that departures from departmental regulations in matters of this kind involve more than mere consideration of procedural irregularities. For in proceedings of this nature, in which the ordinary rules of evidence do not apply, in which matters involving the disclosure of confidential information are withheld, and where it must be recognized that counsel is under practical constraints in the making of objections and in the tactical handling of his case which would not obtain in a cause being tried in a court of law before trained judges, scrupulous observance of departmental procedural safeguards is clearly of particular importance.

Because the proceedings attendant upon petitioner's dismissal from government service on grounds of national security fell substantially short of the requirements of the applicable departmental regulations, we hold that such dismissal was illegal and of no effect.

*****

SUBSTANTIVE RULES, INTERPRETIVE RULES, AND POLICY STATEMENTS

What Is a Rule and Why Does It Matter?

For a variety of reasons, agencies have often issued various kinds of pronouncements that looked like substantive (or legislative) rules within the meaning of the Administrative Procedure Act (APA). If they are substantive rules, then they are not only binding, but must be developed in accordance with APA requirements (in addition to whatever other obligations are imposed by an agency's enabling act or the program's authorization statute). Over time, various courts have wrestled with just which types of agency action fit which categories. The

---

6. Justice Frankfurter wrote a dissent, joined by Justices Clark, Whittaker, and Stewart, agreeing with the essential principle announced by Justice Harlan but arguing that the legislation allowed the secretary authority to act summarily.

following cases present some of that discussion. And as *Public Law and Public Administration, Third Edition* points out, this is a discussion that can sometimes be difficult to follow. What follows are cases that attempt to clarify the situation.

Morton v. Ruiz, 415 U.S. 199 (1974).

INTRODUCTION: This case involved Ramon and Anita Ruiz and their daughter, who were Papago Indians living in Arizona at the time of this case. The Ruiz family moved off the Papago reservation some 15 miles away to the nearby community of Ajo where Mr. Ruiz had found a job at the Phelps–Dodge copper mines. They lived in a part of that community known as "Indian Village," almost all of the residents of which were Papago Indians. They lived there from 1940 until the time of this case. They retained their strong connections with the reservation, lived primarily in the tribal culture, and had limited English proficiency.

When a strike shut down the mine in 1967, Ruiz's income was lost and he applied for assistance from the Bureau of Indian Affairs (BIA), part of the U.S. Department of the Interior. His claim was denied on grounds that the BIA's Indian Affairs Manual limited assistance to those living on reservations. After the administrative appeals were exhausted, Ruiz brought a class action suit, challenging the exclusion from benefits. A critical element of the case goes to the question of the status and nature of the BIA pronouncements in the Bureau of Indian Affairs Manual.

✻✻✻✻✻

JUSTICE BLACKMUN wrote the opinion for the Court.

We are confronted, therefore, with the issues whether the geographical limitation placed on general assistance eligibility by the BIA is consistent with congressional intent and the meaning of the applicable statutes, or, to phrase it somewhat differently, whether the congressional appropriations are properly limited by the BIA's restrictions. The question is whether Congress intended to exclude from the general assistance program these respondents and their class, who are full-blooded, unassimilated Indians living in an Indian community near their native reservation, and who maintain close economic and social ties with that reservation. Except for formal residence outside the physical boundaries of the Papago Reservation, the respondents, as has been conceded, meet all other requirements for the general assistance program.

Our examination of [the relevant] material[s] leads us to a conclusion contrary to that urged by the Secretary.

In actual practice, general assistance clearly has not been limited to reservation Indians. Indeed, the [Bureau of Indian Affairs] Manual's provision itself provides that general assistance is available to nonreservation Indians in Alaska and Oklahoma. There was testimony in several of the hearings that the BIA, in fact, was not limiting general assistance to those within reservation boundaries and, on more than one occasion, Congress was notified that exceptions were being made where they were deemed appropriate. Notwithstanding the Manual, at least three categories of off-reservation Indians outside Alaska and Oklahoma have been treated as eligible for general assistance. Even more important is the fact that, for many years, to and including the appropriation year at issue, the BIA itself made continual representations to the appropriations subcommittees that nonurban Indians living "near" a reservation were eligible for BIA services.

Having found that the congressional appropriation was intended to cover welfare services at least to those Indians residing "on or near" the reservation, it does not necessarily follow that the Secretary is without power to create reasonable classifications and eligibility requirements in order to allocate the limited funds available to him for this purpose. But in such a case the agency must, at a minimum, let the standard be generally known so as to assure that it is being applied consistently and so as to avoid both the reality and the appearance of arbitrary denial of benefits to potential beneficiaries.

Assuming, *arguendo* [for purposes of argument], that the Secretary rationally could limit the "on or near" appropriation to include only the smaller class of Indians who lived directly "on" the reservation, the question that remains is whether this has been validly accomplished. The power of an administrative agency to administer a congressionally created and funded program necessarily requires the formulation of policy and the making of rules to fill any gap left, implicitly or explicitly, by Congress. This agency power to make rules that affect substantial individual rights and obligations carries with it the responsibility not only to remain consistent with the governing legislation, but also to employ procedures that conform to the law. No matter how rational or consistent with congressional intent a particular decision might be, the determination of eligibility cannot be made on an *ad hoc* basis by the dispenser of the funds.

The Administrative Procedure Act was adopted to provide, *inter alia* [among other things] that administrative policies affecting individual rights and obligations be promulgated pursuant to certain stated procedures so as to avoid the inherently arbitrary nature of unpublished ad hoc determinations.

In the instant case the BIA itself has recognized the necessity of formally publishing its substantive policies and has placed itself under the structure of the APA procedures.

Unlike numerous other programs authorized by the Snyder Act and funded by the annual appropriations, the BIA has chosen not to publish its eligibility requirements for general assistance in the *Federal Register* or in the CFR [*Code of Federal Regulations*]. The only official manifestation of this alleged policy of restricting general assistance to those directly on the reservations is the material in the [Bureau of Indian Affairs] Manual which is, by BIA's own admission, solely an internal-operations brochure intended to cover policies that "do not relate to the public." Indeed, at oral argument the Government conceded that for this to be a "real legislative rule," itself endowed with the force of law, it should be published in the *Federal Register*.

Where the rights of individuals are affected, it is incumbent upon agencies to follow their own procedures. This is so even where the internal procedures are possibly more rigorous than otherwise would be required. *Service v. Dulles*, 354

U.S. 363, 388 (1957); *Vitarelli v. Seaton,* 359 U.S. 535, 539-540 (1959). The BIA, by its Manual, has declared that all directives that "inform the public of privileges and benefits available" and of "eligibility requirements" are among those to be published. The requirement that, in order to receive general assistance, an Indian must reside directly "on" a reservation is clearly an important substantive policy that fits within this class of directives.

Before the BIA may extinguish the entitlement of these otherwise eligible beneficiaries, it must comply, at a minimum, with its own internal procedures.

The Secretary has presented no reason why the requirements of the Administrative Procedure Act could not or should not have been met. The BIA itself has not attempted to defend its rule as a valid exercise of its "legislative power," but rather depends on the argument that Congress itself has not appropriated funds for Indians not directly on the reservations. The conscious choice of the Secretary not to treat this extremely significant eligibility requirement, affecting rights of needy Indians, as a legislative-type rule, renders it ineffective so far as extinguishing rights of those otherwise within the class of beneficiaries contemplated by Congress is concerned.

The overriding duty of our Federal Government to deal fairly with Indians wherever located has been recognized by this Court on many occasions. Particularly here, where the BIA has continually represented to Congress, when seeking funds, that Indians living near reservations are within the service area, it is essential that the legitimate expectation of these needy Indians not be extinguished by what amounts to an unpublished *ad hoc* determination of the agency that was not promulgated in accordance with its own procedures, to say nothing of those of the Administrative Procedure Act. Before benefits may be denied to these otherwise entitled Indians, the BIA must first promulgate eligibility requirements according to established procedures.

Even assuming the lack of binding effect of the BIA policy, the Secretary argues that the residential restriction in the Manual is a longstanding interpretation of the Snyder Act by the agency best suited to do this, and that deference is due its interpretation. As we have already noted, however, the BIA, through its own practices and representations, has led Congress to believe that these appropriations covered Indians "on or near" the reservations, and it is too late now to argue that the words "on reservations" in the Manual mean something different from "on or near" when, in fact, the two have been continuously equated by the BIA to Congress.

We have recognized previously that the weight of an administrative interpretation will depend, among other things, upon "its consistency with earlier and later pronouncements" of an agency. In this instance the BIA's somewhat inconsistent posture belies its present assertion. In order for an agency interpretation to be granted deference, it must be consistent with the congressional purpose. It is evident to us that Congress did not itself intend to limit its authorization to only those Indians directly on, in contrast to those "near," the reservation, and that, therefore, the BIA's interpretation must fail.

*****

Fast forward to 1995 and the Court's continuing effort to clarify the nature and status of agency rules. In this instance, the focus was the U.S. Department of Health and Human Services' administration of the Medicare program, and the question of how the agency used what are termed interpretive rules.

Shalala v. Guernsey Memorial Hospital, 514 U.S. 87 (1995).

INTRODUCTION: This complex case arose out of efforts by a hospital to recover losses, in part at least, from Medicare. While the Department of Health and Human Services (HHS) did not dispute that the hospital was entitled to the loss recovery, it disagreed with the accounting method, drawn from the Generally Accepted Accounting Principles (GAAP), used by the hospital to claim the loss all in one year. In this case, the hospital claimed that under the Medicare statute and the existing legislative (substantive) rules, the GAAP principles should be used. However, in rejecting the claim, HHS relied on a section of its Medicare Provider Reimbursement Manual (PRM) for guidance. The department did not maintain that the PRM was a set of substantive rules, and argued that the provision in question was nothing more than an interpretive rule, which explained but did not change the basic rules. It was, HHS contended, therefore not subject to APA rulemaking requirements.

*****

JUSTICE KENNEDY wrote the opinion for the Court.

What begins as a rather conventional accounting problem raises significant questions respecting the interpretation of the Secretary's regulations and her authority to resolve certain reimbursement issues by adjudication and interpretive rules, rather than by regulations that address all accounting questions in precise detail. The particular dispute concerns whether the Medicare regulations require reimbursement according to generally accepted accounting principles (GAAP), and whether the reimbursement guideline the Secretary relied upon is invalid because she did not follow the notice-and-comment provisions of the Administrative Procedure Act (APA) in issuing it. We hold that the Secretary's regulations do not require reimbursement according to GAAP and that her guideline is a valid interpretive rule.

Under the Medicare reimbursement scheme at issue here, participating hospitals furnish services to program beneficiaries and are reimbursed by the Secretary through fiscal intermediaries. Hospitals are reimbursed for "reasonable costs," defined by the statute as "the cost actually incurred, excluding therefrom any part of incurred cost found to be unnecessary in the efficient delivery of needed health services." The Medicare Act authorizes the Secretary to promulgate regulations "establishing the method or methods to be used" for determining reasonable costs, directing her in the process to "consider, among other things, the principles generally applied by national organizations or established prepayment organizations (which have developed such principles) in computing" reimbursement amounts.

The Secretary has promulgated, and updated on an annual basis, regulations establishing the methods for determining reasonable cost reimbursement. Respondent contends that two of these regulations, §§413.20(a) and 413.24, mandate reimbursement according to GAAP, and the Secretary counters that neither does.

The Secretary's reading of her regulations is consistent with the Medicare statute. Rather than requiring adherence to GAAP, the statute merely instructs the Secretary, in establishing the methods for determining reimbursable costs, to "consider, among other things, the principles generally applied by national organizations or established prepayment organizations (which have developed such principles) in computing the amount of payment . . . to providers of services."

Nor is there any basis for suggesting that the Secretary has a statutory duty to promulgate regulations that, either by default rule or by specification, address every conceivable question in the process of determining equitable reimbursement. To the extent the Medicare statute's broad delegation of authority imposes a rulemaking obligation, it is one the Secretary has without doubt discharged. The Secretary has issued regulations to address a wide range of reimbursement questions.

As to particular reimbursement details not addressed by her regulations, the Secretary relies upon an elaborate adjudicative structure which includes the right to review by the Provider Reimbursement Review Board, and, in some instances, the Secretary, as well as judicial review in federal district court of final agency action. That her regulations do not resolve the specific timing question before us in a conclusive way, or "could use a more exact mode of calculating," does not, of course, render them invalid, for the "methods for the estimation of reasonable costs" required by the statute only need be "generalizations [that] necessarily will fail to yield exact numbers." The APA does not require that all the specific applications of a rule evolve by further, more precise rules rather than by adjudication. The Secretary's mode of determining benefits by both rulemaking and adjudication is, in our view, a proper exercise of her statutory mandate.

We also believe it was proper for the Secretary to issue a guideline or interpretive rule in determining that defeasance losses should be amortized. PRM §233 is the means to ensure that capital-related costs allowable under the regulations are reimbursed in a manner consistent with the statute's mandate that the program bear neither more nor less than its fair share of costs. As an application of the statutory ban on cross-subsidization and the regulatory requirement that only the actual cost of services rendered to beneficiaries during a given year be reimbursed, PRM §233 is a prototypical example of an interpretive rule "'issued by an agency to advise the public of the agency's construction of the statutes and rules which it administers.'" *Chrysler Corp. v. Brown,* 441 U.S. 281, 302, n. 31 (1979). Interpretive rules do not require notice and comment, although, as the Secretary recognizes, they also do not have the force and effect of law and are not accorded that weight in the adjudicatory process.

We can agree that APA rulemaking would still be required if PRM §233 adopted a new position inconsistent with any of the Secretary's existing regulations. [However, t]he framework followed in this case is a sensible structure for the complex Medicare reimbursement process. The Secretary has promulgated regulations setting forth the basic principles and methods of reimbursement, and has issued interpretive rules such as PRM §233 that advise providers how she will apply the Medicare statute and regulations in adjudicating particular reimbursement claims. Because the Secretary's regulations do not bind her to make Medicare reimbursements in accordance with GAAP, her determination in PRM §233 to depart from GAAP by requiring bond defeasance losses to be amortized does not amount to a substantive change to the regulations. It is a valid interpretive rule.

JUSTICE O'CONNOR wrote a dissenting opinion joined by JUSTICES SCALIA, SOUTER, and THOMAS

I believe that general Medicare reporting and reimbursement regulations require provider costs to be treated according to "generally accepted accounting principles." As a result, I would hold that contrary guidelines issued by the Secretary of Health and Human Services in an informal policy manual and applied to determine the timing of reimbursement in this case are invalid for failure to comply with the notice and comment procedures established by the Administrative Procedure Act, 5 U.S.C. §553.

I take seriously our obligation to defer to an agency's reasonable interpretation of its own regulations, particularly "when, as here, the regulation concerns 'a complex and highly technical regulatory program,' in which the identification and classification of relevant 'criteria necessarily require significant expertise and entail the exercise of judgment grounded in policy concerns.'" In this case, however, the Secretary advances a view of the regulations that would force us to conclude that she has not fulfilled her statutory duty to promulgate regulations determining the methods by which reasonable Medicare costs are to be calculated. If §413.20 does not incorporate GAAP as the basic method for determining cost reimbursement in the absence of a more specific regulation, then there is no regulation that specifies an overall methodology to be applied in the cost determination process. Given that the regulatory scheme could not operate without such a background method, and given that the statute requires the Secretary to make reimbursement decisions "in accordance with regulations establishing the method or methods to be used," I find the Secretary's interpretation to be unreasonable and unworthy of deference.

Unlike the Court, I would hold that §413.20 requires the costs incurred by Medicare providers to be reimbursed according to GAAP in the absence of a specific regulation providing otherwise. PRM §233, which departs from the GAAP rule concerning advance refunding losses, does not have the force of a regulation because it was promulgated without notice and comment as required by the Administrative Procedure Act. And, contrary to the Secretary's argument, PRM §233 cannot be a valid "interpretation" of the Medicare regulations because it is clearly at odds with the meaning of §413.20 itself. Thus, I would conclude that the Secretary's refusal, premised upon an application of PRM §233 was invalid.

The remaining arguments advanced by the Court in support of the Secretary's position do not alter my view of the regulatory scheme. The Court suggests that requiring the Secretary to comply with the notice and comment provisions of the [APA] in promulgating reimbursement regulations, would impose an insurmountable burden on the Secretary's administration of the Medicare program. I disagree. Congress obviously thought that the Secretary could manage that task when it required that she act by regulation. [N]othing in my position requires the agency to adopt substantive rules addressing every detailed and minute reimbursement issue that might arise. An agency certainly cannot foresee every factual scenario with which it may be presented in administering its programs; to fill in the gaps, it must rely on adjudication of particular cases and other forms of agency action, such as the promulgation of interpretive rules and policy statements, that give effect to the statutory principles and the background methods embodied in the regulations. [T]he Secretary is simply obligated, in making those reimbursement decisions, to abide by whatever ground rules she establishes by regulation.

Congress expressed a clear policy in the Medicare Act that the reimbursement principles selected by the Secretary—whatever they may be—must be adopted subject to the procedural protections of the Administrative Procedure Act. I would require the Secretary to comply with that statutory mandate.

*****

In addition to interpretative rules, the other kind of actions exempted in the APA from regular rulemaking procedures are what are termed policy statements. To many observers, particularly those in the regulated community, it has seemed that agencies have increasingly attempted to label their rules as policy statements in order to avoid the requirements not only of the APA but of the requirements for rulemaking imposed by executive orders on top of the APA obligations. The D.C. Circuit responded to one such claim in the *McLouth Steel Products Corp.* case.

McLouth Steel Products Corp. v. Thomas, 367 F.2d 1317 (D.C. Cir. 1988).

INTRODUCTION: The Environmental Protection Agency (EPA) produced what it termed a policy statement concerning how it would determine whether a firm was to be regulated under the Resource Conservation and Recovery Act (RCRA). The RCRA is the statute regulating the use and disposal of toxic chemicals (as compared with the Superfund program aimed at cleaning up abandoned toxic waste sites). The EPA policy developed a computer model that would be used to process information about a company that had been identified as the target of regulation under RCRA and would determine whether the firm qualified for exemption from regulation. The company complained that the creation and use of the model constituted a substantive (legislative) rule that should have been made by the rulemaking process prescribed by the APA and other relevant requirements.

*****

JUDGE WILLIAMS wrote the opinion for the panel (JUDGES WILLIAMS and HOGAN).

We believe that in [its approach EPA] gave the effect of a rule to its "VHS model"—a systematic approach to computing probable contamination levels—without having exposed the model to the comment opportunities required for rules by the Administrative Procedure Act, 5 U.S.C. §553 (1982). Accordingly, we remand the case to the EPA.

The EPA used its VHS model (referring to "vertical and horizontal spread") to predict the "leachate" [residue that seeps out of waste and into the surrounding ground or water] levels of the hazardous components of McLouth's waste. The model "estimates the ability of an aquifer to dilute the toxicants from a specific volume of waste, and predicts toxicant levels at a receptor well." A user of the model feeds into it data as to the actual leachate concentrations of the constituents of a specific waste, and the amount of waste generated at the site, and the model predicts contamination levels. EPA then compares these predictions with health-based standards for each constituent to determine whether a waste should be delisted.

EPA argues that the model is just a policy, not a rule, and that if a rule its adoption was in compliance with §553. We find that petitioner has the better of the argument.

EPA argues that the VHS model falls under [the APA provision for] "general statements of policy." According to the EPA, the VHS model is merely a "non-binding statement of agency policy" that is "not solely determinative of EPA's action on a delisting petition," but rather is just "one of many tools" it uses in evaluating delisting petitions.

In attempting to flesh out the "tenuous," "blurred," and "fuzzy" distinction between legislative rules and policy statements, we [have] identified two criteria. A policy statement is one that first, does not have "a present-day binding effect," that is, it does not "impose any rights and obligations," and second, "genuinely leaves the agency and its decisionmakers free to exercise discretion." In practice, there appears some overlap in the[se] criteria; the second criterion may well swallow the first. If a statement denies the decisionmaker discretion in the area of its coverage, so that he, she or they will automatically decline to entertain challenges to the statement's position, then the statement is binding, and creates rights or obliga-tions. The question for purposes of §553 is whether a statement is a rule of present binding effect; the answer depends on whether the statement constrains the agency's discretion.

We find that the VHS model meets the definition of a legislative rule under the[se] criteria. For openers, EPA's current claim that "it does not consider itself . . . bound by [the VHS] model" is obviously of little weight. The agency's past characterizations, and more important, the nature of its past applications of the model, are what count.

It is true that in the *Federal Register* notices announcing EPA's intent to employ the VHS model, EPA indicated that it retained discretion to deviate from its use. Yet other language in that notice strongly suggests that EPA will treat the model as a binding norm.

More critically than EPA's language adopting the model, its later conduct applying it confirms its binding character. The agency treated the model as conclusively disposing of certain issues—the relationship between its input (leachate concentrations and amounts of waste) and its output (predicted contamination levels). On those issues, EPA was simply unready to hear new argument. The model thus created a norm with "present-day binding effect" on the rights of delisting petitioners.

EPA's claim to have been open to consideration of other factors does not make the VHS model any less of a rule. If a disposition turns on affirmative answers to two questions, and an agency adopts a rule giving conclusive answers to the first question once certain data are supplied, the rule is a rule even though it does not purport to answer the second question.

The EPA has rested on the policy statement exception to §553's requirements, which we find inapplicable. Though not invoking the exception for interpretive rules, it does couch one point in terms reminiscent of some characterizations of such rules. While the exact definition of an interpretive rule is unclear, it is clear that we don't have one here. The VHS model meets [the] affirmative definition of a legislative rule: it substantially curtails EPA's discretion in delisting decisions and accordingly has present binding effect. While not all rules of thumb are legislative rules, they are when they have these characteristics.

✳✳✳✳✳

Consider one final example of this problem of defining a rule and characterizing its effects in terms of the Administrative Procedure Act requirements for the creation of rules. Once again, the case arose out of action by the Environmental Protection Agency, but this time it concerned something EPA called a "guidance document."

General Electric v. EPA, 290 F.3d 377 (D.C. Cir. 2002).

INTRODUCTION: This case emerged from a challenge by General Electric to an EPA guidance document concerning the cleanup and disposal of polychlorinated biphenyls (PCBs). The guidance assessed methods for evaluating risks in cleanups and disposal. The company challenged EPA's actions on a variety of grounds, but, for present purposes, primarily on allegations that the guidance was, in reality, a legislative rule rather than a policy statement. While the policy statement need not comply with the rulemaking requirements of the APA, legislative rules, of course, must be made in accordance with those procedures.

*****

JUDGE GINSBURG wrote the opinion for the panel.

GE's primary argument is that the Guidance Document is a legislative rule and therefore should have been promulgated only after public notice and an opportunity for comment. Before we can reach the merits, we must consider whether the Document is a "rule" subject to our review under [the Toxic Substances Control Act] TSCA. [W]e conclude that the Guidance Document is indeed a legislative rule.

GE argues that the Guidance Document is a legislative rule rather than a statement of policy or an interpretive rule because it gives substance to the vague language of 40 C.F.R. §761.61(c) ("unreasonable risk of injury to health or the environment)," does so in an obligatory fashion, and is treated by the EPA as "controlling in the field." Although it is not entirely clear what in the EPA's view the Document is, the EPA comes closest to characterizing it as a statement of policy. With the Agency's argument so understood, the question before us can be framed as whether the Guidance Document is a legislative rule or a statement of policy.

[W]here we have attempted to draw the line between legislative rules and statements of policy, we have considered whether the agency action (1) "imposes any rights and obligations" or (2) "genuinely leaves the agency and its decision-makers free to exercise discretion." In *McLouth [Steel Products] v. Thomas,* 367 F.2d 1317 (D.C. Cir. 1988), we recognized that "in practice, there appears some overlap in . . . criteria" because "if a statement denies the decisionmaker discretion in the area of its coverage, so that [the agency] will automatically decline to entertain challenges to the statement's position, then the statement is binding, and creates rights or obligations." We emphasized that an agency announcement has "present-day binding effect" if the agency is "simply unready to hear new argument" in proceedings governed by the announcement.

The EPA urges the court to consider three factors: "(1) the Agency's own characterization of its action; (2) whether the action was published in the *Federal Register* or the *Code of Federal Regulations;* and (3) whether the action has binding effects on private parties or on the agency." *Molycorp, Inc. v. EPA,* 197 F.3d 543, 545 (D.C. Cir. 1999). As the EPA concedes, however, the third factor is the most important: "The ultimate focus of the inquiry is whether the agency action partakes of the fundamental characteristic of a regulation, i.e., that it has the force of law."

The two tests overlap at step three of the *Molycorp* formulation—in which the court determines whether the agency action binds private parties or the agency itself with the "force of law." This common standard has been well stated as follows: "If a document expresses a change in substantive law or policy (that is not an interpretation) which the agency intends to make binding, or administers with binding effect, the agency may not rely upon the statutory exemption for policy statements, but must observe the APA's legislative rulemaking procedures." Robert A. Anthony, "Interpretive Rules, Policy Statements, Guidances, Manuals, and the Like—Should Federal Agencies Use Them to Bind the Public?" 41 *Duke Law Journal* 1311, 1355 (1992). Our cases likewise make clear that an agency pronouncement will be considered binding as a practical matter if it either appears on its face to be binding or is applied by the agency in a way that indicates it is binding. [T]he mandatory language of a document alone can be sufficient to render it binding:

We think it clear that the Guidance Document does purport to bind applicants for approval of a risk-based cleanup plan. If an applicant chooses not to use the 4.0 total toxicity factor, then it "must, at a minimum account for the risk from non-cancer endpoints for neurotoxicity, reproductive and developmental toxicity, immune system suppression, liver damage, skin irritation, and endocrine disruption for each of the commercial mixtures found at the cleanup site." Although the Guidance Document does anticipate and acknowledge [some exceptions], that does not undermine the binding force of the Guidance Document in standard cases. To the applicant reading the Guidance Document the message is clear: in reviewing applications the Agency will not be open to considering approaches other than those prescribed in the Document.

According to the Agency, its position with respect to the total toxicity factor "is a matter of policy" that "can be changed at any time to respond to, *inter alia,* advances in scientific knowledge." But the Guidance Document itself says nothing of the sort. Clearly the EPA's initial response more accurately describes the Agency's approach in the Document: Stating without qualification that an applicant may use a total toxicity factor of 4.0 (mg/kg/day)-1 strongly implies that use of that value will not be questioned; an applicant reasonably could rely upon that implication.

The EPA argues that the Guidance Document "neither adds to EPA's prior position nor imposes any further obligations on EPA or the regulated community." Because we conclude that the Guidance Document does bind the Agency, it follows that the Document does indeed impose a "further obligation on the EPA." Furthermore, the EPA does not contend that in practice it has not treated the Guidance Document as binding in the ways described above.

In sum, the commands of the Guidance Document indicate that it has the force of law. On its face the Guidance Document imposes binding obligations upon applicants to submit applications that conform to the Document and upon the Agency. This is sufficient to render it a legislative rule. Furthermore, the Agency's application of the Document does nothing to demonstrate that the Document has any lesser effect in practice. Consequently, we conclude that the Guidance Document is a legislative rule.

*****

THE LEGISLATIVE VETO

A Demonstration of Louis Fisher's
Constitutional Dialogue

As Chapter 3 of *Public Law and Public Administration, Third Edition* explains, the legislative veto was a longstanding, though very controversial, device that was tolerated a long time and in a limited number of policy arenas. Presidents did not like it particularly, but administrations were willing to work with the

Congress in areas like government reorganization, appropriations issues, and some areas of foreign and military policy. These date back to the New Deal era and World War II. However, starting in the 1970s, the use of the committee and one-house veto provisions proliferated dramatically, to the point where it was almost a standard boilerplate provision in legislation. Even then, most agency staffs consulted informally with legislative staff in an effort to avoid confrontations later on in the process.

However, the Reagan administration came into office facing a legislature controlled by the other party and viewing it as a hostile arena. The Reagan White House almost immediately demonstrated that it was going to use administrative means to accomplish its ends and it was prepared to litigate to recover what Reagan officials regarded as legislative usurpation of executive authority dating at least back to the Watergate era.

Beyond that, there were many interest groups, regulated businesses, and even individuals affected by the politics associated with the legislative veto. In the end, some of these people took the constitutional questions about the legislative veto to court. However, the fact that the Supreme Court struck down the legislative veto was not the end of the story. As Louis Fisher has argued at length, the Court's ruling was part of a constitutional dialogue which continued well after the ruling in the *Chadha* case.[7]

Immigration and Naturalization Service v. Chadha, 462 U.S. 919 (1983).

INTRODUCTION: It was only a matter of time before the challenges to the legislative veto would reach the Supreme Court. In an interesting twist, the first case to get to the Court was not about a rulemaking proceeding, but instead concerned a form of adjudication. It was a one-house legislative veto of the findings of the Immigration and Naturalization Service (INS), concerning deportation of a number of individuals. Even so, the *Chadha* case provided the context in which the Court took on the wider issue of the legislative veto.

NOTE: For students who have been forced to read the *Federalist Papers* or who have constantly heard about the "intent of the framers" in various contexts, it is interesting to note the references in this and other cases to those materials. They are actually still used and, yes, there are surprisingly many cases of first impression (cases presenting an issue to the Court for the first time) under the Constitution even today.

---

7. Louis Fisher, *Constitutional Dialogues: Interpretation as Political Process* (Princeton, NJ: Princeton University Press, 1988). See also his *Constitutional Conflicts Between Congress and the President, 4th Ed. Revised* (Lawrence, KS: University Press of Kansas, 1997).

*****

CHIEF JUSTICE BURGER wrote the opinion for the Court.

[This case] presents a challenge to the constitutionality of the provision in §244(c)(2) of the Immigration and Nationality Act, authorizing one House of Congress, by resolution, to invalidate the decision of the Executive Branch, pursuant to authority delegated by Congress to the Attorney General of the United States, to allow a particular deportable alien to remain in the United States.

III. [T]he fact that a given law or procedure is efficient, convenient, and useful in facilitating functions of government, standing alone, will not save it if it is contrary to the Constitution. Convenience and efficiency are not the primary objectives—or the hallmarks—of democratic government and our inquiry is sharpened rather than blunted by the fact that congressional veto provisions are appearing with increasing frequency in statutes which delegate authority to executive and independent agencies.

Explicit and unambiguous provisions of the Constitution prescribe and define the respective functions of the Congress and of the Executive in the legislative process. Since the precise terms of those familiar provisions are critical to the resolution of these cases, we set them out verbatim. Article I provides: "All legislative Powers herein granted shall be vested in a Congress of the United States, which shall consist of a Senate and House of Representatives." Art. I, §1. [It requires that] "Every Bill which shall have passed the House of Representatives and the Senate, shall, before it becomes a law, be presented to the President of the United States. . . ." Art. I, §7, cl. 2. "Every Order, Resolution, or Vote to which the Concurrence of the Senate and House of Representatives may be necessary . . . shall be presented to the President of the United States; and before the Same shall take Effect, shall be approved by him, or being disapproved by him, shall be repassed by two thirds of the Senate and House of Representatives, according to the Rules and Limitations prescribed in the Case of a Bill." Art. I, §7, cl. 3.

These provisions of Art. I are integral parts of the constitutional design for the separation of powers. We have recently noted that "[the] principle of separation of powers was not simply an abstract generalization in the minds of the Framers: it was woven into the document that they drafted in Philadelphia in the summer of 1787." [W]e see that the purposes underlying the Presentment Clauses, Art. I, §7, cls. 2, 3, and the bicameral requirement of Art. I, §1, and §7, cl. 2, guide our resolution of the important question presented in these cases.

The Presentment Clauses.

The records of the Constitutional Convention reveal that the requirement that all legislation be presented to the President before becoming law was uniformly accepted by the Framers.[8] The decision to provide the President with a limited and qualified power to nullify proposed legislation by veto was based on the pro-

---

8. I. J. Story, *Commentaries on the Constitution of the United States* 611 (3rd ed. 1858). See
   I. M. Farrand, *The Records of the Federal Convention of 1787,* pp. 21, 97–104, 138–140
   (1911) (hereinafter Farrand); id., at 73–80, 181, 298, 301–305.

found conviction of the Framers that the powers conferred on Congress were the powers to be most carefully circumscribed. The President's role in the lawmaking process also reflects the Framers' careful efforts to check whatever propensity a particular Congress might have to enact oppressive, improvident, or ill-considered measures. The Court also has observed that the Presentment Clauses serve the important purpose of assuring that a "national" perspective is grafted on the legislative process.

Bicameralism.

The bicameral requirement of Art. I, §§1, 7, was of scarcely less concern to the Framers than was the Presidential veto and indeed the two concepts are interdependent. By providing that no law could take effect without the concurrence of the prescribed majority of the Members of both Houses, the Framers reemphasized their belief that legislation should not be enacted unless it has been carefully and fully considered by the Nation's elected officials. In the Constitutional Convention debates on the need for a bicameral legislature, James Wilson commented: "If the Legislative authority be not restrained, there can be neither liberty nor stability; and it can only be restrained by dividing it within itself, into distinct and independent branches. In a single house there is no check, but the inadequate one, of the virtue & good sense of those who compose it." I Farrand 254.[9]

Hamilton argued that a Congress comprised of a single House was antithetical to the very purposes of the Constitution. This view was rooted in a general skepticism regarding the fallibility of human nature.

These observations are consistent with what many of the Framers expressed, none more cogently than Madison in pointing up the need to divide and disperse power in order to protect liberty. However familiar, it is useful to recall that apart from their fear that special interests could be favored at the expense of public needs, the Framers were also concerned over the apprehensions of the smaller states. It need hardly be repeated here that the Great Compromise, under which one House was viewed as representing the people and the other the states, allayed the fears of both the large and small states.

We see therefore that the Framers were acutely conscious that the bicameral requirement and the Presentment Clauses would serve essential constitutional functions. The President's participation in the legislative process was to protect the Executive Branch from Congress and to protect the whole people from improvident laws. The division of the Congress into two distinctive bodies assures that the legislative power would be exercised only after opportunity for full study and debate in separate settings. The President's unilateral veto power, in turn, was limited by the power of two-thirds of both Houses of Congress to overrule a veto thereby precluding final arbitrary action of one person.

IV. The Constitution sought to divide the delegated powers of the new Federal Government into three defined categories, Legislative, Executive, and Judicial, to

---

9. NOTE: This citation refers to Max Farrand, *Records of the Federal Convention of 1787* (New Haven: Yale University Press, 1966), Vol. I, p. 254. Farrand is generally regarded as the authoritative work on the proceedings of the constitutional convention.

assure, as nearly as possible, that each branch of government would confine itself to its assigned responsibility. The hydraulic pressure inherent within each of the separate Branches to exceed the outer limits of its power, even to accomplish desirable objectives, must be resisted.

Although not "hermetically" sealed from one another, the powers delegated to the three Branches are functionally identifiable. When any Branch acts, it is presumptively exercising the power the Constitution has delegated to it. When the Executive acts, he presumptively acts in an executive or administrative capacity as defined in Art. II. And when, as here, one House of Congress purports to act, it is presumptively acting within its assigned sphere.

Whether actions taken by either House are, in law and fact, an exercise of legislative power depends not on their form but upon "whether they contain matter which is properly to be regarded as legislative in its character and effect."

Examination of the action taken here by one House pursuant to § 244(c)(2) reveals that it was essentially legislative in purpose and effect. In purporting to exercise power defined in Art. I, §8, cl. 4, to "establish an uniform Rule of Naturalization," the House took action that had the purpose and effect of altering the legal rights, duties, and relations of persons, including the Attorney General, Executive Branch officials and Chadha, all outside the Legislative Branch. The one-House veto operated in these cases to overrule the Attorney General and mandate Chadha's deportation; absent the House action, Chadha would remain in the United States. Congress has acted and its action has altered Chadha's status.

The legislative character of the one-House veto in these cases is confirmed by the character of the congressional action it supplants. After long experience with the clumsy, time-consuming private bill procedure, Congress made a deliberate choice to delegate to the Attorney General, the authority to allow deportable aliens to remain in this country in certain specified circumstances. Congress' decision to deport Chadha—no less than Congress' original choice to delegate to the Attorney General the authority to make that decision, involves determinations of policy that Congress can implement in only one way; bicameral passage followed by presentment to the President. Congress must abide by its delegation of authority until that delegation is legislatively altered or revoked.

[W]hen the Framers intended to authorize either House of Congress to act alone and outside of its prescribed bicameral legislative role, they narrowly and precisely defined the procedure for such action. There are four provisions in the Constitution, explicit and unambiguous, by which one House may act alone with the unreviewable force of law, not subject to the President's veto: (a) The House of Representatives power to initiate impeachments. Art. I, §2, cl. 5; (b) The Senate power to conduct trials following impeachment. Art. I, §3, cl. 6; (c) The Senate power to approve or to disapprove Presidential appointments. Art. II, §2, cl. 2; [and] (d) The Senate power to ratify treaties. Art. II, §2, cl. 2.

Since it is clear that the action by the House under §244(c)(2) was not within any of the express constitutional exceptions authorizing one House to act alone, and equally clear that it was an exercise of legislative power, that action was subject to the standards prescribed in Art. I. The bicameral requirement, the Presentment Clauses, the President's veto, and Congress' power to override a veto were intended to erect enduring checks on each Branch and to protect the people from the improvident exercise of power by mandating certain prescribed steps. To preserve those checks, and maintain the separation of powers, the carefully defined limits on the power of each Branch must not be eroded. To accomplish what has been attempted by one House of Congress in this case requires action in conformity with the express procedures of the Constitution's prescription for legislative action: passage by a majority of both Houses and presentment to the President.

In purely practical terms, it is obviously easier for action to be taken by one House without submission to the President; but it is crystal clear from the records of the Convention, contemporaneous writings and debates, that the Framers ranked other values higher than efficiency. The choices we discern as having been made in the Constitutional Convention impose burdens on governmental processes that often seem clumsy, inefficient, even unworkable, but those hard choices were consciously made. There is no support in the Constitution or decisions of this Court for the proposition that the cumbersomeness and delays often encountered in complying with explicit constitutional standards may be avoided, either by the Congress or by the President. See *Youngstown Sheet & Tube Co. v. Sawyer,* 343 U.S. 579 (1952). With all the obvious flaws of delay, untidiness, and potential for abuse, we have not yet found a better way to preserve freedom than by making the exercise of power subject to the carefully crafted restraints spelled out in the Constitution.

V. We hold that the congressional veto provision in §244(c)(2) is unconstitutional.

JUSTICE POWELL wrote an opinion concurring in the judgment.

The Court's decision will invalidate every use of the legislative veto. The breadth of this holding gives one pause. Congress has included the veto in literally hundreds of statutes, dating back to the 1930's. Congress clearly views this procedure as essential to controlling the delegation of power to administrative agencies. One reasonably may disagree with Congress' assessment of the veto's utility, but the respect due its judgment as a coordinate branch of Government cautions that our holding should be no more extensive than necessary to decide these cases. In my view, the cases may be decided on a narrower ground. When Congress finds that a particular person does not satisfy the statutory criteria for permanent residence in this country it has assumed a judicial function in violation of the principle of separation of powers. Accordingly, I concur only in the judgment.

I. The Framers perceived that "[the] accumulation of all powers legislative, executive and judiciary in the same hands, whether of one, a few or many, and whether hereditary, self appointed, or elective, may justly be pronounced the very definition of tyranny." *The Federalist* No. 47. One abuse that was prevalent during the Confederation was the exercise of judicial power by the state legislatures. The Framers were well acquainted with the danger of subjecting the determination of the rights of one person to the "tyranny of shifting majorities." It was to prevent the recurrence of such abuses that the Framers vested the executive, legislative, and judicial powers in separate branches. Their concern that a legislature should not be able unilaterally to impose a substantial deprivation on one person was expressed not only in this general allocation of power, but also in more specific provisions, such as the Bill of Attainder Clause. This Clause, and the separation-of-powers doctrine generally, reflect the Framers' concern that trial by a legislature lacks the safeguards necessary to prevent the abuse of power.

The Constitution does not establish three branches with precisely defined boundaries. The Court thus has been mindful that the boundaries between each branch should be fixed "according to common sense and the inherent necessities of the governmental coordination." But where one branch has impaired or sought to assume a power central to another branch, the Court has not hesitated to enforce the doctrine.

II. On its face, the House's action appears clearly adjudicatory. The House did not enact a general rule; rather it made its own determination that six specific persons did not comply with certain statutory criteria. It thus undertook the type of decision that traditionally has been left to other branches. Where, as here, Congress has exercised a power "that cannot possibly be regarded as merely in aid of the legislative function of Congress," the decisions of this Court have held that Congress impermissibly assumed a function that the Constitution entrusted to another branch.

In my view . . . Congress . . . exceeded the scope of its constitutionally prescribed authority. I would not reach the broader question whether legislative vetoes are invalid under the Presentment Clauses.

JUSTICE WHITE wrote a dissent.

Today the Court not only invalidates §244(c)(2) of the Immigration and Nationality Act, but also sounds the death knell for nearly 200 other statutory provisions in which Congress has reserved a "legislative veto." For this reason, the Court's decision is of surpassing importance. And it is for this reason that the Court would have been well advised to decide the cases, if possible, on the narrower grounds of separation of powers, leaving for full consideration the constitutionality of other congressional review statutes.

The prominence of the legislative veto mechanism in our contemporary political system and its importance to Congress can hardly be overstated. It has become a central means by which Congress secures the accountability of executive and independent agencies. Without the legislative veto, Congress is faced with a Hobson's choice: either to refrain from delegating the necessary authority, leaving itself with a hopeless task of writing laws with the requisite specificity to cover endless special circumstances across the entire policy landscape, or in the alternative, to abdicate its law-making function to the Executive Branch and independent agencies.

I. The legislative veto developed initially in response to the problems of reorganizing the sprawling Government structure created in response to the Depression. The Reorganization Acts established the chief model for the legislative veto. Shortly after adoption of the Reorganization Act of 1939 Congress and the President applied the legislative veto procedure to resolve the delegation problem for national security and foreign affairs. World War II occasioned the need to transfer greater authority to the President in these areas. The legislative veto offered the means by which Congress could confer additional authority while preserving its own constitutional role.

During the 1970's the legislative veto was important in resolving a series of major constitutional disputes between the President and Congress over claims of the President to broad impoundment, war, and national emergency powers. The key provision of the War Powers Resolution authorizes the termination by concurrent resolution of the use of armed forces in hostilities. A similar measure resolved the problem posed by Presidential claims of inherent power to impound appropriations. Congressional Budget and Impoundment Control Act of 1974. Although the War Powers Resolution was enacted over President Nixon's veto, the Impoundment Control Act was enacted with the President's approval. These statutes were followed by others resolving similar problems: the National Emergencies Act, resolving the longstanding problems with unchecked Executive emergency power; the International Security Assistance and Arms Export Control Act, resolving the problem of foreign arms sales; and the Nuclear Non-Proliferation Act of 1978, resolving the problem of exports of nuclear technology.

Even this brief review suffices to demonstrate that the legislative veto is more than "efficient, convenient, and useful." It is an important if not indispensable political invention that allows the President and Congress to resolve major constitutional and policy differences, assures the accountability of independent regulatory agencies, and preserves Congress' control over lawmaking. Perhaps there are other means of accommodation and accountability, but the increasing reliance of Congress upon the legislative veto suggests that the alternatives to which Congress must now turn are not entirely satisfactory.

The reality of the situation is that the constitutional question posed today is one of immense difficulty over which the Executive and Legislative Branches have understandably disagreed. In my view, neither Art. I of the Constitution nor the doctrine of separation of powers is violated by this mechanism by which our elected Representatives preserve their voice in the governance of the Nation.

If Congress may delegate lawmaking power to independent and Executive agencies, it is most difficult to understand Art. I as prohibiting Congress from also reserving a check on legislative power for itself. Absent the veto, the agencies receiving delegations of legislative or quasi-legislative power may issue regulations having the force of law without bicameral approval and without the President's signature. It is thus not apparent why the reservation of a veto over the exercise of that legislative power must be subject to a more exacting test. In both cases, it is enough that the initial statutory authorizations comply with the Art. I requirements.

✳✳✳✳✳

After the Court ruled in the *Chadha* case, it considered two cases from the U.S. Circuit Court of Appeals for the D.C. Circuit that did involve interventions in rulemaking. The first concerned legislative veto provisions in the natural gas deregulation legislation passed during the Carter administration, and the second involved Federal Trade Commission rules governing used car dealer disclosures of defects. The D.C. Circuit struck down the veto in both cases. *Consumer Energy Council v. Federal Energy Regulatory Commission,* 673 F. 2d 425 (D.C. Cir. 1982); *Consumers Union v. FTC,* 691 F.2d 575 (D.C. Cir. 1982). *The Consumer Energy Council* opinion is far stronger than the *Chadha* opinion and is well worth reading. The Supreme Court affirmed both cases without opinion.[10]

On the other hand, when the Republicans came back into control of the Congress after the 1994 elections, with Democrat Bill Clinton in the White House, they had no difficulty seeking an alternative by which to restore the legislative veto, notwithstanding their opposite position during the Reagan years. They accomplished the task with the passage in 1996 of the Congressional Review Act, 5 U.S.C. §801 et seq.[11]

Chapter 5 of *Public Law and Public Administration, Third Edition* explains the requirements of the Act and they will not be repeated here. The first example of its use came about early in 2001 and involved rules adopted by the Occupational Safety and Health Administration (OSHA) during the Clinton years, requiring employers to seek to prevent repetitive stress injuries to workers through the requirements for ergonomically safe equipment and processes. What follows are the documents required by the Congressional Review Act as they developed in the process of nullifying the ergonomics rules.

First, the General Counsel of the U.S. General Accounting Office (GAO) is required to assess agency compliance with existing law at the time the rules were initially issued. This comes in the form of a letter to the appropriate legislative committees in both houses.

✳✳✳✳✳

B-286818
November 29, 2000
The Honorable James M. Jeffords
Chairman
The Honorable Edward M. Kennedy
Ranking Minority Member
Committee on Health, Education, Labor, and Pensions
United States Senate

---

10. *Process Gas Consumers v. Consumer Energy Council,* 463 U.S. 1216 (1983); *United States Senate v. FTC,* 463 U.S. 1216 (1983).

11. The Congress managed to get this and other controversial legislation passed by attaching it to the Debt Limit Extension Act, which was, as a practical matter, veto proof.

The Honorable William F. Goodling
Chairman
The Honorable William Clay
Ranking Minority Member
Committee on Education and the Workforce
House of Representatives

Subject: Department of Labor, Occupational Safety and Health Administration:
Ergonomics Program

Pursuant to section 801(a)(2)(A) of title 5, United States Code, this is our
report on a major rule promulgated by the Department of Labor, Occupational
Safety and Health Administration (OSHA), entitled "Ergonomics Program" (RIN:
1218-AB36). We received the rule on November 14, 2000. It was published in the
Federal Register as a final rule on November 14, 2000. 65 Fed. Reg. 68262.

The final rule issues a final Ergonomics Program that addresses the risks of
employee exposure to ergonomic risk factors in jobs in general industry workplaces.

The final standard would affect approximately 6.1 million employers and
102 million employees in general industry workplaces.

Enclosed is our assessment of OSHA's compliance with the procedural steps
required by section 801(a)(1)(B)(i) through (iv) of title 5 with respect to the rule.
Our review indicates that OSHA complied with the applicable requirements.

If you have any questions about this report, please contact James W. Vickers,
Assistant General Counsel, at (202) 512-8210. The official responsible for GAO
evaluation work relating to the subject matter of the rule is Cindy Fagnoni,
Managing Director, Education, Workforce, and Income Security. Ms. Fagnoni can
be reached at (202) 512-7215.

Kathleen E. Wannisky
Managing Associate General Counsel

Enclosure
   cc: The Honorable Charles N. Jeffress
   Assistant Secretary
   Department of Labor

*****

ANALYSIS UNDER 5 U.S.C. §801(a)(1)(B)(i)-(iv) OF A MAJOR RULE
ISSUED BY THE
DEPARTMENT OF LABOR,
OCCUPATIONAL SAFETY AND HEALTH ADMINISTRATION
ENTITLED
"ERGONOMICS PROGRAM"
(RIN: 1218-AB36)

(i) Cost-benefit analysis

OSHA performed a Final Economic Analysis, which was furnished to our Office and is summarized in the preamble to the final rule. The analysis considers the costs, benefits, technological and economic feasibility, and economic impacts of the final standard.

In the analysis, all costs are expressed in 1996 dollars and annualized using a 7-percent discount rate and a 10-year annualization period. The analysis shows that the total estimated costs to society for the private sector are $3.4 billion per year, and estimated costs for all affected parties, including state and local governments, are $3.9 billion per year. Estimated costs to employers in the private sector as a whole are $4 billion per year and to all affected sectors are $4.5 billion per year. OSHA states that the distinction between costs to society and costs to employers is necessary because costs associated with the standard's work restriction protection provisions represent a cost to employers, but not to society as a whole.

OSHA believes that the incidence of musculoskeletal disorders (MSDs), which the rule seeks to prevent, is underreported by 50 percent. In the first 10 years, OSHA projects that the standard will avert approximately 2.3 million currently reported MSDs and an additional 2.3 million MSDs not currently reported, for a total of 4.6 million MSDs averted.

OSHA estimates that the direct costs savings associated with each currently reported MSD, including the savings in lost productivity, lost tax payments, and administrative costs for workers' compensation claims, are $27,000 and for not currently reported MSDs $7,000. The difference in amounts reflects OSHA's belief that the MSDs not reported currently are less severe than those being reported. Based on this estimate of direct cost savings with each reported MSD avoided, the annualized benefits accruing in the first 10 years are estimated to be $9.1 billion per year.

(ii) Agency actions relevant to the Regulatory Flexibility Act, 5 U.S.C. §§603-605, 607, and 609.

OSHA prepared a Final Regulatory Flexibility Analysis, which is summarized in the preamble to the final rule. It furnishes the information required by the

Regulatory Flexibility Act, including the reasons for the agency action, an estimate of the number of small entities affected by the rule, reporting and record-keeping requirements, and steps taken to minimize the impact on small entities.

OSHA estimates that there are 4.75 million small establishments in general industry affected by the rule and that 4.2 million of these are very small entities (employing fewer than 20 employees).

Regarding reducing the impact on small entities, OSHA points out that the use of the two-part action trigger will have the effect of decreasing the number of jobs small businesses will need to address through a full ergonomics program or a quick fix. Establishments with fewer than 11 employees do not have to keep records. Existing ergonomic programs will be grandfathered in and considered in compliance with the standards as long as the existing program meets the certain requirements. Finally, OSHA will supply compliance guides for small businesses and a Web-based expert system to guide employers through the applicability of the standard.

(iii) Agency actions relevant to sections 202-205 of the Unfunded Mandates Reform Act of 1995, 2 U.S.C. §§1532-1535

Since the final rule will require the expenditure of approximately $4.0 billion each year by employers in the private sector, the rule establishes a federal private sector mandate within the meaning of section 202 of the Act.

OSHA notes that its standards do not apply to state and local governments except in states that have voluntarily elected to adopt an OSHA State Plan. Therefore, the final rule does not impose an intergovernmental mandate.

OSHA does not anticipate any disproportionate budgetary effects on any particular region, state, local, or tribal government or urban or rural community. The discussion in the Final Economic Analysis concerning benefits and costs and alternatives considered comply with the requirements of the Act.

(iv) Other relevant information or requirements under acts and executive orders.

Administrative Procedure Act, 5 U.S.C. §§551 et seq.

The final rule was issued using the notice and comment procedures contained at 5 U.S.C. 553.

On August 3, 1992, OSHA published an Advanced Notice of Proposed Rulemaking (ANPR) in the Federal Register (57 Fed. Reg. 34192) requesting information for consideration in the development of an ergonomics standard and received 290 comments in response.

Between the issuance of the ANPR and the November 23, 1999, Notice of Proposed Rulemaking (64 Fed. Reg. 65768), OSHA met with various industry, labor and professional groups and organizations. In 1998, OSHA met with 400 stakeholders to discuss the proposed standards. Also, OSHA convened a SBREFA Panel to review and comment on a draft of the standards.

Following the publication of the proposed rule, OSHA extended the time for receipt of comments and held numerous public hearings that resulted in 18,337 page of transcript pages from 714 witnesses. In addition, more than 6,100 comments were received.

Paperwork Reduction Act, 44 U.S.C. §§3501-3520.

The final rule contains information collections that are required to be reviewed and approved by the Office of Management and Budget. OSHA has submitted an Information Collection Request (ICR) to OMB for approval, which contains the required information and is summarized in the preamble to the final rule. The ICR describes the collections of information, the need for and proposed use of the information, the covered employers who will be required to collect and maintain information under the standard, and an estimate of the annual cost and reporting burden.

OSHA notes that the time per response will vary from minimal recordkeeping requirements for a quick fix situation to establishing and implementing a complete ergonomics program. OSHA estimates that the annual burden hours will be 36.5 million hours at an estimated cost of $61 million.

Statutory authorization for the rule.

The final rule was issued pursuant to the authority contained in sections 4, 6, and 8 of the Occupational Safety and Health Act, 29 U.S.C. 653, 655, 657; the Secretary of Labor's Order No. 3-2000 (65 Fed. Reg. 50017); and 29 CFR Part 1911.

Executive Order No. 12866

The final rule was reviewed by the Office of Management and Budget and found to be an "economically significant" regulatory action under the order. Executive Order No. 13132 (Federalism).

OSHA reviewed the final rule in accordance with the Executive Order on Federalism and determined that section 18 of the Occupational Safety and Health Act (OSH Act) expresses Congress' intent to preempt state laws with respect to which federal OSHA has promulgated standards.

Under the OSH Act, a state can avoid preemption only if it submits, and obtains federal approval of, a plan for the development of such standards and their enforcement. These state plans must be at least as effective as the federal standards in providing safe and healthful employment and places of employment.

The preamble to the final rule, regarding the requirement to consult with governmental officials, contains various listings of the numerous governmental representatives that attended various stakeholder meetings and public hearings in formulating the final standard.

*****

With this report in hand, the Congress may, if it wishes, move a joint resolution of disapproval. The reason for the joint resolution as compared with earlier one-house or even committee vetoes is that this form of action requires involvement by both houses and presentation to the president for a possible veto, thus avoiding the bicameralism and Presentment clause difficulties at the core of the *Chadha* ruling. They did so in the case of the ergonomics rule.

*****

PUBLIC LAW 107-5 [S.J. Res. 6]

Joint Resolution

Providing for congressional disapproval of the rule submitted by the Department of Labor under chapter 8 of title 5, United States Code, relating to ergonomics.

Resolved by the Senate and House of Representatives of the United States of America in Congress assembled, That Congress disapproves the rule submitted by the Department of Labor relating to ergonomics (published at 65 Fed. Reg. 68261 (2000)), and such rule shall have no force or effect.

*****

President George W. Bush had followed Presidents Reagan and Bush in promising to attack regulation, and was only too happy to sign the resolution of disapproval. What follows is his statement on signing S.J. 6.

*****

Weekly Compilation of Presidential Documents
Monday, March 26, 2001
Volume 37, Page 477
Statement on Signing Legislation To Repeal Federal Ergonomics Regulations

March 20, 2001

Today I have signed into law S.J. Res. 6, a measure that repeals an unduly burdensome and overly broad regulation dealing with ergonomics. This is the first time the Congressional Review Act has been put to use. This resolution is a good and proper use of the Act because the different branches of our Government need to be held accountable.

There needs to be a balance between and an understanding of the costs and benefits associated with Federal regulations. In this instance, though, in exchange for uncertain benefits, the ergonomics rule would have cost both large and small employers billions of dollars and presented employers with overwhelming compliance challenges. Also, the rule would have applied a bureaucratic one-size-fits-all solution to a broad range of employers and workers—not good government at work.

The safety and health of our Nation's workforce is a priority for my Administration. Together we will pursue a comprehensive approach to ergonomics that addresses the concerns surrounding the ergonomics rule repealed today. We will work with the Congress, the business community, and our Nation's workers to address this important issue.

George W. Bush
The White House,
March 20, 2001.

*****

With that, the ergonomics rules were halted.

ADDITIONAL READINGS

Robert A. Anthony, "Interpretative Rules, Policy Statements, Guidances, Manuals, and the Like—Should Federal Agencies Use Them to Bind the Public?" 41 *Duke L.J.* 1311 (1992).

Barbara Hinckson Craig, *The Legislative Veto* (Boulder, CO: Westport, 1983).

Louis Fisher, *Constitutional Conflicts Between Congress and the President, Fourth Edition Revised* (Lawrence: University Press of Kansas, 1997).

Philip J. Harter, "Assessing the Assessors: The Actual Performance of Negotiated Rulemaking," 9 *N.Y.U. Envtl. L.J.* 32 (2000).

Cornelius M. Kerwin, *Rulemaking: How Government Agencies Write Law and Make Policy, Third Edition* (Washington, D.C.: Congressional Quarterly Press, 2003).

Thomas O. McGarity, "Some Thoughts on 'Deossifying' the Rulemaking Process," 41 *Duke L.J.* 1385 (1992).

Stephen Williams, "Hybrid Rulemaking Under the Administrative Procedure Act: A Legal and Empirical Analysis," 42 *University of Chicago L. Rev.* 401 (1975).

2

⚖️

Administrative
Adjudications*

J ust what happens when government focuses on a particular individual, specific group, or business has changed a good deal since the adoption of the Administrative Procedure Act. In some respects, the way courts and administrators conceptualize the situation is as important as the processes themselves. The shift has been toward a greater emphasis on due process—and particularly on hearings—as devices for fact-finding, as well as a concern with the costs and burdens of these proceedings aimed at resolution of disputes over legally protected rights. As Chapter 6 of *Public Law and Public Administration, Third Edition* explains, that is significantly different from the situation more than three decades ago when the emphasis was on ensuring fundamental fairness and preventing arbitrary behavior whenever people were likely to suffer a grievous loss. That is not to say that there was, in earlier years, an unwillingness to recognize the need for flexible procedures or a lack of awareness of the burdens of adjudicatory processes.[1] Although courts were willing to consider circumstances and take into consideration the nature of the disputes in defining

---

* Related Material in *Public Law and Public Administration, Third Edition,* Chapter 6.

1. See, e.g., *Cafeteria Workers v. McElroy,* 367 U.S. 886 (1961).

when, whether, and what kind of hearing was to be provided, the Supreme Court made clear that it would reject arguments that no protections were needed, simply because what was at issue was a privilege rather than a right. The Court was not prepared in that earlier time to accept administrative efficiency or simplistic balancing tests to deny due process protections.

Starting with *Arnett v. Kennedy*,[2] *Mathews v. Eldridge*,[3] and *Board of Regents v. Roth*,[4] the Burger Court began a significant shift away from expanded due process protections and indeed signaled a retreat from previous rulings. Although a majority of the Court continues to argue that it has not returned to the days of the right/privilege dichotomy and irrebuttable presumptions, other members of the Court, led by Chief Justice Rehnquist and Justice Scalia, argue for precisely that.[5] Litigants who have gone to court expecting the long-touted concern with fundamental fairness and protection from arbitrary behavior have encountered demands that they clearly identify the specific legal rights they claim within a narrower interpretation of liberty or property than before. They must also demonstrate that more or different adjudicative procedures are needed to remedy demonstrated defects in the fact-finding process. Even if they satisfy those two conditions, they still are called upon to demonstrate a favorable cost/benefit balance to obtain enhanced protections.

Of course, the problem with case-by-case assessments of what process is required, and the use of cost/benefit calculations in each instance, is that neither the agency involved, nor the citizen who has a problem with government, can be certain just what the requirements are in any given situation until that case has gone to judicial review. Hence, although the rulings of the past quarter century appear to have moved significantly toward protecting public administrators from increasing demands for more due process protections, the fact is that the situation is far from certain. All that having been said, and beyond constitutional claims, it is important to remember that agencies must meet the requirements of the legislation they administer and the rules they promulgate in designing their adjudicative procedures.

---

2. 416 U.S. 134 (1974).

3. 424 U.S. 319 (1976).

4. 408 U.S. 564 (1972). Ironically, many commentators see *Roth* as part of the expansion of due process protections, but as William Van Alstyne has pointed out, that usually reflects a lack of careful analysis of the earlier cases. William Van Alstyne, "Cracks in 'The New Property': Adjudicative Due Process in the Administrative State," 62 *Cornell Law Review* 445, 489–90 (1977).

5. *Rutan v. Republican Party of Illinois*, 497 U.S. 62, 97 n. 2 (1990), Scalia, J., dissenting.

THE BROAD APPROACH
TO DUE PROCESS RIGHTS
IN ADMINISTRATIVE ADJUDICATIONS

Let us take a step back in time to a few brief statements of the more robust interpretation of due process, beginning with one of the most important of these, *Goldberg v. Kelly.*

Goldberg v. Kelly, 397 U.S. 254 (1970).

INTRODUCTION: The precedents concerning due process adjudication rights cited in this important case trace back all the way to 1914, and from there through the development of procedural due process requirements in administrative adjudications from the early 1950s through the 1960s. During this period, government jobs, contracts, loan programs, licenses, and social service benefits had grown tremendously in number and importance, both for businesses and individuals. So important were these programs, that the Court accepted the assertion that they represented a kind of "new property" (see the opinion below). Second, the experiences of the 1950s and 1960s had demonstrated a host of abuses in which individuals were made to suffer what the Court referred to as a "grievous loss," from arbitrary government behavior. (See *Public Law and Public Administration, Third Edition,* Chapter 4.) Finally, in the decades following the passage of the APA, many agencies had not brought themselves into compliance and had not ensured fundamental fairness in their adjudicative practices.

In *Goldberg,* a group of recipients of Aid to Families with Dependent Children (AFDC)[6] and some receiving the New York State's Home Relief assistance brought suit in federal district court, claiming that they either had been or were in danger of being terminated from the programs without adequate notice or an opportunity for a hearing before the cutoff of benefits. Under the rules that existed at the time the case began, recipients whose benefits were terminated could request a post-termination "fair hearing," but no pre-termination hearing was available.

*****

JUSTICE BRENNAN wrote the opinion for the Court.

The question for decision is whether a State that terminates public assistance payments to a particular recipient without affording him the opportunity for an

---

6. This program was generally referred to as welfare, but has since been substantially
    modified and renamed as the Temporary Assistance for Needy Families (TANF) program.

evidentiary hearing prior to termination denies the recipient procedural due process in violation of the Due Process Clause of the Fourteenth Amendment.

Appellant does not contend that procedural due process is not applicable to the termination of welfare benefits. Such benefits are a matter of statutory entitlement for persons qualified to receive them.[7] Their termination involves state action that adjudicates important rights. The constitutional challenge cannot be answered by an argument that public assistance benefits are "a 'privilege' and not a 'right.'" *Shapiro v. Thompson,* 394 U.S. 618, 627 n. 6 (1969). Relevant constitutional restraints apply as much to the withdrawal of public assistance benefits as to disqualification for unemployment compensation, *Sherbert v. Verner,* 374 U.S. 398 (1963); or to denial of a tax exemption, *Speiser v. Randall,* 357 U.S. 513 (1958); or to discharge from public employment, *Slochower v. Board of Higher Education,* 350 U.S. 551 (1956). The extent to which procedural due process must be afforded the recipient is influenced by the extent to which he may be "condemned to suffer grievous loss," and depends upon whether the recipient's interest in avoiding that loss outweighs the governmental interest in summary adjudication.

We agree with the District Court that when welfare is discontinued, only a pre-termination evidentiary hearing provides the recipient with procedural due process. For qualified recipients, welfare provides the means to obtain essential food, clothing, housing, and medical care. Termination of aid pending resolution of a controversy over eligibility may deprive an eligible recipient of the very means by which to live while he waits. Since he lacks independent resources, his situation becomes immediately desperate. His need to concentrate upon finding the means for daily subsistence, in turn, adversely affects his ability to seek redress from the welfare bureaucracy.

Moreover, important governmental interests are promoted by affording recipients a pre-termination evidentiary hearing. Welfare, by meeting the basic demands of subsistence, can help bring within the reach of the poor the same opportunities that are available to others to participate meaningfully in the life of the community. At the same time, welfare guards against the societal malaise that may flow from a widespread sense of unjustified frustration and insecurity. Public assistance, then, is not mere charity, but a means to "promote the general Welfare, and secure

---

7. It may be realistic today to regard welfare entitlements as more like "property" than a "gratuity." Much of the existing wealth in this country takes the form of rights that do not fall within traditional common-law concepts of property. It has been aptly noted that: "society today is built around entitlement. The automobile dealer has his franchise, the doctor and lawyer their professional licenses, the worker his union membership, contract, and pension rights, the executive his contract and stock options; all are devices to aid security and independence. Many of the most important of these entitlements now flow from government: subsidies to farmers and businessmen, routes for airlines and channels for television stations; long term contracts for defense, space, and education; social security pensions for individuals. Such sources of security, whether private or public, are no longer regarded as luxuries or gratuities; to the recipients they are essentials, fully deserved, and in no sense a form of charity. It is only the poor whose entitlements, although recognized by public policy, have not been effectively enforced." Reich, "Individual Rights and Social Welfare: The Emerging Legal Issues," 74 *Yale L. J.* 1245, 1255 (1965). See also Reich, "The New Property," 73 *Yale L. J.* 733 (1964).

the Blessings of Liberty to ourselves and our Posterity." The same governmental interests that counsel the provision of welfare, counsel as well its uninterrupted provision to those eligible to receive it; pre-termination evidentiary hearings are indispensable to that end.

Appellant does not challenge the force of these considerations but argues that they are outweighed by countervailing governmental interests in conserving fiscal and administrative resources. These interests, the argument goes, justify the delay of any evidentiary hearing until after discontinuance of the grants. Summary adjudication protects the public fisc by stopping payments promptly upon discovery of reason to believe that a recipient is no longer eligible. Since most terminations are accepted without challenge, summary adjudication also conserves both the fisc and administrative time and energy by reducing the number of evidentiary hearings actually held.

The requirement of a prior hearing doubtless involves some greater expense, and the benefits paid to ineligible recipients pending decision at the hearing probably cannot be recouped, since these recipients are likely to be judgment-proof. But the State is not without weapons to minimize these increased costs. Much of the drain on fiscal and administrative resources can be reduced by developing procedures for prompt pre-termination hearings and by skillful use of personnel and facilities. Thus, the interest of the eligible recipient in uninterrupted receipt of public assistance, coupled with the State's interest that his payments not be erroneously terminated, clearly outweighs the State's competing concern to prevent any increase in its fiscal and administrative burdens. As the District Court correctly concluded, "the stakes are simply too high for the welfare recipient, and the possibility for honest error or irritable misjudgment too great, to allow termination of aid without giving the recipient a chance, if he so desires, to be fully informed of the case against him so that he may contest its basis and produce evidence in rebuttal."

"The fundamental requisite of due process of law is the opportunity to be heard." *Grannis v. Ordean,* 234 U.S. 385, 394 (1914). The hearing must be "at a meaningful time and in a meaningful manner." *Armstrong v. Manzo,* 380 U.S. 545, 552 (1965). In the present context these principles require that a recipient have timely and adequate notice detailing the reasons for a proposed termination, and an effective opportunity to defend by confronting any adverse witnesses and by presenting his own arguments and evidence orally. These rights are important in cases such as those before us, where recipients have challenged proposed terminations as resting on incorrect or misleading factual premises or on misapplication of rules or policies to the facts of particular cases.

The city's procedures presently do not permit recipients to appear personally with or without counsel before the official who finally determines continued eligibility. Thus a recipient is not permitted to present evidence to that official orally, or to confront or cross-examine adverse witnesses. These omissions are fatal to the constitutional adequacy of the procedures.

The opportunity to be heard must be tailored to the capacities and circumstances of those who are to be heard. It is not enough that a welfare recipient may present his position to the decision maker in writing or secondhand through his caseworker. Written submissions are an unrealistic option for most recipients, who lack the educational attainment necessary to write effectively and who cannot obtain professional assistance. Moreover, written submissions do not afford the flexibility of oral presentations; they do not permit the recipient to mold his argument to the issues the decision maker appears to regard as important. Particularly where credibility and veracity are at issue, as they must be in many termination proceedings, written submissions are a wholly unsatisfactory basis for decision. The secondhand presentation to the decision maker by the caseworker has its own deficiencies; since the caseworker usually gathers the facts upon which the charge of ineligibility rests, the presentation of the recipient's side of the controversy cannot safely be left to him. Therefore a recipient must be allowed to state his position orally.

In almost every setting where important decisions turn on questions of fact, due process requires an opportunity to confront and cross-examine adverse witnesses. This Court has been zealous to protect these rights from erosion, not only in criminal cases, but also in all types of cases where administrative actions were under scrutiny.

Welfare recipients must therefore be given an opportunity to confront and cross-examine the witnesses relied on by the department. "The right to be heard would be, in many cases, of little avail if it did not comprehend the right to be heard by counsel." We do not say that counsel must be provided at the pre-termination hearing, but only that the recipient must be allowed to retain an attorney if he so desires. Counsel can help delineate the issues, present the factual contentions in an orderly manner, conduct cross-examination, and generally safeguard the interests of the recipient.

Finally, the decision maker's conclusion as to a recipient's eligibility must rest solely on the legal rules and evidence adduced at the hearing. To demonstrate compliance with this elementary requirement, the decision maker should state the reasons for his determination and indicate the evidence he relied on, though his statement need not amount to a full opinion or even formal findings of fact and conclusions of law. And, of course, an impartial decision maker is essential.

JUSTICE BLACK wrote a dissent (joined by CHIEF JUSTICE BURGER).[8]

The more than a million names on the relief rolls in New York, and the more than nine million names on the rolls of all the 50 States were not put there at random. The names are there because state welfare officials believed that those people were eligible for assistance. Doubtless some draw relief checks from time to time who know they are not eligible, either because they are not actually in need or for some other reason. The Court today holds that it would violate the Due Process Clause of the Fourteenth Amendment to stop paying those people weekly or

---

8. There was a companion case, *Wheeler v. Montgomery,* 397 U.S. 280 (1970), that struck down California procedures for terminating old age program benefits on the basis of the reasoning in *Goldberg.* Burger issued a separate dissent in that case as did Stewart that applied to *Goldberg* as well.

monthly allowances unless the government first affords them a full "evidentiary hearing" even though welfare officials are persuaded that the recipients are not rightfully entitled to receive a penny under the law. I do not believe there is any provision in our Constitution that should paralyze the government's efforts to protect itself against making payments to people who are not entitled to them. Particularly do I not think that the Fourteenth Amendment should be given such an unnecessarily broad construction. That Amendment came into being primarily to protect Negroes from discrimination, and while some of its language can and does protect others, all know that the chief purpose behind it was to protect ex-slaves.

This decision is thus only another variant of the view often expressed by some members of this Court that the Due Process Clause forbids any conduct that a majority of the Court believes "unfair," "indecent," or "shocking to their consciences." Neither these words nor any like them appear anywhere in the Due Process Clause. If they did, they would leave the majority of Justices free to hold any conduct unconstitutional that they should conclude on their own to be unfair or shocking to them. A written constitution, designed to guarantee protection against governmental abuses, including those of judges, must have written standards that mean something definite and have an explicit content.

*****

Things changed significantly after *Goldberg*. Probably the single most important case in that trend away from the broad view of adjudicative rights was *Mathews v. Eldridge,* the opinion that set forth the controlling test in this area of the law.

THE DEVELOPMENT
OF THE ELDRIDGE BALANCING TEST

Mathews v. Eldridge, 424 U.S. 319 (1976).

INTRODUCTION: This is a difficult opinion to read (and for that matter to edit) because it begins from very problematic foundations. For reasons explained in the fully developed case study of the *Mathews v. Eldridge* battle in *Public Law and Public Administration, Third Edition,* Justice Powell misunderstood the case and its facts, and, not surprisingly therefore, his opinion misrepresented the case and the parties. Part of this problem stemmed from a very deceptive set of tactics employed by the Solicitor General in his handling of the case and in the oral argument. (This is explained in the case study in the text.) On the other side, a more experienced Supreme Court advocate would likely have seen the importance of this case as a policy matter and would have picked up on the tactics used by the Solicitor General to confuse the facts, the procedural posture of the matter, and the policy issues in the case. Thus, the opinion is edited as much as possible to avoid these problems and focus on the Court's development of the test that has been used ever since to determine on constitutional grounds when, whether, and what kind of process is due in administrative adjudications.

*****

JUSTICE POWELL wrote the opinion for the Court, joined by BURGER, STEWART, WHITE, BLACKMUN, and REHNQUIST. STEVENS did not participate.

The issue in this case is whether the Due Process Clause of the Fifth Amendment requires that prior to the termination of Social Security disability benefit payments the recipient be afforded an opportunity for an evidentiary hearing.

I. The District Court concluded that the administrative procedures pursuant to which the Secretary had terminated Eldridge's [Social Security Disability] benefits abridged his right to procedural due process. The court viewed the interest of the disability recipient in uninterrupted benefits as indistinguishable from that of the welfare recipient in *Goldberg*. It further noted that decisions subsequent to *Goldberg* demonstrated that the due process requirement of pretermination hearings is not limited to situations involving the deprivation of vital necessities. See *Fuentes v. Shevin,* 407 U.S. 67, 88-89 (1972); *Bell v. Burson,* 402 U.S. 535, 539 (1971). Reasoning that disability determinations may involve subjective judgments based on conflicting medical and nonmedical evidence, the District Court held that prior to termination of benefits Eldridge had to be afforded an evidentiary hearing of the type required for welfare beneficiaries under Title IV of the Social Security Act. The Court of Appeals for the Fourth Circuit affirmed the injunction barring termination of Eldridge's benefits prior to an evidentiary hearing. 493 F.2d 1230 (4th Cir. 1974). We reverse.

III. Procedural due process imposes constraints on governmental decisions which deprive individuals of "liberty" or "property" interests within the meaning of the Due Process Clause of the Fifth or Fourteenth Amendment. The Secretary does not contend that procedural due process is inapplicable to terminations of Social Security disability benefits. He recognizes, as has been implicit in our prior decisions, that the interest of an individual in continued receipt of these benefits is a statutorily created "property" interest protected by the Fifth Amendment. Rather, the Secretary contends that the existing administrative procedures provide all the process that is constitutionally due before a recipient can be deprived of that interest.

This Court consistently has held that some form of hearing is required before an individual is finally deprived of a property interest. See *Dent v. West Virginia,* 129 U.S. 114, 124-125 (1889). The "right to be heard before being condemned to suffer grievous loss of any kind, even though it may not involve the stigma and hardships of a criminal conviction, is a principle basic to our society." *Joint Anti-Fascist Comm. v. McGrath,* 341 U.S. 123, 168 (1951) (Frankfurter, J., concurring). The fundamental requirement of due process is the opportunity to be heard "at a meaningful time and in a meaningful manner." *Armstrong v. Manzo,* 380 U.S. 545, 552 (1965). See *Grannis v. Ordean,* 234 U.S. 385, 394 (1914). Eldridge agrees that the review procedures available to a claimant before the initial determination of ineligibility becomes final would be adequate if disability benefits were not terminated until after the evidentiary hearing stage of the administrative process. The dispute centers upon what process is due prior to the initial termination of benefits, pending review.

In recent years this Court increasingly has had occasion to consider the extent to which due process requires an evidentiary hearing prior to the deprivation of some type of property interest even if such a hearing is provided thereafter. In only one case, *Goldberg v. Kelly,* has the Court held that a hearing closely approximating a judicial trial is necessary. More recently, in *Arnett v. Kennedy,* we sustained the validity of procedures by which a federal employee could be dismissed for cause. They included notice of the action sought, a copy of the charge, reasonable time for filing a written response, and an opportunity for an oral appearance. Following dismissal, an evidentiary hearing was provided.

These decisions underscore the truism that "'[d]ue process,' unlike some legal rules, is not a technical conception with a fixed content unrelated to time, place and circumstances.'"'[D]ue process is flexible and calls for such procedural protections as the particular situation demands." Accordingly, resolution of the issue whether the administrative procedures provided here are constitutionally sufficient requires analysis of the governmental and private interests that are affected. More precisely, our prior decisions indicate that identification of the specific dictates of due process generally requires consideration of three distinct factors: First, the private interest that will be affected by the official action; second, the risk of an erroneous deprivation of such interest through the procedures used, and the probable value, if any, of additional or substitute procedural safeguards; and finally, the Government's interest, including the function involved and the fiscal and administrative burdens that the additional or substitute procedural requirement would entail.

The disability insurance program is administered jointly by state and federal agencies. State [vocational rehabilitation] agencies, in most cases, make the initial determination whether a disability exists, when it began, and when it ceased. The standards applied and the procedures followed are prescribed by the Secretary of HHS [Health and Human Services] who has delegated his responsibilities and powers under the Act to the SSA [Social Security Administration].

In order to establish initial and continued entitlement to disability benefits a worker must demonstrate that he is unable "to engage in any substantial gainful activity by reason of any medically determinable physical or mental impairment which can be expected to result in death or which has lasted or can be expected to last for a continuous period of not less than 12 months . . ."

To satisfy this test the worker bears a continuing burden of showing, by means of "medically acceptable clinical and laboratory diagnostic techniques," that he has a physical or mental impairment of such severity that "he is not only unable to do his previous work but cannot, considering his age, education, and work experience, engage in any other kind of substantial gainful work which exists in the national economy, regardless of whether such work exists in the immediate area in which he lives, or whether a specific job vacancy exists for him, or whether he would be hired if he applied for work."

Information regarding the recipient's current condition is also obtained from his sources of medical treatment. Whenever the agency's tentative assessment of the beneficiary's condition differs from his own assessment, the beneficiary is informed that benefits may be terminated, provided a summary of the evidence upon which the proposed determination to terminate is based, and afforded an opportunity to review the medical reports and other evidence in his case file. He also may respond in writing and submit additional evidence.

If the recipient seeks reconsideration by the state agency and the determination is adverse, the SSA reviews the reconsideration determination and notifies the recipient of the decision. He then has a right to an evidentiary hearing before an SSA administrative law judge.

Should it be determined at any point after termination of benefits, that the claimant's disability extended beyond the date of cessation initially established, the worker is entitled to retroactive payments. If, on the other hand, a beneficiary receives any payments to which he is later determined not to be entitled, the statute authorizes the Secretary to attempt to recoup these funds in specified circumstances.

The courts below held these [administrative procedures] to be constitutionally inadequate, concluding that due process requires an evidentiary hearing prior to termination. In light of the private and governmental interests at stake here and the nature of the existing procedures, we think this was error.

Since a recipient whose benefits are terminated is awarded full retroactive relief if he ultimately prevails, his sole interest is in the uninterrupted receipt of this source of income pending final administrative decision on his claim. His potential injury is thus similar in nature to that of the welfare recipient in *Goldberg,* the nonprobationary federal employee in *Arnett,* and the wage earner in *Sniadach.*

It was emphasized in *Goldberg* that welfare assistance is given to persons on the very margin of subsistence: "The crucial factor in this context—a factor not present in the case of . . . virtually anyone else whose governmental entitlements are ended—is that termination of aid pending resolution of a controversy over eligibility may deprive an eligible recipient of the very means by which to live while he waits."

Eligibility for disability benefits, in contrast, is not based upon financial need. As *Goldberg* illustrates, the degree of potential deprivation that may be created by a particular decision is a factor to be considered in assessing the validity of any administrative decisionmaking process. The potential deprivation here is generally likely to be less than in *Goldberg,* although the degree of difference can be overstated. As the District Court emphasized, to remain eligible for benefits a recipient must be "unable to engage in substantial gainful activity." Thus, in contrast to the discharged federal employee in *Arnett,* there is little possibility that the terminated recipient will be able to find even temporary employment to ameliorate the interim loss.

An additional factor to be considered here is the fairness and reliability of the existing pretermination procedures, and the probable value, if any, of additional procedural safeguards. In order to remain eligible for benefits the disabled worker must demonstrate by means of "medically acceptable clinical and laboratory diagnostic techniques," that he is unable "to engage in any substantial gainful activity by reason of any medically determinable physical or mental impairment." In short, a medical assessment of the worker's physical or mental condition is required. This is a more sharply focused and easily documented decision than the typical determination of welfare entitlement. In the latter case, a wide variety of information may be deemed relevant, and issues of witness credibility and veracity often are critical to the decisionmaking process. *Goldberg* noted that in such circumstances "written submissions are a wholly unsatisfactory basis for decision."

By contrast, the decision whether to discontinue disability benefits will turn, in most cases, upon "routine, standard, and unbiased medical reports by physician specialists." To be sure, credibility and veracity may be a factor in the ultimate disability assessment in some cases. But procedural due process rules are shaped by the risk of error inherent in the truthfinding process as applied to the generality of cases, not the rare exceptions. The potential value of an evidentiary hearing, or even oral presentation to the decisionmaker, is substantially less in this context than in *Goldberg*.[9]

The decision in *Goldberg* also was based on the Court's conclusion that written submissions were an inadequate substitute for oral presentation because they did not provide an effective means for the recipient to communicate his case to the decisionmaker. Written submissions were viewed as an unrealistic option, for most recipients lacked the "educational attainment necessary to write effectively" and could not afford professional assistance. In addition, such submissions would not provide the "flexibility of oral presentations" or "permit the recipient to mold his argument to the issues the decision maker appears to regard as important." In the context of the disability-benefits-entitlement assessment the administrative procedures under review here fully answer these objections.

Despite these carefully structured procedures, *amici* point to the significant reversal rate for appealed cases as clear evidence that the current process is inadequate. Thus, although we view such information as relevant, it is certainly not controlling in this case.

In striking the appropriate due process balance the final factor to be assessed is the public interest. This includes the administrative burden and other societal costs that would be associated with requiring, as a matter of constitutional right, an evidentiary hearing upon demand in all cases prior to the termination of disability benefits. The most visible burden would be the incremental cost resulting from

---

9. NOTE: All of the evidence developed during the time *Eldridge* was pending was to the contrary. Congress has found the disability process rife with error prone and unfair decision characteristics, including poor preparation of the record by those handling the paper review. That was one of the reasons for reversal rates in excess of 60% once claimants actually received a hearing. The details are laid out in the case study in *Public Law and Public Administration, Third Edition*. Congress ultimately agreed and reversed the Supreme Court ruling by statute, requiring continuation of payments pending appeals. It is worth noting, however, that notwithstanding all of the studies, there continue to be difficulties in *Social Security* Disability processing. U.S. General Accounting Office, *Social Security Disability: Efforts to Improve Claims Process Have Fallen Short and Further Action is Needed* (Washington, D.C.: General Accounting Office, 2002).

the increased number of hearings and the expense of providing benefits to ineligible recipients pending decision. No one can predict the extent of the increase, but the fact that full benefits would continue until after such hearings would assure the exhaustion in most cases of this attractive option. Nor would the theoretical right of the Secretary to recover undeserved benefits result, as a practical matter, in any substantial offset to the added outlay of public funds. The parties submit widely varying estimates of the probable additional financial cost. We only need say that experience with the constitutionalizing of government procedures suggests that the ultimate additional cost in terms of money and administrative burden would not be insubstantial.

Financial cost alone is not a controlling weight in determining whether due process requires a particular procedural safeguard prior to some administrative decision. But the Government's interest, and hence that of the public, in conserving scarce fiscal and administrative resources is a factor that must be weighed. At some point the benefit of an additional safeguard to the individual affected by the administrative action and to society in terms of increased assurance that the action is just, may be outweighed by the cost. Significantly, the cost of protecting those whom the preliminary administrative process has identified as likely to be found undeserving may in the end come out of the pockets of the deserving since resources available for any particular program of social welfare are not unlimited. We conclude that an evidentiary hearing is not required prior to the termination of disability benefits and that the present administrative procedures fully comport with due process.

JUSTICE BRENNAN wrote a dissent joined by MARSHALL.

For the reasons stated in my dissenting opinion in *Richardson v. Wright*, 405 U.S. 208, 212 (1972), [see the *Richardson v. Wright* dissent below] I agree with the District Court and the Court of Appeals that, prior to termination of benefits, Eldridge must be afforded an evidentiary hearing of the type required for welfare beneficiaries under Title IV of the Social Security Act. I would add that the Court's consideration that a discontinuance of disability benefits may cause the recipient to suffer only a limited deprivation is no argument. It is speculative. Moreover, the very legislative determination to provide disability benefits, without any prerequisite determination of need in fact, presumes a need by the recipient which is not this Court's function to denigrate. Indeed, in the present case, it is indicated that because disability benefits were terminated there was a foreclosure upon the Eldridge home and the family's furniture was repossessed, forcing Eldridge, his wife, and their children to sleep in one bed. Finally, it is also no argument that a worker, who has been placed in the untenable position of having been denied disability benefits, may still seek other forms of public assistance.

*****

Richardson v. Wright, 405 U.S. 208 (1972).

INTRODUCTION: Brennan had written a dissent in *Richardson v. Wright,* which was a 1972 case in which the Court had ducked the same issue later presented in *Eldridge.* The agency was in the process of promulgating new rules for the program while the case was in progress and the Court used that as a way to avoid decision at that time. However, Brennan had written an opinion for himself, Marshall and Douglas dissenting in that case. Because Brennan had been the author of the *Goldberg* opinion and because he relied upon it as his dissent in *Eldridge,* it is reproduced here.

JUSTICE BRENNAN wrote the dissent joined by DOUGLAS AND MARSHALL.

The Secretary's new regulations permit discontinuance of disability benefits without affording beneficiaries procedural due process either in the form mandated by *Goldberg v. Kelly.* The regulations require only that the beneficiary be informed of the proposed suspension or termination and the information upon which it is based and be given an opportunity to submit a written response before benefits are cut off. This procedure does not afford the beneficiary, as *Goldberg* requires for welfare and old-age recipients, an evidentiary hearing at which he may personally appear to offer oral evidence and confront and cross-examine adverse witnesses.

[T]he Secretary insists that the "hearing on paper" afforded to disability beneficiaries by his new regulations is constitutionally sufficient. The Secretary does not contend that disability beneficiaries differ from welfare and old-age recipients with respect to their entitlement to benefits or the drastic consequences that may befall them if their benefits are erroneously discontinued. The only distinctions urged are that the evidence ordinarily adduced to support suspension and termination of disability benefits differs markedly from that relied upon to cut off welfare benefits and that an undue monetary and administrative burden would result if prior hearings were required. Neither distinction withstands analysis.

First. The Secretary seriously misconstrues the holding in *Goldberg.* The Court there said that "the pre-termination hearing has one function only: to produce an initial determination of the validity of the welfare department's grounds for discontinuance of payments in order to protect a recipient against an erroneous termination of his benefits." The Secretary does not deny that due process safeguards fulfill the same function in disability cases. In *Goldberg,* the Court held that welfare recipients were entitled to hearings because decisions to discontinue benefits were challenged "as resting on incorrect or misleading factual premises or on misapplication of rules or policies to the facts of particular cases." The Court expressly put aside consideration of situations "where there are no factual issues in dispute or where the application of the rule of law is not intertwined with factual issues." However reliable the evidence upon which a disability determination is normally based, and however rarely it involves questions of credibility and veracity, it is plain that, as with welfare and old-age determinations, the determination that an individual is or is not "disabled" will frequently depend upon the resolution of factual issues and the application of legal rules to the facts found. It is precisely for that reason that a hearing must be held.

[T]he Secretary insists that the decision to discontinue disability benefits differs from the decision to discontinue welfare benefits because the latter "may" be based upon "personal and social situations brought to the attention of the authorities by tips, rumor or gossip." Yet it is irrelevant how the matter is "brought to the attention of the authorities," whether "by tips, rumor or gossip" or otherwise. The question in a welfare determination, as in a disability determination, is simply whether the recipient continues to be eligible for benefits.

To support the assertion that pre-termination hearings are required in welfare cases because "credibility and veracity" are in issue, the Secretary focuses upon certain language in *Goldberg*. He first quotes the statement that "particularly where credibility and veracity are at issue, as they must be in many termination proceedings, written submissions are a wholly unsatisfactory basis for decision." Apart from the obvious fact that that was not an absolute statement intended to limit hearings solely to those instances, it was but one of three reasons given to demonstrate that written submissions are insufficient. The Court also said that written submissions "are an unrealistic option for most recipients, who lack the educational attainment necessary to write effectively and who cannot obtain professional assistance" and that they "do not afford the flexibility of oral presentations; they do not permit the recipient to mold his argument to the issues the decision-maker appears to regard as important." Significantly, the Secretary does not deny that those reasons are as fully applicable to disability beneficiaries as to welfare recipients.

The premise of the Secretary's entire argument is that disability benefits are discontinued "only on the basis of an objective consideration—that the previous disability has ceased—and that conclusion rests on reliable information." Whether or not the information is reliable, the premise is questionable. The Secretary himself emphasizes that disability determinations require "specialized medical and vocational evaluations" and not simply the acquisition of "medical and other relevant data." In any event, there are three grounds, pertinent here, upon which disability can be found to have ceased. None can fairly be characterized by the term "objective."

First, cessation of disability may be found if the beneficiary refuses to cooperate with the social security authorities. That judgment, of course, could be wholly subjective, as the Secretary points out with reference to welfare cases.

Second, cessation may be found if the beneficiary "has regained his ability to engage in substantial gainful activity . . . as demonstrated by work activity." That decision does not, as the Secretary appears to assert, rest solely "upon regular reports made by [the beneficiary's] employers to the government." Rather, "the work performed" by the beneficiary "may demonstrate" that he is no longer disabled, but only if it "is both substantial and gainful." "Substantial work activity involves the performance of significant physical or mental duties, or a combination of both, productive in nature." A finding of "substantial gainful activity" depends upon the nature of the work performed, the adequacy of the performance, and the special conditions, if any, of the employment, as well as an evaluation of the time spent and the amount of money earned by the beneficiary.

Third, cessation of disability may be found if the evidence establishes medical recovery. That decision, of course, will be based upon medical examinations, but it does not follow that it is necessarily "objective." "The function of deciding whether or not an individual is under a disability is the responsibility of the Secretary," and a medical conclusion that the beneficiary is or is not disabled "shall not be determinative of the question." The Secretary's decision that a beneficiary's impairment "is no longer of such severity as to prevent him from engaging in any substantial gainful activity," obviously depends upon more than an "objective" medical report, for the application of the legal standard necessarily requires the exercise of judgment. And, of course, multiple conflicting medical reports are "not uncommon." *Richardson v. Perales,* 402 U.S. 389, 399 (1971).

Finally, the post-termination reversal rate for disability determinations makes the asserted "objectivity" even more doubtful. According to the Secretary's figures for 1971, 37% of the requests for reconsideration resulted in reversal of the determination that disability had ceased. Moreover, 55% of the beneficiaries who exercised their right to a hearing won reversal. While, as the Secretary says, these figures may attest to the fairness of the system, they also appear to confirm that the Court's reference in *Goldberg* to "the welfare bureaucracy's difficulties in reaching correct decisions on eligibility," is fully applicable to the administration of the disability program.

The Secretary also contends that affording disability beneficiaries the opportunity to participate in evidentiary hearings before discontinuance of their benefits will result in great expense and a vast disruption of the administrative system. This justification for denial of pre-termination hearings was, of course, specifically rejected in *Goldberg* and the Secretary offers no new considerations to support its acceptance here.

In *Goldberg,* the Court pointed out "that termination of aid pending resolution of a controversy over eligibility may deprive an eligible recipient of the very means by which to live while he waits." That statement applies equally to eligible disability beneficiaries, for, as the District Court noted and the Secretary does not deny, "a disability beneficiary is by definition unable to engage in substantial gainful activity and he would, therefore, be liable to sustain grievous loss while awaiting the resolution of his claim." In view of that result, the District Court concluded that the "fiscal and administrative expenses to the government, whatever their magnitude, are insufficient justification considering the crippling blow that could be dealt to an individual in these circumstances."

Except for bald assertion, the Secretary offers nothing to indicate that any great burden upon the system would result if the state agencies conducted the hearings. Moreover, the Secretary omits even to mention the existence of the current post-termination hearing procedures. It is reasonable to assume that the only "restructuring" necessary would be a change in the timing of the hearings. That was apparently the method by which the Secretary required the States to comply with *Goldberg* in the administration of various other social security programs, and it would seem to be an equally available response here. While the administration of the disability program to provide prior hearings may involve "some greater expense," as the Court noted in *Goldberg,* that expense should not be exaggerated in order to deprive disability beneficiaries of their right to "rudimentary due process."

I do not deny that prior hearings will entail some additional administrative burdens and expense. Administrative fairness usually does. But the Secretary "is not without weapons to minimize these increased costs." Despite the Secretary's protestations to the contrary, I believe that in the disability, as in the welfare, area "much of the drain on fiscal and administrative resources can be reduced by developing procedures for prompt pre-termination hearings and by skillful use of personnel and facilities." The Court's conclusion on this point in *Goldberg* is fully applicable here: "Indeed, the very provision for a post-termination evidentiary hearing . . . is itself cogent evidence that the State recognizes the primacy of the public interest in correct eligibility determinations and therefore in the provision of procedural safeguards. Thus, the interest of the eligible recipient in uninterrupted receipt of public assistance, coupled with the State's interest that his payments not be erroneously terminated, clearly outweighs the State's competing concern to prevent any increase in its fiscal and administrative burdens."

*****

DUE PROCESS QUESTIONS
AFTER ELDRIDGE

By this point, there was speculation about just how far the Court would go in the due process reaction. Clearly, Justices Rehnquist and Scalia wanted to go further than most other members of the Court. It was a combined case from the Cleveland area that presented the first opportunity to read the Court's direction.

Cleveland Board of Education v. Loudermill, 470 U.S. 532 (1985).

INTRODUCTION: The Court's opinion provides a summary of the facts in this important decision. This is a set of opinions that requires a careful reading. At first blush, it appears that there is significant agreement among members of the Court. However, the more carefully one reads the various perspectives on the case, the more apparent it is that there is far from consensus on the contemporary requirements of due process.

*****

JUSTICE WHITE wrote the opinion for the Court. BURGER, BLACKMUN, POWELL, STEVENS, and O'CONNOR joined.

In these cases we consider what pretermination process must be accorded a public employee who can be discharged only for cause.

I. In 1979 the Cleveland Board of Education hired James Loudermill as a security guard. On his job application, Loudermill stated that he had never been convicted of a felony. Eleven months later, as part of a routine examination of his employment records, the Board discovered that in fact Loudermill had been convicted of grand larceny in 1968. By letter dated November 3, 1980, the Board's Business Manager informed Loudermill that he had been dismissed because of his dishonesty in filling out the employment application. Loudermill was not afforded an opportunity to respond to the charge of dishonesty or to challenge his dismissal. On November 13, the Board adopted a resolution officially approving the discharge.

Under Ohio law, Loudermill was a "classified civil servant." Such employees can be terminated only for cause, and may obtain administrative review if discharged. Loudermill filed an appeal with the Cleveland Civil Service Commission on November 12. The Commission appointed a referee, who held a hearing on January 29, 1981. Loudermill argued that he had thought that his 1968 larceny conviction was for a misdemeanor rather than a felony. The referee recommended reinstatement. On July 20, 1981, the full Commission heard argument and orally announced that it would uphold the dismissal. Proposed findings of fact and conclusions of law followed on August 10, and Loudermill's attorneys were advised of the result by mail on August 21.

Although the Commission's decision was subject to judicial review in the state courts, Loudermill instead brought the present suit in the Federal District Court for the Northern District of Ohio. The complaint alleged that [the Ohio termination law] was unconstitutional on its face because it did not provide the employee an opportunity to respond to the charges against him prior to removal. As a result, discharged employees were deprived of liberty and property without due process. The complaint also alleged that the provision was unconstitutional as applied because discharged employees were not given sufficiently prompt post-removal hearings.

The other case before us arises on similar facts and followed a similar course. Richard Donnelly was a bus mechanic for the Parma Board of Education. In August 1977, Donnelly was fired because he had failed an eye examination. He was offered a chance to retake the examination but did not do so. Like Loudermill, Donnelly appealed to the Civil Service Commission. After a year of wrangling about the timeliness of his appeal, the Commission heard the case. It ordered Donnelly reinstated, though without back pay. In a complaint essentially identical to Loudermill's, Donnelly challenged the constitutionality of the dismissal procedures. The District Court dismissed, relying on its opinion in Loudermill.

[T]he Court of Appeals found that both respondents had been deprived of due process. It concluded that the compelling private interest in retaining employment, combined with the value of presenting evidence prior to dismissal, outweighed the added administrative burden of a pretermination hearing. With regard to the alleged deprivation of liberty, and Loudermill's 9-month wait for an administrative decision, the court affirmed the District Court, finding no constitutional violation.

We affirm in all respects.

II. Respondents' federal constitutional claim depends on their having had a property right in continued employment. If they did, the State could not deprive them of this property without due process.

Property interests are not created by the Constitution, "they are created and their dimensions are defined by existing rules or understandings that stem from an independent source such as state law...." *Board of Regents v. Roth.* The Ohio statute plainly creates such an interest. Respondents were "classified civil service employees," entitled to retain their positions "during good behavior and efficient service," who could not be dismissed "except ... for ... misfeasance, malfeasance, or nonfeasance in office." The statute plainly supports the conclusion, reached by both lower courts, that respondents possessed property rights in continued employment.

The Parma Board argues, however, that the property right is defined by, and conditioned on, the legislature's choice of procedures for its deprivation. The procedures were adhered to in these cases. According to petitioner, "[to] require additional procedures would in effect expand the scope of the property interest itself."

This argument has its genesis in the plurality opinion in *Arnett v. Kennedy. Arnett* involved a challenge by a former federal employee to the procedures by which he was dismissed. The plurality reasoned that where the legislation conferring the substantive right also sets out the procedural mechanism for enforcing that right, the two cannot be separated: "The employee's statutorily defined right is not a guarantee against removal without cause in the abstract, but such a guarantee as enforced by the procedures which Congress has designated for the determination of cause.... [Where] the grant of a substantive right is inextricably intertwined with the limitations on the procedures which are to be employed in determining that right, a litigant in the position of appellee must take the bitter with the sweet."

This view garnered three votes in *Arnett,* but was specifically rejected by the other six Justices. Since then, this theory has at times seemed to gather some additional support. More recently, however, the Court has clearly rejected it. In *Vitek v. Jones,* 445 U.S. 480, 491 (1980), we pointed out that "minimum [procedural] requirements [are] a matter of federal law, they are not diminished by the fact that the State may have specified its own procedures that it may deem adequate for determining the preconditions to adverse official action."

In light of these holdings, it is settled that the "bitter with the sweet" approach misconceives the constitutional guarantee. If a clearer holding is needed, we provide it today. The point is straightforward: the Due Process Clause provides that certain substantive rights—life, liberty, and property—cannot be deprived except pursuant to constitutionally adequate procedures. The categories of substance and procedure are distinct. Were the rule otherwise, the Clause would be reduced to a mere tautology. "Property" cannot be defined by the procedures provided for its deprivation any more than can life or liberty. The right to due process "is conferred, not by legislative grace, but by constitutional guarantee. While the legislature may elect not to confer a property interest in [public] employment, it may not constitutionally authorize the deprivation of such an interest, once conferred, without appropriate procedural safeguards."

In short, once it is determined that the Due Process Clause applies, "the question remains what process is due." The answer to that question is not to be found in the Ohio statute.

III. An essential principle of due process is that a deprivation of life, liberty, or property "be preceded by notice and opportunity for hearing appropriate to the nature of the case." *Mullane v. Central Hanover Bank & Trust Co.,* 339 U.S. 306, 313 (1950). We have described "the root requirement" of the Due Process Clause as being "that an individual be given an opportunity for a hearing before he is deprived of any significant property interest." This principle requires "some kind of a hearing" prior to the discharge of an employee who has a constitutionally protected property interest in his employment. As we pointed out last Term, this rule has been settled for some time now. Even decisions finding no constitutional violation in termination procedures have relied on the existence of some pretermination opportunity to respond. For example, in *Arnett* six Justices found constitutional minima satisfied where the employee had access to the material upon which the charge was based and could respond orally and in writing and present rebuttal affidavits.

The need for some form of pretermination hearing, recognized in these cases, is evident from a balancing of the competing interests at stake. These are the private interest in retaining employment, the governmental interest in the expeditious removal of unsatisfactory employees and the avoidance of administrative burdens, and the risk of an erroneous termination. See *Mathews v. Eldridge,* 424 U.S. 319, 335 (1976).

First, the significance of the private interest in retaining employment cannot be gainsaid. While a fired worker may find employment elsewhere, doing so will take some time and is likely to be burdened by the questionable circumstances under which he left his previous job.

Second, some opportunity for the employee to present his side of the case is recurringly of obvious value in reaching an accurate decision. Dismissals for cause will often involve factual disputes. Even where the facts are clear, the appropriateness or necessity of the discharge may not be; in such cases, the only meaningful opportunity to invoke the discretion of the decision maker is likely to be before the termination takes effect.

Both respondents [here] had plausible arguments to make that might have prevented their discharge. The fact that the Commission saw fit to reinstate Donnelly suggests that an error might have been avoided had he been provided an opportunity to make his case to the Board. As for Loudermill, given the Commission's ruling we cannot say that the discharge was mistaken. Nonetheless, in light of the referee's recommendation, neither can we say that a fully informed decisionmaker might not have exercised its discretion and decided not to dismiss him, notwithstanding its authority to do so. In any event, the termination involved arguable issues, and the right to a hearing does not depend on a demonstration of certain success.

The governmental interest in immediate termination does not outweigh these interests. As we shall explain, affording the employee an opportunity to respond prior to termination would impose neither a significant administrative burden nor intolerable delays. Furthermore, the employer shares the employee's interest in avoiding disruption and erroneous decisions; and until the matter is settled, the employer would continue to receive the benefit of the employee's labors. It is preferable to keep a qualified employee on than to train a new one. A governmental employer also has an interest in keeping citizens usefully employed rather than taking the possibly erroneous and counterproductive step of forcing its employees onto the welfare rolls. Finally, in those situations where the employer perceives a significant hazard in keeping the employee on the job, it can avoid the problem by suspending with pay.

IV. The foregoing considerations indicate that the pretermination "hearing," though necessary, need not be elaborate. We have pointed out that "[the] formality and procedural requisites for the hearing can vary, depending upon the importance of the interests involved and the nature of the subsequent proceedings." In general, "something less" than a full evidentiary hearing is sufficient prior to adverse administrative action. Under state law, respondents were later entitled to a full administrative hearing and judicial review. The only question is what steps were required before the termination took effect.

[T]he pretermination hearing need not definitively resolve the propriety of the discharge. It should be an initial check against mistaken decisions—essentially, a determination of whether there are reasonable grounds to believe that the charges against the employee are true and support the proposed action.

The essential requirements of due process are notice and an opportunity to respond. The opportunity to present reasons, either in person or in writing, why proposed action should not be taken is a fundamental due process requirement. The tenured public employee is entitled to oral or written notice of the charges against him, an explanation of the employer's evidence, and an opportunity to present his side of the story. To require more than this prior to termination would intrude to an unwarranted extent on the government's interest in quickly removing an unsatisfactory employee.

V. Our holding rests in part on the provisions in Ohio law for a full post-termination hearing. In his cross-petition Loudermill asserts, as a separate constitutional violation, that his administrative proceedings took too long.[10] The Court of Appeals held otherwise, and we agree. The Due Process Clause requires provision of a hearing "at a meaningful time." At some point, a delay in the post-termination hearing would become a constitutional violation. A 9-month adjudication is not, of course, unconstitutionally lengthy per se. Yet Loudermill offers no indication that his wait was unreasonably prolonged other than the fact that it took nine months.

---

10. Loudermill's hearing before the referee occurred two and one-half months after he filed his appeal. The Commission issued its written decision six and one-half months after that. Administrative proceedings in Donnelly's case, once it was determined that they could proceed at all, were swifter. A writ of mandamus requiring the Commission to hold a hearing was issued on May 9, 1978; the hearing took place on May 30; the order of reinstatement was issued on July 6.

VI. We conclude that all the process that is due is provided by a pretermination opportunity to respond, coupled with post-termination administrative procedures as provided by the Ohio statute. Because respondents allege in their complaints that they had no chance to respond, the District Court erred in dismissing for failure to state a claim. The judgment of the Court of Appeals is affirmed, and the case is remanded for further proceedings consistent with this opinion.

JUSTICE MARSHALL concurred in part in the opinion and concurred in the judgment of the Court.

I agree wholeheartedly with the Court's express rejection of the theory of due process that a public employee who may be discharged only for cause may be discharged by whatever procedures the legislature chooses. I therefore join Part II of the opinion for the Court. I also agree that, before discharge, the respondent employees were entitled to the opportunity to respond to the charges against them (which is all they requested), and that the failure to accord them that opportunity was a violation of their constitutional rights. Because the Court holds that the respondents were due all the process they requested, I concur in the judgment of the Court.

I write separately, however, to reaffirm my belief that public employees who may be discharged only for cause are entitled, under the Due Process Clause of the Fourteenth Amendment, to more than respondents sought in this case. I continue to believe that before the decision is made to terminate an employee's wages, the employee is entitled to an opportunity to test the strength of the evidence "by confronting and cross-examining adverse witnesses and by presenting witnesses on his own behalf, whenever there are substantial disputes in testimonial evidence." Because the Court suggests that even in this situation due process requires no more than notice and an opportunity to be heard before wages are cut off, I am not able to join the Court's opinion in its entirety.

To my mind, the disruption caused by a loss of wages may be so devastating to an employee that, whenever there are substantial disputes about the evidence, additional predeprivation procedures are necessary to minimize the risk of an erroneous termination. That is, I place significantly greater weight than does the Court on the public employee's substantial interest in the accuracy of the pretermination proceeding. After wage termination, the employee often must wait months before his case is finally resolved, during which time he is without wages from his public employment. By limiting the procedures due prior to termination of wages, the Court accepts an impermissibly high risk that a wrongfully discharged employee will be subjected to this often lengthy wait for vindication, and to the attendant and often traumatic disruptions to his personal and economic life.

Considerable amounts of time may pass between the termination of wages and the decision in a post-termination evidentiary hearing—indeed, in this case nine months passed before Loudermill received a decision from his postdeprivation hearing. During this period the employee is left in limbo, deprived of his livelihood and of wages on which he may well depend for basic sustenance. In that time, his ability to secure another job might be hindered, either because of the nature of the charges against him, or because of the prospect that he will return to his prior public employment if permitted. Similarly, his access to unemployment benefits might seriously be constrained, because many States deny unemployment compensation to workers discharged for cause. Absent an interim source of wages, the employee might be unable to meet his basic, fixed costs, such as food, rent or mortgage payments. He would be forced to spend his savings, if he had any, and to convert his possessions to cash before becoming eligible for public assistance. Even in that instance "[the] substitution of a meager welfare grant for a regular paycheck may bring with it painful and irremediable personal as well as financial dislocations. A child's education may be interrupted, a family's home lost, a person's relationship with his friends and even his family may be irrevocably affected. The costs of being forced, even temporarily, onto the welfare rolls because of a wrongful discharge from tenured Government employment cannot be so easily discounted."

Moreover, it is in no respect certain that a prompt post-deprivation hearing will make the employee economically whole again, and the wrongfully discharged employee will almost inevitably suffer irreparable injury. Even if reinstatement is forthcoming, the same might not be true of back pay—as it was not to respondent Donnelly in this case—and the delay in receipt of wages would thereby be transformed into a permanent deprivation. Of perhaps equal concern, the personal trauma experienced during the long months in which the employee awaits decision, during which he suffers doubt, humiliation, and the loss of an opportunity to perform work, will never be recompensed, and indeed probably could not be with dollars alone.

That these disruptions might fall upon a justifiably discharged employee is unfortunate; that they might fall upon a wrongfully discharged employee is simply unacceptable. Yet in requiring only that the employee have an opportunity to respond before his wages are cut off, without affording him any meaningful chance to present a defense, the Court is willing to accept an impermissibly high risk of error with respect to a deprivation that is substantial.

Were there any guarantee that the post-deprivation hearing and ruling would occur promptly, such as within a few days of the termination of wages, then this minimal predeprivation process might suffice. But there is no such guarantee. On a practical level, if the employer had to pay the employee until the end of the proceeding, the employer obviously would have an incentive to resolve the issue expeditiously. The employer loses this incentive if the only suffering as a result of the delay is borne by the wage earner, who eagerly awaits the decision on his livelihood. Nor has this Court grounded any guarantee of this kind in the Constitution. Indeed, this Court has in the past approved, at least implicitly, an average 10- or 11-month delay in the receipt of a decision on Social Security benefits, and, in the case of respondent Loudermill, the Court gives a stamp of approval to a process that took nine months. The hardship inevitably increases as the days go by, but nevertheless the Court countenances such delay. The adequacy of the pre-deprivation and post-deprivation procedures are inevitably intertwined, and only a constitutional guarantee that the latter will be immediate and complete might alleviate my concern about the possibility of a wrongful termination of wages.

The opinion for the Court does not confront this reality. I cannot and will not close my eyes today—as I could not 10 years ago—to the economic situation of great numbers of public employees, and to the potentially traumatic effect of a wrongful discharge on a working person. Given that so very much is at stake, I am unable to accept the Court's narrow view of the process due to a public employee before his wages are terminated, and before he begins the long wait for a public agency to issue a final decision in his case.

JUSTICE BRENNAN concurred in part and dissented in part.

Today the Court puts to rest any remaining debate over whether public employers must provide meaningful notice and hearing procedures before discharging an employee for cause. As the Court convincingly demonstrates, the employee's right to fair notice and an opportunity to "present his side of the story" before discharge is not a matter of legislative grace, but of "constitutional guarantee."

Accordingly, I concur in Parts I–IV of the Court's opinion. I write separately to comment on two issues the Court does not resolve today, and to explain my dissent from the result in Part V of the Court's opinion.

First, the Court today does not prescribe the precise form of required pretermination procedures in cases where an employee disputes the facts proffered to support his discharge. The cases at hand involve, as the Court recognizes, employees who did not dispute the facts but had "plausible arguments to make that might have prevented their discharge." In such cases, notice and an "opportunity to present reasons," are sufficient to protect the important interests at stake.

As the Court also correctly notes, other cases "will often involve factual disputes" such as allegedly erroneous records or false accusations. As Justice Marshall has previously noted and stresses again today where there exist not just plausible arguments to be made, but also "substantial disputes in testimonial evidence," due process may well require more than a simple opportunity to argue or deny. When factual disputes are involved, therefore, an employee may deserve a fair opportunity before discharge to produce contrary records or testimony, or even to confront an accuser in front of the decisionmaker.

II. The second issue not resolved today is that of administrative delay. In holding that Loudermill's administrative proceedings did not take too long, the Court plainly does not state a flat rule that 9-month delays in deciding discharge appeals will pass constitutional scrutiny as a matter of course. To the contrary, the Court notes that a full post-termination hearing and decision must be provided at "a meaningful time" and that "[at] some point, a delay in the post-termination hearing would become a constitutional violation." For example, in *Barry v. Barchi,* 443 U.S. 55 (1979), we disapproved as "constitutionally infirm" the shorter administrative delays that resulted under a statute that required "prompt" postsuspension hearings for suspended racehorse trainers with decision to follow within 30 days of the hearing. As Justice Marshall demonstrates, when an employee's wages are terminated pending administrative decision, "hardship inevitably increases as the days go by."

III. Recognizing the limited scope of the holding in Part V, I must still dissent from its result, because the record in this case is insufficiently developed to permit an informed judgment on the issue of overlong delay. Loudermill's complaint was dismissed without answer from the respondent Cleveland Civil Service Commission. Loudermill alleged that it took the Commission over two and one-half months simply to hold a hearing in his case, over two months more to issue a nonbinding interim decision, and more than three and one-half months after that to deliver a final decision. The Commission provided no explanation for these significant gaps in the administrative process; we do not know if they were due to an overabundance of appeals, Loudermill's own foot-dragging, bad faith on the part of the Commission, or any other of a variety of reasons that might affect our analysis. We do know, however, that under Ohio law the Commission is obligated to hear appeals like Loudermill's "within thirty days." I cannot conclude on this record that Loudermill could prove "no set of facts" that might have entitled him to relief after nine months of waiting.

Disposal of Loudermill's complaint without examining the competing interests involved marks an unexplained departure from the careful multifaceted analysis of the facts we consistently have employed in the past. I therefore would remand the delay issue to the District Court for further evidentiary proceedings consistent with the *Mathews* approach. I respectfully dissent from the Court's contrary decision in Part V.

JUSTICE REHNQUIST wrote a dissent.

In *Arnett v. Kennedy*, six Members of this Court agreed that a public employee could be dismissed for misconduct without a full hearing prior to termination. A plurality of Justices agreed that the employee was entitled to exactly what Congress gave him, and no more.

[I]n one legislative breath Ohio has conferred upon civil service employees such as respondents in these cases a limited form of tenure during good behavior, and prescribed the procedures by which that tenure may be terminated. Here, as in *Arnett,* "[the] employee's statutorily defined right is not a guarantee against removal without cause in the abstract, but such a guarantee as enforced by the procedures which [the Ohio Legislature] has designated for the determination of cause."

Having concluded that Ohio has created a property right in the respondents in these cases, the Court naturally proceeds to inquire what process is "due" before the respondents may be divested of that right. This customary "balancing" inquiry conducted by the Court in these cases reaches a result that is quite unobjectionable, but it seems to me that it is devoid of any principles which will either instruct or endure. The balance is simply an ad hoc weighing which depends to a great extent upon how the Court subjectively views the underlying interests at stake. The results in previous cases and in these cases have been quite unpredictable. The results from today's balance certainly do not jibe with the result in *Goldberg* or *Eldridge.* The lack of any principled standards in this area means that these procedural due process cases will recur time and again. Every different set of facts will present a new issue on what process was due and when. One way to avoid this subjective and varying interpretation of the Due Process Clause in cases such as these is to hold that one who avails himself of government entitlements accepts the grant of tenure along with its inherent limitations.

Because I believe that the Fourteenth Amendment of the United States Constitution does not support the conclusion that Ohio's effort to confer a limited form of tenure upon respondents resulted in the creation of a "property right" in their employment, I dissent.

*****

If observers thought that *Loudermill* represented a softening of efforts to constrain due process protections, they were mistaken. In 1997, Justice Scalia wrote for a unanimous Court in a case seeking to determine what process was due before suspension without pay of a public employee.

Gilbert v. Homar, 520 U.S. 924 (1997).

INTRODUCTION: An East Stroudsburg University police officer was arrested in a drug raid while a visitor in someone else's home. While state police filed marijuana possession and also criminal conspiracy (a felony) charges against him, the allegations against him were dropped less than a week later.

In the interim, the university suspended Homar without pay. Even though the charges were dropped, the university continued his suspension. When he met with his supervisor and the police chief, he was told that the state police had provided them with incriminating information, but he was not told at that time about the substance of that information. He therefore could not respond. Some three weeks later, Homar was told that he was to be demoted with a cut in pay and would be retained as a groundskeeper.

*****

JUSTICE SCALIA wrote the opinion for the unanimous Court.

This case presents the question whether a State violates the Due Process Clause of the Fourteenth Amendment by failing to provide notice and a hearing before suspending a tenured public employee without pay.

II. The protections of the Due Process Clause apply to government deprivation of those perquisites of government employment in which the employee has a constitutionally protected "property" interest. Although we have previously held that public employees who can be discharged only for cause have a constitutionally protected property interest in their tenure and cannot be fired without due process, we have not had occasion to decide whether the protections of the Due Process Clause extend to discipline of tenured public employees short of termination.

In *Loudermill*, we concluded that a public employee dismissible only for cause was entitled to a very limited hearing prior to his termination, to be followed by a more comprehensive post-termination hearing. Stressing that the pretermination hearing "should be an initial check against mistaken decisions—essentially, a determination of whether there are reasonable grounds to believe that the charges against the employee are true and support the proposed action," we held that pretermination process need only include oral or written notice of the charges, an explanation of the employer's evidence, and an opportunity for the employee to tell his side of the story. In the course of our assessment of the governmental interest in immediate termination of a tenured employee, we observed that "in those situations where the employer perceives a significant hazard in keeping the employee on the job, it can avoid the problem by suspending with pay."

Relying on this dictum, the Court of Appeals adopted a categorical prohibition: "[A] governmental employer may not suspend an employee without pay unless that suspension is preceded by some kind of pre-suspension hearing, providing the employee with notice and an opportunity to be heard." [U]nder our precedents such an absolute rule is indefensible.

It is by now well established that "'due process,' unlike some legal rules, is not a technical conception with a fixed content unrelated to time, place and circumstances." This Court has recognized, on many occasions, that where a State must act quickly, or where it would be impractical to provide predeprivation process, postdeprivation process satisfies the requirements of the Due Process Clause. In *FDIC v. Mallen,* 486 U.S. 230, 240 (1988), we said: "An important government interest, accompanied by a substantial assurance that the deprivation is not baseless or unwarranted, may in limited cases demanding prompt action justify postponing the opportunity to be heard until after the initial deprivation."

The dictum in *Loudermill* relied upon by the Court of Appeals is of course not inconsistent with these precedents. To say that when the government employer perceives a hazard in leaving the employee on the job it "can avoid the problem by suspending with pay" is not to say that that is the only way of avoiding the problem. Whatever implication the phrase "with pay" might have conveyed is far outweighed by the clarity of our precedents which emphasize the flexibility of due process.

To determine what process is constitutionally due, we have generally balanced three distinct factors: "First, the private interest that will be affected by the official action; second, the risk of an erroneous deprivation of such interest through the procedures used, and the probable value, if any, of additional or substitute procedural safeguards; and finally, the Government's interest." *Eldridge.*

[W]hile our opinions have recognized the severity of depriving someone of the means of his livelihood, they have also emphasized that in determining what process is due, account must be taken of "the length" and "finality of the deprivation." Unlike the employee in *Loudermill,* who faced termination, respondent faced only a temporary suspension without pay. So long as the suspended employee receives a sufficiently prompt postsuspension hearing, the lost income is relatively insubstantial (compared with termination), and fringe benefits such as health and life insurance are often not affected at all.

On the other side of the balance, the State has a significant interest in immediately suspending, when felony charges are filed against them, employees who occupy positions of great public trust and high public visibility, such as police officers. Respondent contends that this interest in maintaining public confidence could have been accommodated by suspending him with pay until he had a hearing. We think, however, that the government does not have to give an employee charged with a felony a paid leave at taxpayer expense. If his services to the government are no longer useful once the felony charge has been filed, the Constitution does not require the government to bear the added expense of hiring a replacement while still paying him. ESU's interest in preserving public confidence in its police force is at least as significant as the State's interest in preserving the integrity of the sport of horse racing, an interest we "deemed sufficiently important . . . to justify a brief period of suspension prior to affording the suspended trainer a hearing."

The last factor in the *Mathews* balancing, and the factor most important to resolution of this case, is the risk of erroneous deprivation and the likely value of any additional procedures. [T]he State had no constitutional obligation to provide respondent with a presuspension hearing. We noted in *Loudermill* that the purpose of a pre-termination hearing is to determine "whether there are reasonable grounds to believe the charges against the employee are true and support the proposed action." By parity of reasoning, the purpose of any pre-suspension hearing would be to assure that there are reasonable grounds to support the suspension without pay. But here that has already been assured by the arrest and the filing of charges.

Whether respondent was provided an adequately prompt post-suspension hearing in the present case is a separate question. Although the charges against respondent were dropped on September 1 (petitioners apparently learned of this on September 2), he did not receive any sort of hearing until September 18. Once the charges were dropped, the risk of erroneous deprivation increased substantially, and, as petitioners conceded at oral argument, there was likely value in holding a prompt hearing. Because neither the Court of Appeals nor the District Court addressed whether, under the particular facts of this case, petitioners violated due process by failing to provide a sufficiently prompt postsuspension hearing, we will not consider this issue in the first instance, but remand for consideration by the Court of Appeals.

*****

CONTRACTED OUT ADJUDICATIONS
AND THE DUE PROCESS CLAUSE

It is surprising to some to learn that contracting out has extended even into the area of adjudications. Consider two examples: one from the federal level and one in a state.

Schweiker v. McClure, 456 U.S. 188 (1982).

INTRODUCTION: The Medicare program has a Part A which deals with hospital and nursing home charges and a Part B that dealing with "Supplementary Medical Insurance Benefits for the Aged and Disabled." Part B deals with a variety of physicians' bills and other outpatient charges. Some 27 million Americans participate in the Part B program and are paid claims of more than $10 billion each year. Congress authorized contracts with private insurance firms to operate the Part B claims process.

Claimants can request a review in support of which they can submit arguments and information. The review is conducted by a different employee of the insurance firm contracted to process claims under this program. For larger claims, those in excess of $100, a claimant can obtain a hearing, but that hearing is conducted by another employee of the insurance firm contracted to the federal government. There is no other review provided under the program.

This case arose as a class action brought by three people whose claims were denied by contractors.

JUSTICE POWELL wrote the opinion for the unanimous Court.

The question is whether Congress, consistently with the requirements of due process, may provide that hearings on disputed claims for certain Medicare payments be held by private insurance carriers, without a further right of appeal.

II. This case arose as a result of decisions by hearing officers against three claimants. The claimants, here appellees, sued to challenge the constitutional adequacy of the hearings afforded them. The District Court concluded that the Part B hearing procedures violated appellees' right to due process "insofar as the final, unappealable decision regarding claims disputes is made by carrier appointees. . . ."

The court reached its conclusion of unconstitutionality by alternative lines of argument. The first rested upon the principle that tribunals must be impartial. The court thought that the impartiality of the carrier's hearing officers was compromised by their "prior involvement and pecuniary interest." "Pecuniary interest" was shown, the District Court said, by the fact that "their incomes as hearing officers are entirely dependent upon the carrier's decisions regarding whether, and how often, to call upon their services." Respecting "prior involvement," the court acknowledged that hearing officers personally had not been previously involved in the cases they decided. But it noted that hearing officers "are appointed by, and serve at the will of, the carrier [that] has not only participated in the prior stages of each case, but has twice denied the claims [that] are the subject of the hearing," and that five out of seven of Blue Shield's past and present hearing officers "are former or current Blue Shield employees." The District Court thought these links between the carriers and their hearing officers sufficient to create a constitutionally intolerable risk of hearing officer bias against claimants.

The District Court's alternative reasoning assessed the costs and benefits of affording claimants a hearing before one of the Secretary's administrative law judges, "either subsequent to or substituting for the hearing conducted by a carrier appointee." The court noted that *Eldridge* makes three factors relevant to such an inquiry: "First, the private interest that will be affected by the official action; second, the risk of an erroneous deprivation of such interest through the procedures used, and the probable value, if any, of additional or substitute procedural safeguards; and finally, the Government's interest, including the function involved and the fiscal and administrative burdens that the additional or substitute procedural requirement would entail."

Considering the first *Mathews* factor, the court listed three considerations tending to show that the private interest at stake was not overwhelming. The court then stated, however, that "it cannot be gainsaid" that denial of a Medicare beneficiary's claim to reimbursement may impose "considerable hardship."

As to the second *Mathews* factor of risk of erroneous deprivation and the probable value of added process, the District Court found the record "inconclusive." The court cited statistics showing that the two available Part B appeal procedures frequently result in reversal of the carriers' original disposition.[11] But it criticized these statistics for failing to distinguish between partial and total reversals. The court stated that hearing officers were required neither to receive training nor to satisfy "threshold criteria such as having a law degree." On this basis it held that "it must be assumed that additional safeguards would reduce the risk of erroneous deprivation of Part B benefits."

On the final *Mathews* factor involving the Government's interest, the District Court noted that carriers processed 124 million Part B claims in 1978. The court stated that "[only] a fraction of those claimants pursue their currently-available appeal remedies," and that "there is no indication that anything but an even smaller group of claimants will actually pursue [an] additional remedy" of appeal to the Secretary. Moreover, the court said, the Secretary already maintained an appeal procedure using administrative law judges for appeals by Part A claimants. Increasing the number of claimants who could use this Part A administrative appeal "would not be a cost-free change from the status quo, but neither should it be a costly one."

Weighing the three *Mathews* factors, the court concluded that due process required additional procedural protection over that presently found in the Part B hearing procedure. The court ordered that the appellees were entitled to a *de novo* hearing of record conducted by an administrative law judge of the Social Security Administration. We noted probable jurisdiction and now reverse.

III. The hearing officers involved in this case serve in a quasi-judicial capacity, similar in many respects to that of administrative law judges. As this Court repeatedly has recognized, due process demands impartiality on the part of those who function in judicial or quasi-judicial capacities. We must start, however, from the presumption that the hearing officers who decide Part B claims are unbiased. This presumption can be rebutted by a showing of conflict of interest or some other specific reason for disqualification. But the burden of establishing a disqualifying interest rests on the party making the assertion.

---

11. "[B]etween 1975 and 1978, carriers wholly or partially reversed, upon 'review determination,' their initial determinations in 51–57 percent of the cases considered. Of the adverse determination decisions brought before hearing officers, 42–51 percent of the carriers' decisions were reversed in whole or in part." [503 F. Supp. at 416].

Fairly interpreted, the factual findings made in this case do not reveal any disqualifying interest under the standard of our cases. The District Court relied almost exclusively on generalized assumptions of possible interest, placing special weight on the various connections of the hearing officers with the private insurance carriers. The difficulty with this reasoning is that these connections would be relevant only if the carriers themselves are biased or interested. We find no basis in the record for reaching such a conclusion. As previously noted, the carriers pay all Part B claims from federal, and not their own, funds. Similarly, the salaries of the hearing officers are paid by the Federal Government. Further, the carriers operate under contracts that require compliance with standards prescribed by the statute and the Secretary. In the absence of proof of financial interest on the part of the carriers, there is no basis for assuming a derivative bias among their hearing officers.

Appellees further argued that due process requires an additional administrative or judicial review by a Government rather than a carrier-appointed hearing officer. Specifically, the District Court ruled that "[existing] Part B procedures might remain intact so long as aggrieved beneficiaries would be entitled to appeal carrier appointees' decisions to Part A administrative law judges." In reaching this conclusion, the District Court applied the familiar test prescribed in *Mathews*. We may assume that the District Court was correct in viewing the private interest in Part B payments as "considerable," though "not quite as precious as the right to receive welfare or social security benefits." We likewise may assume, in considering the third *Mathews* factor, that the additional cost and inconvenience of providing administrative law judges would not be unduly burdensome.

We focus narrowly on the second *Mathews* factor that considers the risk of erroneous decision and the probable value, if any, of the additional procedure. The District Court's reasoning on this point consisted only of this sentence: "In light of [appellees'] undisputed showing that carrier-appointed hearing officers receive little or no formal training and are not required to satisfy any threshold criteria such as having a law degree, it must be assumed that additional safeguards would reduce the risk of erroneous deprivation of Part B benefits."

Again, the record does not support these conclusions. The Secretary has directed carriers to select as a hearing officer: "'an attorney or other qualified individual with the ability to conduct formal hearings and with a general understanding of medical matters and terminology. The [hearing officer] must have a thorough knowledge of the Medicare program and the statutory authority and regulations upon which it is based, as well as rulings, policy statements, and general instructions pertinent to the Medicare Bureau.'"

The District Court did not identify any specific deficiencies in the Secretary's selection criteria. By definition, a "qualified" individual already possessing "ability" and "thorough knowledge" would not require further training. The court's further general concern that hearing officers "are not required to satisfy any threshold criteria" overlooks the Secretary's quoted regulation. Moreover, the District Court apparently gave no weight to the qualifications of hearing officers about whom there is information in the record. Their qualifications tend to undermine rather than to support the contention that accuracy of Part B decisionmaking may suffer by reason of carrier appointment of unqualified hearing officers. Appellees simply have not shown that the procedures prescribed by Congress and the Secretary are not fair or that different or additional procedures would reduce the risk of erroneous deprivation of Part B benefits.

*****

American Manufacturers Mutual Insurance Co. v. Sullivan, 526 U.S. 40 (1999).

INTRODUCTION: This case is another example of contracted adjudication, but one that is even more complex than the Part B Medicare example. In this instance, the issue is due process once again, but this time it concerns workers' compensation processing. Even though the claim goes through the Workers' Compensation Bureau of the Pennsylvania Department of Labor and Industry, that agency, if requested by an employer, turns the claim over to a "utilization review organization." The problem arises because that review is usually critical to a claim, but the claimant could not obtain any kind of procedural protections in terms of the manner in which the utilization review was conducted. The case raises the question of when a contractor can be said to be acting in the place of the state for purposes of due process protections, the so-called state action doctrine. If the contractor is a state actor, then the due process clause applies. If not, then no such due process protections are available unless they are provided by statute or regulation, which they were not in the Pennsylvania case.

JUSTICE REHNQUIST wrote the opinion for the Court. O'CONNOR, SCALIA, KENNEDY, SOUTER, THOMAS, and BREYER joined Parts I and II of the opinion. O'CONNOR, KENNEDY, THOMAS, and GINSBURG joined Part III.

Pennsylvania provides in its workers' compensation regime that an employer or insurer may withhold payment for disputed medical treatment pending an independent review to determine whether the treatment is reasonable and necessary. We hold that the insurers are not "state actors" under the Fourteenth Amendment, and that the Pennsylvania regime does not deprive disabled employees of property within the meaning of that Amendment.

I. [The] Pennsylvania's Workers' Compensation Act creates a system of no-fault liability for work-related injuries and makes employers' liability under this system "exclusive . . . of any and all other liability." All employers subject to the Act must either (1) obtain workers' compensation insurance from a private insurer, (2) obtain such insurance through the State Workers' Insurance Fund (SEIF), or (3) seek permission from the state to self-insure. Once an employer becomes liable for an employee's work-related injury—because liability either is not contested or is no longer at issue—the employer or its insurer must pay for all "reasonable" and "necessary" medical treatment, and must do so within 30 days of receiving a bill. To assure that insurers pay only for medical care that meets these criteria, and in an attempt to control costs, Pennsylvania amended its workers' compensation system, creat[ing] a "utilization review" procedure under which the reasonableness and necessity of an employee's past, ongoing, or prospective medical treatment could be reviewed before a medical bill must be paid. Under this system, if an insurer "disputes the reasonableness or necessity of the treatment provided," it may request utilization review by filing a one-page form with the Workers' Compensation Bureau of the Pennsylvania Department of Labor and Industry (Bureau). The form identifies the employee, the medical provider, the date of the employee's injury, and the medical treatment to be reviewed. The Bureau makes no attempt to "address the legitimacy or lack thereof of the request," but merely determines whether the form is "properly completed." Upon the proper filing of a request, an insurer may withhold payment to health care providers for the particular services being challenged.

The Bureau then notifies the parties that utilization review has been requested and forwards the request to a randomly selected "utilization review organization" (URO). UROs are private organizations consisting of health care providers who are "licensed in the same profession and have the same or similar specialty as that of the provider of the treatment under review." The purpose of utilization review, and the sole authority conferred upon a URO, is to determine "whether the treatment under review is reasonable or necessary for the medical condition of the employee" in light of "generally accepted treatment protocols." Reviewers must examine the treating provider's medical records and must give the provider an opportunity to discuss the treatment under review. Any doubt as to the reasonableness and necessity of a given procedure must be resolved in favor of the employee.

UROs are instructed to complete their review and render a determination within 30 days of a completed request. If the URO finds in favor of the insurer, the employee may appeal the determination to a workers' compensation judge for a *de novo* review, but the insurer need not pay for the disputed services unless the URO's determination is overturned by the judge, or later by the courts. If the URO finds in favor of the employee, the insurer must pay the disputed bill immediately, with 10 percent annual interest, as well as the cost of the utilization review.

Respondents are 10 individual employees and 2 organizations representing employees who received medical benefits under the Act.[12] They claimed to have had payment of particular benefits withheld pursuant to the utilization review procedure set forth in the Act. They sued under 42 U.S.C. § 1983, acting individually and on behalf of a class of similarly situated employees. Named as defendants were various Pennsylvania officials who administer the Act, the director of the SEIF, the School District of Philadelphia (which self-insures), and a number of private insurance companies who provide workers' compensation coverage in

---

12. In addition to the 10 named employees, the 2 named organizations are the Philadelphia Area Project on Occupational Safety and Health, a nonprofit group composed of over 2,000 unions and their members, and the Philadelphia Federation of Teachers, a labor organization representing approximately 20,000 employees of the School District of Philadelphia.

Pennsylvania. Respondents alleged that in withholding workers' compensation benefits without predeprivation notice and an opportunity to be heard, the state and private defendants, acting "under color of state law," deprived them of property in violation of due process. They sought declaratory and injunctive relief, as well as damages.

The District Court dismissed the private insurers from the lawsuit on the ground that they are not "state actors," and later dismissed the state officials who remained as defendants, as well as the school district, on the ground that the Act does not violate due process.

The Court of Appeals for the Third Circuit disagreed on both issues. It held that a private insurer's decision to suspend payment under the Act constitutes state action. The court reasoned:

> In creating and executing this system of entitlements, the [State] has enacted a complex and interwoven regulatory web enlisting the Bureau, the employers, and the insurance companies. The [State] extensively regulates and controls the Workers' Compensation system. Although the insurance companies are private entities, when they act under the construct of the Workers' Compensation system, they are providing public benefits which honor state entitlements. In effect, they become an arm of the State, fulfilling a uniquely governmental obligation under an entirely state-created, self-contained public benefit system. . . .
>
> The right to stop payments, is a power that traditionally was held in the hands of the State. When insurance companies [suspend] an employee's medical benefits, they compromise an employee's state-created entitlements. The insurers have no power to deprive or terminate such benefits without the permission and participation of the [State]. More importantly, however, the [State] is intimately involved in any decision by an insurer to terminate an employee's constitutionally protected benefits because an insurer cannot suspend medical payments without first obtaining authorization from the Bureau. However this authorization may be characterized, any deprivation that occurs is predicated upon the State's involvement.

On the due process issue, the Court of Appeals did not address whether respondents have a protected property interest in workers' compensation medical benefits, stating that "neither party disputes" this point. Thus focusing on what process is "due," the court held that payment of bills may not be withheld until employees have had an opportunity to submit their view in writing as to the reasonableness and necessity of the disputed treatment to the URO. The court then determined that the relevant statutory language permitting the suspension of payment during utilization review was severable and struck it from the statute.

II. To state a claim for relief in an action brought under §1983, respondents must establish that they were deprived of a right secured by the Constitution or laws of the United States, and that the alleged deprivation was committed under color of state law. Like the state-action requirement of the Fourteenth Amendment, the under-color-of-state-law element of §1983 excludes from its reach "'merely private conduct, no matter how discriminatory or wrongful,'"

[S]tate action requires both an alleged constitutional deprivation "caused by the exercise of some right or privilege created by the State or by a rule of conduct imposed by the State or by a person for whom the State is responsible," and that "the party charged with the deprivation must be a person who may fairly be said to be a state actor." *Lugar v. Edmondson Oil Co.,* 457 U.S. 922, 937, (1982). In this case, while it may fairly be said that private insurers act "'with knowledge of and pursuant to'" the state statute, thus satisfying the first requirement, respondents still must satisfy the second, whether the allegedly unconstitutional conduct is fairly attributable to the State.

Our approach to this latter question begins by identifying "the specific conduct of which the plaintiff complains." Here, respondents named as defendants both public officials and a class of private insurers and self-insured employers. Also named is the director of the SEIF, and the School District of Philadelphia, a municipal corporation. The complaint alleged that the state and private defendants, acting under color of state law and pursuant to the Act, deprived them of property in violation of due process by withholding payment for medical treatment without prior notice and an opportunity to be heard. All agree that the public officials responsible for administering the workers' compensation system and the director of SEIF are state actors. Thus, the issue we address, in accordance with our cases, is whether a private insurer's decision to withhold payment for disputed medical treatment may be fairly attributable to the State so as to subject insurers to the constraints of the Fourteenth Amendment. Our answer to that question is "no."

In cases involving extensive state regulation of private activity, we have consistently held that "the mere fact that a business is subject to state regulation does not by itself convert its action into that of the State for purposes of the Fourteenth Amendment." Faithful application of the state-action requirement in these cases ensures that the prerogative of regulating private business remains with the States and the representative branches, not the courts. Thus, the private insurers in this case will not be held to constitutional standards unless "there is a sufficiently close nexus between the State and the challenged action of the regulated entity so that the latter may be fairly treated as that of the State itself." Whether such a "close nexus" exists, our cases state, depends on whether the State "has exercised coercive power or has provided such significant encouragement, either overt or covert, that the choice must in law be deemed to be that of the State." Action taken by private entities with the mere approval or acquiescence of the State is not state action.

We do not doubt that the State's decision to provide insurers the option of deferring payment for unnecessary and unreasonable treatment pending review can in some sense be seen as encouraging them to do just that. But, as petitioners note, this kind of subtle encouragement is no more significant than that which inheres in the State's creation or modification of any legal remedy. We have never held that the mere availability of a remedy for wrongful conduct, even when the private use of that remedy serves important public interests, so significantly encourages the private activity as to make the State responsible for it. It bears repeating that a finding of state action on this basis would be contrary to the "essential dichotomy," between public and private acts that our cases have consistently recognized.

The State's decision to allow insurers to withhold payments pending review can just as easily be seen as state inaction, or more accurately, a legislative decision not to intervene in a dispute between an insurer and an employee over whether a particular treatment is reasonable and necessary. The most that can be said of the statutory scheme, therefore, is that whereas it previously prohibited insurers from withholding payment for disputed medical services, it no longer does so. Such permission of a private choice cannot support a finding of state action. As we have said before, our cases will not tolerate "the imposition of Fourteenth Amendment restraints on private action by the simple device of characterizing the State's inaction as 'authorization' or 'encouragement.'"

Nor does the State's role in creating, supervising, and setting standards for the URO process differ in any meaningful sense from the creation and administration of any forum for resolving disputes. While the decision of a URO, like that of any judicial official, may properly be considered state action, a private party's mere use of the State's dispute resolution machinery, without the "overt, significant assistance of state officials" cannot.

We also reject the notion that the challenged decisions are state action because insurers must first obtain "authorization" or "permission" from the Bureau before withholding payment. We [have] rejected the notion that the State, "by requiring completion of a form," is responsible for the private party's decision. The additional "paper shuffling" performed by the Bureau here in response to an insurers' request does not alter that conclusion.

Respondents next contend that state action is present because the State has delegated to insurers "powers traditionally exclusively reserved to the State." Their argument here is twofold. [R]espondents first argue that workers' compensation benefits are state-mandated "public benefits," and that the State has delegated the provision of these "public benefits" to private insurers. They also contend that the State has delegated to insurers the traditionally exclusive government function of determining whether and under what circumstances an injured worker's medical benefits may be suspended.

[N]othing in Pennsylvania's constitution or statutory scheme obligates the State to provide either medical treatment or workers' compensation benefits to injured workers. Nor is there any merit in respondents' argument that the State has delegated to insurers the traditionally exclusive governmental function of deciding whether to suspend payment for disputed medical treatment. Historical practice, as well as the state statutory scheme, does not support respondents' characterization. It is no doubt true that before the 1993 amendments an insurer who sought to withhold payment for disputed medical treatment was required to petition the Bureau, and could withhold payment only upon a favorable ruling by a workers' compensation judge, and then only for prospective treatment.... But before Pennsylvania ever adopted its workers' compensation law, an insurer under contract with an employer to pay for its workers' reasonable and necessary medical expenses could withhold payment, for any reason or no reason, without any authorization or involvement of the State.

The Court of Appeals, in response to the various arguments advanced by respondents, seems to have figuratively thrown up its hands and fallen back on language in our decision in *Burton v. Wilmington Parking Authority,* 365 U.S. 715 (1961). The Pennsylvania system, that court said, "inextricably entangles the insurance companies in a partnership with the Commonwealth such that they become an integral part of the state in administering the statutory scheme."

Burton was one of our early cases dealing with "state action" under the Fourteenth Amendment, and later cases have refined the vague "joint participation" test embodied in that case. [Later cases] have established that "privately owned enterprises providing services that the State would not necessarily provide, even though they are extensively regulated, do not fall within the ambit of *Burton.*"

We conclude that an insurer's decision to withhold payment and seek utilization review of the reasonableness and necessity of particular medical treatment is not fairly attributable to the State. Respondents have therefore failed to satisfy an essential element of their §1983 claim.

III. Though our resolution of the state-action issue would be sufficient by itself to reverse the judgment of the Court of Appeals, we believe the court fundamentally misapprehended the nature of respondents' property interest at stake in this case, with ramifications not only for the state officials who are concededly state actors, but also for the private insurers who (under our holding in Part II) are not. [The second problem to be resolved, then is as follows:] "Whether the Due Process Clause requires workers' compensation insurers to pay disputed medical bills prior to a determination that the medical treatment was reasonable and necessary."

The first inquiry in every due process challenge is whether the plaintiff has been deprived of a protected interest in "property" or "liberty." *Mathews v. Eldridge.* Only after finding the deprivation of a protected interest do we look to see if the State's procedures comport with due process.

Here, respondents contend that Pennsylvania's workers' compensation law confers upon them a protected property interest in workers' compensation medical benefits. Under state law, respondents assert, once an employer's liability is established for a particular work-related injury, the employer is obligated to pay for certain benefits, including partial wage replacement, compensation for permanent injury or disability, and medical care. It follows from this, the argument goes, that medical benefits are a state-created entitlement, and thus an insurer cannot withhold payment of medical benefits without affording an injured worker due process.

In *Goldberg,* we held that an individual receiving federal welfare assistance has a statutorily created property interest in the continued receipt of those benefits. Likewise, in *Mathews,* we recognized that the same was true for an individual receiving Social Security disability benefits. In both cases, an individual's entitlement to benefits had been established, and the question presented was whether predeprivation notice and a hearing were required before the individual's interest in continued payment of benefits could be terminated.

While they indeed have established their initial eligibility for medical treatment, they have yet to make good on their claim that the particular medical treatment they received was reasonable and necessary. Consequently, they do not have a property interest in having their providers paid for treatment that has yet to be found reasonable and necessary.

The judgment of the Court of Appeals is reversed.

JUSTICE STEVENS wrote and opinion concurring in part and dissenting in part.[13]

Because the individual respondents suffered work-related injuries, they are entitled to have their employers, or the employers' insurers, pay for whatever "reasonable" and "necessary" treatment they may need. That right—whether described as a "claim for payment or a "cause of action"—is unquestionably a species of property protected by the Due Process Clause of the Fourteenth Amendment. Disputes over the reasonableness or necessity of particular treatments are resolved by decisionmakers who are state actors and who must follow procedures established by Pennsylvania law. Because the resolution of such disputes determines the scope of the claimants' property interests, the Constitution requires that the procedure be fair. That is true whether the claim is asserted against a private insurance carrier or against a public entity that self-insures. It is equally clear that the State's duty to establish and administer a fair procedure for resolving the dispute obtains whether the dispute is initiated by the filing of a claim or by an insurer's decision to withhold payment until the reasonableness issue is resolved.

In my judgment the significant questions raised by this case are: (1) whether Pennsylvania's procedure was fair when the case was commenced, and (2) if not, whether it was fair after the State modified its rules in response to the Court of Appeals' decision. In my opinion the Court of Appeals correctly concluded that the original procedure was deficient because it did not give employees either notice that a request for utilization review would automatically suspend their benefits or an opportunity to provide relevant evidence and argument to the state actor vested with initial decisional authority. I would therefore affirm the judgment of the Court of Appeals insofar as it mandated the change described in the Court's footnote 3. I do not, however, find any constitutional defect in the procedures that are now in place, and therefore agree that the judgment should be reversed to the extent that it requires any additional modifications. It is not unfair, in and of itself, for a State to allow either a private or a publicly owned party to withhold payment of a state-created entitlement pending resolution of a dispute over its amount.

Thus, although I agree with much of what the Court has written, I do not join its opinion for two reasons. First, I think it incorrectly assumes that the question whether the insurance company is a state actor is relevant to the controlling question whether the state procedures are fair. The relevant state actors, rather than the particular parties to the payment disputes, are the state-appointed deci-

---

13. Justices Ginsburg and Breyer wrote opinions concurring in part and in the judgment.

sionmakers who implement the exclusive procedure that the State has created to protect respondents' rights. These state actors are defendants in this suit. Second, the Court fails to answer either the question whether the State's procedures were fair when the case was filed or the question whether they are fair now.

*****

EX PARTE COMMUNICATIONS

One of the difficulties involved in administrative adjudications, regardless of who is responsible for the ruling, is the question of attempts at inappropriate influence in that decisionmaking by one side or the other; or, for that matter, by some outside party. An effort to sway an adjudicator outside the normal process is known as an *ex parte* communication, meaning a contact on behalf of a party. The general rule provided in the APA is that "'*ex parte* communication' means an oral or written communication not on the public record with respect to which reasonable prior notice to all parties is not given, but it shall not include requests for status reports on any matter or proceeding covered by this subchapter." 5 U.S.C. §551(14). The APA goes on to warn that:

(A) no interested person outside the agency shall make or knowingly cause to be made to any member of the comprising the agency, administrative law judge, or other employee who is reasonably be expected to, be involved in the decisional process of the proceeding, an *ex parte* communication relevant to the merits of the proceeding;

(B) no member of the body comprising the agency, administrative law judge, or other employee who is or may reasonably be expected to be involved in the decisional process of the proceeding, shall make or knowingly cause to be made to any interested person outside the agency an *ex parte* communication relevant to the merits of the proceeding;

(C) a member of the body comprising the agency, administrative law judge, or other employee who is or may reasonably be expected to be involved in the decisional process of such proceedings who receives, or who makes or knowingly causes to be made, a communication prohibited by this subsection shall place on the public record of the proceeding;

(i) all such written communications;

(ii) memoranda stating the substance of all such oral communications; and

(iii) all written responses, and memoranda stating the substance of all oral responses, to the materials described in clauses (i) and (ii) of this subparagraph;

(D) upon receipt of a communication knowingly made or knowingly caused to be made by a party in violation of this subsection, the agency, administrative law judge, or other employee presiding at the hearing may, to the extent consistent with the interests of justice and the policy of the underlying statutes, require the party to show cause why his claim or interest in the proceeding should not be dismissed, denied, disregarded, or otherwise adversely affected on account of such violation; and

(E) the prohibitions of this subsection shall apply beginning at such time as the agency may designate, but in no case shall they begin to apply later an the time at which proceeding is noticed for hearing unless the person responsible for the communication has knowledge that it will be noticed, in which case the prohibitions shall apply beginning at the time of this acquisition of such knowledge. 5 U.S.C. §557 (d)(1).

However, the problem confronting the adjudicator can be more complex than a seemingly simple and direct effort by one of the named parties to an adjudication to communicate with the decisionmaker. And even when the nature and extent of an *ex parte* violation are clear, what sanction will be imposed, given that it could be the basis for the ruling against the offending party? These matters were raised in a particularly controversial case involving the Professional Air Traffic Controllers' Organization. That case provided an opportunity for the D.C. Circuit to explore the boundaries of the *ex parte* concept.

Professional Air Traffic Controllers Organization v. Federal Labor Relations Authority, 685 F.2d 547 (D.C. Cir. 1982).

INTRODUCTION: This case grew out of the extremely controversial Professional Air Traffic Controllers' Organization (PATCO) strike. Federal employees, of course, do not have a right to strike, and this job action was all the more controversial because it involved employees in an essential national safety field. On the other hand, controllers had argued loudly and often that the system was not safe and that something had to be done to increase the number of available controllers, to reduce stress and fatigue for existing workers, and to update the totally inadequate technical systems available to the controllers. Yet they saw that the deregulated airlines were going to move toward ever more flights with little or no improvement in the national flight control system.

The Reagan administration announced that either air traffic controllers would return to work immediately or they would be fired. Indeed, it began immediately to terminate strikers. (So precipitous were these actions that the administration was forced to back up and institute appropriate due process steps before actually terminating workers.) The administration also brought an action before the Federal Labor Relations Authority (FLRA) to decertify the PATCO union, effectively killing it. The administration was determined to assert control over public servants, union or not, and it called for swift action by the FLRA.

In fact, the Secretary of Transportation went so far as to call members of the FLRA and press them for a rapid decision, reasserting the importance that the administration attached to their ruling.

Not surprisingly, many in organized labor saw the attack on PATCO as part of a dramatically anti-union position by the Reagan White House. This issue was not just what would happen with PATCO but what union would be the next target? With that in mind, a well-known labor advocate planned a dinner with an FLRA member who was a long-time acquaintance and used it to argue for lenient treatment for PATCO. Both this action and the Secretary of Transportation's contacts raised serious questions about *ex parte* communications that might undermine whatever decision FLRA reached.

The full opinion of the D.C. Circuit addressed two issues. The first concerned the discretion of the FLRA to decertify the union. The court affirmed that action. The second issue, however, is the focus of this discussion. That concerned whether there were *ex parte* communications. If so, what steps should the FLRA have taken?

JUSTICE EDWARDS wrote the opinion for the court.

After the Professional Air Traffic Controllers Organization (PATCO) called a nationwide strike of air traffic controllers against the Federal Aviation Administration (FAA) in the summer of 1981, the Authority revoked PATCO's status as exclusive bargaining representative for the controllers. For the reasons set forth below, we affirm the decision of the Authority.

II. *EX PARTE* COMMUNICATIONS DURING THE FLRA PROCEEDINGS

Only a day before oral argument [on the challenge to the FLRA ruling], the Department of Justice, which represents the FAA in this review, informed the court that the Department of Justice Criminal Division and the FBI had investigated allegations of an improper contact between a "well-known labor leader" and FLRA Member Applewhaite during the pendency of the PATCO case. We were understandably concerned about the suggestion that attempts had been made to influence the Authority improperly and about the possible inference that the Authority's decision might have been affected by these attempts.

[W]e invoked a procedure that this court has occasionally employed in like situations in the past. [W]e ordered the FLRA "to hold, with the aid of a specially-appointed administrative law judge, an evidentiary hearing to determine the nature, extent, source and effect of any and all ex parte communications and other approaches that may have been made to any member or members of the FLRA while the PATCO case was pending before it."

John M. Vittone, an Administrative Law Judge with the Civil Aeronautics Board, made extensive findings regarding all possibly relevant approaches to and communications with FLRA Members. A.L.J. Vittone's inquiry led to the disclosure of a number of communications with FLRA Members that were at least arguably related to the Authority's consideration of the PATCO case. We find the vast majority of these communications unobjectionable. Three occurrences, however, are somewhat more troubling and require our careful review and discussion.

On August 10, 1981 (one week after the unfair labor practice complaint against PATCO was filed), H. Stephan Gordon, the FLRA General Counsel, was in Member Applewhaite's office discussing administrative matters unrelated to the PATCO case. During Gordon's discussion with Member Applewhaite, Ms. Ellen Stern, an attorney with the FLRA Solicitor's office, entered Member Applewhaite's office to deliver a copy of a memorandum entitled "Decertification of Labor Organization Participating in the Conduct of a Strike in Violation of Section 7116(b) (7) of the Statute." Ms. Stern had prepared the memo at the request of Member Frazier. With General Counsel Gordon present, Ms. Stern proceeded to discuss her memorandum, which dealt with whether the Civil Service Reform Act makes revocation of a striking union's exclusive recognition status mandatory or discretionary and, assuming it is discretionary, what other disciplinary actions might be taken. While the conversation at least implicitly focused on the PATCO case, the facts of the case and the appropriate disposition were not discussed. The discussion ended after ten or fifteen minutes. A.L.J. Vittone concluded that "the conversation had no effect or impact on Member Applewhaite's ultimate decision in the PATCO case."

During the morning of August 13, 1981, Secretary of Transportation Andrew L. Lewis, Jr. telephoned Member Frazier. Secretary Lewis stated that he was not calling about the substance of the PATCO case, but wanted Member Frazier to know that, contrary to some news reports, no meaningful efforts to settle the strike were underway. Secretary Lewis also stated that the Department of Transportation would appreciate expeditious handling of the case. Not wanting to discuss the PATCO case with Secretary Lewis, Member Frazier replied, "I understand your position perfectly, Mr. Secretary." Secretary Lewis then inquired whether Member Applewhaite was in Washington, D.C. at that time. Member Frazier replied that he was, but that Chairman Haughton was out of town. Although Member Frazier offered to convey the Secretary's message to Member Applewhaite, Secretary Lewis stated that he would call personally.

Member Frazier discussed Secretary Lewis' call with FLRA Solicitor Robert Freehling, describing it as relating to status and settlement. Solicitor Freehling advised Member Frazier that the communication did not fall within the ex parte prohibitions of the FLRA Rules.

Member Frazier also advised Member Applewhaite of Secretary Lewis' telephone call. In anticipation of a call, Member Applewhaite located the FLRA Rules regarding the time limits for processing an appeal from an A.L.J. decision in an unfair labor practice case. When Secretary Lewis telephoned and stated his concern that the case not be delayed, Member Applewhaite interrupted the Secretary to inform him that if he wished to obtain expedited handling of the case, he would have to comply with the FLRA Rules and file a written motion. Secretary Lewis stated that he was unaware that papers had to be filed and that he would contact his General Counsel immediately. The conversation ended without further discussion.

Since 1974 Albert Shanker has been President of the American Federation of Teachers, a large public-sector labor union, and a member of the Executive Council of the AFL-CIO. Since 1964 Mr. Shanker has been President of the AFT's New York City Local, the United Federation of Teachers. Before joining the FLRA, Member Applewhaite had been associated with the New York Public Employment Relations Board. Through their contacts in New York, Mr. Shanker and Member Applewhaite had become professional and social friends.

The Applewhaite/Shanker Dinner. On September 21, Mr. Shanker made arrangements to have dinner with Member Applewhaite that evening. Although he did not inform Member Applewhaite of his intentions when he made the arrangements, Mr. Shanker candidly admitted that he wanted to have dinner with Member Applewhaite because he felt strongly about the PATCO case and wanted to communicate directly to Member Applewhaite his sentiments, previously expressed in public statements, that PATCO should not be severely punished for its strike. In particular, Mr. Shanker believed that revocation of PATCO's exclusive recognition status would be an excessive punishment. After accepting the invitation, Member Applewhaite informed Member Frazier and Chairman Haughton that he was having dinner with Mr. Shanker.

The two men discussed various approaches to public employee strikes in New York, Pennsylvania and the federal government. Mr. Shanker expressed his view that the punishment of a striking union should fit the crime and that revocation of certification as a punishment for an illegal strike was tantamount to "killing a union." The record is clear that Mr. Shanker made no threats or promises to Member Applewhaite; likewise, the evidence also indicates that Member Applewhaite never revealed his position regarding the PATCO case.

Near the end of their conversation, Member Applewhaite commented that because the PATCO case was hotly contested, he would be viewed with disfavor by whichever side he voted against. Member Applewhaite also observed that he was concerned about his prospects for reappointment to the FLRA in July 1982. Mr. Shanker, in turn, responded that Member Applewhaite had no commitments from anyone and urged him to vote without regard to personal considerations.

The FLRA Decisional Process. On the afternoon of September 21, before the Applewhaite/Shanker dinner, the FLRA Members had had their first formal conference on the PATCO case, which had been argued to them five days earlier. Members Frazier and Applewhaite both favored revocation of PATCO's exclusive recognition status and took the position that PATCO would no longer be a labor organization within the meaning of the Civil Service Reform Act. Member Frazier favored an indefinite revocation; Member Applewhaite favored a revocation for a fixed period of one to three years. Chairman Haughton agreed that an illegal strike had occurred, but favored suspension, not revocation, of PATCO's collective bargaining status.

After September 21, Member Applewhaite considered other remedies, short of revocation, to deal with the PATCO strike. For over two weeks Member Applewhaite sought to find common ground with Chairman Haughton. Those efforts to agree on an alternative solution failed and, on October 9, Member

Applewhaite finally decided to vote with Member Frazier for revocation. (Member Applewhaite apparently was concerned that the FLRA have a majority favoring one remedy, rather than render three opinions favoring three different dispositions.) All three Members drafted their final opinions by October 19. The drafts were exchanged and responses inserted. With some polishing, but no substantive change of positions, the opinions issued on October 22, 1981.

Member Frazier later asked Solicitor Freehling if Member Applewhaite had discussed his dinner with Mr. Shanker. Solicitor Freehling told Member Frazier that they had talked and that Member Applewhaite had concluded that there were no problems involved. Despite these assurances, Member Frazier contacted his personal attorney. Sometime in early October, Member Frazier's attorney contacted the FBI. The FBI interviewed Member Frazier on October 17 and then other FLRA Members and staff. FBI agents interviewed Member Applewhaite on October 22, the day the FLRA Decision issued.

The Parties' Positions. Each of the FLRA Members argue that their individual contacts with persons outside of the Authority were not improper. In addition, each of the Members supports A.L.J. Vittone's findings that the various contacts, their own and their colleagues,' had no effect on the ultimate decision of the PATCO case. Member Applewhaite alone disputes A.L.J. Vittone's finding that his dinner with Mr. Shanker may have had a transitory effect on his consideration of the case. Mr. Shanker also argues that his dinner with Member Applewhaite was not inappropriate and that it had no effect on the decision. In addition to the individual Members and Mr. Shanker, the FLRA (represented by its Acting Solicitor) and the FAA agree with the finding of no effect on the decision in the case.

PATCO, amicus Skirlick, and amici McClure, Hough and Tierney are less sanguine about the implications of Judge Vittone's findings. Each of them argue that the disclosed communications were improper and require remedial action. The amici contend that, due to the ex parte contacts, the Authority had an irrational sense of urgency about the case. This, they argue, prejudiced their ability to participate in the unfair labor practice proceeding and to protect the interests of nonstriking controllers. PATCO contends that the contacts with Authority Members by General Counsel Gordon and Secretary Lewis require a remand with instructions that the FLRA General Counsel and the FAA be required to show cause why the complaint should not be dismissed.

Applicable Legal Standards.

1. The Statutory Prohibition of Ex Parte Contacts and the FLRA Rules

The Civil Service Reform Act requires that FLRA unfair labor practice hearings, to the extent practicable, be conducted in accordance with the provisions of the Administrative Procedure Act. The APA Section 557(d) prohibits ex parte communications "relevant to the merits of the proceeding" between an 'interested person' and an agency decisionmaker, requires the agency decisionmaker to place any prohibited communications on the public record, grants the agency the authority to require an infringing party "to show cause why his claim or interest should not be dismissed, denied, disregarded, or otherwise adversely affected on account of [a] violation," and defines the time period during which the statutory prohibitions are applicable. The FLRA has adopted rules that parallel the requirements of section 557(d).

Three features of the prohibition on ex parte communications in agency adjudications are particularly relevant to the contacts here at issue. First, by its terms, section 557(d) applies only to ex parte communications to or from an "interested person." Congress did not intend, however, that the prohibition on ex parte communications would therefore have only a limited application. A House Report explained: "The term "interested person" is intended to be a wide, inclusive term covering any individual or other person with an interest in the agency proceeding that is greater than the general interest the public as a whole may have. The interest need not be monetary, nor need a person to [sic] be a party to, or intervenor in, the agency proceeding to come under this section. The term includes, but is not limited to, parties, competitors, public officials, and nonprofit or public interest organizations and associations with a special interest in the matter regulated."

Second, the Act defines an ex parte communication as "an oral or written communication not on the public record to which reasonable prior notice to all parties is not given, but . . . not includ[ing] requests for status reports on any matter or proceeding. . . ." Nevertheless, the legislative history of the Act cautions: "A request for a status report or a background discussion may in effect amount to an indirect or subtle effort to influence the substantive outcome of the proceedings. The judgment will have to be made whether a particular communication could affect the agency's decision on the merits. In doubtful cases the agency official should treat the communication as ex parte so as to protect the integrity of the decision making."

Third, and in direct contrast to status reports, section 557(d) explicitly prohibits communications "relevant to the merits of the proceeding." The congressional reports state that the phrase should "be construed broadly and . . . include more than the phrase 'fact in issue' currently used in [section 554(d) (1) of] the Administrative Procedure Act."

In sum, Congress sought to establish common-sense guidelines to govern ex parte contacts in administrative hearings, rather than rigidly defined and woodenly applied rules. The disclosure of ex parte communications serves two distinct interests. Disclosure is important in its own right to prevent the appearance of impropriety from secret communications in a proceeding that is required to be decided on the record. Disclosure is also important as an instrument of fair decisionmaking; only if a party knows the arguments presented to a decisionmaker can the party respond effectively and ensure that its position is fairly considered. When these interests of openness and opportunity for response are threatened by an ex parte communication, the communication must be disclosed. It matters not whether the communication comes from someone other than a formal party or if the communication is clothed in the guise of a procedural inquiry. If, however, the communication is truly not relevant to the merits of an adjudication and, therefore, does not threaten the interests of openness and effective response, disclosure is unnecessary. Congress did not intend to erect meaningless procedural barriers to effective agency action. It is thus with these interests in mind that the statutory prohibition on ex parte communications must be applied.

Remedies for Ex Parte Communications.

Section 557(d) contains two possible administrative remedies for improper ex parte communications. The first is disclosure of the communication and its content. The second requires the violating party to "show cause why his claim or interest in the proceeding should not be dismissed, denied, disregarded, or otherwise adversely affected on account of [the] violation." Congress did not intend, however, that an agency would require a party to "show cause" after every violation or that an agency would dismiss a party's interest more than rarely.

The Act contains no specific provisions for judicial remedy of improper ex parte communications. Under the case law in this Circuit, improper ex parte communications, even when undisclosed during agency proceedings, do not necessarily void an agency decision. Rather, agency proceedings that have been blemished by ex parte communications have been held to be voidable. In enforcing this standard, a court must consider whether, as a result of improper ex parte communications, the agency's decisionmaking process was irrevocably tainted so as to make the ultimate judgment of the agency unfair, either to an innocent party or to the public interest that the agency was obliged to protect. In making this determination, a number of considerations may be relevant: the gravity of the ex parte communications; whether the contacts may have influenced the agency's ultimate decision; whether the party making the improper contacts benefited from the agency's ultimate decision; whether the contents of the communications were unknown to opposing parties, who therefore had no opportunity to respond; and whether vacation of the agency's decision and remand for new proceedings would serve a useful purpose. Since the principal concerns of the court are the integrity of the process and the fairness of the result, mechanical rules have little place in a judicial decision whether to vacate a voidable agency proceeding. Instead, any such decision must of necessity be an exercise of equitable discretion.

After extensive review of the three troubling incidents describe[d] above, we believe that they too provide insufficient reason to vacate the FLRA Decision or to remand this case for further proceedings before the Authority. We conclude that at least one and possibly two of the contacts documented by the A.L.J. probably infringed the statutory prohibitions on ex parte communications. The incidents reported by the A.L.J. also included some evident, albeit unintended, indiscretions in a highly charged and widely publicized case. Nevertheless, we agree with A.L.J. Vittone that the ex parte contacts here at issue had no effect on the ultimate decision of the FLRA. Moreover, we conclude that the statutory infringements and other indiscretions are not so serious as to require us to vacate the FLRA Decision or to remand the case to the Authority. On the facts of this case, we believe that to vacate and remand would be a gesture of futility.

Of course, the most troublesome ex parte communication in this case occurred during the September 21 dinner meeting between Member Applewhaite and American Federation of Teachers President Albert Shanker. We agree—as do all the parties before us—with A.L.J. Vittone's finding that the dinner had no effect on the FLRA Decision in the case. After thorough consideration, we further conclude that the incident does not require a remand to the Authority.

Even if we were to adopt Mr. Shanker's position that he was not an interested person, we are astonished at his claim that he did nothing wrong. Mr. Shanker frankly concedes that he "desired to have dinner with Member Applewhaite because he felt strongly about the PATCO case and he wished to communicate directly to Member Applewhaite sentiments he had previously expressed in public." While we appreciate Mr. Shanker's forthright admission, we must wonder whether it is a product of candor or a failure to comprehend that his conduct was improper. In case any doubt still lingers, we take the opportunity to make one thing clear: It is simply unacceptable behavior for any person directly to attempt to influence the decision of a judicial officer in a pending case outside of the formal, public proceedings. This is true for the general public, for "interested persons," and for the formal parties to the case. This rule applies to administrative adjudications as well as to cases in Article III courts.

We think it a mockery of justice to even suggest that judges or other decisionmakers may be properly approached on the merits of a case during the pendency of an adjudication. Administrative and judicial adjudications are viable only so long as the integrity of the decisionmaking processes remains inviolate. There would be no way to protect the sanctity of adjudicatory processes if we were to condone direct attempts to influence decisionmakers through ex parte contacts.

We do not hold, however, that Member Applewhaite committed an impropriety when he accepted Mr. Shanker's dinner invitation. Member Applewhaite and Mr. Shanker were professional and social friends. We recognize, of course, that a judge "must have neighbors, friends and acquaintances, business and social relations, and be a part of his day and generation." Similarly, Member Applewhaite was not required to renounce his friendships, either personal or professional, when he was appointed to the FLRA. When Mr. Shanker called Member Applewhaite on September 21, Member Applewhaite was unaware of Mr. Shanker's purpose in arranging the dinner. He therefore had no reason to reject the invitation.

The majority of the dinner conversation was unrelated to the PATCO case. Only in the last fifteen minutes of the dinner did the discussion become relevant to the PATCO dispute, apparently when Mr. Shanker raised the topic of local approaches to public employee strikes in New York and Pennsylvania. At this point, and as the conversation turned to the discipline appropriate for a striking union like PATCO, Member Applewhaite should have promptly terminated the discussion. Had Mr. Shanker persisted in discussing his views of the PATCO case, Member Applewhaite should have informed him in no uncertain terms that such behavior was inappropriate. Unfortunately, he did not do so.

In these circumstances, we do not believe that it is necessary to vacate the FLRA Decision and remand the case. First, while Mr. Shanker's purpose and conduct were improper, and while Member Applewhaite should not have entertained Mr. Shanker's views on the desirability of decertifying a striking union, no threats or promises were made. Though plainly inappropriate, the ex parte communication was limited to a ten or fifteen minute discussion, often couched in general terms, of the appropriate discipline for a striking public employee union.

Second, A.L.J. Vittone found that the Applewhaite/Shanker dinner had no effect on the ultimate decision of Member Applewhaite or of the FLRA as a whole in the PATCO case.

Third, no party benefited from the improper contact. The ultimate decision was adverse to PATCO, the party whose interests were most closely aligned with Mr. Shanker's position. The final decision also rejected the position taken by the AFL-CIO as amicus curiae and by Mr. Shanker in his dinner conversation with Member Applewhaite.

Finally, we cannot say that the parties were unfairly deprived of an opportunity to refute the arguments propounded in the ex parte communication. PATCO has not identified any manner in which it was denied a reasonable opportunity to respond or any new arguments which it would present to the FLRA if given an opportunity. Understandably, the FAA does not complain that its interests were injured. Moreover, Mr. Shanker's arguments regarding the severity of decertification paralleled PATCO's own arguments before the FLRA. The FAA and the FLRA General Counsel had a full opportunity to refute these arguments before the Authority.

We in no way condone Mr. Shanker's behavior in this case. Nor do we approve Member Applewhaite's failure to avoid discussion of a case pending before the Authority. Nevertheless, we do not believe that the Applewhaite/Shanker dinner, as detailed in A.L.J. Vittone's findings, irrevocably tainted the Authority's decisionmaking process or resulted in a decision unfair either to the parties or to the public interest.

Our review of the record of the special evidentiary hearing, and of the findings of Judge Vittone, leads us to a simple conclusion: There is no reason to vacate the FLRA decision or to remand the case to the FLRA for any further proceedings. We have not found any ex parte communications that irrevocably tainted the Authority's decision. Nor have the proceedings effected procedural unfairness on any of the parties.

This is not to say that the Authority's handling of the case has been a paragon of administrative procedure. We have carefully examined the alleged indiscretions and improprieties. Although we have found one (or possibly two) statutory infringements, we conclude that no parties have been prejudiced by the flaws in the proceedings.

For the foregoing reasons, we find that the conclusion of the Federal Labor Relations Authority that PATCO committed unfair labor practices by striking in violation of the Civil Service Reform Act is supported by substantial evidence. We also hold that the Federal Labor Relations Authority did not abuse its discretion in denying PATCO a continuance to prepare evidence in potential mitigation of remedy, or in revoking PATCO's exclusive recognition status pursuant to section 7120(f). As a result, we deny PATCO's petition for review and affirm the Decision and Order of the Federal Labor Relations Authority.

Finally, because the ex parte contacts issue already has been fully and adequately addressed during the special evidentiary hearing before Judge Vittone, and because the facts of this case are free from any arguable taint, we have concluded that a remand of this case would be a futile gesture.

CHIEF JUDGE ROBINSON wrote an opinion concurring in part and concurring in the judgment.

I join my colleagues in their construction of the relevant provisions of Title VII of the Civil Service Reform Act, and in their application of those statutory sections to the action of the Federal Labor Relations Authority (FLRA) in this case. I also agree, on review of the extensive record compiled and the careful findings proposed by Administrative Law Judge Vittone, that the ex parte communications which sullied FLRA's handling of the case did not affect its members' ultimate decision, and therefore do not call for a remand. I thus concur in Parts I, III and IV of the court's opinion. I cannot, however, subscribe to Part II. The treatment there accorded the most conspicuous contacts and the tone pervading the discussion tend, I fear, to minify the gravity of the improprieties that occurred, and to understate the culpability of those who initiated and those who received ex parte pleas and approaches.

From the special hearing emerges an appalling chronicle of attorneys, high government officials, and interested outsiders apparently without compunction about intervening in the course of FLRA's decision-making by means of private communications with those charged with resolving the case on the merits. We have an even more distressing picture of agency decisionmakers—whose role in this formal adjudication concededly approximated that of judges—seemingly ignorant of the substance of the ex parte rules, insensitive to the compromising potentialities of certain official and social contacts, and unwilling to silence peremptorily and firmly improper discussions that did transpire. Although the special hearing disclosed no such taint on the agency's ultimate decision as would require additional corrective proceedings, I feel compelled to review several of these incidents, for in my view the court's opinion administers a mild chiding where a ringing condemnation is in order.

I pause only briefly over Shanker's conduct. His deliberate crusade to sway through private importunity the decision of one acting as judge in a pending case is so far beyond the pale of legally tolerable activity that even the most caustic criticism could not overstate the magnitude of the impropriety. Suffice it to say, I join in the court's conclusion that Shanker was, beyond cavil, an interested party, and in its condemnation of his behavior as an egregious violation of the APA. Far more necessitous of extended comment, in my view, is the conduct of Member Applewhaite. This court should not hesitate to allocate blame squarely where it belongs: at the doorstep of one acting as a judicial officer who, with a solemn responsibility to preserve both the fact and appearance of complete impartiality, first subjected himself to a palpable risk of contamination, and then made no effort to arrest forbidden advocacy when it came.

I cannot accede to the assertion that, by itself, a private dinner engagement between Applewhaite and Shanker was not improper. I would have thought it unnecessary this late in the day to defend the precept that one who judges should avoid even the appearance of impropriety. Shanker was a prominent labor official who had been vocal in his partisanship of PATCO's cause; moreover, the powerful labor organization on whose Executive Board he sat was amicus curiae in the case. Can the public really be expected to believe in the fairness and neutrality of the agency's formal adjudicatory processes when one of its decisionmakers permits an outspoken, highly visible official of a participating union to wine and dine him during deliberations on the case?

Going beyond questions about the propriety of Applewhaite's agreement to dine privately with Shanker during the critical deliberative phase of the case, there can be no doubt that their after-dinner discussion of the merits of decertifying PATCO violated the express prohibition of Section 557(d) of the APA. Applewhaite's failure to "steer the conversation away from PATCO" thus was far more than a mere "indiscretion." The moment that Shanker broached the topic of public employee strikes, Applewhaite should have enjoined conversation on that score. While it might be possible to attribute Applewhaite's actions in placing himself in a compromising position to thoughtless imprudence, his unprotesting submission to blatant ex parte advocacy on the merits of a case then pending before the members defies explanation.

We are unanimous in our acceptance of Judge Vittone's several determinations that none of the above-described contacts tainted FLRA's final decision. I fear, however, that in announcing that we find no reason to send this case back, the court's opinion comes perilously close to intimating that we discover nothing seriously wrong. Such suggestion, in my view, would be a gross mischaracterization. The record before us may be free of instances of sensational wrongdoing, but it is filled with a pattern of insidious lapses. The casualness with which interested persons privately approached decisionmakers engaged in formal adjudication; the thoughtlessness with which the decisionmakers exposed themselves to such approaches and permitted them to proceed unchecked; the ignorance of, and unconcern for, the principles that underlie the ex parte rules—all these things signal something fundamentally awry.

The laxness with which FLRA protected the integrity of its adjudicatory processes in this case ought be a matter of deep concern for this court, which routinely is asked to accord substantial deference to the decisions rendered by the agency on questions of considerable import to federal employees. It ought be a matter of even deeper concern to the agency itself. FLRA will have the respect of the public only when its personnel have sufficient respect for their especial mission to rebuff any attempt to influence or corrupt it. Ultimately, an agency must be the guardian of its own honor. If it permits interested persons to show contempt for its formal adjudicatory processes by the subversion of ex parte pleas and approaches, then those processes will indeed become contemptible.

JUSTICE MACKINNON wrote a concurring opinion.

Subject to the fact that I might differ in the characterization of some of the ex parte contacts, I concur in Judge Edwards' opinion but wish to record some additional comments.

The number of ex parte contacts that were disclosed at the remand hearing is appalling, as are the statements by counsel that such contacts were nothing more than what is normal and usual in administrative agencies and even in courts of law. That statement is categorically denied insofar as our courts are concerned. If that ever turns out to be true some very severe penalties are going to be meted out. The conduct of Shanker, as described above, was the most serious, but the telephone calls by the Secretary of Transportation were also objectionable. Union and cabinet officers, and all citizens, will have to realize that officials of the administrative agencies engaged in adjudicating rights and interests are not their hand maidens. In deciding such cases the government officials act in a quasi-judicial capacity and ex parte contacts that attempt to "back door" the adjudicative process, with respect to the merits or discipline, are highly improper and illegal. Shanker argues that his dinner with member Applewhaite "had no effect on the decision" and hence is of no moment. That is like the man charged with attempted murder asserting the indictment should be dismissed because his shot missed the intended victim. In my opinion Shanker and his Teacher's Union were both "interested parties" within the meaning of 5 U.S.C. 557(d) of the Administrative Procedure Act.

*****

ADDITIONAL READINGS

Henry J. Friendly, "Some Kind of a Hearing," 123 *U. Pennsylvania L. Rev.* 1267 (1975).

Jerry L. Mashaw, *Due Process in the Administrative State* (New Haven: Yale University Press, 1985).

Carrie Menkel-Meadow, "Symposium—Alternative Dispute Resolution: When Dispute Resolution Begets Disputes of Its Own," *44 UCLA L. Rev.* 1871 (1997).

William Van Alstyne, "Cracks in 'The New Property': Adjudicative Due Process in the Administrative State," 62 *Cornell L. Rev.* 445 (1977).

3

⚖

Judicial Review*

he cases on judicial review represent the ongoing effort by judges to find
the right approach to review and determine the kinds of cases that
should be before them. The purpose is to ensure that the review is adequate to protect citizens from arbitrary and capricious behavior; keep officials
operating within their lawfully delegated authority; and maintain the constitutional, statutory, and procedural requirements needed to integrate the decisions
of administrators with the larger body of law.

At the same time, judges are aware that their rulings are part of a larger dialogue, what Louis Fisher refers to as a "constitutional dialogue," a continuing
conversation among the other branches of government.[1] The courts rule,
Congress responds, the executive branch reacts in turn, and the matter then
comes back to court once more. For example, led by the D.C. Circuit, judges
responded to criticisms of agencies for failing to use proper rulemaking proceedings under the APA and moved to ensure that notice, opportunity for participation, and consideration of input were real and seriously contemplated by

---

* Related Material in *Public Law and Public Administration, Third Edition,* Chapter 7.

1. Louis Fisher, *Constitutional Dialogues: Interpretation as Political Process* (Princeton, NJ:
Princeton University Press, 1988). See also Fisher, *Constitutional Conflicts Between Congress
and the President, Fourth Edition Revised* (Lawrence: University Press of Kansas, 1997).

administrators. They pressed agencies to employ what came to be known as hybrid rulemaking.[2] However, the Supreme Court admonished the lower courts that they had no business requiring additional procedures from administrative agencies beyond those required by statute.[3] However, by that time, Congress was mandating hybrid rulemaking in virtually all new programs that called for rulemaking. The White House mandated it for all executive branch agencies and recommended it for independent commissions as well.[4]

GETTING THROUGH
THE COURTHOUSE DOOR

Judges also participate in the dialogue by setting the rules that determine whether and when a case will be reviewed. Some of these rules grow out of the Constitution's Article III command that the judicial power is the power to decide "cases" and "controversies" that are properly presented, while others are the result of what the Supreme Court has termed "prudential considerations." Thus, there are situations in which a challenger may have met all of the requirements for a proper case or controversy but the Court nevertheless exercises its discretion to deny review. This has been an expanding area with many important opinions, but this chapter provides only two excerpts that are illustrative of the issues that arise in the decision whether a case will be heard. *Public Law and Public Administration, Third Edition*, Chapter 7 discusses the full range of such issues.

Lujan v. National Wildlife Federation, 497 U.S. 871 (1990).

INTRODUCTION: The National Wildlife Federation challenged officials of the Department of the Interior in 1985 based on a "land withdrawal review program." The Federation argued that the program and process by which it was developed violated the Federal Land Policy and Management Act, the National Environmental Policy Act, and the APA. As the Court explained it, "In its complaint, respondent averred generally that the reclassification of some withdrawn

---

2. *Mobil Oil Corp. v. FPC*, 483 F.2d 1238 (D.C.Cir. 1973); *International Harvester Co. v. Ruckelshaus*, 478 F.2d 615 (D.C.Cir. 1973); *Appalachian Power Co. v. EPA*, 477 F.2d 495 (4th Cir. 1973); *Walter Holm & Co. v. Hardin*, 449 F.2d 1009 (D.C.Cir. 1971); *American Airlines, Inc. v. CAB*, 359 F.2d 624 (D.C.Cir. 1966).

3. *Vermont Yankee Nuclear Power Corp. v. Natural Resources Defense Council*, 435 U.S. 519 (1978).

4. 43 Fed. Reg. 12661 (1978).

lands and the return of others to the public domain would open the lands up to mining activities, thereby destroying their natural beauty. Respondent alleged that petitioners, in the course of administering the Nation's public lands, had violated the FLPMA by failing to 'develop, maintain, and, when appropriate, revise land use plans which provide by tracts or areas for the use of the public lands;' failing to submit recommendations as to withdrawals in the 11 Western States to the President; failing to consider multiple uses for the disputed lands, focusing inordinately on such uses as mineral exploitation and development; and failing to provide public notice of decisions. . . . Finally, respondent alleged that all of the above actions were 'arbitrary, capricious, an abuse of discretion, or otherwise not in accordance with law,' and should therefore be set aside pursuant to the APA."

This opinion focuses on the issue of ripeness, which concerns the readiness of a case for judicial review. The fact that a policy may result in a problem that would justify judicial examination at some future time is not sufficient. In the process of explaining ripeness, the Court discusses the general requirements of review.

✳✳✳✳✳

Justice Scalia wrote the opinion for the Court.

In this case we must decide whether respondent, the National Wildlife Federation is a proper party to challenge actions of the Federal Government relating to certain public lands.

We first address respondent's claim that the Peterson and Erman affidavits alone suffice to establish respondent's right to judicial review of petitioners' actions. Respondent claims a right to judicial review under §10(a) of the APA, which provides: "A person suffering legal wrong because of agency action, or adversely affected or aggrieved by agency action within the meaning of a relevant statute, is entitled to judicial review thereof." 5 U.S.C. §702.

This provision contains two separate requirements. First, the person claiming a right to sue must identify some "agency action" that affects him in the specified fashion; it is judicial review "thereof" to which he is entitled. When, as here, review is sought not pursuant to specific authorization in the substantive statute, but only under the general review provisions of the APA, the "agency action" in question must be "final agency action."

Second, the party seeking review under §702 must show that he has "suffered legal wrong" because of the challenged agency action, or is "adversely affected or aggrieved" by that action "within the meaning of a relevant statute." [T]o be "adversely affected or aggrieved . . . within the meaning" of a statute, the plaintiff must establish that the injury he complains of (his aggrievement, or the adverse effect upon him) falls within the "zone of interests" sought to be protected by the statutory provision whose violation forms the legal basis for his complaint.

We turn, then, to whether the specific facts alleged in the two affidavits considered by the District Court raised a genuine issue of fact as to whether an "agency action" taken by petitioners caused respondent to be "adversely affected or aggrieved . . . within the meaning of a relevant statute." We assume, since it has been uncontested, that the allegedly affected interests set forth in the affidavits—"recreational use and aesthetic enjoyment"—are sufficiently related to the purposes of respondent association that respondent meets the requirements of §702 if any of its members do.

As for the "agency action" requirement, we think that each of the affidavits can be read, as the Court of Appeals believed, to complain of a particular "agency action" as that term is defined in §551.

We also think that whatever "adverse effect" or "aggrievement" is established by the affidavits was "within the meaning of the relevant statute"—i.e., met the "zone of interests" test. We have no doubt that "recreational use and aesthetic enjoyment" are among the sorts of interests those statutes were specifically designed to protect. The only issue, then, is whether the facts alleged in the affidavits showed that those interests of Peterson and Erman were actually affected.

Respondent alleges that violation of the law is rampant within this program—failure to revise land use plans in proper fashion, failure to submit certain recommendations to Congress, failure to consider multiple use, inordinate focus upon mineral exploitation, failure to provide required public notice, failure to provide adequate environmental impact statements. Perhaps so. But respondent cannot seek wholesale improvement of this program by court decree, rather than in the offices of the Department or the halls of Congress, where programmatic improvements are normally made. Under the terms of the APA, respondent must direct its attack against some particular "agency action" that causes it harm. Some statutes permit broad regulations to serve as the "agency action," and thus to be the object of judicial review directly, even before the concrete effects normally required for APA review are felt. Absent such a provision, however, a regulation is not ordinarily considered the type of agency action "ripe" for judicial review under the APA until the scope of the controversy has been reduced to more manageable proportions, and its factual components fleshed out, by some concrete action applying the regulation to the claimant's situation in a fashion that harms or threatens to harm him.

In the present case, the individual actions of the BLM identified in the six affidavits can be regarded as rules of general applicability announcing, with respect to vast expanses of territory that they cover, the agency's intent to grant requisite permission for certain activities, to decline to interfere with other activities, and to take other particular action if requested. It may well be, then, that even those individual actions will not be ripe for challenge until some further agency action or inaction more immediately harming the plaintiff occurs. But it is at least entirely certain that the flaws in the entire "program"—consisting principally of the many individual actions referenced in the complaint, and presumably actions yet to be taken as well—cannot be laid before the courts for wholesale correction under the APA, simply because one of them that is ripe for review adversely affects one of respondent's members.

The case-by-case approach that this requires is understandably frustrating to an organization such as respondent, which has as its objective across-the-board protection of our Nation's wildlife and the streams and forests that support it. But this is the traditional, and remains the normal mode of operation of the courts. Except where Congress explicitly provides for our correction of the administrative process at a higher level of generality, we intervene in the administration of the laws only when, and to the extent that, a specific "final agency action" has an actual or immediately threatened effect. Such an intervention may ultimately have the effect of requiring a regulation, a series of regulations, or even a whole "program" to be revised by the agency in order to avoid the unlawful result that the court discerns. But it is assuredly not as swift or as immediately far-reaching a corrective process as those interested in systemic improvement would desire. Until confided to us, however, more sweeping actions are for the other branches.

JUSTICE BLACKMUN wrote a dissent joined by BRENNAN, MARSHALL, and STEVENS.

The Federation's asserted injury in this case rested upon its claim that the Government actions challenged here would lead to increased mining on public lands; that the mining would result in damage to the environment; and that the recreational opportunities of NWF's members would consequently be diminished. Abundant record evidence supported the Federation's assertion that on lands newly opened for mining, mining in fact would occur. Similarly, the record furnishes ample support for NWF's contention that mining activities can be expected to cause severe environmental damage to the affected lands.

The majority, like the District Court, holds that the averments of Peterson and Erman were insufficiently specific to withstand a motion for summary judgment. Although these affidavits were not models of precision, I believe that they were adequate at least to create a genuine issue of fact as to the organization's injury.

*****

Lujan v. Defenders of Wildlife, 504 U.S. 555 (1992).

INTRODUCTION: This is a case concerned with standing to sue. It involved a challenge under the Endangered Species Act of 1973. During the Carter administration, the Department of Interior and the Department of Commerce adopted a rule that applied the Endangered Species Act requirements to the departments' involvement in projects around the world. However, in 1979, the agencies began a reconsideration of the rule, and during the Reagan administration in 1983, launched an action to limit the rule to the United States.

*****

JUSTICE SCALIA wrote the opinion for the Court.

The preliminary issue, and the only one we reach, is whether respondents here, plaintiffs below, have standing to seek judicial review of the rule.

Shortly [after the agencies proposed the limitation on the former rule], respondents, organizations dedicated to wildlife conservation and other environmental causes, filed this action against the Secretary of the Interior, seeking a declaratory judgment that the new regulation is in error as to the geographic scope of §7(a)(2) and an injunction requiring the Secretary to promulgate a new regulation restoring the initial interpretation.

Over the years, our cases have established that the irreducible constitutional minimum of standing contains three elements. First, the plaintiff must have suffered an "injury in fact"—an invasion of a legally protected interest which is (a) concrete and particularized; and (b) actual or imminent, not 'conjectural' or 'hypothetical.'" Second, there must be a causal connection between the injury and the conduct complained of—the injury has to be "fairly . . . trace[able] to the challenged action of the defendant, and not . . . the result [of] the independent action of some third party not before the court."Third, it must be "likely," as opposed to merely "speculative," that the injury will be "redressed by a favorable decision."

The party invoking federal jurisdiction bears the burden of establishing these elements.

When the suit is one challenging the legality of government action or inaction, the nature and extent of facts that must be averred (at the summary judgment stage) or proved (at the trial stage) in order to establish standing depends considerably upon whether the plaintiff is himself an object of the action (or forgone action) at issue. If he is, there is ordinarily little question that the action or inaction has caused him injury, and that a judgment preventing or requiring the action will redress it. When, however, as in this case, a plaintiff's asserted injury arises from the government's allegedly unlawful regulation (or lack of regulation) of someone else, much more is needed. In that circumstance, causation and redressability ordinarily hinge on the response of the regulated (or regulable) third party to the government action or inaction—and perhaps on the response of others as well. Thus, when the plaintiff is not himself the object of the government action or inaction he challenges, standing is not precluded, but it is ordinarily "substantially more difficult" to establish.

We think the Court of Appeals failed to apply the foregoing principles in denying the Secretary's motion for summary judgment. Respondents had not made the requisite demonstration of (at least) injury and redressability.

Respondents' claim to injury is that the lack of consultation with respect to certain funded activities abroad "increas[es] the rate of extinction of endangered and threatened species." Of course, the desire to use or observe an animal species, even for purely esthetic purposes, is undeniably a cognizable interest for purpose of standing. "But the 'injury in fact' test requires more than an injury to a cognizable interest. It requires that the party seeking review be himself among the injured." To survive the Secretary's summary judgment motion, respondents had to submit affidavits or other evidence showing, through specific facts, not only that listed species were in fact being threatened by funded activities abroad, but also that one or more of respondents' members would thereby be "directly" affected apart from their "'special interest' in the subject."

With respect to this aspect of the case, the Court of Appeals focused on the affidavits of two Defenders' members—Joyce Kelly and Amy Skilbred. Ms. Kelly stated that she traveled to Egypt in 1986 and "observed the traditional habitat of the endangered Nile crocodile there and intend[s] to do so again, and hope[s] to observe the crocodile directly," and that she "will suffer harm in fact as the result of [the] American . . . role . . . in overseeing the rehabilitation of the Aswan High Dam on the Nile . . . and [in] developing . . . Egypt's . . . Master Water Plan." Ms. Skilbred averred that she traveled to Sri Lanka in 1981 and "observed the habitat" of "endangered species such as the Asian elephant and the leopard" at what is now the site of the Mahaweli project funded by the Agency for International Development (AID), although she "was unable to see any of the endangered species"; "this development project," she continued, "will seriously reduce endangered, threatened, and endemic species habitat including areas that I visited . . . [, which] may severely shorten the future of these species"; that threat, she concluded, harmed her because she "intend[s] to return to Sri Lanka in the future and hope[s] to be more fortunate in spotting at least the endangered elephant and leopard." When Ms. Skilbred was asked at a subsequent deposition if and when she had any plans to return to Sri Lanka, she reiterated that "I intend to go back to Sri Lanka," but confessed that she had no current plans: "I don't know [when]. There is a civil war going on right now. I don't know. Not next year, I will say. In the future."

We shall assume for the sake of argument that these affidavits contain facts showing that certain agency-funded projects threaten listed species—though that is questionable. They plainly contain no facts, however, showing how damage to the species will produce "imminent" injury to Mses. Kelly and Skilbred. That the women "had visited" the areas of the projects before the projects commenced proves nothing. As we have said in a related context, "'Past exposure to illegal conduct does not in itself show a present case or controversy regarding injunctive relief . . . if unaccompanied by any continuing, present adverse effects.'" And the affiants' profession of an "intent" to return to the places they had visited before is simply not enough. Such "some day" intentions do not support a finding of the "actual or imminent" injury that our cases require.

Besides relying upon the Kelly and Skilbred affidavits, respondents propose a series of novel standing theories. The first, inelegantly styled "ecosystem nexus," proposes that any person who uses any part of a "contiguous ecosystem" adversely affected by a funded activity has standing even if the activity is located a great distance away. This approach, as the Court of Appeals correctly observed, is inconsistent with our opinion in *National Wildlife Federation,* which held that a plaintiff claiming injury from environmental damage must use the area affected by the challenged activity and not an area roughly "in the vicinity" of it. To say that the Act protects ecosystems is not to say that the Act creates (if it were possible) rights of action in persons who have not been injured in fact, that is, persons who use portions of an ecosystem not perceptibly affected by the unlawful action in question.

Respondents' other theories are called, alas, the "animal nexus" approach, whereby anyone who has an interest in studying or seeing the endangered animals anywhere on the globe has standing; and the "vocational nexus" approach, under which anyone with a professional interest in such animals can sue. Under these theories, anyone who goes to see Asian elephants in the Bronx Zoo, and anyone who is a keeper of Asian elephants in the Bronx Zoo, has standing to sue because the Director of the Agency for International Development (AID) did not consult with the Secretary regarding the AID-funded project in Sri Lanka. This is beyond all reason. Standing is not "an ingenious academic exercise in the conceivable," but as we have said requires, at the summary judgment stage, a factual showing of perceptible harm. It is clear that the person who observes or works with a particular animal threatened by a federal decision is facing perceptible harm, since the very subject of his interest will no longer exist. It is even plausible to think that a person who observes or works with animals of a particular species in the very area of the world where that species is threatened by a federal decision is facing such harm, since some animals that might have been the subject of his interest will no longer exist. It goes beyond the limit, however, and into pure speculation and fantasy, to say that anyone who observes or works with an endangered species, anywhere in the world, is appreciably harmed by a single project affecting some portion of that species with which he has no more specific connection.

The most obvious problem in the present case is redressability. Since the agencies funding the projects were not parties to the case, the District Court could accord relief only against the Secretary: He could be ordered to revise his regulation to require consultation for foreign projects. But this would not remedy respondents' alleged injury unless the funding agencies were bound by the Secretary's regulation, which is very much an open question.

Respondents assert that this did not affect redressability (and hence standing) because the District Court itself could resolve the issue of the Secretary's authority as a necessary part of its standing inquiry. The short of the matter is that redress of the only injury in fact respondents complain of requires action (termination of funding until consultation) by the individual funding agencies; and any relief the District Court could have provided in this suit against the Secretary was not likely to produce that action.

A further impediment to redressability is the fact that the agencies generally supply only a fraction of the funding for a foreign project. AID, for example, has provided less than 10% of the funding for the Mahaweli project. Respondents have produced nothing to indicate that the projects they have named will either be suspended, or do less harm to listed species, if that fraction is eliminated. It is entirely conjectural whether the non-agency activity that affects respondents will be altered or affected by the agency activity they seek to achieve. There is no standing.

The Court of Appeals found that respondents had standing for an additional reason: because they had suffered a "procedural injury." The so-called "citizen-suit" provision of the ESA provides, in pertinent part, that "any person may commence a civil suit on his own behalf (A) to enjoin any person, including the United States and any other governmental instrumentality or agency . . . who is alleged to be in violation of any provision of this chapter." The court held that, because §7(a)(2) requires interagency consultation, the citizen-suit provision creates a "procedural right" to consultation in all "persons"—so that anyone can file suit in federal court to challenge the Secretary's (or presumably any other official's) failure to follow the assertedly correct consultative procedure. This is not a case where plaintiffs are seeking to enforce a procedural requirement the disregard of which could impair a separate concrete interest of theirs (e.g., the procedural requirement for a hearing prior to denial of their license application, or the procedural requirement for an environmental impact statement before a federal facility is constructed next door to them). Nor is it simply a case where concrete injury has been suffered by many persons, as in mass fraud or mass tort situations. Nor, finally, is it the unusual case in which Congress has created a concrete private interest in the outcome of a suit against a private party for the Government's benefit, by providing a cash bounty for the victorious plaintiff. Rather, the court held that the injury-in-fact requirement had been satisfied by congressional conferral upon all persons of an abstract, self-contained, noninstrumental "right" to have the Executive observe the procedures required by law. We reject this view.

We have consistently held that a plaintiff raising only a generally available grievance about government—claiming only harm to his and every citizen's interest in proper application of the Constitution and laws, and seeking relief that no more directly and tangibly benefits him than it does the public at large—does not state an Article III case or controversy.

To be sure, our generalized-grievance cases have typically involved Government violation of procedures assertedly ordained by the Constitution rather than the Congress. But there is absolutely no basis for making the Article III inquiry turn on the source of the asserted right. Whether the courts were to act on their own, or at the invitation of Congress, in ignoring the concrete injury requirement described in our cases, they would be discarding a principle fundamental to the separate and distinct constitutional role of the Third Branch—one of the essential elements that identifies those "Cases" and "Controversies" that are the business of the courts rather than of the political branches.

We hold that respondents lack standing to bring this action and that the Court of Appeals erred in denying the summary judgment motion filed by the United States.[5]

JUSTICE BLACKMUN wrote a dissent joined by JUSTICE O'CONNOR.

I part company with the Court in this case in two respects. First, I believe that respondents have raised genuine issues of fact—sufficient to survive summary judgment—both as to injury and as to redressability. Second, I question the Court's breadth of language in rejecting standing for "procedural" injuries. I fear the Court seeks to impose fresh limitations on the constitutional authority of Congress to allow citizen suits in the federal courts for injuries deemed "procedural" in nature. I dissent.

To survive petitioner's motion for summary judgment on standing, respondents need not prove that they are actually or imminently harmed. They need show only a "genuine issue" of material fact as to standing. A "genuine issue" exists so long as "the evidence is such that a reasonable jury could return a verdict for the nonmoving party [respondents]." This Court's "function is not [it]self to

---

5. Justice Kennedy issued a concurring opinion joined by Stevens.

weigh the evidence and determine the truth of the matter but to determine whether there is a genuine issue for trial."

Were the Court to apply the proper standard for summary judgment, I believe it would conclude that the sworn affidavits and deposition testimony of Joyce Kelly and Amy Skilbred advance sufficient facts to create a genuine issue for trial concerning whether one or both would be imminently harmed by the Aswan and Mahaweli projects. In the first instance, as the Court itself concedes, the affidavits contained facts making it at least "questionable" that certain agency funded projects threaten listed species. The only remaining issue, then, is whether Kelly and Skilbred have shown that they personally would suffer imminent harm.

I think a reasonable finder of fact could conclude from the information in the affidavits and deposition testimony that either Kelly or Skilbred will soon return to the project sites, thereby satisfying the "actual or imminent" injury standard. The Court dismisses Kelly's and Skilbred's general statements that they intended to revisit the project sites as "simply not enough." But those statements did not stand alone. A reasonable finder of fact could conclude, based not only upon their statements of intent to return, but upon their past visits to the project sites, as well as their professional backgrounds, that it was likely that Kelly and Skilbred would make a return trip to the project areas.

By requiring a "description of concrete plans" or "specification of when the some day [for a return visit] will be," the Court, in my view, demands what is likely an empty formality. No substantial barriers prevent Kelly or Skilbred from simply purchasing plane tickets to return to the Aswan and Mahaweli projects.

I fear the Court's demand for detailed descriptions of future conduct will do little to weed out those who are genuinely harmed from those who are not. More likely, it will resurrect a code-pleading formalism in federal court summary judgment practice, as federal courts, newly doubting their jurisdiction, will demand more and more particularized showings of future harm.

The Court also concludes that injury is lacking, because respondents' allegations of "ecosystem nexus" failed to demonstrate sufficient proximity to the site of the environmental harm. Many environmental injuries, however, cause harm distant from the area immediately affected by the challenged action. It cannot seriously be contended that a litigant's failure to use the precise or exact site where animals are slaughtered or where toxic waste is dumped into a river means he or she cannot show injury.

The Court also rejects respondents' claim of vocational or professional injury. The Court says that it is "beyond all reason" that a zoo "keeper" of Asian elephants would have standing to contest his Government's participation in the eradication of all the Asian elephants in another part of the world. I am unable to see how the distant location of the destruction necessarily mitigates the harm to the elephant keeper. If there is no more access to a future supply of the animal that sustains a keeper's livelihood, surely there is harm.

A plurality of the Court suggests that respondents have not demonstrated redressability: a likelihood that a court ruling in their favor would remedy their injury. The plurality identifies two obstacles. The first is that the "action agencies" (e.g., AID) cannot be required to undertake consultation with petitioner Secretary, because they are not directly bound as parties to the suit and are otherwise not indirectly bound by being subject to petitioner Secretary's regulation. Petitioner, however, officially and publicly has taken the position that his regulations regarding consultation under §7 of the Act are binding on action agencies. I cannot agree with the plurality that the Secretary is now free, for the convenience of this appeal, to disavow his prior public and litigation positions. More generally, I cannot agree that the Government is free to play "Three-Card Monte" with its description of agencies' authority to defeat standing against the agency given the lead in administering a statutory scheme.

Emphasizing that none of the action agencies are parties to this suit, the plurality concludes that "there is no reason they should be obliged to honor an incidental legal determination the suit produced." I am not as willing as the plurality is to assume that agencies at least will not try to follow the law.

The second redressability obstacle relied on by the plurality is that "the [action] agencies generally supply only a fraction of the funding for a foreign project." What this Court might "generally" take to be true does not eliminate the existence of a genuine issue of fact to withstand summary judgment. Even if the action agencies supply only a fraction of the funding for a particular foreign project, it remains at least a question for the finder of fact whether threatened withdrawal of that fraction would affect foreign government conduct sufficiently to avoid harm to listed species.

I find myself unable to agree with the plurality's analysis of redressability, based as it is on its invitation of executive lawlessness, ignorance of principles of collateral estoppel, unfounded assumptions about causation, and erroneous conclusions about what the record does not say. In my view, respondents have satisfactorily shown a genuine issue of fact as to whether their injury would likely be redressed by a decision in their favor.

The Court concludes that any "procedural injury" suffered by respondents is insufficient to confer standing. It rejects the view that the "injury-in-fact requirement [is] satisfied by congressional conferral upon all persons of an abstract, self-contained, noninstrumental 'right' to have the Executive observe the procedures required by law." Whatever the Court might mean with that very broad language, it cannot be saying that "procedural injuries" as a class are necessarily insufficient for purposes of Article III standing.

Most governmental conduct can be classified as "procedural." Many injuries caused by governmental conduct, therefore, are categorizable at some level of generality as "procedural" injuries. Yet, these injuries are not categorically beyond the pale of redress by the federal courts.

In conclusion, I cannot join the Court on what amounts to a slash-and-burn expedition through the law of environmental standing. In my view, "the very essence of civil liberty certainly consists in the right of every individual to claim the protection of the laws, whenever he receives an injury." *Marbury v. Madison,* 5 U.S. 137, 163 (1803).

*****

THE BASIC APPROACH TO REVIEW

Notwithstanding the continuing debates over barriers to judicial review, many cases do get through the courthouse door. It is therefore important to consider the basic approach to judicial review explained in *Citizens to Preserve Overton Park v. Volpe* and *Vermont Yankee Nuclear Power Corp. v. Natural Resources Defense Council*. Later opinions in this chapter flesh out the contours and character of judicial review of administrative action, but these two cases set the foundations.

Citizens to Preserve Overton Park v. Volpe, 401 U.S. 402 (1971).

INTRODUCTION: The opinion provides a useful summary of the facts in this interesting case. Despite the fact that much has happened since this important decision was delivered, it remains a core ruling on the basics of judicial review of administrative action.

Although the case initially was heard to review the decision of the Secretary of Transportation to approve a highway, the events unfolded in a more complex story. After the Supreme Court remanded the case, concluding that it would require a proper administrative record so that a full review of the decision to build the highway through a Memphis park could proceed, the district court called attorneys in the case to provide that record. Ultimately, the district court determined, after considerable stalling by the agency, that there really had never been an adequate record constructed at the time of the decision and, hence, the Secretary's decision had to fall. However, the state and city went back to court to turn the tables, demanding that the Department of Transportation carry the burden for finding a feasible and prudent alternative. The circuit court of appeals rejected their efforts some three years after the Supreme Court ruling, *Citizens to Preserve Overton Park v. Brinegar*, 494 F.2d 1212 (6th Cir. 1974).

✹✹✹✹✹

JUSTICE MARSHALL for the Court (joined by BURGER, HARLAN, STEWART, WHITE, and BLACKMUN). DOUGLAS did not participate.

We are concerned in this case with §4 (f) of the Department of Transportation Act of 1966 and §18 (a) of the Federal-Aid Highway Act of 1968 [which] prohibit the Secretary of Transportation from authorizing the use of federal funds to finance the construction of highways through public parks if a "feasible and prudent" alternative route exists. If no such route is available, the statutes allow him to approve construction through parks only if there has been "all possible planning to minimize harm" to the park.

Petitioners, private citizens as well as local and national conservation organizations, contend that the Secretary has violated these statutes by authorizing federal funds for a six-lane interstate highway through a public park in Memphis, Tennessee. Their claim was rejected by the District Court which granted the Secretary's motion for summary judgment, and the Court of Appeals for the Sixth Circuit affirmed. We now reverse the judgment below and remand for further proceedings in the District Court.

Overton Park is a 342-acre city park located near the center of Memphis. The park contains a zoo, a nine-hole municipal golf course, an outdoor theater, nature trails, a bridle path, an art academy, picnic areas, and 170 acres of forest. The proposed highway, which is to be a six-lane, high-speed, expressway, will sever the zoo from the rest of the park. Although the roadway will be depressed below ground level except where it crosses a small creek, 26 acres of the park will be destroyed. The highway is to be a segment of Interstate Highway I-40, part of the National System of Interstate and Defense Highways. I-40 will provide Memphis with a major east-west expressway which will allow easier access to downtown Memphis from the residential areas on the eastern edge of the city.

Although the route through the park was approved by the Bureau of Public Roads in 1956 and by the Federal Highway Administrator in 1966, the enactment of §4 (f) of the Department of Transportation Act prevented distribution of federal funds for the section of the highway designated to go through Overton Park until the Secretary of Transportation determined whether the requirements of §4 (f) had been met. Federal funding for the rest of the project was, however, available; and the state acquired a right-of-way on both sides of the park. In April 1968, the Secretary announced that he concurred in the judgment of local officials that I-40 should be built through the park. And in September 1969 the State acquired the right-of-way inside Overton Park from the city. Final approval for the project— the route as well as the design—was not announced until November 1969, after Congress had reiterated in §138 of the Federal-Aid Highway Act that highway construction through public parks was to be restricted. Neither announcement approving the route and design of I-40 was accompanied by a statement of the Secretary's factual findings. He did not indicate why he believed there were no feasible and prudent alternative routes or why design changes could not be made to reduce the harm to the park.

A threshold question—whether petitioners are entitled to any judicial review—is easily answered. Section 701 of the Administrative Procedure Act provides that the action of "each authority of the Government of the United States," which includes the Department of Transportation, is subject to judicial review except where there is a statutory prohibition on review or where "agency action is committed to agency discretion by law." In this case, there is no indication that Congress sought to prohibit judicial review and there is most certainly no "showing of 'clear and convincing evidence' of a . . . legislative intent" to restrict access to judicial review. *Abbott Laboratories v. Gardner*, 387 U.S. 136, 141 (1967).

Similarly, the Secretary's decision here does not fall within the exception for action "committed to agency discretion." This is a very narrow exception. The legislative history of the Administrative Procedure Act indicates that it is applicable in those rare instances where "statutes are drawn in such broad terms that in a given case there is no law to apply."

[T]he Department of Transportation Act and the Federal-Aid Highway Act bar the use of federal funds for construction of highways through parks—only the most unusual situations are exempted. Despite the clarity of the statutory language, respondents argue that the Secretary has wide discretion. They recognize that the requirement that there be no "feasible" alternative route admits of little administrative discretion. For this exemption to apply the Secretary must find that as a matter of sound engineering it would not be feasible to build the highway along any other route. Respondents argue, however, that the requirement that there be no other "prudent" route requires the Secretary to engage in a wide-ranging balancing of competing interests.

But no such wide-ranging endeavor was intended. It is obvious that in most cases considerations of cost, directness of route, and community disruption will indicate that parkland should be used for highway construction whenever possible. Although it may be necessary to transfer funds from one jurisdiction to another, there will always be a smaller outlay required from the public purse when parkland is used since the public already owns the land and there will be no need to pay for right-of-way. And since people do not live or work in parks, if a highway is built on parkland no one will have to leave his home or give up his business. Such factors are common to substantially all highway construction. Thus, if Congress intended these factors to be on an equal footing with preservation of parkland there would have been no need for the statutes. [T]he very existence of the statutes indicates that protection of parkland was to be given paramount importance.

[T]he existence of judicial review is only the start: the standard for review must also be determined. For that we must look to §706 of the APA which provides that a "reviewing court shall . . . hold unlawful and set aside agency action, findings, and conclusions found" not to meet six separate standards. In all cases agency action must be set aside if the action was "arbitrary, capricious, an abuse of discretion, or otherwise not in accordance with law" or if the action failed to meet statutory, procedural, or constitutional requirements. In certain narrow, specifically limited situations, the agency action is to be set aside if the action was not supported by "substantial evidence." And in other equally narrow circumstances the reviewing court is to engage in a de novo review of the action and set it aside if it was "unwarranted by the facts."

The court is first required to decide whether the Secretary acted within the scope of his authority. This determination naturally begins with a delineation of the scope of the Secretary's authority and discretion. As has been shown, Congress has specified only a small range of choices that the Secretary can make. Also involved in this initial inquiry is a determination of whether on the facts the Secretary's decision can reasonably be said to be within that range. The reviewing court must consider whether the Secretary properly construed his authority to approve the use of parkland as limited to situations where there are no feasible alternative routes or where feasible alternative routes involve uniquely difficult problems. And the reviewing court must be able to find that the Secretary could have reasonably believed that in this case there are no feasible alternatives or that alternatives do involve unique problems.

Scrutiny of the facts does not end, however, with the determination that the Secretary has acted within the scope of his statutory authority. Section 706 (2)(A) requires a finding that the actual choice made was not "arbitrary, capricious, an abuse of discretion, or otherwise not in accordance with law." To make this finding the court must consider whether the decision was based on a consideration of the relevant factors and whether there has been a clear error of judgment. Although this inquiry into the facts is to be searching and careful, the ultimate standard of review is a narrow one. The court is not empowered to substitute its judgment for that of the agency.

The final inquiry is whether the Secretary's action followed the necessary procedural requirements. Here the only procedural error alleged is the failure of the Secretary to make formal findings and state his reason for allowing the highway to be built through the park.

Undoubtedly, review of the Secretary's action is hampered by his failure to make such findings, but the absence of formal findings does not necessarily require that the case be remanded to the Secretary. Neither the Department of Transportation Act nor the Federal-Aid Highway Act requires such formal findings.

The Secretary's administrative record is not, however, before us. The lower courts based their review on the litigation affidavits that were presented. These affidavits were merely *"post hoc"* rationalizations, *Burlington Truck Lines v. United States,* 371 U.S. 156, 168–169 (1962), [prepared for the litigation and not at the time of decision] which have traditionally been found to be an inadequate basis for review. *SEC v. Chenery Corp.,* 318 U.S. 80, 87 (1943). And they clearly do not constitute the "whole record" compiled by the agency: the basis for review required by §706 of the Administrative Procedure Act.

Thus it is necessary to remand this case to the District Court for plenary review of the Secretary's decision. That review is to be based on the full administrative record that was before the Secretary at the time he made his decision.[6]

✳✳✳✳✳

Although *Overton Park* laid down the basic scope and limitations on judicial review, that was but part of an ongoing conversation among the courts, Congress, and administrative agencies about the real character and boundaries of judicial review. Agencies performed an increasing array of complex and often controversial tasks that courts were then called upon to review. Judges, like the famous Harold Leventhal of the U.S. Circuit Court of Appeals for the D.C. Circuit, tried to find the middle ground between interference in the workings of the agencies and excessive deference that would fall short of the purposes of

---

6. Justice Black (joined by Justice Brennan) concluded the Secretary was plainly in
   violation of statute and would have remanded the matter directly to the agency rather
   than returning it to the district court.

judicial review. Leventhal originated what has come to be known as the "Hard Look" doctrine which sought to focus judicial review on one critical question. "What counts is the reality of an opportunity to submit an effective presentation, to assure that the Secretary and his assistants will take a hard look at the problems in the light of [the record]."[7]

To be sure, the idea of taking a "hard look" was intuitively satisfying, but different judges could have very different views as to exactly what that hard look should entail. Another famous judge of the D.C. Circuit, Judge David L. Bazelon, faced just such a range of interpretation in what was to become a very important case on judicial review ultimately decided by the U. S. Supreme Court. The *Vermont Yankee* opinion became, along with *Overton Park,* the basic instructions to judges about review and to administrators as to what they could expect.

In order to understand this continuing conversation about the proper character of review, it is useful to consider both the D.C. Circuit opinion as well as the Supreme Court *Vermont Yankee* decision. What is now known as the *Vermont Yankee* ruling came about as the result of challenges to decisions of the U.S. Nuclear Regulatory Commission.

Natural Resources Defense Council v. U.S. Nuclear Regulatory Commission, 547 F.2d 633 (D.C. Cir. 1976).

INTRODUCTION: The *Vermont Yankee* case began with a question quite different from what was to become the focus of the case. Initially, this matter was about a challenge to licensing applications from nuclear power plants. In the course of the dispute over the licenses, attention focused on the degree to which the Nuclear Regulation Commission (NRC) was required by the National Environmental Policy Act (NEPA) to address issues associated with the handling and disposal of nuclear fuel for the plants in making decisions about construction and operation permits for those facilities. The NRC undertook a rulemaking proceeding to determine how to address those issues. In so doing, the Commission employed what is now known as a hybrid rulemaking proceeding. (See Chapter 5 of *Public Law and Public Administration, Third Edition.*) Knowing that its decision, whatever it was, would be controversial, the NRC created a docket, made the record available for inspection by the public, and scheduled hearings to consider evidence. None of these steps was required by its enabling statute.

However, things became particularly difficult when commission members refused to allow environmental groups to cross-examine the key government

---

7. *Walter Holm & Co. v. Hardin,* 449 F.2d 1009, 1016 (D.C. Cir. 1971).

witness, a Dr. Pittman, who provided assurances, but virtually no serious evidence, that the disposal problem would be addressed. The commission provided opportunity for the groups to submit their own evidence, but the groups challenged the rulemaking. Some eighty public interest groups brought together and called the Consolidated National Intervenors (CNI) joined the Natural Resources Defense Council and the New England Coalition on Nuclear Pollution to challenge the rulemaking in the D.C. Circuit. They alleged that the NRC decision was arbitrary and capricious because of the Commission's unwillingness to take a hard look at the evidence, particularly the weaknesses of Pittman's testimony so important to the agency decision.

✷✷✷✷✷

CHIEF JUDGE BAZELON wrote for the court joined by EDWARDS.

This appeal involves a rulemaking proceeding. The purpose of the rulemaking was to reconsider whether environmental effects of all stages of the uranium fuel cycle should be included in the cost-benefit analysis for licensing individual reactors. The Commission concluded the environmental effects of the fuel cycle, including waste disposal, were "relatively insignificant," but that it was preferable to take them into account. Therefore, a rule was promulgated requiring a series of specified numerical values (set out as Table S–3 accompanying the rule) be factored into the cost-benefit analysis for an individual reactor.

It is undisputed that a reactor licensing is a "major Federal action significantly affecting the quality of the human environment" which requires a "detailed" environmental impact statement under NEPA. We were informed at argument that the Vermont Yankee plant will produce approximately 160 pounds of plutonium wastes annually during its 40-year life span. Plutonium is generally accepted as among the most toxic substances known; inhalation of a single microscopic particle is thought to be sufficient to cause cancer. Moreover, with a half-life of 25,000 years, plutonium must be isolated from the environment for 250,000 years before it becomes harmless. Operation of the facility in question will also produce substantial quantities of other "high-level" radioactive wastes in the form of strontium-90 and cesium-137 which, with their shorter, 30-year half-lives, must be isolated from the environment for "only" 600 to 1000 years. As more and more reactors producing more and more waste are brought into being, "irretrievable commitments [are] being made and options precluded," and the agency must predict the environmental consequences of its decisions as it makes them.

The notice of proposed rulemaking suggested that a series of specified numerical values (set out as Table S–3 in the notice) be factored into the cost-benefit analysis for individual reactors. An "informal rulemaking hearing" of the "legislative-type" was scheduled to receive comments in the form of "oral or written statements." By subsequent notice, the Commission designated a three-member hearing board to preside, and reiterated, "The procedural format for the hearing will follow the legislative pattern, and no discovery or cross-examination will be utilized."

A few general observations are in order concerning the role of a court in this area. Absent extraordinary circumstances, it is not proper for a reviewing court to prescribe the procedural format which an agency must use to explore a given set of issues. Unless there are statutory directives to the contrary, an agency has discretion to select procedures which it deems best to compile a record illuminating the issues. Courts are no more expert at fashioning administrative procedures than they are in the substantive areas of responsibility which are left to agency discretion. What a reviewing court can do, however, is scrutinize the record as a whole to insure that genuine opportunities to participate in a meaningful way were provided, and that the agency has taken a good, hard look at the major questions before it.

We have sometimes suggested that elucidation of certain types of issues, by their very nature, might require particular procedures, including cross-examination. In fact, we have been more concerned with making sure that the record developed by agency procedures discloses a thorough ventilation of the issues than with what devices the agency used to create the dialogue.

In order to determine whether an agency has lived up to these responsibilities, a reviewing court must examine the record in detail to determine that a real give and take was fostered on the key issues. This does not give the court a license to judge for itself how much weight should be given particular pieces of scientific or technical data, a task for which it is singularly ill-suited. It does require, however, that the court examine the record so that it may satisfy itself that the decision was based "on a consideration of the relevant factors." Where only one side of a controversial issue is developed in any detail, the agency may abuse its discretion by deciding the issues on an inadequate record.

A reviewing court must assure itself not only that a diversity of informed opinion was heard, but that it was genuinely considered. "The dialogue that the APA's rulemaking section contemplates cannot be a sham." Since a reviewing court is incapable of making a penetrating analysis of highly scientific or technical subject matter on its own, it must depend on the agency's expertise, as reflected in the statement of basis and purpose, to organize the record, to distill the major issues which were ventilated and to articulate its reasoning with regard to each of them.

An agency need not respond to frivolous or repetitive comment it receives. However, where apparently significant information has been brought to its attention, or substantial issues of policy or gaps in its reasoning raised, the statement of basis and purpose must indicate why the agency decided the criticisms were invalid. An agency may abuse its discretion by proceeding to a decision which the record before it will not sustain, in the sense that it raises fundamental questions for which the agency has adduced no reasoned answers.

With these observations in mind, we turn to our examination of this record. The significance of Table S–3 is that it expresses in numerical terms the conclusion that the environmental effects of the fuel cycle, including waste disposal, are insubstantial. The only discussion of high-level waste disposal techniques was supplied by a 20-page statement by Dr. Frank K. Pittman, Director of the AEC's Division of Waste Management and Transportation. Dr. Pittman began his statement by acknowledging that he was "broadly involved" with the subject of high-level waste management since he heads the division of the AEC charged with "responsibility for the development, construction and operation of facilities for ultimate management of commercial high-level waste."

Dr. Pittman proceeded to describe for the first time in public the "design concepts" for a federal surface repository for retrievable storage of high-level waste. This is essentially a warehouse in which sealed canisters containing cylinders of solidified nuclear wastes can be stored in water-filled basins recessed into the ground on a temporary basis (up to 100 years), until such time as a permanent waste disposal scheme is devised, when they can be removed. While the "intended life" of the facility is only 100 years, some high-level wastes must be isolated for up to 250,000 years.

Until recently the AEC planned to dispose of wastes by burying them deep inside abandoned salt mines. These plans were postponed indefinitely after a series of technical difficulties, including the discovery the salt mines might be susceptible to underground flooding.

Dr. Pittman's description of the new plan—now also postponed indefinitely— to build a surface storage facility can only fairly be described as vague, but glowing. In less than two pages, he set out a very general description of what the facility is supposed to do accompanied by several schematic drawings. These show the facility will have a cooling system, a transfer area and storage basins, but do not attempt to describe how they will be built and operated, what materials will be used, where such a facility might be located, or what it might cost to build and operate. No citations are given for studies [mentioned by Pittman that would address the serious technical issues he recognized in handling the waste]; in fact, there are no references to back-up materials supporting any of Pittman's statement, or those portions of the Revised Environmental Survey drawn from it. Again without benefit of details, Dr. Pittman offers conclusory reassurances that the proposed facility will be designed so that the possibility of a "meltdown" can be dismissed as "incredible."

Other than the broad reference to "structural strength, plant security, etc., to withstand credible overt forces of man," there is no discussion of how the facility would be protected from terrorism. While Dr. Pittman says "various corrective actions" might be taken to prevent a meltdown, none are specified.

When Dr. Pittman finished, no questions were put to him by the hearing board. No cross-examination was permitted.

[B]ased on the information in Dr. Pittman's statement, the Commission concluded that the future environmental effects from the disposal of high-level nuclear wastes are negligible. This conclusion is in turn embodied in Table S-3, and further consideration of the issue terminated. We do not dispute these conclusions. We may not uphold them, however, lacking a thorough explanation and a meaningful opportunity to challenge the judgments underlying them. Our duty is to insure that the reasoning on which such judgments depend, and the data supporting them, are spread out in detail on the public record. Society must depend largely on oversight by the technically-trained members of the agency and the scientific community at large to monitor technical decisions. The problem with the conclusory quality of Dr. Pittman's statement—and the complete absence of any probing of its underlying basis—is that it frustrates oversight by anyone: Commission, intervenors, court, legislature or public.

After reviewing the record, the presiding hearing board isolated several areas of controversy which it felt ought to be addressed by the Commission in issuing the proposed rule. The Commission disposed of these issues summarily in its state- ment of basis and purpose accompanying the promulgation of the rule without attempting to articulate responses to any of the points which had been raised regarding waste disposal. Thus, to the limited extent that any give-and-take was fostered on the nuclear waste issues, the Commission, in its final decision, failed to address major contentions that were raised. Without a thorough exploration of the problems involved in waste disposal, including past mistakes, and a forthright assessment of the uncertainties and differences in expert opinion, this type of agency action cannot pass muster as reasoned decisionmaking.

Many procedural devices for creating a genuine dialogue on these issues were available to the agency—including informal conferences between intervenors and staff, document discovery, interrogatories, technical advisory committees com- prised of outside experts with differing perspectives, limited cross-examination, funding independent research by intervenors, detailed annotation of technical reports, surveys of existing literature, memoranda explaining methodology. We do not presume to intrude on the agency's province by dictating to it which, if any, of these devices it must adopt to flesh out the record. It may be that no combination of the procedures mentioned above will prove adequate, and the agency will be required to develop new procedures to accomplish the innovative task of imple- menting NEPA through rulemaking. On the other hand, the procedures the agency adopted in this case, if administered in a more sensitive, deliberate manner, might suffice. Whatever techniques the Commission adopts, before it promulgates a rule limiting further consideration of waste disposal and reprocessing issues, it must in one way or another generate a record in which the factual issues are fully developed.

The Commission may well reach the same conclusion on remand. But if it does so on such a record, the Congress, the courts, and the public will all know where we stand.

The Commission's action in cutting off consideration of waste disposal and reprocessing issues in licensing proceedings based on the cursory development of the facts which occurred in this proceeding was capricious and arbitrary. The por- tions of the rule pertaining to these matters are set aside and remanded.

Concurring opinion of BAZELON

I add a word of my own on some of the broader implications of Judge Tamm's concurrence. I agree that courts should be reluctant to impose particular proce- dures on an agency. For example, requiring cross-examination in a rulemaking proceeding is radical therapy, which may cause the patient to suffer a slow, painful death. But I reject the implication that any techniques beyond rudimentary notice and comment are needless "over-formalization" of informal rulemaking.

Despite the controversy surrounding the proper standard of review in informal rulemaking cases, there is less disagreement on this essential point than meets the eye. With customary perspicacity, Judge Friendly has observed that often it does not really matter much whether a court says the record is remanded because the procedures used did not develop sufficient evidence, or because the procedures were inadequate. From the standpoint of the administrator, the point is the same: the procedures prescribed by §553 will not automatically produce an adequate record. Thus, although Judge Tamm vehemently opposes the concept of procedural review of informal rulemaking, he agrees to send this case back for a fuller development of the facts even though the dictates of §553 were followed.

Of course, important differences remain from the standpoint of a reviewing court. I am convinced that in highly technical areas, where judges are institutionally incompetent to weigh evidence for themselves, a focus on agency procedures will prove less intrusive, and more likely to improve the quality of decisionmaking, than judges "steeping" themselves "in technical matters to determine whether the agency has exercised a reasoned discretion."

Concurring opinion by TAMM

I agree with the majority that NEPA requires the Commission fully to assure itself that safe and adequate storage methods are technologically and economically feasible. It forbids reckless decisions to mortgage the future for the present, glibly assuring critics that technological advancement can be counted upon to save us from the consequences of our decisions. I further agree with the conclusion of the majority that it is impossible to determine from the record before us whether the Commission has fulfilled its statutory obligation under NEPA in adopting the S-3 table. Accordingly, the inadequacy of the record demands that we remand this case to the Commission in order to ensure that it has taken a hard look at the waste storage issue. I cannot, however, without qualification, endorse the approach the majority has taken to reach this result or its suggested disposition on remand.

The majority appears to require the Commission to institute further procedures of a more adversarial nature than those customarily required for informal rulemaking by the Administrative Procedure Act. The Commission chose to proceed by "hybrid" rulemaking below, allowing petitioners to present oral arguments before the Commission and subjecting participants to questions, but not permitting participants to cross-examine. By so proceeding the Commission exceeded the minimum procedural requirements of section 553. In my view, the deficiency is not with the type of proceeding below, but with the completeness of the record generated. More procedure will not, in this case, guarantee a better record, and a better record can be generated without reopening the oral proceeding at this time.

I am also troubled by two other aspects of the majority opinion. First, I am distressed because I believe the majority opinion fails to inform the Commission in precise terms what it must do in order to comply with the court's ad hoc standard of review. The majority sends the waste storage issue back to the Commission for a "thorough ventilation." This language, of course, means very little in procedural terms. In order to aid the Commission in filling in the gaps in the record, the majority enumerates a number of procedural alternatives in varying degrees of formality, some less intrusive into agency prerogatives than others.

Then, heeding the Supreme Court's admonition that we may not, except in extraordinary circumstances, specify agency procedures on remand, the majority declines to give the Commission any direction as to which procedure or combination of them, will suffice.

Second, the majority's insistence upon increased adversariness and procedural rigidity, uneasily combined with its non-direction toward any specific procedures, continues a distressing trend toward over-formalization of the administrative decisionmaking process which ultimately will impair its utility. Fearing reversal, administrators will tend to over-formalize, clothing their actions "in the full wardrobe of adjudicatory procedures," until the advantages of informal rulemaking as an administrative tool are lost in a heap of judicially imposed procedure. The majority's reliance upon the so-called "hybrid rulemaking" cases for its conclusion that the procedures prescribed by section 553 are inadequate for resolution of the complex issues involved in this case and its insistence that the Commission adopt more formal adversary procedures are, I believe, misplaced.

The appropriate remedy at this point is not to impose ad hoc procedural requirements in an attempt to raise the level of petitioners' participation, already adequate under section 553, but to remand for an explanation of the basis of Dr. Pittman's statements and of the staff's numerical conclusions, i.e. for the documentation which the majority finds so conspicuously lacking. The Commission should be able to supply the court with a statement of the methods by which its staff arrived at the figures embodied in Table S-3 and by which Dr. Pittman concluded that the waste storage problem is already technologically and economically soluble. If it cannot, then we will have no choice but to invalidate the Commission's rule under the "arbitrary, capricious" standard; if it can, we should defer to the administrative weighing of risks and benefits of additional reactors.

*****

From the D.C. Circuit to the Supreme Court

So the question then becomes: which approach is correct? Was Bazelon right that judges have no business delving into the substantive technical arguments in the record to decide for themselves whether the Commission reached a supportable conclusion? Was his approach—ensuring that the agency's rulemaking process had to make meaningful the notice, participation, and consideration requirements set forth in the APA—the proper way to address administrative decisionmaking? Or was Tamm correct in rejecting Bazelon's inquiry into the way the record was developed and focusing instead on a substantive assessment of that record to determine whether the Commission's behavior was arbitrary and capricious? The unanimous ruling by the U.S. Supreme Court in the *Vermont Yankee* case would seem to have resolved this question definitively, but did it really?

Vermont Yankee Nuclear Power Corp. v. Natural Resources Defense Council, 435 U.S. 519 (1978).

JUSTICE REHNQUIST wrote for the Court.[8]

In 1946, Congress enacted the Administrative Procedure Act, which was not only "a new, basic and comprehensive regulation of procedures in many agencies," but was also a legislative enactment which settled "long-continued and hard-fought contentions, and enacts a formula upon which opposing social and political forces have come to rest." Section 553, dealing with rulemaking, requires that "notice of proposed rule making shall be published in the Federal Register," describes the contents of that notice, and goes on to require that after the notice the agency "shall give interested persons an opportunity to participate in the rule making through submission of written data, views, or arguments with or without opportunity for oral presentation. After consideration of the relevant matter presented, the agency shall incorporate in the rules adopted a concise general statement of their basis and purpose." We [have] held that generally speaking this section of the Act established the maximum procedural requirements which Congress was willing to have the courts impose upon agencies in conducting rulemaking procedures. Agencies are free to grant additional procedural rights in the exercise of their discretion, but reviewing courts are generally not free to impose them if the agencies have not chosen to grant them.

Even apart from the Administrative Procedure Act this Court has for more than four decades emphasized that the formulation of procedures was basically to be left within the discretion of the agencies to which Congress had confided the responsibility for substantive judgments. It is in the light of this background of statutory and decisional law that we granted certiorari to review two judgments of the Court of Appeals for the District of Columbia Circuit because of our concern that they had seriously misread or misapplied this statutory and decisional law cautioning reviewing courts against engrafting their own notions of proper procedures upon agencies entrusted with substantive functions by Congress. The Court of Appeals has done just that in these cases, and we therefore remand them to it for further proceedings.

As we read the opinion of the Court of Appeals, its view that reviewing courts may in the absence of special circumstances justifying such a course of action impose additional procedural requirements on agency action raises questions of such significance in this area of the law as to warrant our granting certiorari and deciding the case. Since the vast majority of challenges to administrative agency action are brought to the Court of Appeals for the District of Columbia Circuit, the decision of that court in this case will serve as precedent for many more proceedings for judicial review of agency actions than would the decision of another Court of Appeals.

[B]efore determining whether the Court of Appeals reached a permissible result, we must determine exactly what result it did reach, and in this case that is

---

8. Justices Blackmun and Powell did not participate.

no mean feat. Vermont Yankee argues that the court invalidated the rule because of the inadequacy of the procedures employed in the proceedings. Respondents, on the other hand, labeling petitioner's view of the decision a "straw man," argue to this Court that the court merely held that the record was inadequate to enable the reviewing court to determine whether the agency had fulfilled its statutory obligation. After a thorough examination of the opinion itself, we conclude that while the matter is not entirely free from doubt, the majority of the Court of Appeals struck down the rule because of the perceived inadequacies of the procedures employed in the rulemaking proceedings. The court frame[d] the issue for decision thus: "Thus, we are called upon to decide whether the procedures provided by the agency were sufficient to ventilate the issues."

The court conceded that absent extraordinary circumstances it is improper for a reviewing court to prescribe the procedural format an agency must follow, but it likewise clearly thought it entirely appropriate to "scrutinize the record as a whole to insure that genuine opportunities to participate in a meaningful way were provided." The court also refrained from actually ordering the agency to follow any specific procedures, but there is little doubt in our minds that the ineluctable mandate of the court's decision is that the procedures afforded during the hearings were inadequate. The exploration of the record and the statement regarding its insufficiency might initially lead one to conclude that the court was only examining the sufficiency of the evidence, but the remaining portions of the opinion dispel any doubt that this was certainly not the sole or even the principal basis of the decision. Accordingly, we feel compelled to address the opinion on its own terms, and we conclude that it was wrong.

Absent constitutional constraints or extremely compelling circumstances the "administrative agencies should be free to fashion their own rules of procedure and to pursue methods of inquiry capable of permitting them to discharge their multitudinous duties." Indeed, our cases could hardly be more explicit in this regard. We have continually repeated this theme through the years. "At least in the absence of substantial justification for doing otherwise, a reviewing court may not, after determining that additional evidence is requisite for adequate review, proceed by dictating to the agency the methods, procedures, and time dimension of the needed inquiry and ordering the results to be reported to the court without opportunity for further consideration on the basis of the new evidence by the agency. Such a procedure clearly runs the risk of '[propelling] the court into the domain which Congress has set aside exclusively for the administrative agency.' *SEC v. Chenery Corp.*, 332 U.S. 194, 196 (1947)."

Respondent NRDC argues that §553 merely establishes lower procedural bounds and that a court may routinely require more than the minimum when an agency's proposed rule addresses complex or technical factual issues or "Issues of Great Public Import." We have, however, previously shown that our decisions reject this view. We also think the legislative history does not bear out its contention. And the Attorney General's Manual on the Administrative Procedure Act further confirms that view. In short, all of this leaves little doubt that Congress intended that the discretion of the agencies and not that of the courts be exercised in determining when extra procedural devices should be employed.

There are compelling reasons for construing §553 in this manner. In the first place, if courts continually review agency proceedings to determine whether the agency employed procedures which were, in the court's opinion, perfectly tailored to reach what the court perceives to be the "best" or "correct" result, judicial review would be totally unpredictable. And the agencies, operating under this vague injunction to employ the "best" procedures and facing the threat of reversal if they did not, would undoubtedly adopt full adjudicatory procedures in every instance. Not only would this totally disrupt the statutory scheme, through which Congress enacted "a formula upon which opposing social and political forces have come to rest," but all the inherent advantages of informal rulemaking would be totally lost.

Secondly, it is obvious that the court in these cases reviewed the agency's choice of procedures on the basis of the record actually produced at the hearing, and not on the basis of the information available to the agency when it made the decision to structure the proceedings in a certain way. This sort of Monday morning quarterbacking not only encourages but almost compels the agency to conduct all rulemaking proceedings with the full panoply of procedural devices normally associated only with adjudicatory hearings.

Finally, and perhaps most importantly, this sort of review fundamentally misconceives the nature of the standard for judicial review of an agency rule. The court below uncritically assumed that additional procedures will automatically result in a more adequate record because it will give interested parties more of an opportunity to participate in and contribute to the proceedings. But informal rulemaking need not be based solely on the transcript of a hearing held before an agency. Indeed, the agency need not even hold a formal hearing. Thus, the adequacy of the "record" in this type of proceeding is not correlated directly to the type of procedural devices employed, but rather turns on whether the agency has followed the statutory mandate of the Administrative Procedure Act or other relevant statutes. In sum, this sort of unwarranted judicial examination of perceived procedural shortcomings of a rulemaking proceeding can do nothing but seriously interfere with that process prescribed by Congress.

In short, nothing in the APA, NEPA, the circumstances of this case, the nature of the issues being considered, past agency practice, or the statutory mandate under which the Commission operates permitted the court to review and overturn the rulemaking proceeding on the basis of the procedural devices employed (or not employed) by the Commission so long as the Commission employed at least the statutory minima, a matter about which there is no doubt in this case.

There remains, of course, the question of whether the challenged rule finds sufficient justification in the administrative proceedings that it should be upheld by the reviewing court. Judge Tamm, concurring in the result reached by the majority of the Court of Appeals, thought that it did not. There are also intimations in the majority opinion which suggest that the judges who joined it likewise may have thought the administrative proceedings an insufficient basis upon which to predicate the rule in question. We accordingly remand so that the Court of Appeals may review the rule as the Administrative Procedure Act provides. We have made it abundantly clear before that when there is a contemporaneous explanation of the agency decision, the validity of that action must "stand or fall on the propriety of that finding, judged, of course, by the appropriate standard of review." The court should engage in this kind of review and not stray beyond the judicial province to explore the procedural format or to impose upon the agency its own notion of which procedures are "best" or most likely to further some vague, undefined public good.

*****

THE ARBITRARY
AND CAPRICIOUS STANDARD

There has been a good deal of discussion of the basic arbitrary and capricious standard for judicial review of administrative action. But what does that standard really entail? The Supreme Court provided one of its clearest explanations of that standard and the one that remains the controlling law in the so-called "Airbags Case," *Motor Vehicle Manufacturers Association v. State Farm Mutual Automobile Insurance Co.*

Motor Vehicle Manufacturers Association v. State Farm Mutual Automobile Insurance Co., 463 U.S. 29 (1983).

INTRODUCTION: The Airbags Case is an interesting example of an important and ongoing problem in decisionmaking. It is a case that involved decisions about automotive safety rules that spanned several presidential administrations with very different regulatory philosophies and political appointees to implement those views. Just what constitutes arbitrary and capricious decisionmaking in the context of political change is a recurring problem at all levels of government, from cases like the Airbags battle at the national level to city council control over sign ordinances.

There is one more feature that is significant about this opinion. Most often, agencies have been challenged because they reached out to assert regulatory authority over someone or a firm. In this instance, the controversy concerns a decision to step back, to rescind a rule. Part of the debate concerned the question of whether courts have similar obligations when agencies rescind a rule as when they create a new one.

*****

JUSTICE WHITE wrote the opinion for the Court.

Since 1929, motor vehicles have been the leading cause of accidental deaths and injuries in the United States. Before changes in automobile design could be mandated, the effectiveness of these changes had to be studied, their costs examined, and public acceptance considered. This task called for considerable expertise and Congress responded by enacting the National Traffic and Motor Vehicle Safety Act of 1966. The Act, created for the purpose of "[reducing] traffic accidents and deaths and injuries to persons resulting from traffic accidents," directs the Secretary of Transportation or his delegate to issue motor vehicle safety standards that "shall be practicable, shall meet the need for motor vehicle safety, and shall be stated in objective terms." In issuing these standards, the Secretary is directed to consider "relevant available motor vehicle safety data," whether the proposed standard "is reasonable, practicable and appropriate" for the particular type of motor vehicle, and the "extent to which such standards will contribute to carrying out the purposes" of the Act.

The Act also authorizes judicial review under the provisions of the Administrative Procedure Act (APA) of all "orders establishing, amending, or revoking a Federal motor vehicle safety standard." Under this authority, we review today whether NHTSA acted arbitrarily and capriciously in revoking the requirement in Motor Vehicle Safety Standard 208 that new motor vehicles produced after September 1982 be equipped with passive restraints to protect the safety of the occupants of the vehicle in the event of a collision. Briefly summarized, we hold that the agency failed to present an adequate basis and explanation for rescinding the passive restraint requirement and that the agency must either consider the matter further or adhere to or amend Standard 208 along lines which its analysis supports.

The regulation whose rescission is at issue bears a complex and convoluted history. As originally issued by the Department of Transportation in 1967, Standard 208 simply required the installation of seatbelts in all automobiles. It soon became apparent that the level of seatbelt use was too low to reduce traffic injuries to an acceptable level. The Department therefore began consideration of "passive occupant restraint systems"—devices that do not depend for their effectiveness upon any action taken by the occupant except that necessary to operate the vehicle. Two types of automatic crash protection emerged: automatic seatbelts and airbags. The lifesaving potential of these devices was immediately recognized.

In 1969, the Department formally proposed a standard requiring the installation of passive restraints, thereby commencing a lengthy series of proceedings. In 1970, the agency revised Standard 208 to include passive protection requirements, and in 1972, the agency amended the Standard to require full passive protection for all front seat occupants of vehicles manufactured after August 15, 1975. In the interim, vehicles built between August 1973 and August 1975 were to carry either passive restraints or lap and shoulder belts coupled with an "ignition interlock" that would prevent starting the vehicle if the belts were not connected. On review, the agency's decision to require passive restraints was found to be supported by "substantial evidence" and upheld [in] *Chrysler Corp. v. Department of Transportation,* 472 F.2d 659 (6th Cir. 1972).

In preparing for the upcoming model year, most car makers chose the "ignition interlock" option, a decision which was highly unpopular, and led Congress to amend the Act to prohibit a motor vehicle safety standard from requiring or permitting compliance by means of an ignition interlock or a continuous buzzer designed to indicate that safety belts were not in use. The Motor Vehicle and Schoolbus Safety Amendments of 1974 provided that any safety standard that could be satisfied by a system other than seatbelts would have to be submitted to Congress where it could be vetoed by concurrent resolution of both Houses.

The effective date for mandatory passive restraint systems was extended for a year until August 31, 1976. But in June 1976, Secretary of Transportation William T. Coleman, Jr., initiated a new rulemaking on the issue. After hearing testimony and reviewing written comments, Coleman extended the optional alternatives indefinitely and suspended the passive restraint requirement. Although he found passive restraints technologically and economically feasible, the Secretary based his decision on the expectation that there would be widespread public resistance to the new systems. He instead proposed a demonstration project involving up to 500,000 cars installed with passive restraints, in order to smooth the way for public acceptance of mandatory passive restraints at a later date.

Coleman's successor as Secretary of Transportation disagreed. Within months of assuming office, Secretary Brock Adams decided that the demonstration project was unnecessary. He issued a new mandatory passive restraint regulation, known as Modified Standard 208. The Modified Standard mandated the phasing in of passive restraints beginning with large cars in model year 1982 and extending to all cars by model year 1984. The two principal systems that would satisfy the Standard were airbags and passive belts; the choice of which system to install was left to the manufacturers. In *Pacific Legal Foundation v. Department of Transportation,* 593 F.2d 1338 (D.C. Cir. 1979) the Court of Appeals upheld Modified Standard 208 as a rational, nonarbitrary regulation consistent with the agency's mandate under the Act. The Standard also survived scrutiny by Congress, which did not exercise its authority under the legislative veto provision of the 1974 Amendments.

Over the next several years, the automobile industry geared up to comply with Modified Standard 208. In February 1981, however, Secretary of Transportation Andrew Lewis reopened the rulemaking due to changed economic circumstances and, in particular, the difficulties of the automobile industry. Two months later, the agency ordered a one-year delay in the application of the Standard to large cars, extending the deadline to September 1982, and at the same time, proposed the possible rescission of the entire Standard. After receiving written comments and holding public hearings, NHTSA issued a final rule (Notice 25) that rescinded the passive restraint requirement contained in Modified Standard 208.

In a statement explaining the rescission, NHTSA maintained that it was no longer able to find, as it had in 1977, that the automatic restraint requirement would produce significant safety benefits. This judgment reflected not a change of opinion on the effectiveness of the technology, but a change in plans by the automobile industry. In 1977, the agency had assumed that airbags would be installed in 60% of all new cars and automatic seatbelts in 40%. By 1981 it became apparent that automobile manufacturers planned to install the automatic seatbelts in approximately 99% of the new cars. For this reason, the lifesaving potential of airbags would not be realized. Moreover, it now appeared that the overwhelming majority of passive belts planned to be installed by manufacturers could be detached easily and left that way permanently. Passive belts, once detached, then required "the same type of affirmative action that is the stumbling block to obtaining high usage levels of manual belts." For this reason, the agency concluded that there was no longer a basis for reliably predicting that the Standard would lead to any significant increased usage of restraints at all.

State Farm Mutual Automobile Insurance Co. and the National Association of Independent Insurers filed petitions for review of NHTSA's rescission of the passive restraint Standard. The United States Court of Appeals for the District of Columbia Circuit held that the agency's rescission of the passive restraint requirement was arbitrary and capricious for three reasons. First, the court found insufficient as a basis for rescission NHTSA's conclusion that it could not reliably predict an increase in belt usage under the Standard. The court held that there was insufficient evidence in the record to sustain NHTSA's position on this issue, and that, "only a well justified refusal to seek more evidence could render rescission non-arbitrary." Second, a majority of the panel concluded that NHTSA inadequately considered the possibility of requiring manufacturers to install nondetachable rather than detachable passive belts. Third, the majority found that the agency acted arbitrarily and capriciously by failing to give any consideration whatever to requiring compliance with Modified Standard 208 by the installation of airbags.

Petitioner Motor Vehicle Manufacturers Association (MVMA) contend[s] that the rescission of an agency rule should be judged by the same standard a court would use to judge an agency's refusal to promulgate a rule in the first place—a standard petitioner believes considerably narrower than the traditional arbitrary-and-capricious test. We reject this view. The Act expressly equates orders "revoking" and "establishing" safety standards; neither that Act nor the APA suggests that revocations are to be treated as refusals to promulgate standards. Petitioner's view would render meaningless Congress' authorization for judicial review of orders revoking safety rules. Moreover, the revocation of an extant regulation is substantially different than a failure to act. Revocation constitutes a reversal of the agency's former views as to the proper course. A "settled course of behavior embodies the agency's informed judgment that, by pursuing that course, it will carry out the policies committed to it by Congress. There is, then, at least a presumption that those policies will be carried out best if the settled rule is adhered to." Accordingly, an agency changing its course by rescinding a rule is obligated to supply a reasoned analysis for the change beyond that which may be required when an agency does not act in the first instance.

In so holding, we fully recognize that "[regulatory] agencies do not establish rules of conduct to last forever," and that an agency must be given ample latitude to "adapt their rules and policies to the demands of changing circumstances." But the forces of change do not always or necessarily point in the direction of deregulation. In the abstract, there is no more reason to presume that changing circumstances require the rescission of prior action, instead of a revision in or even the extension of current regulation. If Congress established a presumption from which judicial review should start, that presumption—contrary to petitioners' views—is not against safety regulation, but against changes in current policy that are not justified by the rulemaking record. While the removal of a regulation may not entail the monetary expenditures and other costs of enacting a new standard, and, accordingly, it may be easier for an agency to justify a deregulatory action, the direction in which an agency chooses to move does not alter the standard of judicial review established by law.

The scope of review under the "arbitrary and capricious" standard is narrow and a court is not to substitute its judgment for that of the agency. Nevertheless, the agency must examine the relevant data and articulate a satisfactory explanation for its action including a "rational connection between the facts found and the choice made." In reviewing that explanation, we must "consider whether the decision was based on a consideration of the relevant factors and whether there has been a clear error of judgment." Normally, an agency rule would be arbitrary and capricious if the agency has relied on factors which Congress has not intended it to consider, entirely failed to consider an important aspect of the problem, offered an explanation for its decision that runs counter to the evidence before the agency, or is so implausible that it could not be ascribed to a difference in view or the product of agency expertise. The reviewing court should not attempt itself to make up for such deficiencies; we may not supply a reasoned basis for the agency's action that the agency itself has not given. We will, however, "uphold a decision of less than ideal clarity if the agency's path may reasonably be discerned." For purposes of these cases, it is also relevant that Congress required a record of the rulemaking proceedings to be compiled and submitted to a reviewing court and intended that agency findings under the Act would be supported by "substantial evidence on the record considered as a whole."

The ultimate question before us is whether NHTSA's rescission of the passive restraint requirement of Standard 208 was arbitrary and capricious. We conclude, as did the Court of Appeals, that it was. The first and most obvious reason for finding the rescission arbitrary and capricious is that NHTSA apparently gave no consideration whatever to modifying the Standard to require that airbag technology be utilized. Standard 208 sought to achieve automatic crash protection by requiring automobile manufacturers to install either of two passive restraint devices: airbags or automatic seatbelts. There was no suggestion in the long rulemaking process that led to Standard 208 that if only one of these options were feasible, no passive restraint standard should be promulgated.

The agency has now determined that the detachable automatic belts will not attain anticipated safety benefits because so many individuals will detach the mechanism. Even if this conclusion were acceptable in its entirety, standing alone it would not justify any more than an amendment of Standard 208 to disallow compliance by means of the one technology which will not provide effective passenger protection. It does not cast doubt on the need for a passive restraint standard or upon the efficacy of airbag technology.

Given the effectiveness ascribed to airbag technology by the agency, the mandate of the Act to achieve traffic safety would suggest that the logical response to the faults of detachable seatbelts would be to require the installation of airbags. At the very least this alternative way of achieving the objectives of the Act should have been addressed and adequate reasons given for its abandonment. But the agency not only did not require compliance through airbags, it also did not even consider the possibility in its 1981 rulemaking. "There are no findings and no analysis here to justify the choice made, no indication of the basis on which the [agency] exercised its expert discretion. We are not prepared to and the Administrative Procedure Act will not permit us to accept such . . . practice. . . . Expert discretion is the lifeblood of the administrative process, but 'unless we make the requirements for administrative action strict and demanding, expertise, the strength of modern government, can become a monster which rules with no practical limits on its discretion.'"

We have frequently reiterated that an agency must cogently explain why it has exercised its discretion in a given manner and we reaffirm this principle again today.

We do not require today any specific procedures which NHTSA must follow. Nor do we broadly require an agency to consider all policy alternatives in reaching decision. We hold only that given the judgment made in 1977 that airbags are an effective and cost-beneficial life-saving technology, the mandatory passive restraint rule may not be abandoned without any consideration whatsoever of an airbags-only requirement. Accordingly, we vacate the judgment of the Court of Appeals and remand the cases to that court with directions to remand the matter to the NHTSA for further consideration consistent with this opinion.

JUSTICE REHNQUIST wrote concurring in part and dissenting in part joined by BURGER, POWELL, and O'CONNOR.

I join Parts I, II, III, IV, and V-A of the Court's opinion. In particular, I agree that, since the airbag and continuous spool automatic seatbelt were explicitly approved in the Standard the agency was rescinding, the agency should explain why it declined to leave those requirements intact. In this case, the agency gave no explanation at all. Of course, if the agency can provide a rational explanation, it may adhere to its decision to rescind the entire Standard.

I do not believe, however, that NHTSA's view of detachable automatic seatbelts was arbitrary and capricious. The agency adequately explained its decision to rescind the Standard insofar as it was satisfied by detachable belts.

The agency's changed view of the standard seems to be related to the election of a new President of a different political party. It is readily apparent that the responsible members of one administration may consider public resistance and uncertainties to be more important than do their counterparts in a previous administration. A change in administration brought about by the people casting their votes is a perfectly reasonable basis for an executive agency's reappraisal of the costs and benefits of its programs and regulations. As long as the agency remains within the bounds established by Congress, it is entitled to assess administrative records and evaluate priorities in light of the philosophy of the administration.

*****

THE CHALLENGE OF JUDICIAL DEFERENCE

Running through all of these issues is the question of just how much deference judges should show to administrative decisions. It might seem as if the cases considered to this point would resolve that matter, but that simply is not the case. Within this general discussion, two elements of the problem produce recurring debate: the situation in which an agency seeks deference for its interpretation of a statute, and the question of deference to an agency's technical expertise.

The Supreme Court has often addressed these questions of deference, but it laid down a standard for approaching such problems in *Chevron U.S.A., Inc. v. Natural Resources Defense Council*.

Chevron U.S.A., Inc. v. Natural Resources Defense Council, 467 U.S. 837 (1984).

INTRODUCTION: This case arose from standards established by the EPA under the Clean Air Act Amendments of 1977. It focused on the question of how the agency's interpretation of the statute should be reviewed. Although *Chevron* continues to be the controlling standard for this kind of question, its meaning and application in any given setting have often been matters of debate both within the Court and outside of it. Note, for example, that Justice Stevens wrote the opinion for the Court in *Chevron* and that then Justice Rehnquist did not participate. Later, in *Rust v. Sullivan* (discussed later in this chapter), Rehnquist wrote for a sharply divided Court, making a quite different interpretation and application in *Chevron,* with Stevens in dissent.

*****

JUSTICE STEVENS wrote the opinion for the Court (MARSHALL, REHNQUIST, and O'CONNOR did not participate in the decision).

In the Clean Air Act Amendments of 1977, Congress enacted certain requirements applicable to States that had not achieved the national air quality standards established by the Environmental Protection Agency (EPA) pursuant to earlier legislation. The amended Clean Air Act required these "nonattainment" States to establish a permit program regulating "new or modified major stationary sources" of air pollution. Generally, a permit may not be issued for a new or modified major stationary source unless several stringent conditions are met. The EPA regulation promulgated to implement this permit requirement allows a State to adopt a plantwide definition of the term "stationary source." Under this definition, an existing plant that contains several pollution-emitting devices may install or modify one piece of equipment without meeting the permit conditions if the alteration will not increase the total emissions from the plant. The question presented by these cases is whether EPA's decision to allow States to treat all of the pollution-emitting devices within the same industrial grouping as though they were encased within a single "bubble" is based on a reasonable construction of the statutory term "stationary source."

The EPA regulations containing the plantwide definition of the term stationary source were promulgated on October 14, 1981. The Court of Appeals set aside the regulations. The court observed that the relevant part of the amended Clean Air Act "does not explicitly define what Congress envisioned as a 'stationary source,' to which the permit program . . . should apply," and further stated that the precise issue was not "squarely addressed in the legislative history." In light of its conclusion that the legislative history bearing on the question was "at best contradictory," it reasoned that "the purposes of the non-attainment program should guide our decision here." Based on two of its precedents concerning the applicability of the bubble concept to certain Clean Air Act programs, the court stated that the bubble concept was "mandatory" in programs designed merely to maintain existing air quality, but held that it was "inappropriate" in programs enacted to improve air quality. Since the purpose of the permit program—its "raison d'etre," in the court's view—was to improve air quality, the court held that the bubble concept was inapplicable in these cases under its prior precedents. It therefore set aside the regulations embodying the bubble concept as contrary to law. We now reverse.

The basic legal error of the Court of Appeals was to adopt a static judicial definition of the term "stationary source" when it had decided that Congress itself had not commanded that definition. We must determine whether the Court of Appeals' legal error resulted in an erroneous judgment on the validity of the regulations.

When a court reviews an agency's construction of the statute which it administers, it is confronted with two questions. First, always, is the question whether Congress has directly spoken to the precise question at issue. If the intent of Congress is clear, that is the end of the matter; for the court, as well as the agency, must give effect to the unambiguously expressed intent of Congress. If, however, the court determines Congress has not directly addressed the precise question at issue, the court does not simply impose its own construction on the statute, as would be necessary in the absence of an administrative interpretation. Rather, if the statute is silent or ambiguous with respect to the specific issue, the question for the court is whether the agency's answer is based on a permissible construction of the statute.

If Congress has explicitly left a gap for the agency to fill, there is an express delegation of authority to the agency to elucidate a specific provision of the statute by regulation. Such legislative regulations are given controlling weight unless they are arbitrary, capricious, or manifestly contrary to the statute. Sometimes the legislative delegation to an agency on a particular question is implicit rather than explicit. In such a case, a court may not substitute its own construction of a statutory provision for a reasonable interpretation made by the administrator of an agency.

We have long recognized that considerable weight should be accorded to an executive department's construction of a statutory scheme it is entrusted to administer, and the principle of deference to administrative interpretations has been consistently followed by this Court whenever decision as to the meaning or reach of a statute has involved reconciling conflicting policies, and a full understanding of the force of the statutory policy in the given situation has depended upon more than ordinary knowledge respecting the matters subjected to agency regulations.

In light of these well-settled principles it is clear that the Court of Appeals misconceived the nature of its role in reviewing the regulations at issue. Once it determined, after its own examination of the legislation, that Congress did not actually have an intent regarding the applicability of the bubble concept to the permit program, the question before it was not whether in its view the concept is "inappropriate" in the general context of a program designed to improve air quality, but whether the Administrator's view that it is appropriate in the context of this particular program is a reasonable one. Based on the examination of the legislation and its history which follows, we agree with the Court of Appeals that Congress did not have a specific intention on the applicability of the bubble concept in these cases, and conclude that the EPA's use of that concept here is a reasonable policy choice for the agency to make.

In these cases the Administrator's interpretation represents a reasonable accommodation of manifestly competing interests and is entitled to deference: the regulatory scheme is technical and complex, the agency considered the matter in a detailed and reasoned fashion, and the decision involves reconciling conflicting policies.

Judges are not experts in the field, and are not part of either political branch of the Government. Courts must, in some cases, reconcile competing political interests, but not on the basis of the judges' personal policy preferences. In contrast, an agency to which Congress has delegated policymaking responsibilities may, within the limits of that delegation, properly rely upon the incumbent administration's views of wise policy to inform its judgments. While agencies are not directly accountable to the people, the Chief Executive is, and it is entirely appropriate for this political branch of the Government to make such policy choices—resolving the competing interests which Congress itself either inadvertently did not resolve, or intentionally left to be resolved by the agency charged with the administration of the statute in light of everyday realities.

When a challenge to an agency construction of a statutory provision, fairly conceptualized, really centers on the wisdom of the agency's policy, rather than whether it is a reasonable choice within a gap left open by Congress, the challenge must fail. In such a case, federal judges—who have no constituency—have a duty to respect legitimate policy choices made by those who do. The responsibilities for assessing the wisdom of such policy choices and resolving the struggle between competing views of the public interest are not judicial ones: "Our Constitution vests such responsibilities in the political branches."

We hold that the EPA's definition of the term "source" is a permissible construction of the statute which seeks to accommodate progress in reducing air pollution with economic growth. The judgment of the Court of Appeals is reversed.

*****

Rust v. Sullivan, **500 U.S. 173 (1991).**

INTRODUCTION: *Rust* was a case that developed amidst dramatic controversy over abortion. It raised important questions of constitutional law in terms of the right to privacy and also First Amendment questions of freedom of speech. Not nearly as well noticed at the time, though, was the fact that it was an important case concerning deference in the aftermath of the *Chevron* ruling and about the approach to review of significant policy change growing out of electoral politics. The case began during the last year of the Reagan administration, when the Secretary of Health and Human Services issued new rules that dramatically reversed previous policy concerning federally funded family planning clinics under Title X of the Public Health Service Act of 1970.

The new regulations held that "Title X project may not provide counseling concerning the use of abortion as a method of family planning or provide referral for abortion as a method of family planning." As the Court recognized, while "Title X projects must refer every pregnant client 'for appropriate prenatal and/or social services by furnishing a list of available providers that promote the welfare of mother and unborn child,' [the] list may not be used indirectly to encourage or promote abortion, 'such as by weighing the list of referrals in favor of health care providers which perform abortions, by including on the list of referral providers health care providers whose principal business is the provision of abortions, by excluding available providers who do not provide abortions, or by 'steering' clients to providers who offer abortion as a method of family planning." The Title X project is expressly prohibited from referring a pregnant woman to an abortion provider, even upon specific request. Second, the regulations broadly prohibit a Title X project from engaging in activities that "encourage, promote or advocate abortion as a method of family planning. Forbidden activities include lobbying for legislation that would increase the availability of abortion as a method of family planning, developing or disseminating materials advocating abortion as a method of family planning, providing speakers to promote abortion as a method of family planning, using legal action to make abortion available in any way as a method of family planning, and paying dues to any group that advocates abortion as a method of family planning as a substantial part of its activities. Third, the regulations require that Title X projects be organized so that they are 'physically and financially separate' from prohibited abortion activities."

Challenges were promptly brought in New York, Colorado, and Massachusetts, but the differences among the circuits on the validity of the new rules virtually ensured consideration by the U.S. Supreme Court. The portions of the opinion provided below focus on the deference to administrative discretion and review of major policy change.

Justice Rehnquist wrote for the five person majority, moving his arguments about the acceptability of major change through rulemaking that he had written in his Airbags separate opinion into a majority opinion. Citing the deference statement from *Chevron* and reading the Airbags ruling and his interpretation of it very broadly, he concluded that since agencies must be able to change rules, no deference was due to existing administrative practice, even one that was longstanding and based upon interpretation of the same statutory language. Four members of the Court dissented. Of course, in this case, there was no issue of deference to technical expertise, and the dramatic reversal of statutory interpretation here made *Rust* a very different case. Justice Stevens, author of the *Chevron* decision, dissented in *Rust* and took exception to Rehnquist's application of *Chevron* in this case. Rehnquist, of course, had not participated in *Chevron*.

*****

JUSTICE REHNQUIST wrote the opinion for the Court.

We turn first to petitioners' contention that the regulations exceed the Secretary's authority under Title X and are arbitrary and capricious. We need not dwell on the plain language of the statute because we agree with every court to have addressed the issue that the language is ambiguous. If a statute is "silent or ambiguous with respect to the specific issue, the question for the court is whether the agency's answer is based on a permissible construction of the statute." *Chevron*.

The Secretary's construction of Title X may not be disturbed as an abuse of discretion if it reflects a plausible construction of the plain language of the statute and does not otherwise conflict with Congress' expressed intent. In determining whether a construction is permissible, "the court need not conclude that the agency construction was the only one it permissibly could have adopted . . . or even the reading the court would have reached if the question initially had arisen in a judicial proceeding." Rather, substantial deference is accorded to the interpretation of the authorizing statute by the agency authorized with administering it.

The broad language of Title X plainly allows the Secretary's construction of the statute. When we find, as we do here, that the legislative history is ambiguous and unenlightening on the matters with respect to which the regulations deal, we customarily defer to the expertise of the agency. Petitioners argue, however, that the regulations are entitled to little or no deference because they "reverse a long-standing agency policy that permitted nondirective counseling and referral for abortion" and thus represent a sharp break from the Secretary's prior construction of the statute. Petitioners argue that the agency's prior consistent interpretation of §1008 to permit nondirective counseling and to encourage coordination with local and state family planning services is entitled to substantial weight.

This Court has rejected the argument that an agency's interpretation "is not entitled to deference because it represents a sharp break with prior interpretations" of the statute in question. In *Chevron*, we held that a revised interpretation deserves deference because "an initial agency interpretation is not instantly carved

in stone" and "the agency, to engage in informed rulemaking, must consider varying interpretations and the wisdom of its policy on a continuing basis." An agency
is not required to "establish rules of conduct to last forever," *Motor Vehicle Mfrs.
Assn. v. State Farm,* but rather "must be given ample latitude to 'adapt [its] rules
and policies to the demands of changing circumstances.'"

The Secretary's regulations are a permissible construction of Title X and do
not violate either the First or Fifth Amendments to the Constitution. Accordingly,
the judgment of the Court of Appeals is affirmed.

JUSTICE STEVENS wrote a dissent.

In my opinion, the Court has not paid sufficient attention to the language of
the controlling statute or to the consistent interpretation accorded the statute by
the responsible cabinet officers during four different Presidencies and 18 years.
The original regulations promulgated in 1971 by the Secretary of Health,
Education, and Welfare so interpreted the statute. This "contemporaneous construction of [the] statute by the men charged with the responsibility of setting its
machinery in motion" is entitled to particular respect. The regulations described
the kind of services that grant recipients had to provide in order to be eligible for
federal funding, but they did not purport to regulate or restrict the kinds of advice
or information that recipients might make available to their clients. The same is
true of the regulations promulgated in 1986 by the Secretary of Health and
Human Services.

The entirely new approach adopted by the Secretary in 1988 was not, in my
view, authorized by the statute. The new regulations did not merely reflect a
change in a policy determination that the Secretary had been authorized by
Congress to make. Rather, they represented an assumption of policymaking
responsibility that Congress had not delegated to the Secretary. I would hold the
challenged regulations invalid and reverse the judgment of the Court of Appeals.[9]

✳✳✳✳✳

Ever since the *Chevron* ruling, there appeared to be a growing trend toward a
doctrine of deference that called for more presumptions in favor of administrative interpretations of statutes, even if not all courts actually applied the doctrine in that way. However, in *United States v. Mead,* the Court took a very
different approach to judicial deference, one that Justice Scalia in dissent
referred to as "one of the most significant opinions ever rendered by the Court
dealing with the judicial review of administrative action."

United States v. Mead Corp., 533 U.S. 218 (2001).

INTRODUCTION: The case developed from a tariff classification ruling produced by the U.S. Customs Service as to the proper way to classify "day planners"

---

9. Justices Blackmun and O'Connor also wrote dissents.

imported by the Mead Corporation. The company appealed the change in the classification of its products. Once in the United States Court of Appeals for the Federal Circuit, the focus of the case turned to whether the court should apply the *Chevron* deference approach. The Supreme Court, in an opinion for all members of the Court except Scalia, concluded that *Chevron* deference should not apply. In fact, the Court went well beyond the previous approach to judicial deference to agency discretion.

*****

JUSTICE SOUTER wrote for the Court.

The question is whether a tariff classification ruling by the United States Customs Service deserves judicial deference. The Federal Circuit rejected Customs's invocation of *Chevron* in support of such a ruling, to which it gave no deference. We agree that a tariff classification has no claim to judicial deference under *Chevron,* there being no indication that Congress intended such a ruling to carry the force of law, but we hold that under *Skidmore v. Swift & Co.,* 323 U.S. 134 (1944), the ruling is eligible to claim respect according to its persuasiveness.

The Mead Corporation imports "day planners," three-ring binders with pages having room for notes of daily schedules and phone numbers and addresses, together with a calendar and suchlike. Between 1989 and 1993, Customs repeatedly treated day planners under the "other" HTSUS [Harmonized Tariff Schedule of the United States] subheading. In January 1993, however, Customs changed its position, and issued a Headquarters ruling letter classifying Mead's day planners as "Diaries . . . bound" subject to tariff under subheading 4820.10.20. Customs rejected Mead's [protests].

The Federal Circuit reversed the Court of International Trade and held that Customs classification rulings should not get *Chevron* deference, owing to differences from the regulations at issue in [*United States v. Haggar Apparel Co.,* 526 U.S. 380 (1999)]. Rulings are not preceded by notice and comment as under the Administrative Procedure Act (APA), 5 U.S.C. §553, they "do not carry the force of law and are not, like regulations, intended to clarify the rights and obligations of importers beyond the specific case under review." The Court of Appeals accordingly gave no deference at all to the ruling classifying the Mead day planners and rejected the agency's reasoning.

We granted certiorari in order to consider the limits of *Chevron* deference owed to administrative practice in applying a statute. We hold that administrative implementation of a particular statutory provision qualifies for *Chevron* deference when it appears that Congress delegated authority to the agency generally to make rules carrying the force of law, and that the agency interpretation claiming deference was promulgated in the exercise of that authority. Delegation of such authority may be shown in a variety of ways, as by an agency's power to engage in adjudication or notice-and-comment rulemaking, or by some other indication of a comparable congressional intent. The Customs ruling at issue here fails to qualify, although the possibility that it deserves some deference under *Skidmore* leads us to vacate and remand.

When Congress has "explicitly left a gap for an agency to fill, there is an express delegation of authority to the agency to elucidate a specific provision of the statute by regulation," *Chevron,* and any ensuing regulation is binding in the courts unless procedurally defective, arbitrary or capricious in substance, or manifestly contrary to the statute. But whether or not they enjoy any express delegation of authority on a particular question, agencies charged with applying a statute necessarily make all sorts of interpretive choices, and while not all of those choices bind judges to follow them, they certainly may influence courts facing questions the agencies have already answered. "The well-reasoned views of the agencies implementing a statute 'constitute a body of experience and informed judgment to which courts and litigants may properly resort for guidance,'" *Bragdon v. Abbott,* 524 U.S. 624, 642 (1998), and "we have long recognized that considerable weight should be accorded to an executive department's construction of a statutory scheme it is entrusted to administer. . . ." *Chevron.* The fair measure of deference to an agency administering its own statute has been understood to vary with circumstances, and courts have looked to the degree of the agency's care, its consistency, formality, and relative expertness, and to the persuasiveness of the agency's position, see *Skidmore.* The approach has produced a spectrum of judicial responses, from great respect at one end to near indifference at the other. Justice Jackson summed things up in *Skidmore:* "The weight [accorded to an administrative] judgment in a particular case will depend upon the thoroughness evident in its consideration, the validity of its reasoning, its consistency with earlier and later pronouncements, and all those factors which give it power to persuade, if lacking power to control."

Since 1984, we have identified a category of interpretive choices distinguished by an additional reason for judicial deference. This Court in *Chevron* recognized that Congress not only engages in express delegation of specific interpretive authority, but that "sometimes the legislative delegation to an agency on a particular question is implicit." We have recognized a very good indicator of delegation meriting *Chevron* treatment in express congressional authorizations to engage in the process of rulemaking or adjudication that produces regulations or rulings for which deference is claimed. It is fair to assume generally that Congress contemplates administrative action with the effect of law when it provides for a relatively formal administrative procedure tending to foster the fairness and deliberation that should underlie a pronouncement of such force. Thus, the overwhelming number of our cases applying *Chevron* deference have reviewed the fruits of notice-and-comment rulemaking or formal adjudication. That said, and as significant as notice-and-comment is in pointing to *Chevron* authority, the want of that procedure here does not decide the case, for we have sometimes found reasons for *Chevron* deference even when no such administrative formality was required and none was afforded. The fact that the tariff classification here was not a product of such formal process does not alone, therefore, bar the application of *Chevron.*

There are, nonetheless, ample reasons to deny *Chevron* deference here. The authorization for classification rulings, and Customs's practice in making them, present a case far removed not only from notice-and-comment process, but from any other circumstances reasonably suggesting that Congress ever thought of classification rulings as deserving the deference claimed for them here.

It is difficult, in fact, to see in the agency practice itself any indication that Customs ever set out with a lawmaking pretense in mind when it undertook to make classifications like these. Customs does not generally engage in notice-and-comment practice when issuing them, and their treatment by the agency makes it clear that a letter's binding character as a ruling stops short of third parties; Customs has regarded a classification as conclusive only as between itself and the importer to whom it was issued, and even then only until Customs has given advance notice of intended change.

Indeed, to claim that classifications have legal force is to ignore the reality that 46 different Customs offices issue 10,000 to 15,000 of them each year. Any suggestion that rulings intended to have the force of law are being churned out at a rate of 10,000 a year at an agency's 46 scattered offices is simply self-refuting. Although the circumstances are less startling here, with a Headquarters letter in issue, none of the relevant statutes recognizes this category of rulings as separate or different from others; there is thus no indication that a more potent delegation might have been understood as going to Headquarters even when Headquarters provides developed reasoning, as it did in this instance.

Nor do the amendments to the statute made effective after this case arose disturb our conclusion. The new law requires Customs to provide notice-and-comment procedures only when modifying or revoking a prior classification ruling or modifying the treatment accorded to substantially identical transactions; and under its regulations, Customs sees itself obliged to provide notice-and-comment procedures only when "changing a practice" so as to produce a tariff increase, or in the imposition of a restriction or prohibition, or when Customs Headquarters determines that "the matter is of sufficient importance to involve the interests of domestic industry." The statutory changes reveal no new congressional objective of treating classification decisions generally as rulemaking with force of law, nor do they suggest any intent to create a *Chevron* patchwork of classification rulings, some with force of law, some without.

In sum, classification rulings are best treated like "interpretations contained in policy statements, agency manuals, and enforcement guidelines." They are beyond the *Chevron* pale.

To agree with the Court of Appeals that Customs ruling letters do not fall within *Chevron* is not, however, to place them outside the pale of any deference whatever. *Chevron* did nothing to eliminate *Skidmore's* holding that an agency's interpretation may merit some deference whatever its form, given the "specialized experience and broader investigations and information" available to the agency, and given the value of uniformity in its administrative and judicial understandings of what a national law requires, "at least some added persuasive force" where *Chevron* is inapplicable.

There is room at least to raise a *Skidmore* claim here, where the regulatory scheme is highly detailed, and Customs can bring the benefit of specialized experience to bear on the subtle questions in this case: whether the daily planner with room for brief daily entries falls under "diaries," when diaries are grouped with "notebooks and address books, bound; memorandum pads, letter pads and similar articles;" and whether a planner with a ring binding should qualify as "bound," when a binding may be typified by a book, but also may have "reinforcements or fittings of metal, plastics, etc." A classification ruling in this situation may therefore at least seek a respect proportional to its "power to persuade." Such a ruling may surely claim the merit of its writer's thoroughness, logic and expertness, its fit with prior interpretations, and any other sources of weight.

Although we all accept the position that the Judiciary should defer to at least some of this multifarious administrative action, we have to decide how to take account of the great range of its variety. If the primary objective is to simplify the judicial process of giving or withholding deference, then the diversity of statutes authorizing discretionary administrative action must be declared irrelevant or minimized. If, on the other hand, it is simply implausible that Congress intended such a broad range of statutory authority to produce only two varieties of administrative action, demanding either *Chevron* deference or none at all, then the breadth of the spectrum of possible agency action must be taken into account.

[I]n holding here that *Chevron* left *Skidmore* intact and applicable where statutory circumstances indicate no intent to delegate general authority to make rules with force of law, or where such authority was not invoked, we hold nothing more than we said last Term in response to the particular statutory circumstances in *Christensen,* to which Justice Scalia then took exception, just as he does again today.

We think, in sum, that Justice Scalia's efforts to simplify ultimately run afoul of Congress's indications that different statutes present different reasons for considering respect for the exercise of administrative authority or deference to it. Without being at odds with congressional intent much of the time, we believe that judicial responses to administrative action must continue to differentiate between *Chevron* and *Skidmore,* and that continued recognition of *Skidmore* is necessary for just the reasons Justice Jackson gave when that case was decided.

Since the *Skidmore* assessment called for here ought to be made in the first instance by the Court of Appeals for the Federal Circuit or the Court of International Trade, we go no further than to vacate the judgment and remand the case for further proceedings consistent with this opinion.

JUSTICE SCALIA wrote a dissent.

Today's opinion makes an avulsive change in judicial review of federal administrative action. Whereas previously a reasonable agency application of an ambiguous statutory provision had to be sustained so long as it represented the agency's authoritative interpretation, henceforth such an application can be set aside unless "it appears that Congress delegated authority to the agency generally to make rules carrying the force of law," as by giving an agency "power to engage in adjudication or notice-and-comment rulemaking, or . . . some other [procedure] indicating comparable congressional intent," and "the agency interpretation claiming deference was promulgated in the exercise of that authority." What was previously a general presumption of authority in agencies to resolve ambiguity in the statutes they have been authorized to enforce has been changed to a presumption of no such authority, which must be overcome by affirmative legislative intent to the contrary. We will be sorting out the consequences of the *Mead* doctrine, which has today replaced the *Chevron* doctrine, for years to come. I would adhere to our established jurisprudence, defer to the reasonable interpretation the Customs

Service has given to the statute it is charged with enforcing, and reverse the judgment of the Court of Appeals.

Today the Court collapses [the *Chevron*] doctrine, announcing instead a presumption that agency discretion does not exist unless the statute, expressly or impliedly, says so. While the Court disclaims any hard-and-fast rule for determining the existence of discretion-conferring intent, it asserts that "a very good indicator [is] express congressional authorizations to engage in the process of rulemaking or adjudication that produces regulations or rulings for which deference is claimed." Only when agencies act through "adjudication[,] notice-and-comment rulemaking, or . . . some other [procedure] indicating comparable congressional intent [whatever that means]" is *Chevron* deference applicable—because these "relatively formal administrative procedures [designed] to foster . . . fairness and deliberation" bespeak (according to the Court) congressional willingness to have the agency, rather than the courts, resolve statutory ambiguities. Once it is determined that *Chevron* deference is not in order, the uncertainty is not at an end—and indeed is just beginning. Litigants cannot then assume that the statutory question is one for the courts to determine, according to traditional interpretive principles and by their own judicial lights. No, the Court now resurrects, in full force, the pre-*Chevron* doctrine of *Skidmore* deference, whereby "the fair measure of deference to an agency administering its own statute . . . varies with circumstances," including "the degree of the agency's care, its consistency, formality, and relative expertness, and . . . the persuasiveness of the agency's position." The Court has largely replaced *Chevron,* in other words, with that test most beloved by a court unwilling to be held to rules (and most feared by litigants who want to know what to expect): the old "totality of the circumstances" test. The Court's new doctrine is neither sound in principle nor sustainable in practice.

The basis in principle for today's new doctrine can be described as follows: The background rule is that ambiguity in legislative instructions to agencies is to be resolved not by the agencies but by the judges. Specific congressional intent to depart from this rule must be found—and while there is no single touchstone for such intent it can generally be found when Congress has authorized the agency to act through (what the Court says is) relatively formal procedures such as informal rulemaking and formal (and informal?) adjudication, and when the agency in fact employs such procedures.

As for the practical effects of the new rule:

(1) The principal effect will be protracted confusion. The one test for *Chevron* deference that the Court enunciates is wonderfully imprecise: whether "Congress delegated authority to the agency generally to make rules carrying the force of law, . . . as by . . . adjudication[,] notice-and-comment rulemaking, or . . . some other [procedure] indicating comparable congressional intent." It is hard to know what the lower courts are to make of today's guidance.

(2) Another practical effect of today's opinion will be an artificially induced increase in informal rulemaking. Buy stock in the GPO. Since informal rulemaking and formal adjudication are the only more-or-less safe harbors from the storm that the Court has unleashed; and since formal adjudication is not an option but must be mandated by statute or constitutional command;

informal rulemaking—which the Court was once careful to make voluntary unless required by statute—will now become a virtual necessity.

(3) Worst of all, the majority's approach will lead to the ossification of large portions of our statutory law. Where *Chevron* applies, statutory ambiguities remain ambiguities subject to the agency's ongoing clarification. They create a space, so to speak, for the exercise of continuing agency discretion.

I know of no case, in the entire history of the federal courts, in which we have allowed a judicial interpretation of a statute to be set aside by an agency—or have allowed a lower court to render an interpretation of a statute subject to correction by an agency.

(4) And finally, the majority's approach compounds the confusion it creates by breathing new life into the anachronism of *Skidmore,* which sets forth a sliding scale of deference owed an agency's interpretation of a statute that is dependent "upon the thoroughness evident in [the agency's] conside-ration, the validity of its reasoning, its consistency with earlier and later pronouncements, and all those factors which give it power to persuade, if lacking power to control"; in this way, the appropriate measure of deference will be accorded the "body of experience and informed judgment" that such interpretations often embody.

It was possible to live with the indeterminacy of *Skidmore* deference in earlier times. But in an era when federal statutory law administered by federal agencies is pervasive, and when the ambiguities (intended or unintended) that those statutes contain are innumerable, totality-of-the-circumstances *Skidmore* deference is a recipe for uncertainty, unpredictability, and endless litigation.

I respectfully dissent from the Court's judgment. I dissent even more vigor-ously from the reasoning that produces the Court's judgment, and that makes today's decision one of the most significant opinions ever rendered by the Court dealing with the judicial review of administrative action. Its consequences will be enormous, and almost uniformly bad.

*****

ADDITIONAL READINGS

Abram Chayes, "The Role of the Judge in Public Law Litigation," 89 *Harvard L. Rev.* 1281 (1976).

Robert Choo, "Judicial Review of Negotiated Rulemaking: Should Chevron Deference Apply?" 52 *Rutgers L. Rev.* 1069 (2000).

Phillip J. Cooper, *Hard Judicial Choices* (New York: Oxford University Press, 1988).

Louis Fisher, *Constitutional Dialogues* (Princeton, NJ: Princeton University Press, 1988).

Carl McGowan, "Reflections on Rulemaking Review," 53 *Tulane L. Rev.* 681 (1979).

Richard J. Pierce, Jr., "The Special Contributions of the D.C. Circuit to Administrative Law," 90 *Geo. L.J.* 779 (2002)

Richard J. Pierce, Sidney A. Shapiro, Paul R. Verkuil, *Administrative Law and Process, Third Edition* (New York: Foundation Press, 1999).

4

⚖️

The Law and
Public Employees*

For many years, it was assumed that the Supreme Court had read the Constitution such that the protections available to public employees were broad and would continue to expand. That was particularly true after many in the legal community interpreted *Board of Regents v. Roth*,[1] *Perry v. Sindermann*,[2] and *Pickering v. Board of Education*[3] very broadly. However, as William Van Alstyne noted, many of these interpretations seemed to ignore much of what had come before and misread the precedents.[4] In a number of respects, these cases set limits on employee protections and presaged more limits yet to come. Even so, many public administrators saw the Court as launching a kind of ongoing assault on the flexibility of managers to supervise their people and operate their organizations. In fact, many still seem to have that view.

However, the Supreme Court has led a trend away from protections of public employees and toward greater deference to management discretion. As

---

* Related Material in *Public Law and Public Administration, Third Edition*, Chapter 12.

1. *Board of Regents v. Roth*, 408 U.S. 564 (1972).

2. *Perry v. Sindermann*, 408 U.S. 593 (1972).

3. *Pickering v. Board of Education*, 391 U.S. 563 (1968).

4. William Van Alstyne, "Cracks in 'The New Property': Adjudicative Due Process in the Administrative State," 62 *Cornell Law Review* 445, 489–90 (1977).

Chapter 12 of *Public Law and Public Administration, Third Edition* points out, though, neither managers nor public employees are truly able to have a sense of security in their decisions in light of the expanded use of a loose set of balancing tests to determine the outer boundaries of public employee protections. This chapter focuses on the trend since the early 1980's, beginning with *Connick v. Myers.*

FIRST AMENDMENT
AND PUBLIC EMPLOYEE SPEECH

Connick v. Myers, 461 U.S. 138 (1983).

INTRODUCTION: Sheila Myers was an assistant district attorney in New Orleans for five and a half years. She was told that she was to be reassigned. However, she objected to the transfer because she would be prosecuting cases before a judge with whom she had been working on diversion programs. She indicated that there were ethical concerns. She complained that the heavy handed behavior exhibited toward her was part of a pattern of management problems in the office, including such abuses as pressuring employees to participate in fund raising and campaigning for the district attorney. While she conferred with her supervisor about this, she continued to carry out her duties competently. In speaking with her immediate supervisor, Myers was told that her frustrations about the management of the office were not shared by others. She then prepared a questionnaire that she gave to other employees. When her supervisor learned of this, he notified Connick, the district attorney, that there was a "mini-insurrection" in progress. Myers was then summarily fired because she had refused the transfer. The district court found that she had been terminated in violation of her First Amendment–protected free speech rights and the court of appeals affirmed.

*****

JUSTICE WHITE wrote the opinion for the Court.

In *Pickering v. Board of Education*, 391 U.S. 563 (1968), we stated that a public employee does not relinquish First Amendment rights to comment on matter of public interest by virtue of government employment. We also recognized that the State's interests as an employer in regulating the speech of its employees "differ significantly from those it possesses in connection with regulation of the speech of the citizenry in general." The problem, we thought, was arriving "at a balance between the interests of the [employee], as a citizen, in commenting upon matters of public concern and the interest of the State, as an employer, in promoting the efficiency of the public services it performs through its employees." We return to this problem today and consider whether the First and Fourteenth Amendments prevent the discharge of a state employee for circulating a questionnaire concerning internal office affairs.

II. For at least 15 years, it has been settled that a State cannot condition public employment on a basis that infringes the employee's constitutionally protected interest in freedom of expression. *Keyishian v. Board of Regents,* 385 U.S. 589, 605–606 (1967); *Pickering v. Board of Education,* 391 U.S. 563 (1968); *Perry v. Sindermann,* 408 U.S. 593, 597 (1972). Our task, as we defined it in *Pickering,* is to seek "a balance between the interests of the [employee], as a citizen, in commenting upon matters of public concern and the interest of the State, as an employer, in promoting the efficiency of the public services it performs through its employees." The [courts below] misapplied our decision in *Pickering* [in this case] and erred in striking the balance for respondent.

The District Court got off on the wrong foot in this case by initially finding that, "[taken] as a whole, the issues presented in the questionnaire relate to the effective functioning of the District Attorney's Office and are matters of public importance and concern." Connick contends at the outset that no balancing of interests is required in this case because Myers' questionnaire concerned only internal office matters and that such speech is not upon a matter of "public concern," as the term was used in *Pickering.* Although we do not agree that Myers' communication in this case was wholly without First Amendment protection, there is much force to Connick's submission. The repeated emphasis in *Pickering* on the right of a public employee "as a citizen, in commenting upon matters of public concern," was not accidental. This language reflects both the historical evolvement of the rights of public employees, and the common-sense realization that government offices could not function if every employment decision became a constitutional matter.

For most of this century, the unchallenged dogma was that a public employee had no right to object to conditions placed upon the terms of employment—including those which restricted the exercise of constitutional rights. The classic formulation of this position was that of Justice Holmes, who, when sitting on the Supreme Judicial Court of Massachusetts, observed: "[A policeman] may have a constitutional right to talk politics, but he has no constitutional right to be a policeman." *McAuliffe v. Mayor of New Bedford,* 29 N. E. 517, 517 (1892). For many years, Holmes' epigram expressed this Court's law.

The Court cast new light on the matter in a series of cases arising from the widespread efforts in the 1950's and early 1960's to require public employees, particularly teachers, to swear oaths of loyalty to the State and reveal the groups with which they associated. The Court held that a State could not require its employees to establish their loyalty by extracting an oath denying past affiliation with Communists. [We also] recognized that the government could not deny employment because of previous membership in a particular party. By the time *Sherbert v. Verner,* 374 U.S. 398 (1963), was decided, it was already "too late in the day to doubt that the liberties of religion and expression may be infringed by the denial of or placing of conditions upon a benefit or privilege." It was therefore no surprise when in *Keyishian v. Board of Regents, supra,* the Court invalidated New York statutes barring employment on the basis of membership in "subversive" organizations, observing that the theory that public employment which may be denied altogether may be subjected to any conditions, regardless of how unreasonable, had been uniformly rejected.

In all of these cases the invalidated statutes and actions sought to suppress the rights of public employees to participate in public affairs. *Pickering,* its antecedents, and its progeny lead us to conclude that if Myers' questionnaire cannot be fairly characterized as constituting speech on a matter of public concern, it is unnecessary for us to scrutinize the reasons for her discharge. When employee expression cannot be fairly considered as relating to any matter of political, social, or other concern to the community, government officials should enjoy wide latitude in managing their offices, without intrusive oversight by the judiciary in the name of the First Amendment. Perhaps the government employer's dismissal of the worker may not be fair, but ordinary dismissals from government service which violate no fixed tenure or applicable statute or regulation are not subject to judicial review even if the reasons for the dismissal are alleged to be mistaken or unreasonable.

[W]hen a public employee speaks not as a citizen upon matters of public concern, but instead as an employee upon matters only of personal interest, absent the most unusual circumstances, a federal court is not the appropriate forum in which to review the wisdom of a personnel decision taken by a public agency allegedly in reaction to the employee's behavior. Whether an employee's speech addresses a matter of public concern must be determined by the content, form, and context of a given statement, as revealed by the whole record. In this case, with but one exception,[5] the questions posed by Myers to her co-workers do not fall under the rubric of matters of "public concern." We view the questions pertaining to the confidence and trust that Myers' co-workers possess in various supervisors, the level of office morale, and the need for a grievance committee as mere extensions of Myers' dispute over her transfer to another section of the criminal court.

To presume that all matters which transpire within a government office are of public concern would mean that virtually every remark—and certainly every criticism directed at a public official—would plant the seed of a constitutional case. While as a matter of good judgment, public officials should be receptive to constructive criticism offered by their employees, the First Amendment does not require a public office to be run as a roundtable for employee complaints over internal office affairs.

Because one of the questions in Myers' survey touched upon a matter of public concern and contributed to her discharge, we must determine whether Connick was justified in discharging Myers. *Pickering* unmistakably states that the State's bur-

---

5. The Court went on to note that: "Question 11 inquires if assistant district attorneys 'ever feel pressured to work in political campaigns on behalf of office supported candidates.' [W]e believe it apparent that the issue of whether assistant district attorneys are pressured to work in political campaigns is a matter of interest to the community upon which it is essential that public employees be able to speak freely without fear of retaliatory dismissal."

den in justifying a particular discharge varies depending upon the nature of the employee's expression. Although such particularized balancing is difficult, the courts must reach the most appropriate possible balance of the competing interests.

The *Pickering* balance requires full consideration of the government's interest in the effective and efficient fulfillment of its responsibilities to the public. One hundred years ago, the Court noted the government's legitimate purpose in "[promoting] efficiency and integrity in the discharge of official duties, and [in] [maintaining] proper discipline in the public service." "To this end, the Government, as an employer, must have wide discretion and control over the management of its personnel and internal affairs. This includes the prerogative to remove employees whose conduct hinders efficient operation and to do so with dispatch. Prolonged retention of a disruptive or otherwise unsatisfactory employee can adversely affect discipline and morale in the work place, foster disharmony, and ultimately impair the efficiency of an office or agency."

We agree with the District Court that there is no demonstration here that the questionnaire impeded Myers' ability to perform her responsibilities. Connick's judgment, and apparently also that of his first assistant Dennis Waldron, who characterized Myers' actions as causing a "mini-insurrection," was that Myers' questionnaire was an act of insubordination which interfered with working relationships. When close working relationships are essential to fulfilling public responsibilities, a wide degree of deference to the employer's judgment is appropriate. Furthermore, we do not see the necessity for an employer to allow events to unfold to the extent that the disruption of the office and the destruction of working relationships is manifest before taking action.

JUSTICE BRENNAN wrote a dissent joined by JUSTICES MARSHALL, BLACKMUN, and STEVENS.

Sheila Myers was discharged for circulating a questionnaire to her fellow Assistant District Attorneys seeking information about the effect of petitioner's personnel policies on employee morale and the overall work performance of the District Attorney's Office. The Court concludes that her dismissal does not violate the First Amendment, primarily because the questionnaire addresses matters that, in the Court's view, are not of public concern. It is hornbook law, however, that speech about "the manner in which government is operated or should be operated" is an essential part of the communications necessary for self-governance the protection of which was a central purpose of the First Amendment. Because the questionnaire addressed such matters and its distribution did not adversely affect the operations of the District Attorney's Office or interfere with Myers' working relationship with her fellow employees, I dissent.

I. The Court correctly reaffirms the long-established principle that the government may not constitutionally compel persons to relinquish their First Amendment rights as a condition of public employment. *Pickering* held that the First Amendment protects the rights of public employees "as citizens to comment on matters of public interest" in connection with the operation of the government agencies for which they work.

The balancing test articulated in *Pickering* comes into play only when a public employee's speech implicates the government's interests as an employer. When public employees engage in expression unrelated to their employment while away from the workplace, their First Amendment rights are, of course, no different from those of the general public. Thus, whether a public employee's speech addresses a matter of public concern is relevant to the constitutional inquiry only when the statements at issue—by virtue of their content or the context in which they were made—may have an adverse impact on the government's ability to perform its duties efficiently.

The Court's decision today is flawed in three respects. First, the Court distorts the balancing analysis required under *Pickering* by suggesting that one factor, the context in which a statement is made, is to be weighed twice—first in determining whether an employee's speech addresses a matter of public concern and then in deciding whether the statement adversely affected the government's interest as an employer. Second, in concluding that the effect of respondent's personnel policies on employee morale and the work performance of the District Attorney's Office is not a matter of public concern, the Court impermissibly narrows the class of subjects on which public employees may speak out without fear of retaliatory dismissal. Third, the Court misapplies the *Pickering* balancing test in holding that Myers could constitutionally be dismissed for circulating a questionnaire addressed to at least one subject that was "a matter of interest to the community," in the absence of evidence that her conduct disrupted the efficient functioning of the District Attorney's Office.

II. The standard announced by the Court suggests that the manner and context in which a statement is made must be weighed on both sides of the *Pickering* balance. It is beyond dispute that how and where a public employee expresses his views are relevant in the second half of the *Pickering* inquiry—determining whether the employee's speech adversely affects the government's interests as an employer. In my view, whether a particular statement by a public employee is addressed to a subject of public concern does not depend on where it was said or why. The First Amendment affords special protection to speech that may inform public debate about how our society is to be governed—regardless of whether it actually becomes the subject of a public controversy.

Unconstrained discussion concerning the manner in which the government performs its duties is an essential element of the public discourse necessary to informed self-government. The constitutionally protected right to speak out on governmental affairs would be meaningless if it did not extend to statements expressing criticism of governmental officials. In *Pickering* we held that the First Amendment affords similar protection to critical statements by a public school teacher directed at the Board of Education for whom he worked. In so doing, we recognized that "free and open debate" about the operation of public schools "is vital to informed decision-making by the electorate." We also acknowledged the importance of allowing teachers to speak out on school matters.

Applying these principles, I would hold that Myers' questionnaire addressed matters of public concern because it discussed subjects that could reasonably be expected to be of interest to persons seeking to develop informed opinions about the manner in which the Orleans Parish District Attorney, an elected official charged with managing a vital governmental agency, discharges his responsibilities. Because I believe the First Amendment protects the right of public employees to discuss such matters so that the public may be better informed about how their elected officials fulfill their responsibilities, I would affirm the District Court's conclusion that the questionnaire related to matters of public importance and concern.

Based on its own narrow conception of which matters are of public concern, the Court implicitly determines that information concerning employee morale at an important government office will not inform public debate. To the contrary, the First Amendment protects the dissemination of such information so that the people, not the courts, may evaluate its usefulness. The proper means to ensure that the courts are not swamped with routine employee grievances mischaracterized as First Amendment cases is not to restrict artificially the concept of "public concern," but to require that adequate weight be given to the public's important interests in the efficient performance of governmental functions and in preserving employee discipline and harmony sufficient to achieve that end.

III. Although the Court finds most of Myers' questionnaire unrelated to matters of public interest, it does hold that one question—asking whether Assistants felt pressured to work in political campaigns on behalf of office-supported candidates—addressed a matter of public importance and concern. The Court also recognizes that this determination of public interest must weigh heavily in the balancing of competing interests required by *Pickering*. Having gone that far, however, the Court misapplies the *Pickering* test and holds—against our previous authorities—that a public employer's mere apprehension that speech will be disruptive justifies suppression of that speech when all the objective evidence suggests that those fears are essentially unfounded.

The Court responds that an employer need not wait until the destruction of working relationships is manifest before taking action. In the face of the District Court's finding that the circulation of the questionnaire had no disruptive effect, the Court holds that respondent may be dismissed because petitioner "reasonably believed [the action] would disrupt the office, undermine his authority, and destroy close working relationships." Even though the District Court found that the distribution of the questionnaire did not impair Myers' working relationship with her supervisors, the Court bows to petitioner's judgment because "[when] close working relationships are essential to fulfilling public responsibilities, a wide degree of deference to the employer's judgment is appropriate."

Such extreme deference to the employer's judgment is not appropriate when public employees voice critical views concerning the operations of the agency for which they work. Although an employer's determination that an employee's statements have undermined essential working relationships must be carefully weighed in the *Pickering* balance, we must bear in mind that "the threat of dismissal from public employment is . . . a potent means of inhibiting speech." If the employer's judgment is to be controlling, public employees will not speak out when what they have to say is critical of their supervisors. In order to protect public employees'

First Amendment right to voice critical views on issues of public importance, the courts must make their own appraisal of the effects of the speech in question.

Because the speech at issue addressed matters of public importance, a similar standard should be applied here. After reviewing the evidence, the District Court found that "it cannot be said that the defendant's interest in promoting the efficiency of the public services performed through his employees was either adversely affected or substantially impeded by plaintiff's distribution of the questionnaire." Based on these findings the District Court concluded that the circulation of the questionnaire was protected by the First Amendment. The District Court applied the proper legal standard and reached an acceptable accommodation between the competing interests. I would affirm its decision and the judgment of the Court of Appeals.

IV. The Court's decision today inevitably will deter public employees from making critical statements about the manner in which government agencies are operated for fear that doing so will provoke their dismissal. As a result, the public will be deprived of valuable information with which to evaluate the performance of elected officials. Because protecting the dissemination of such information is an essential function of the First Amendment, I dissent.

*****

For a time, it was uncertain how far down this road toward greater deference to employers the Court would go. However, it became clear that a majority of the justices were going to push the envelope still further when the Court rendered its ruling in *Waters v. Churchill* in 1994.

Waters v. Churchill, 511 U.S. 661 (1994).

INTRODUCTION: This case arose from a dinner conversation in a hospital cafeteria involving two nurses that was overheard by others. Although the supervisor did not consult other witnesses to the conversation to resolve the very different versions of the conversation, Churchill was ultimately dismissed.

*****

JUSTICE O'CONNOR wrote the opinion for the Court.

Churchill was in the obstetrics department, and Perkins-Graham was considering transferring to that department. Petitioners heard about [their conversation] and fired Churchill, allegedly because of it. There is, however, a dispute about what Churchill actually said, and therefore about whether petitioners were constitutionally permitted to fire Churchill for her statements.

The conversation was overheard in part by two other nurses, Mary Lou Ballew and Jean Welty, and by Dr. Thomas Koch, the clinical head of obstetrics. A few days later, Ballew told Cynthia Waters, Churchill's supervisor, about the incident. According to Ballew, Churchill took "the cross trainee into the kitchen for ... at least 20 minutes to talk about [Waters] and how bad things are in [obstetrics] in general." Ballew said that Churchill's statements led Perkins-Graham to no longer be interested in switching to the department.

Shortly after this, Waters met with Ballew a second time for confirmation of Ballew's initial report. Ballew said that Churchill "was knocking the department" and that "in general [Churchill] was saying what a bad place [obstetrics] is to work." Ballew said she heard Churchill say Waters "was trying to find reasons to fire her." Ballew also said Churchill described a patient complaint for which Waters had supposedly wrongly blamed Churchill.

Waters, together with petitioner Kathleen Davis, the hospital's vice president of nursing, also met with Perkins-Graham, who told them that Churchill "had indeed said unkind and inappropriate negative things about [Waters]." Also, according to Perkins-Graham, Churchill mentioned a negative evaluation that Waters had given Churchill, which arose out of an incident in which Waters had cited Churchill for an insubordinate remark. The evaluation stated that Churchill "'promotes an unpleasant atmosphere and hinders constructive communication and cooperation,'" and "'exhibits negative behavior towards [Waters] and [Waters'] leadership through her actions and body language'"; the evaluation said Churchill's work was otherwise satisfactory. Churchill allegedly told Perkins-Graham that she and Waters had discussed the evaluation, and that Waters "wanted to wipe the slate clean . . . but [Churchill thought] this wasn't possible." Churchill also allegedly told Perkins-Graham "that just in general things were not good in OB and hospital administration was responsible." Churchill specifically mentioned Davis, saying Davis "was ruining MDH." Perkins-Graham told Waters that she knew Davis and Waters "could not tolerate that kind of negativism."

Churchill's version of the conversation is different. For several months, Churchill had been concerned about the hospital's "cross-training" policy, under which nurses from one department could work in another when their usual location was overstaffed. Churchill believed this policy threatened patient care because it was designed not to train nurses but to cover staff shortages, and she had complained about this to Davis and Waters. According to Churchill, the conversation with Perkins-Graham primarily concerned the crosstraining policy. Churchill denies that she said some of what Ballew and Perkins-Graham allege she said. She does admit she criticized Davis, saying her staffing policies threatened to "ruin" the hospital because they "'seemed to be impeding nursing care.'" She claims she actually defended Waters and encouraged Perkins-Graham to transfer to obstetrics.

Koch's and Welty's recollections of the conversation match Churchill's. Davis and Waters, however, never talked to Koch or Welty about this, and they did not talk to Churchill until the time they told her she was fired. Moreover, Churchill claims, Ballew was biased against Churchill because of an incident in which Ballew apparently made an error and Churchill had to cover for her.

After she was discharged, Churchill filed an internal grievance. The president of the hospital, petitioner Stephen Hopper, met with Churchill in regard to this and heard her side of the story. He then reviewed Waters' and Davis' written reports of their conversations with Ballew and Perkins-Graham, and had Bernice Magin, the hospital's vice president of human resources, interview Ballew one more time. After considering all this, Hopper rejected Churchill's grievance.

Churchill then sued, claiming that the firing violated her First Amendment rights because her speech was protected under *Connick v. Myers,* 461 U.S. 138 (1983). In May 1991, the United States District Court for the Central District of Illinois granted summary judgment to petitioners. The court held that neither version of the conversation was protected under *Connick:* Regardless of whose story was accepted, the speech was not on a matter of public concern, and even if it was on a matter of public concern, its potential for disruption nonetheless stripped it of First Amendment protection. Therefore, the court held, management could fire Churchill for the conversation with impunity.

The United States Court of Appeals for the Seventh Circuit reversed [and] held that Churchill's speech, viewed in the light most favorable to her, was protected speech under the *Connick* test: It was on a matter of public concern—"the hospital's [alleged] violation of state nursing regulations as well as the quality and level of nursing care it provides its patients,"—and it was not disruptive.

In *Connick v. Myers,* we set forth a test for determining whether speech by a government employee may, consistently with the First Amendment, serve as a basis for disciplining or discharging that employee. In this case, we decide whether the *Connick* test should be applied to what the government employer thought was said, or to what the trier of fact ultimately determines to have been said.

II. There is no dispute in this case about when speech by a government employee is protected by the First Amendment: To be protected, the speech must be on a matter of public concern, and the employee's interest in expressing herself on this matter must not be outweighed by any injury the speech could cause to "'the interest of the State, as an employer, in promoting the efficiency of the public services it performs through its employees.'" *Connick.* The dispute is over how the factual basis for applying the test—what the speech was, in what tone it was delivered, what the listener's reactions were—is to be determined. Should the court apply the *Connick* test to the speech as the government employer found it to be, or should it ask the jury to determine the facts for itself?

[Our] cases establish a basic First Amendment principle: Government action based on protected speech may under some circumstances violate the First Amendment even if the government actor honestly believes the speech is unprotected. And though Justice Scalia suggests that this principle be limited to licensing schemes and to "deprivation[s] of the freedom of speech specifically through the judicial process," we do not think the logic of the cases supports such a limitation. Speech can be chilled and punished by administrative action as much as by judicial processes; in no case have we asserted or even implied the contrary.

Nonetheless, not every procedure that may safeguard protected speech is constitutionally mandated. True, the procedure adopted by the Court of Appeals may lower the chance of protected speech being erroneously punished. A speaker is more protected if she has two opportunities to be vindicated—first by the employer's investigation and then by the jury—than just one. But each procedure involves a different mix of administrative burden, risk of erroneous punishment of protected speech, and risk of erroneous exculpation of unprotected speech. Though the First Amendment creates a strong presumption against punishing protected speech even inadvertently, the balance need not always be struck in that direction.

We have never set forth a general test to determine when a procedural safeguard is required by the First Amendment and we do not purport to do so now. But though we agree with Justice Scalia that the lack of such a test is inconvenient, this does not relieve us of our responsibility to decide the case that is before us today. Both Justice Scalia and we agree that some procedural requirements are mandated by the First Amendment and some are not. None of us have discovered a general principle to determine where the line is to be drawn. We must therefore reconcile ourselves to answering the question on a case-by-case basis, at least until some workable general rule emerges.

Accordingly, all we say today is that the propriety of a proposed procedure must turn on the particular context in which the question arises—on the cost of the procedure and the relative magnitude and constitutional significance of the risks it would decrease and increase. And to evaluate these factors here we have to return to the issue we dealt with in *Connick* and in the cases that came before it: What is it about the government's role as employer that gives it a freer hand in regulating the speech of its employees than it has in regulating the speech of the public at large?

B. We have never explicitly answered this question, though we have always assumed that its premise is correct—that the government as employer indeed has far broader powers than does the government as sovereign. This assumption is amply borne out by considering the practical realities of government employment, and the many situations in which, we believe, most observers would agree that the government must be able to restrict its employees' speech.

To begin with, even many of the most fundamental maxims of our First Amendment jurisprudence cannot reasonably be applied to speech by government employees. [W]hen an employee counsels her co-workers to do their job in a way with which the public employer disagrees, her managers may tell her to stop, rather than relying on counterspeech. [T]hough a private person is perfectly free to uninhibitedly and robustly criticize a state governor's legislative program, we have never suggested that the Constitution bars the governor from firing a high-ranking deputy for doing the same thing.

Government employee speech must be treated differently with regard to procedural requirements as well. [S]urely a public employer may, consistently with the First Amendment, prohibit its employees from being "rude to customers," a standard almost certainly too vague when applied to the public at large.

Likewise, we have consistently given greater deference to government predictions of harm used to justify restriction of employee speech than to predictions of harm used to justify restrictions on the speech of the public at large. Few of the examples we have discussed involve tangible, present interference with the agency's operation. The danger in them is mostly speculative. One could make a respectable argument that political activity by government employees is generally not harmful or that high officials should allow more public dissent by their subordinates or that even in a government workplace the free market of ideas is superior to a command economy. But we have given substantial weight to government employers' reasonable predictions of disruption, even when the speech involved is on a matter of public concern, and even though when the government is acting as sovereign our review of legislative predictions of harm is considerably less deferential. Similarly, we have refrained from intervening in government employer decisions that are based on speech that is of entirely private concern. Doubtless some such speech is sometimes nondisruptive; doubtless it is sometimes of value to the speakers and the listeners. But we have declined to question government employers' decisions on such matters.

This does not, of course, show that the First Amendment should play no role in government employment decisions. Government employees are often in the best position to know what ails the agencies for which they work; public debate may gain much from their informed opinions. And a government employee, like any citizen, may have a strong, legitimate interest in speaking out on public matters. In many such situations the government may have to make a substantial showing that the speech is, in fact, likely to be disruptive before it may be punished. Moreover, the government may certainly choose to give additional protections to its employees beyond what is mandated by the First Amendment, out of respect for the values underlying the First Amendment, values central to our social order as well as our legal system.

But the above examples do show that constitutional review of government employment decisions must rest on different principles than review of speech restraints imposed by the government as sovereign. The restrictions discussed above are allowed not just because the speech interferes with the government's operation. Speech by private people can do the same, but this does not allow the government to suppress it.

Rather, the extra power the government has in this area comes from the nature of the government's mission as employer. Government agencies are charged by law with doing particular tasks. Agencies hire employees to help do those tasks as effectively and efficiently as possible. When someone who is paid a salary so that she will contribute to an agency's effective operation begins to do or say things that detract from the agency's effective operation, the government employer must have some power to restrain her. The reason the governor may, in the example given above, fire the deputy is not that this dismissal would somehow be narrowly tailored to a compelling government interest. It is that the governor and the governor's staff have a job to do, and the governor justifiably feels that a quieter subordinate would allow them to do this job more effectively.

The key to First Amendment analysis of government employment decisions, then, is this: The government's interest in achieving its goals as effectively and efficiently as possible is elevated from a relatively subordinate interest when it acts as sovereign to a significant one when it acts as employer. The government cannot restrict the speech of the public at large just in the name of efficiency. But where the government is employing someone for the very purpose of effectively achieving its goals, such restrictions may well be appropriate.

The Court of Appeals' decision, we believe, gives insufficient weight to the government's interest in efficient employment decisionmaking. In other First

Amendment contexts the need to safeguard possibly protected speech may indeed outweigh the government's efficiency interests. But where the government is acting as employer, its efficiency concerns should, as we discussed above, be assigned a greater value.

The problem with the Court of Appeals' approach is that it would force the government employer to come to its factual conclusions through procedures that substantially mirror the evidentiary rules used in court. But employers, public and private, often do rely on hearsay, on past similar conduct, on their personal knowledge of people's credibility, and on other factors that the judicial process ignores. Such reliance may sometimes be the most effective way for the employer to avoid future recurrences of improper and disruptive conduct. What works best in a judicial proceeding may not be appropriate in the employment context. If one employee accuses another of misconduct, it is reasonable for a government manager to credit the allegation more if it is consistent with what the manager knows of the character of the accused. Likewise, a manager may legitimately want to discipline an employee based on complaints by patrons that the employee has been rude, even though these complaints are hearsay.

It is true that these practices involve some risk of erroneously punishing protected speech. The government may certainly choose to adopt other practices, by law or by contract. But we do not believe that the First Amendment requires it to do so. Government employers should be allowed to use personnel procedures that differ from the evidentiary rules used by courts, without fear that these differences will lead to liability.

On the other hand, we do not believe that the court must apply the *Connick* test only to the facts as the employer thought them to be, without considering the reasonableness of the employer's conclusions. Even in situations where courts have recognized the special expertise and special needs of certain decisionmakers, the deference to their conclusions has never been complete. It is necessary that the decisionmaker reach its conclusion about what was said in good faith, rather than as a pretext; but it does not follow that good faith is sufficient. Justice Scalia is right in saying that we have often held various laws to require only an inquiry into the decisionmaker's intent, but this has not been our view of the First Amendment.

We think employer decisionmaking will not be unduly burdened by having courts look to the facts as the employer reasonably found them to be. It may be unreasonable, for example, for the employer to come to a conclusion based on no evidence at all. Likewise, it may be unreasonable for an employer to act based on extremely weak evidence when strong evidence is clearly available.[6]

Of course, there will often be situations in which reasonable employers would disagree about who is to be believed, or how much investigation needs to be done, or how much evidence is needed to come to a particular conclusion. In

---

6. NOTE: What the Court does not say, however, is that this was exactly the situation in the case before it. There were independent and highly credible witnesses who could have testified as to the nature of the disputed conversations, but they were not asked for their information by the supervisor.

those situations, many different courses of action will necessarily be reasonable. Only procedures outside the range of what a reasonable manager would use may be condemned as unreasonable.

III. Applying the foregoing to this case, it is clear that if petitioners really did believe Perkins-Graham's and Ballew's story, and fired Churchill because of it, they must win. Their belief, based on the investigation they conducted, would have been entirely reasonable. After getting the initial report from Ballew, who overheard the conversation, Waters and Davis approached and interviewed Perkins-Graham, and then interviewed Ballew again for confirmation. In response to Churchill's grievance, Hopper met directly with Churchill to hear her side of the story, and instructed Magin to interview Ballew one more time. Management can spend only so much of their time on any one employment decision. By the end of the termination process, Hopper, who made the final decision, had the word of two trusted employees, the endorsement of those employees' reliability by three hospital managers, and the benefit of a face-to-face meeting with the employee he fired. With that in hand, a reasonable manager could have concluded that no further time needed to be taken.

And under the *Connick* test, Churchill's speech as reported by Perkins-Graham and Ballew was unprotected. Even if Churchill's criticism of cross-training reported by Perkins-Graham and Ballew was speech on a matter of public concern the potential disruptiveness of the speech as reported was enough to outweigh whatever First Amendment value it might have had. According to Ballew, Churchill's speech may have substantially dampened Perkins-Graham's interest in working in obstetrics. As a matter of law, this potential disruptiveness was enough to outweigh whatever First Amendment value the speech might have had.

This is so even if, as Churchill suggests, Davis and Waters were "deliberately indifferent," to the possibility that much of the rest of the conversation was solely about cross-training. So long as Davis and Waters discharged Churchill only for the part of the speech that was either not on a matter of public concern, or on a matter of public concern but disruptive, it is irrelevant whether the rest of the speech was, unbeknownst to them, both on a matter of public concern and nondisruptive. An employee who makes an unprotected statement is not immunized from discipline by the fact that this statement is surrounded by protected statements.

Nonetheless, we agree with the Court of Appeals that the District Court erred in granting summary judgment in petitioners' favor. Though Davis and Waters would have been justified in firing Churchill for the statements outlined above, there remains the question whether Churchill was actually fired because of those statements, or because of something else.

Churchill has produced enough evidence to create a material issue of disputed fact about petitioners' actual motivation. A reasonable factfinder might therefore, on this record, conclude that petitioners actually fired Churchill not because of the disruptive things she said to Perkins-Graham, but because of nondisruptive statements about cross-training that they thought she may have made in the same conversation, or because of other statements she may have made earlier. If this is so, then the court will have to determine whether those statements were protected speech, a different matter than the one before us now.

JUSTICE SOUTER wrote a concurring opinion.

I join the plurality opinion stating that, under the Free Speech Clause, a public employer who reasonably believes a third-party report that an employee engaged in constitutionally unprotected speech may punish the employee in reliance on that report, even if it turns out that the employee's actual remarks were constitutionally protected. I add these words to emphasize that, in order to avoid liability, the public employer must not only reasonably investigate the third-party report, but must also actually believe it. Under the plurality's opinion, an objectively reasonable investigation that fails to convince the employer that the employee actually engaged in disruptive or otherwise unprotected speech does not inoculate the employer against constitutional liability. A public employer violates the Free Speech Clause, that is, by invoking a third-party report to penalize an employee when the employer, despite the report and the reasonable investigation into it, believes or genuinely suspects that the employee's speech was protected in its entirety or in that part on which the employer purports to rely in taking disciplinary action; or if the employer invokes the third-party report merely as a pretext to shield disciplinary action taken because of protected speech the employer believes or genuinely suspects that the employee uttered at another time.

Accordingly, even though petitioners conducted an objectively reasonable investigation into Ballew's report about respondent Churchill's conversation with Perkins-Graham, I believe that petitioners' dismissal of Churchill would have violated the Free Speech Clause if after the investigation they doubted the accuracy of the report and fired Churchill for speech, or for a portion of her speech, that they genuinely suspected was nondisruptive (assuming that the speech was actually on a matter of public concern).

JUSTICE SCALIA wrote a concurring opinion joined by JUSTICES KENNEDY and THOMAS.

The central issue in this case is whether we shall adhere to our previously stated rule that a public employer's disciplining of an employee violates the Speech and Press Clause of the First Amendment only if it is in retaliation for the employee's speech on a matter of public concern. Justice O'Connor would add to this prohibition a requirement that the employer conduct an investigation before taking disciplinary action in certain circumstances. This recognition of a broad new First Amendment procedural right is in my view unprecedented, superfluous to the decision in the present case, unnecessary for protection of public-employee speech on matters of public concern, and unpredictable in its application and consequences.

JUSTICE STEVENS wrote a dissent joined by JUSTICE BLACKMUN.

This is a free country. Every American has the right to express an opinion on issues of public significance. In the private sector, of course, the exercise of that right may entail unpleasant consequences. Absent some contractual or statutory provision limiting its prerogatives, a private-sector employer may discipline or fire employees for speaking their minds. The First Amendment, however, demands that the government respect its employees' freedom to express their opinions on issues of public importance. As long as that expression is not unduly disruptive, it simply may not provide the basis for discipline or termination. The critical issues in a case of this kind are (1) whether the speech is protected, and (2) whether it was the basis for the sanction imposed on the employee.

Applying these standards to the case before us is quite straightforward. Everyone agrees that respondent Cheryl Churchill was fired because of what she said in a conversation with co-workers during a dinner break. Given the posture in which this case comes to us, we must assume that Churchill's statements were fully protected by the First Amendment. Nevertheless, the plurality concludes that a dismissal for speech is valid as a matter of law as long as the public employer reasonably believed that the employee's speech was unprotected. This conclusion is erroneous because it provides less protection for a fundamental constitutional right than the law ordinarily provides for less exalted rights, including contractual and statutory rights applicable in the private sector.

Government agencies are often the site of sharp differences over a wide range of important public issues. In offices where the First Amendment commands respect for candid deliberation and individual opinion, such disagreements are both inevitable and desirable. When those who work together disagree, reports of speech are often skewed, and supervisors are apt to misconstrue even accurate reports. The plurality, observing that managers "can spend only so much of their time on any one employment decision," adopts a rule that invites discipline, rather than further discussion, when such disputes arise. That rule is unwise, for deliberation within the government, like deliberation about it, is an essential part of our "profound national commitment" to the freedom of speech. A proper regard for that principle requires that, before firing a public employee for her speech, management get its facts straight.

*****

FOURTH AMENDMENT
SEARCHES AND SEIZURES

Another of the areas in which there has been a move toward a greater recognition of the claims of employers has been in the field of searches and seizures. However, in this field, as in the areas of due process and freedom of expression, the use of a balancing test has meant a tendency to weigh decisions in favor of supervisors, but a nagging lack of predictability from situation to situation. The starting point for understanding these issues is the ruling of the Court in *O'Connor v. Ortega*.

O'Connor v. Ortega, 480 U.S. 709 (1987).

INTRODUCTION: This case began with an investigation of a psychiatrist at Napa State Hospital. Dr. Magno Ortega had been with the hospital for some

17 years and was director of the residency training program. An investigation was launched even though there were no specific charges lodged against Ortega. He agreed to take a vacation during the investigation, not a paid leave pending the action. However, during that vacation he was told that he was being placed on leave and forbidden to return to the hospital until the investigation had been completed. An investigative team was formed from hospital personnel. Without a warrant they searched his office and seized items from his desk and files, including a variety of personal materials including a Valentine's Day card, photographs, and a book of poetry. There was no effort by those involved to make distinctions between his personal property and state materials. One of the people who searched the office indicated that "trying to sort State from non-State, it was too much to do, so I gave it up and boxed it up."

Neither were these searches undertaken with a warrant, though there was more than sufficient time to obtain one, but there was never any clear foundation put forward to the search and seizure at the time. The state changed its story during the course of litigation, claiming at one point that it was done "pursuant to a Hospital policy of conducting a routine inventory of state property in the office of a terminated employee." Of course, Ortega had not been terminated at the time and indeed no charges had even been filed against him. No inventory was done of the materials searched or seized. Later the state admitted that there was no policy regarding searches of other employee offices on leave or otherwise. At another point, officials suggested that the search was done to secure a computer, but those doing the search indicated that the computer was not the purpose or target of their search. All of this tended to support Ortega's claim that the search was simply an effort by superiors to try to find some way to get him. Ultimately, superiors indicated that they were investigating possible abuses by Ortega, including sexual harassment and improper disciplining of residents.

Ortega brought suit, claiming *inter alia* that the search violated his Fourth Amendment rights. The district court upheld the search on summary judgment and the appellate court affirmed in part and reversed in part.

✳✳✳✳✳

JUSTICE O'CONNOR wrote the opinion for the Court.

This suit under 42 U. S. C. §1983 presents two issues concerning the Fourth Amendment rights of public employees. First, we must determine whether the respondent, a public employee, had a reasonable expectation of privacy in his office, desk, and file cabinets at his place of work. Second, we must address the appropriate Fourth Amendment standard for a search conducted by a public employer in areas in which a public employee is found to have a reasonable expectation of privacy.

II. The strictures of the Fourth Amendment, applied to the States through the Fourteenth Amendment, have been applied to the conduct of governmental officials in various civil activities. *New Jersey v. T. L. O.,* 469 U.S. 325, 334–335 (1985).[7] Searches and seizures by government employers or supervisors of the private property of their employees, therefore, are subject to the restraints of the Fourth Amendment.

The Fourth Amendment protects the "right of the people to be secure in their persons, houses, papers, and effects, against unreasonable searches and seizures. . . ." Our cases establish that Dr. Ortega's Fourth Amendment rights are implicated only if the conduct of the Hospital officials at issue in this case infringed "an expectation of privacy that society is prepared to consider reasonable." We have no talisman that determines in all cases those privacy expectations that society is prepared to accept as reasonable. Instead, "the Court has given weight to such factors as the intention of the Framers of the Fourth Amendment, the uses to which the individual has put a location, and our societal understanding that certain areas deserve the most scrupulous protection from government invasion."

Because the reasonableness of an expectation of privacy, as well as the appropriate standard for a search, is understood to differ according to context, it is essential first to delineate the boundaries of the workplace context. The workplace includes those areas and items that are related to work and are generally within the employer's control. At a hospital, for example, the hallways, cafeteria, offices, desks, and file cabinets, among other areas, are all part of the workplace. These areas remain part of the workplace context even if the employee has placed personal items in them, such as a photograph placed in a desk or a letter posted on an employee bulletin board.

Not everything that passes through the confines of the business address can be considered part of the workplace context, however. An employee may bring closed luggage to the office prior to leaving on a trip, or a handbag or briefcase each workday. While whatever expectation of privacy the employee has in the existence and the outward appearance of the luggage is affected by its presence in the workplace, the employee's expectation of privacy in the contents of the luggage is not affected in the same way. The appropriate standard for a workplace search does not necessarily apply to a piece of closed personal luggage, a handbag, or a briefcase that happens to be within the employer's business address.

Within the workplace context, this Court has recognized that employees may have a reasonable expectation of privacy against intrusions by police. As with the expectation of privacy in one's home, such an expectation in one's place of work is "based upon societal expectations that have deep roots in the history of the Amendment."

Given the societal expectations of privacy in one's place of work expressed in [our earlier rulings], we reject the contention that public employees can never have a reasonable expectation of privacy in their place of work. Individuals do not

---

7. NOTE: Whether it was intended or not, the Court sent quite a message to public
    employees when it employed this case involving searches of school children as a basis for
    the discussion of the rights of adult public employees.

lose Fourth Amendment rights merely because they work for the government instead of a private employer. The operational realities of the workplace, however, may make some employees' expectations of privacy unreasonable when an intrusion is by a supervisor rather than a law enforcement official. Public employees' expectations of privacy in their offices, desks, and file cabinets, like similar expectations of employees in the private sector, may be reduced by virtue of actual office practices and procedures, or by legitimate regulation. An office is seldom a private enclave free from entry by supervisors, other employees, and business and personal invitees. Instead, in many cases offices are continually entered by fellow employees and other visitors during the workday for conferences, consultations, and other work-related visits. Simply put, it is the nature of government offices that others may have frequent access to an individual's office. We agree that "[constitutional] protection against unreasonable searches by the government does not disappear merely because the government has the right to make reasonable intrusions in its capacity as employer," but some government offices may be so open to fellow employees or the public that no expectation of privacy is reasonable. Given the great variety of work environments in the public sector, the question whether an employee has a reasonable expectation of privacy must be addressed on a case-by-case basis.

The Court of Appeals concluded that Dr. Ortega had a reasonable expectation of privacy in his office, and five Members of this Court agree with that determination. Because the record does not reveal the extent to which Hospital officials may have had work-related reasons to enter Dr. Ortega's office, we think the Court of Appeals should have remanded the matter to the District Court for its further determination. But regardless of any legitimate right of access the Hospital staff may have had to the office as such, we recognize that the undisputed evidence suggests that Dr. Ortega had a reasonable expectation of privacy in his desk and file cabinets. The undisputed evidence discloses that Dr. Ortega did not share his desk or file cabinets with any other employees. Dr. Ortega had occupied the office for 17 years and he kept materials in his office, which included personal correspondence, medical files, correspondence from private patients unconnected to the Hospital, personal financial records, teaching aids and notes, and personal gifts and mementos. The files on physicians in residency training were kept outside Dr. Ortega's office. Indeed, the only items found by the investigators were apparently personal items because, with the exception of the items seized for use in the administrative hearings, all the papers and effects found in the office were simply placed in boxes and made available to Dr. Ortega. Finally, we note that there was no evidence that the Hospital had established any reasonable regulation or policy discouraging employees such as Dr. Ortega from storing personal papers and effects in their desks or file cabinets, although the absence of such a policy does not create an expectation of privacy where it would not otherwise exist. On the basis of this undisputed evidence, we accept the conclusion of the Court of Appeals that Dr. Ortega had a reasonable expectation of privacy at least in his desk and file cabinets.

III. Having determined that Dr. Ortega had a reasonable expectation of privacy in his office, the Court of Appeals simply concluded without discussion that the "search . . . was not a reasonable search under the fourth amendment." Thus, we must determine the appropriate standard of reasonableness applicable to the search. A determination of the standard of reasonableness applicable to a particular class of searches requires "[balancing] the nature and quality of the intrusion on the individual's Fourth Amendment interests against the importance of the governmental interests alleged to justify the intrusion." In the case of searches conducted by a public employer, we must balance the invasion of the employees' legitimate expectations of privacy against the government's need for supervision, control, and the efficient operation of the workplace.

In our view, requiring an employer to obtain a warrant whenever the employer wished to enter an employee's office, desk, or file cabinets for a work-related purpose would seriously disrupt the routine conduct of business and would be unduly burdensome. Imposing unwieldy warrant procedures in such cases upon supervisors, who would otherwise have no reason to be familiar with such procedures, is simply unreasonable. Under these circumstances, the imposition of a warrant requirement would conflict with "the common-sense realization that government offices could not function if every employment decision became a constitutional matter." *Connick v. Myers,* 461 U.S. 138, 143 (1983).

Whether probable cause is an inappropriate standard for public employer searches of their employees' offices presents a more difficult issue. Thus, "[where] a careful balancing of governmental and private interests suggests that the public interest is best served by a Fourth Amendment standard of reasonableness that stops short of probable cause, we have not hesitated to adopt such a standard." We have concluded, for example, that the appropriate standard for administrative searches is not probable cause in its traditional meaning. Instead, an administrative warrant can be obtained if there is a showing that reasonable legislative or administrative standards for conducting an inspection are satisfied.

The governmental interest justifying work-related intrusions by public employers is the efficient and proper operation of the workplace. [T]he work of these agencies would suffer if employers were required to have probable cause before they entered an employee's desk for the purpose of finding a file or piece of office correspondence. Indeed, it is difficult to give the concept of probable cause, rooted as it is in the criminal investigatory context, much meaning when the purpose of a search is to retrieve a file for work-related reasons. To ensure the efficient and proper operation of the agency, therefore, public employers must be given wide latitude to enter employee offices for work-related, noninvestigatory reasons.

We come to a similar conclusion for searches conducted pursuant to an investigation of work-related employee misconduct. In contrast to law enforcement officials public employers are not enforcers of the criminal law; instead, public employers have a direct and overriding interest in ensuring that the work of the agency is conducted in a proper and efficient manner. In our view, therefore, a probable cause requirement for searches of the type at issue here would impose intolerable burdens on public employers. Additionally, while law enforcement officials are expected to "[school] themselves in the niceties of probable cause," no such expectation is generally applicable to public employers, at least when the search is not used to gather evidence of a criminal offense.

Balanced against the substantial government interests in the efficient and proper operation of the workplace are the privacy interests of government employees in their place of work which, while not insubstantial, are far less than those found at home or in some other contexts.

In sum, we conclude that the "special needs, beyond the normal need for law enforcement make the . . . probable-cause requirement impracticable," for legitimate work-related, noninvestigatory intrusions as well as investigations of work-related misconduct. A standard of reasonableness will neither unduly burden the efforts of government employers to ensure the efficient and proper operation of the workplace, nor authorize arbitrary intrusions upon the privacy of public employees. We hold, therefore, that public employer intrusions on the constitutionally protected privacy interests of government employees for noninvestigatory, work-related purposes, as well as for investigations of work-related misconduct, should be judged by the standard of reasonableness under all the circumstances. Under this reasonableness standard, both the inception and the scope of the intrusion must be reasonable.

Ordinarily, a search of an employee's office by a supervisor will be "justified at its inception" when there are reasonable grounds for suspecting that the search will turn up evidence that the employee is guilty of work-related misconduct, or that the search is necessary for a noninvestigatory work-related purpose such as to retrieve a needed file. Because petitioners had an "individualized suspicion" of misconduct by Dr. Ortega, we need not decide whether individualized suspicion is an essential element of the standard of reasonableness that we adopt today. The search will be permissible in its scope when "the measures adopted are reasonably related to the objectives of the search and not excessively intrusive in light of . . . the nature of the [misconduct]."

IV. In the procedural posture of this case, we do not attempt to determine whether the search of Dr. Ortega's office and the seizure of his personal belongings satisfy the standard of reasonableness we have articulated in this case. No evidentiary hearing was held in this case because the District Court acted on cross-motions for summary judgment, and granted petitioners summary judgment. On remand, therefore, the District Court must determine the justification for the search and seizure, and evaluate the reasonableness of both the inception of the search and its scope.

JUSTICE SCALIA wrote a concurring opinion.

Although I share the judgment that this case must be reversed and remanded, I disagree with the reason for the reversal given by the plurality opinion, and with the standard it prescribes for the Fourth Amendment inquiry.

The plurality opinion instructs the lower courts that existence of Fourth Amendment protection for a public employee's business office is to be assessed "on a case-by-case basis," in light of whether the office is "so open to fellow employees or the public that no expectation of privacy is reasonable." No clue is provided as to how open "so open" must be; much less is it suggested how police officers are to gather the facts necessary for this refined inquiry. Even if I did not disagree with the plurality as to what result the proper legal standard should produce in the case before us, I would object to the formulation of a standard so devoid of content that it produces rather than eliminates uncertainty in this field.

Whatever the plurality's standard means, however, it must be wrong if it leads to the conclusion on the present facts that if Hospital officials had extensive "work-related reasons to enter Dr. Ortega's office" no Fourth Amendment protection existed. Constitutional protection against unreasonable searches by the government does not disappear merely because the government has the right to make reasonable intrusions in its capacity as employer.

I cannot agree, moreover, with the plurality's view that the reasonableness of the expectation of privacy changes "when an intrusion is by a supervisor rather than a law enforcement official." The identity of the searcher is relevant not to whether Fourth Amendment protections apply, but only to whether the search of a protected area is reasonable.

The case turns, therefore, on whether the Fourth Amendment was violated—i.e., whether the governmental intrusion was reasonable. It is here that the government's status as employer, and the employment-related character of the search, become relevant. While as a general rule warrantless searches are per se unreasonable, we have recognized exceptions when "special needs, beyond the normal need for law enforcement, make the warrant and probable-cause requirement impracticable. . . ." Such "special needs" are present in the context of government employment. I would hold that government searches to retrieve work-related materials or to investigate violations of workplace rules—searches of the sort that are regarded as reasonable and normal in the private-employer context—do not violate the Fourth Amendment. Because the conflicting and incomplete evidence in the present case could not conceivably support summary judgment that the search did not have such a validating purpose, I agree with the plurality that the decision must be reversed and remanded.

JUSTICE BLACKMUN wrote a dissent joined by JUSTICES BRENNAN, MARSHALL, and STEVENS.

The facts of this case are simple and straightforward. Dr. Ortega had an expectation of privacy in his office, desk, and file cabinets. Because there was no "special need," I would evaluate the search by applying this traditional standard. Under that standard, this search clearly violated Dr. Ortega's Fourth Amendment rights.

[I]n this case the plurality acknowledges that Dr. Ortega had an expectation of privacy in his desk and file cabinets and that, as the plurality concedes, the majority of this Court holds that he had a similar expectation in his office. However, I am disturbed by the plurality's suggestion that routine entries by visitors might completely remove this expectation.

[A]s the plurality appears to recognize the precise extent of an employee's expectation of privacy often turns on the nature of the search. Thus, although an employee might well have no reasonable expectation of privacy with respect to an occasional visit by a fellow employee, he would have such an expectation as to an after hours search of his locked office by an investigative team seeking materials to be used against him at a termination proceeding.

Finally and most importantly, the reality of work in modern time, whether done by public or private employees, reveals why a public employee's expectation of privacy in the workplace should be carefully safeguarded and not lightly set aside. It is, unfortunately, all too true that the workplace has become another home for most working Americans. As a result, the tidy distinctions between the workplace and professional affairs, on the one hand, and personal possessions and private activities, on the other, do not exist in reality. Not all of an employee's private possessions will stay in his or her briefcase or handbag. Thus, the plurality's remark that the "employee may avoid exposing personal belongings at work by simply leaving them at home," reveals on the part of the Members of the plurality a certain insensitivity to the "operational realities of the workplace."

Given the facts of this case, no "special need" exists here to justify dispensing with the warrant and probable-cause requirements. As observed above, the facts suggest that this was an investigatory search undertaken to obtain evidence of charges of mismanagement at a time when Dr. Ortega was on administrative leave and not permitted to enter the Hospital's grounds. There was no special practical need that might have justified dispensing with the warrant and probable-cause requirements. Without sacrificing their ultimate goal of maintaining an effective institution devoted to training and healing, to which the disciplining of Hospital employees contributed, petitioners could have taken any evidence of Dr. Ortega's alleged improprieties to a magistrate in order to obtain a warrant.

Furthermore, this seems to be exactly the kind of situation where a neutral magistrate's involvement would have been helpful in curtailing the infringement upon Dr. Ortega's privacy. Petitioners would have been forced to articulate their exact reasons for the search and to specify the items in Dr. Ortega's office they sought, which would have prevented the general rummaging through the doctor's office, desk, and file cabinets. Thus, because no "special need" in this case demanded that the traditional warrant and probable-cause requirements be dispensed with, petitioners' failure to conduct the search in accordance with the traditional standard of reasonableness should end the analysis, and the judgment of the Court of Appeals should be affirmed.

Even were I to accept the proposition that this case presents a situation of "special need" calling for an exception to the warrant and probable-cause standard, I believe that the plurality's balancing of the public employer's and the employee's respective interests to arrive at a different standard is seriously flawed. A careful balancing with respect to the warrant requirement is absent from the plurality's opinion, an absence that is inevitable in light of the gulf between the plurality's analysis and any concrete factual setting. It is certainly correct that a public employer cannot be expected to obtain a warrant for every routine entry into an employee's workplace. This situation, however, should not justify dispensing with a warrant in all searches by the employer.

✻✻✻✻✻

That was not the end of the story. The worst predictions of both sets of critics of the Court's *Ortega* ruling proved to be accurate. Following on the dissenters' predictions, the *Ortega* ruling was cited in a variety of important opinions in the lower courts. It was also significant to the Court's 1989 ruling in the drug testing case, *National Treasury Employees v. Von Raab*, discussed next. For many public employees, the *Ortega* case meant a serious loss of protections previously available to them.

On the other hand, Justice Scalia's fear that the *Ortega* opinion did not provide enough certainty for employers was borne out when the case was sent back to the district court for further action. The Supreme Court plurality opinion remanded the *Ortega* case because there had been no proceeding to make findings about the precise justification for the searches and seizures and whether they were reasonable in nature and scope. That was in 1987. As *Public Law and Public Administration, Third Edition* explained, the case was not ultimately resolved until 1998. By that point, a jury had rendered a verdict against the two hospital supervisors in the amount of $376,000 in compensatory damages and an additional $25,000 against O'Connor and $35,000 against Friday in punitive damages and that ruling was upheld by the circuit court of appeals. The Supreme Court plurality's decision ultimately meant a reduction in protections for both sides, with juries now able to determine "reasonableness" for themselves on a case-by-case basis, assuming that an employee can mount a challenge and sustain it for years.

National Treasury Employees Union v. Von Raab, 489 U.S. 656 (1989).

INTRODUCTION: This case came to the Court as one of two presenting issues of employee drug testing, both decided on the same day. The first case, *Skinner v. Railway Labor Executives' Assn.*, which the Court upheld, concerned a program administered for train crews that had been in an accident. The second case was very different on its facts and the nature of the drug screening program involved.

In the fall of 1986, President Reagan issued the Drug-Free Workplace Executive Order 12564. However, ten months earlier the Commissioner of Customs had launched an anti-drug effort, establishing a task force to consider a drug-testing program for Customs employees. A program was put into place in May 1986 with the screening process to be conducted by an outside contractor. It is perhaps ironic that the primary focus of the testing was on those employees identified for promotion to sensitive positions. The person to be subjected to the test was to be given five days notice before the test and persons already in the positions covered by the testing were not screened. The union brought suit to challenge the testing program.

*****

JUSTICE KENNEDY wrote the opinion for the Court.

We granted certiorari to decide whether it violates the Fourth Amendment for the United States Customs Service to require a urinalysis test from employees who seek transfer or promotion to certain positions.

In *Skinner v. Railway Labor Executives' Assn.*, decided today, we held that federal regulations requiring employees of private railroads to produce urine samples for chemical testing implicate the Fourth Amendment, as those tests invade reasonable expectations of privacy. Our earlier cases have settled that the Fourth Amendment protects individuals from unreasonable searches conducted by the Government, even when the Government acts as an employer, *O'Connor v. Ortega,* and, in view of our holding in Railway Labor Executives that urine tests are searches, it follows that the Customs Service's drug-testing program must meet the reasonableness requirement of the Fourth Amendment.

While we have often emphasized that a search must be supported, as a general matter, by a warrant issued upon probable cause, our decision in *Railway Labor Executives* reaffirms the longstanding principle that neither a warrant nor probable cause, nor, indeed, any measure of individualized suspicion, is an indispensable component of reasonableness in every circumstance. [O]ur cases establish that where a Fourth Amendment intrusion serves special governmental needs, beyond the normal need for law enforcement, it is necessary to balance the individual's privacy expectations against the Government's interests to determine whether it is impractical to require a warrant or some level of individualized suspicion in the particular context.

The purposes of the program are to deter drug use among those eligible for promotion to sensitive positions within the Service and to prevent the promotion of drug users to those positions. These substantial interests, no less than the Government's concern for safe rail transportation at issue in *Railway Labor Executives,* present a special need that may justify departure from the ordinary warrant and probable-cause requirements.

Petitioners do not contend that a warrant is required by the balance of privacy and governmental interests in this context, nor could any such contention withstand scrutiny. We have recognized before that requiring the Government to procure a warrant for every work-related intrusion "would conflict with 'the common-sense realization that government offices could not function if every employment decision became a constitutional matter.'" *O'Connor v. Ortega,* quoting *Connick v. Myers.*

Furthermore, a warrant would provide little or nothing in the way of additional protection of personal privacy. Under the Customs program, every employee who seeks a transfer to a covered position knows that he must take a drug test, and is likewise aware of the procedures the Service must follow in administering the test. A covered employee is simply not subject "to the discretion of the official in the field." The process becomes automatic when the employee elects to apply for, and thereafter pursue, a covered position. Because the Service does not make a discretionary determination to search based on a judgment that certain conditions are present, there are simply "no special facts for a neutral magistrate to evaluate."

Even where it is reasonable to dispense with the warrant requirement in the particular circumstances, a search ordinarily must be based on probable cause. Our cases teach, however, that the probable-cause standard "is peculiarly related to criminal investigations." In particular, the traditional probable-cause standard may be unhelpful in analyzing the reasonableness of routine administrative functions, especially where the Government seeks to prevent the development of hazardous conditions or to detect violations that rarely generate articulable grounds for searching any particular place or person. Our precedents have settled that, in certain limited circumstances, the Government's need to discover such latent or hidden conditions, or to prevent their development, is sufficiently compelling to justify the intrusion on privacy entailed by conducting such searches without any measure of individualized suspicion. We think the Government's need to conduct the suspicionless searches required by the Customs program outweighs the privacy interests of employees engaged directly in drug interdiction, and of those who otherwise are required to carry firearms.

The Customs Service is our Nation's first line of defense against one of the greatest problems affecting the health and welfare of our population. Many of the Service's employees are often exposed to this criminal element and to the controlled substances it seeks to smuggle into the country. The physical safety of these employees may be threatened, and many may be tempted not only by bribes from the traffickers with whom they deal, but also by their own access to vast sources of valuable contraband seized and controlled by the Service.

It is readily apparent that the Government has a compelling interest in ensuring that front-line interdiction personnel are physically fit, and have unimpeachable integrity and judgment.

The public interest likewise demands effective measures to prevent the promotion of drug users to positions that require the incumbent to carry a firearm, even if the incumbent is not engaged directly in the interdiction of drugs. We agree with the Government that the public should not bear the risk that employees who may suffer from impaired perception and judgment will be promoted to positions where they may need to employ deadly force.

Against these valid public interests we must weigh the interference with individual liberty that results from requiring these classes of employees to undergo a urine test. The interference with individual privacy that results from the collection of a urine sample for subsequent chemical analysis could be substantial in some circumstances. We have recognized, however, that the "operational realities of the workplace" may render entirely reasonable certain work-related intrusions by supervisors and co-workers that might be viewed as unreasonable in other contexts. See *O'Connor v. Ortega.*

We think Customs employees who are directly involved in the interdiction of illegal drugs or who are required to carry firearms in the line of duty likewise have a diminished expectation of privacy in respect to the intrusions occasioned by a urine test. Unlike most private citizens or government employees in general, employees involved in drug interdiction reasonably should expect effective inquiry into their fitness and probity. Much the same is true of employees who are required to carry firearms.

Without disparaging the importance of the governmental interests that support the suspicionless searches of these employees, petitioners nevertheless contend that the Service's drug-testing program is unreasonable in two particulars. First, petitioners argue that the program is unjustified because it is not based on a belief that testing will reveal any drug use by covered employees. In pressing this argument, petitioners point out that the Service's testing scheme was not implemented in response to any perceived drug problem among Customs employees, and that the program actually has not led to the discovery of a significant number of drug users. Second, petitioners contend that the Service's scheme is not a "sufficiently productive mechanism to justify [its] intrusion upon Fourth Amendment interests," because illegal drug users can avoid detection with ease by temporary abstinence or by surreptitious adulteration of their urine specimens. These contentions are unpersuasive.

The mere circumstance that all but a few of the employees tested are entirely innocent of wrongdoing does not impugn the program's validity. Where, as here, the possible harm against which the Government seeks to guard is substantial, the need to prevent its occurrence furnishes an ample justification for reasonable searches calculated to advance the Government's goal.

When the Government's interest lies in deterring highly hazardous conduct, a low incidence of such conduct, far from impugning the validity of the scheme for implementing this interest, is more logically viewed as a hallmark of success.

We think petitioners' second argument—that the Service's testing program is ineffective because employees may attempt to deceive the test by a brief abstention before the test date, or by adulterating their urine specimens—overstates the case. [C]ontrary to petitioners' suggestion, no employee reasonably can expect to deceive the test by the simple expedient of abstaining after the test date is assigned. Nor can he expect attempts at adulteration to succeed, in view of the precautions taken by the sample collector to ensure the integrity of the sample.

In sum, we believe the Government has demonstrated that its compelling interests in safeguarding our borders and the public safety outweigh the privacy expectations of employees who seek to be promoted to positions that directly involve the interdiction of illegal drugs or that require the incumbent to carry a firearm. We hold that the testing of these employees is reasonable under the Fourth Amendment.

We are unable, on the present record, to assess the reasonableness of the Government's testing program insofar as it covers employees who are required "to handle classified material." We readily agree that the Government has a compelling interest in protecting truly sensitive information from those who, "might compromise [such] information." It is not clear, however, whether the category defined by the Service's testing directive encompasses only those Customs employees likely to gain access to sensitive information. Employees who are tested under the Service's scheme include those holding such diverse positions as "Accountant," "Accounting Technician," "Animal Caretaker," "Attorney (All)," "Baggage Clerk," "Co-op Student (All)," "Electric Equipment Repairer," "Mail Clerk/Assistant," and "Messenger."

We hold that the suspicionless testing of employees who apply for promotion to positions directly involving the interdiction of illegal drugs, or to positions that require the incumbent to carry a firearm, is reasonable. We do not decide whether testing those who apply for promotion to positions where they would handle "classified" information is reasonable because we find the record inadequate for this purpose.

The judgment of the Court of Appeals for the Fifth Circuit is affirmed in part and vacated in part, and the case is remanded for further proceedings consistent with this opinion.

JUSTICE MARSHALL wrote a dissent joined by JUSTICE BRENNAN.

For the reasons stated in my dissenting opinion in *Skinner v. Railway Labor Executives' Assn.*, I also dissent from the Court's decision in this case. Here, as in *Skinner,* the Court's abandonment of the Fourth Amendment's express requirement that searches of the person rest on probable cause is unprincipled and unjustifiable. But even if I believed that balancing analysis was appropriate under the Fourth Amendment, I would still dissent from today's judgment for the reasons stated by Justice Scalia in his dissenting opinion and for the reasons noted by the dissenting judge below relating to the inadequate tailoring of the Customs Service's drug-testing plan.

JUSTICE SCALIA wrote a dissent joined by JUSTICE STEVENS.

The issue in this case is not whether Customs Service employees can constitutionally be denied promotion, or even dismissed, for a single instance of unlawful drug use, at home or at work. They assuredly can. The issue here is what steps can constitutionally be taken to detect such drug use. The Government asserts it can demand that employees perform "an excretory function traditionally shielded by great privacy," while "a monitor of the same sex . . . remains close at hand to listen for the normal sounds," and that the excretion thus produced be turned over to the Government for chemical analysis. The Court agrees that this constitutes a search for purposes of the Fourth Amendment—and I think it obvious that it is a type of search particularly destructive of privacy and offensive to personal dignity.

Until today this Court had upheld a bodily search separate from arrest and without individualized suspicion of wrongdoing only with respect to prison inmates. Today, in *Skinner,* we allow a less intrusive bodily search of railroad employees involved in train accidents. I joined the Court's opinion there because the demonstrated frequency of drug and alcohol use by the targeted class of employees, and the demonstrated connection between such use and grave harm, rendered the search a reasonable means of protecting society. I decline to join the Court's opinion in the present case because neither frequency of use nor connection to harm is demonstrated or even likely. In my view the Customs Service rules are a kind of immolation of privacy and human dignity in symbolic opposition to drug use.

The Court's opinion in the present case will be searched in vain for real evidence of a real problem that will be solved by urine testing of Customs Service employees. The only pertinent points, it seems to me, [in the Court's support for the Service's need for the program] are supported by nothing but speculation, and not very plausible speculation at that. It is not apparent to me that a Customs Service employee who uses drugs is significantly more likely to be bribed by a drug smuggler, any more than a Customs Service employee who wears diamonds is significantly more likely to be bribed by a diamond smuggler—unless perhaps, the addiction to drugs is so severe, and requires so much money to maintain, that it would be detectable even without benefit of a urine test. Nor is it apparent to me that Customs officers who use drugs will be appreciably less "sympathetic" to their drug-interdiction mission, any more than police officers who exceed the speed limit in their private cars are appreciably less sympathetic to their mission of enforcing the traffic laws. Nor, finally, is it apparent to me that urine tests will be even marginally more effective in preventing gun-carrying agents from risking "impaired perception and judgment" than is their current knowledge that, if impaired, they may be shot dead in unequal combat with unimpaired smugglers— unless, again, their addiction is so severe that no urine test is needed for detection.

What is absent in the Government's justifications—notably absent, revealingly absent, and as far as I am concerned dispositively absent—is the recitation of even a single instance in which any of the speculated horribles actually occurred.

Today's decision would be wrong, but at least of more limited effect, if its approval of drug testing were confined to that category of employees assigned specifically to drug interdiction duties. Relatively few public employees fit that description. But in extending approval of drug testing to that category consisting of employees who carry firearms, the Court exposes vast numbers of public employees to this needless indignity. Logically, of course, if those who carry guns can be treated in this fashion, so can all others whose work, if performed under the influence of drugs may endanger others—automobile drivers, operators of other potentially dangerous equipment, construction workers, school crossing guards.

There is irony in the Government's citation, in support of its position, of Justice Brandeis' statement in *Olmstead v. United States,* 277 U.S. 438, 485 (1928) that "for good or for ill, [our Government] teaches the whole people by its example." Brandeis was there dissenting from the Court's admission of evidence obtained through an unlawful Government wiretap. He was not praising the Government's example of vigor and enthusiasm in combating crime, but condemning its example that "the end justifies the means."

✳✳✳✳✳

Interestingly, the Court took a quite different approach when it came to a program designed to screen political candidates standing for election.

Chandler v. Miller, 520 U.S. 305 (1997).

INTRODUCTION: Georgia enacted a statute in 1990 that orders that "each candidate seeking to qualify for nomination or election to a state office shall as a condition of such qualification be required to certify that such candidate has tested negative for illegal drugs." The statute allowed candidates to present a certificate to the Secretary of State providing the results of a drug test taken within the previous 30 days. The candidate was given the choice of having the test done at his or her physician's office or at a laboratory approved by the state.

Walker Chandler was the candidate for Lieutenant Governor on the Libertarian Party ticket. He challenged the testing law and was joined by a number of other candidates.

*****

JUSTICE GINSBURG wrote the opinion for the Court.

Georgia requires candidates for designated state offices to certify that they have taken a drug test and that the test result was negative. We confront in this case the question whether that requirement ranks among the limited circumstances in which suspicionless searches are warranted. Georgia's requirement that candidates for state office pass a drug test, we hold, does not fit within the closely guarded category of constitutionally permissible suspicionless searches.

Georgia's drug-testing requirement, imposed by law and enforced by state officials, effects a search within the meaning of the Fourth and Fourteenth Amendments. Because "these intrusions [are] searches under the Fourth Amendment," we focus on the question: Are the searches reasonable?

To be reasonable under the Fourth Amendment, a search ordinarily must be based on individualized suspicion of wrongdoing. But particularized exceptions to the main rule are sometimes warranted based on "special needs, beyond the normal need for law enforcement." When such "special needs"—concerns other than crime detection—are alleged in justification of a Fourth Amendment intrusion, courts must undertake a context-specific inquiry, examining closely the competing private and public interests advanced by the parties.

Skinner concerned Federal Railroad Administration (FRA) regulations that required blood and urine tests of rail employees involved in train accidents; the regulations also authorized railroads to administer breath and urine tests to employees who violated certain safety rules. The FRA adopted the drug-testing program in response to evidence of drug and alcohol abuse by some railroad employees, the obvious safety hazards posed by such abuse, and the documented link between drug- and alcohol-impaired employees and the incidence of train accidents.

In *Von Raab,* the Court sustained a United States Customs Service program that made drug tests a condition of promotion or transfer to positions directly involving drug interdiction or requiring the employee to carry a firearm. While the Service's regime was not prompted by a demonstrated drug abuse problem, it was developed for an agency with an "almost unique mission," as the "first line of defense" against the smuggling of illicit drugs into the United States.

Finally, in *Vernonia* [*School Dist. 47J v. Acton*, 515 U.S. 646 (1995)], the Court sustained a random drug-testing program for high school students engaged in interscholastic athletic competitions. The program's context was critical, for local governments bear large "responsibilities, under a public school system, as guardian and tutor of children entrusted to its care." Our decision noted that "students within the school environment have a lesser expectation of privacy than members of the population generally."

Respondents urge that the precedents just examined are not the sole guides for assessing the constitutional validity of the Georgia statute. The "special needs" analysis, they contend, must be viewed through a different lens because §21-2-140 implicates Georgia's sovereign power, reserved to it under the Tenth Amendment, to establish qualifications for those who seek state office. We are aware of no precedent suggesting that a State's power to establish qualifications for state offices diminishes the constraints on state action imposed by the Fourth Amendment.

Turning to those guides, we note, first, that the testing method the Georgia statute describes is relatively noninvasive; therefore, if the "special need" showing had been made, the State could not be faulted for excessive intrusion. Because the State has effectively limited the invasiveness of the testing procedure, we concentrate on the core issue: Is the certification requirement warranted by a special need?

Our precedents establish that the proffered special need for drug testing must be substantial—important enough to override the individual's acknowledged privacy interest, sufficiently vital to suppress the Fourth Amendment's normal requirement of individualized suspicion. Georgia has failed to show, in justification of § 21-2-140, a special need of that kind.

Respondents' defense of the statute rests primarily on the incompatibility of unlawful drug use with holding high state office. The statute is justified, respondents contend, because the use of illegal drugs draws into question an official's judgment and integrity; jeopardizes the discharge of public functions, including antidrug law enforcement efforts; and undermines public confidence and trust in elected officials. Notably lacking in respondents' presentation is any indication of a concrete danger demanding departure from the Fourth Amendment's main rule.

What is left, after close review of Georgia's scheme, is the image the State seeks to project. By requiring candidates for public office to submit to drug testing, Georgia displays its commitment to the struggle against drug abuse. The suspicionless tests, according to respondents, signify that candidates, if elected, will be fit to serve their constituents free from the influence of illegal drugs. But Georgia asserts no evidence of a drug problem among the State's elected officials, those officials typically do not perform high-risk, safety-sensitive tasks, and the required certification immediately aids no interdiction effort. The need revealed, in short, is symbolic, not "special," as that term draws meaning from our case law.

However well meant, the candidate drug test Georgia has devised diminishes personal privacy for a symbol's sake. The Fourth Amendment shields society against that state action.

CHIEF JUSTICE REHNQUIST wrote a dissent.

I fear that the novelty of this Georgia law has led the Court to distort Fourth Amendment doctrine in order to strike it down. The Court notes, impliedly turning up its nose, that "Georgia was the first, and apparently remains the only, State to condition candidacy for state office on a drug test." But novelty itself is not a vice. These novel experiments, of course, must comply with the United States Constitution; but their mere novelty should not be a strike against them.

Few would doubt that the use of illegal drugs and abuse of legal drugs is one of the major problems of our society. It would take a bolder person than I to say that such widespread drug usage could never extend to candidates for public office such as Governor of Georgia. The Court says that "nothing in the record hints that the hazards respondents broadly describe are real and not simply hypothetical for Georgia's polity." But surely the State need not wait for a drug addict, or one inclined to use drugs illegally, to run for or actually become Governor before it installs a prophylactic mechanism.

The test under the Fourth Amendment, as these cases have held, is whether the search required by the Georgia statute is "reasonable." Today's opinion speaks of a "closely guarded" class of permissible suspicionless searches which must be justified by a "special need." Under our precedents, if there was a proper governmental purpose other than law enforcement, there was a "special need," and the Fourth Amendment then required the familiar balancing between that interest and the individual's privacy interest.

Under normal Fourth Amendment analysis, the individual's expectation of privacy is an important factor in the equation. But here, the Court perversely relies on the fact that a candidate for office gives up so much privacy—"candidates for public office . . . are subject to relentless scrutiny as a reason for sustaining a Fourth Amendment claim." The Court says, in effect, that the kind of drug test for candidates required by the Georgia law is unnecessary, because the scrutiny to which they are already subjected by reason of their candidacy will enable people to detect any drug use on their part. But the clear teaching of those cases is that the government is not required to settle for that sort of a vague and uncanalized scrutiny; if in fact preventing persons who use illegal drugs from concealing that fact from the public is a legitimate government interest, these cases indicate that the government may require a drug test.

Nothing in the Fourth Amendment or in any other part of the Constitution prevents a State from enacting a statute whose principal vice is that it may seem misguided or even silly to the members of this Court.

*****

DEVELOPING PUBLIC EMPLOYEE ISSUES

Because public employees represent an interesting mix of many of the diverse characteristics of the nation, and given the continuing dynamics of social change, they bring with them novel contemporary issues, many of which find their way to court. The first example is one of the few cases on the question of restrictions on Internet access by public employees.

Urofsky v. Gilmore, 216 F.3d 401 (4th Cir. 2000).

INTRODUCTION: The state of Virginia enacted a statute that prohibited state employees from using state computers to access Internet sites containing "sexually explicit material," a term subsequently defined at length in the legislation. A number of academics working in public universities brought a challenge to the statute on First Amendment grounds, led by a well-known scholar of public law and the U.S. Supreme Court. These were professors who alleged that their professional research required them to access a variety of material that might violate the statute. In one instance, the concern was checking on materials cited by students in their papers on such matters as constitutional rights and liberties. Other faculty members became involved, including some who taught human sexuality courses and another who was a scholar of poetry. The statute did provide for a process to request permission to access materials, but the challengers argued that censoring their research violated both the First Amendment freedom of expression and their academic freedom, which was also protected by the First Amendment.

*****

JUDGE WILKINS wrote the opinion for the court sitting en banc.

The central provision of the Act states: "Except to the extent required in conjunction with a bona fide, agency-approved research project or other agency approved undertaking, no agency employee shall utilize agency-owned or agency-leased computer equipment to access, download, print or store any information infrastructure files or services having sexually explicit content. Such agency approvals shall be given in writing by agency heads, and any such approvals shall be available to the public under the provisions of the Virginia Freedom of Information Act." Another section of the Act defines "sexually explicit content." When the district court ruled, and when the panel initially considered this appeal, the Act defined "sexually explicit content" to include: (i) any description of or (ii) any picture, photograph, drawing, motion picture film, digital image or similar visual representation depicting sexual bestiality, a lewd exhibition of nudity, as nudity is defined in §18.2-390, sexual excitement, sexual conduct or sadomasochistic abuse, as also defined in §18.2-390, coprophilia, urophilia, or fetishism."

Following our panel decision, the Virginia General Assembly amended the definition of "sexually explicit content" to add the [following] language: "content having as a dominant theme (i) any lascivious description of or (ii) any lascivious picture, photograph, drawing, motion picture film, digital image or similar visual representation depicting sexual bestiality, a lewd exhibition of nudity, as nudity is defined in §18.2-390, sexual excitement, sexual conduct or sadomasochistic abuse, as also defined in §18.2-390, coprophilia, urophilia, or fetishism."[8]

---

8. Section 18.2-390 provides in pertinent part: "'(2) "Nudity" means a state of undress so as to expose the human male or female genitals, pubic area or buttocks with less than a full opaque covering, or the showing of the female breast with less than a fully opaque covering of any portion thereof below the top of the nipple, or the depiction of covered or uncovered male genitals in a discernibly turgid state. (3) "Sexual conduct" means actual or explicitly simulated acts of masturbation, homosexuality, sexual intercourse, or physical contact in an act of apparent sexual stimulation or gratification with a persons clothed or unclothed genitals, pubic area, buttocks or, if such be female, breast. (4) "Sexual excitement" means the condition of human male or female genitals when in a state of sexual stimulation or arousal. (5) "Sadomasochistic abuse" means actual or explicitly simulated flagellation or torture by or upon a person who is nude or clad in undergarments, a mask or bizarre costume, or the condition of being fettered, bound or otherwise physically restrained on the part of one so clothed.'"

As its language makes plain, the Act restricts access by state employees to lascivious sexually explicit material on computers owned or leased by the state. But, the Act does not prohibit all access by state employees to such materials, for a state agency head may give permission for a state employee to access such information on computers owned or leased by the state if the agency head deems such access to be required in connection with a bona fide research project or other undertaking. Further, state employees remain free to access sexually explicit materials from their personal or other computers not owned or leased by the state. Thus, the Act prohibits state employees from accessing sexually explicit materials only when the employees are using computers that are owned or leased by the state and permission to access the material has not been given by the appropriate agency head.

None of the Appellees has requested or been denied permission to access sexually explicit materials pursuant to the Act. Indeed, the record indicates that no request for access to sexually explicit materials on computers owned or leased by the state has been declined.

Appellees maintain that the restriction imposed by the Act violates the First Amendment rights of state employees. Appellees do not assert that state employees possess a First Amendment right to access sexually explicit materials on state-owned or leased computers for their personal use; rather, Appellees confine their challenge to the restriction of access to sexually explicit materials for work-related purposes. Appellees' challenge to the Act is twofold: They first maintain that the Act is unconstitutional as to all state employees; failing this, they argue more particularly that the Act violates academic employees' right to academic freedom. [NOTE: Because the purpose of the discussion of this case is to consider the general approach to computer controls for public employees, the large and important section of this opinion that focuses on the nature and boundaries of academic freedom has been eliminated.]

It is well settled that citizens do not relinquish all of their First Amendment rights by virtue of accepting public employment. Nevertheless, the state, as an employer, undoubtedly possesses greater authority to restrict the speech of its employees than it has as sovereign to restrict the speech of the citizenry as a whole.

The threshold inquiry thus is whether the Act regulates speech by state employees in their capacity as citizens upon matters of public concern. If a public employee's speech made in his capacity as a private citizen does not touch upon a matter of public concern, the state, as employer, may regulate it without infringing any First Amendment protection. Whether speech is that of a private citizen addressing a matter of public concern is a question of law for the court and, accordingly, we review the matter de novo.

To determine whether speech involves a matter of public concern, we examine the content, context, and form of the speech at issue in light of the entire record. Speech involves a matter of public concern when it involves an issue of social, political, or other interest to a community. An inquiry into whether a matter is of public concern does not involve a determination of how interesting or important the subject of an employee's speech is. Further, the place where the speech occurs is irrelevant: An employee may speak as a citizen on a matter of public concern at the workplace, and may speak as an employee away from the workplace.

The Supreme Court has made clear that the concern is to maintain for the government employee the same right enjoyed by his privately employed counterpart. To this end, in its decisions determining speech to be entitled to First Amendment protection the Court has emphasized the unrelatedness of the speech at issue to the speaker's employment duties. Thus, critical to a determination of whether employee speech is entitled to First Amendment protection is whether the speech is "made primarily in the [employee's] role as citizen or primarily in his role as employee."

This focus on the capacity of the speaker recognizes the basic truth that speech by public employees undertaken in the course of their job duties will frequently involve matters of vital concern to the public, without giving those employees a First Amendment right to dictate to the state how they will do their jobs.

The speech at issue here—access to certain materials using computers owned or leased by the state for the purpose of carrying out employment duties—is clearly made in the employee's role as employee. Therefore, the challenged aspect of the Act does not regulate the speech of the citizenry in general, but rather the speech of state employees in their capacity as employees. It cannot be doubted that in order to pursue its legitimate goals effectively, the state must retain the ability to control the manner in which its employees discharge their duties and to direct its employees to undertake the responsibilities of their positions in a specified way. The essence of Appellees' claim is that they are entitled to access sexually explicit material in their capacity as state employees by using equipment owned or leased by the state. Because, as Appellees acknowledge, the challenged aspect of the Act does not affect speech by Appellees in their capacity as private citizens speaking on matters of public concern, it does not infringe the First Amendment rights of state employees.

*****

There were a number of lengthy and fascinating concurring and dissenting opinions in response to Judge Wilkinson's opinion for the court (including one that is a concurring opinion to his own majority opinion by Wilkinson himself). However, for present purposes, the majority opinion in this case is provided to prompt discussion; the separate opinions have been excluded.

The *Urofsky* case specifically concerned controls on behavior associated with public employees' use of public property. However, there have been a variety of situations in which public employers have sought to extend the reach of their control beyond the workplace and public duties. Consider the following opinion by the Florida Supreme Court.

City of North Miami v. Kurtz, 653 So. 2d 1025 (Fla 1995).

INTRODUCTION: The City of North Miami calculated that it could save a considerable amount of money, some $4,611 per employee per year, in insurance and related costs, if it could ensure that its employees did not smoke. Toward that end, the city adopted a regulation that mandated that all job applicants—

though not those presently employed—were required to execute an affidavit, attesting that they had not used tobacco or tobacco products for at least one year before applying for the position. Nothing prevents a person from beginning to smoke after he or she had been hired.

Arlene Kurtz was an applicant for a clerk-typist job. During the interview she was told of the smoking rule and indicated that she was a smoker and could not provide the required affidavit. She was denied employment and sued to challenge the rule.

*****

JUDGE OVERTON wrote the opinion of the court, joined by JUDGES HARDING, WELLS, and ANSTEAD.

After the district court issued [a] decision, it certified, in a separate order, the following question as one of great public importance: DOES ARTICLE I, SECTION 23 OF THE FLORIDA CONSTITUTION PROHIBIT A MUNICIPALITY FROM REQUIRING JOB APPLICANTS TO REFRAIN FROM USING TOBACCO OR TOBACCO PRODUCTS FOR ONE YEAR BEFORE APPLYING FOR, AND AS A CONDITION FOR BEING CONSIDERED FOR EMPLOYMENT, EVEN WHERE THE USE OF TOBACCO IS NOT RELATED TO JOB FUNCTION IN THE POSITION SOUGHT BY THE APPLICANT?

This question involves the issue of whether applicants seeking government employment have a reasonable expectation of privacy under article I, section 23, as to their smoking habits. For the reasons expressed, we answer the certified question in the negative, finding that Florida's constitutional privacy provision does not afford Arlene Kurtz, the job applicant in this case, protection under the circumstances presented.

In ruling on a motion for summary judgment, the trial judge recognized that Kurtz has a fundamental right of privacy under article I, section 23, of the Florida Constitution. The trial judge noted that Kurtz had presented the issue in the narrow context of whether she has a right to smoke in her own home. While he agreed that such a right existed, he concluded that the true issue to be decided was whether the City, as a governmental entity, could regulate smoking through employment. Because he found that there is no expectation of privacy in employment and that the regulation did not violate any provision of either the Florida or the federal constitutions, summary judgment was granted in favor of the City.

The Third District Court of Appeal reversed. The district court first determined that Kurtz'[s] privacy rights are involved when the City requires her to refrain from smoking for a year prior to being considered to employment. The district court then found that, although the City does have an interest in saving taxpayers money by decreasing insurance costs and increasing productivity, such interest is insufficient to outweigh the intrusion into Kurtz'[s] right of privacy and has no relevance to the performance of the duties involved with a clerk-typist.

Consequently, the district court concluded that the regulation violated Kurtz's privacy rights under article I, section 23, of the Florida Constitution. We disagree.

Florida's constitutional privacy provision, which is contained in article I, section 23, provides as follows: "Right of privacy.—Every natural person has the right to be let alone and free from governmental intrusion into his private life except as otherwise provided herein. This section shall not be construed to limit the public's right of access to public records and meetings as provided by law."

This right to privacy protects Florida's citizens from the government's uninvited observation of or interference in those areas that fall within the ambit of the zone of privacy afforded under this provision. Unlike the implicit privacy right of the federal constitution, Florida's privacy provision is, in and of itself, a fundamental one that, once implicated, demands evaluation under a compelling state interest standard. The federal privacy provision, on the other hand, extends only to such fundamental interests as marriage, procreation, contraception, family relationships, and the rearing and educating of children.

Although Florida's privacy right provides greater protection than the federal constitution, it was not intended to be a guarantee against all intrusion into the life of an individual. First, the privacy provision applies only to government action, and the right provided under that provision is circumscribed and limited by the circumstances in which it is asserted. Further, "determining 'whether an individual has a legitimate expectation of privacy in any given case must be made by considering all the circumstances, especially objective manifestations of that expectation.'" Thus, to determine whether Kurtz, as a job applicant, is entitled to protection under article I, section 23, we must first determine whether a governmental entity is intruding into an aspect of Kurtz's life in which she as a "legitimate expectation of privacy." If we find in the affirmative, we must then look to whether a compelling interest exists to justify that intrusion and, if so, whether the least intrusive means is being used to accomplish the goal.

In this case, we find that the City's action does not intrude into an aspect of Kurtz'[s] life in which she has a legitimate expectation of privacy. In today's society, smokers are constantly required to reveal whether they smoke. When individuals are seated in a restaurant, they are asked whether they want a table in a smoking or non-smoking section. When individuals rent hotel or motel rooms, they are asked if they smoke so that management may ensure that certain rooms remain free from the smell of smoke odors. Likewise, when individuals rent cars, they are asked if they smoke so that rental agencies can make proper accommodations to maintain vehicles for non-smokers. Further, employers generally provide smoke-free areas for non-smokers, and employees are often prohibited from smoking in certain areas. Given that individuals must reveal whether they smoke in almost every aspect of life in today's society, we conclude that individuals have no reasonable expectation of privacy in the disclosure of that information when applying for a government job and, consequently, that Florida's right of privacy is not implicated under these unique circumstances.

In reaching the conclusion that the right to privacy is not implicated in this case, however, we emphasize that our holding is limited to the narrow issue presented. Notably, we are not addressing the issue of whether an applicant, once hired, could be compelled by a government agency to stop smoking. Equally as important, neither are we holding today that a governmental entity can ask any type of information it chooses of prospective job applicants.

Having determined that Kurtz has no legitimate expectation of privacy in revealing that she is a smoker under the Florida constitution, we turn now to her claim that the regulation violates her rights under the federal constitution. As noted, the federal constitution's implicit privacy provision extends only to such fundamental interests as marriage, procreation, contraception, family relationships, and the rearing and educating of children. Clearly, the "right to smoke" is not included within the penumbra of fundamental rights protected under that provision. *Grusendorf v. City of Oklahoma City,* 816 F.2d 539 (10th Cir. 1987). Moreover, even if we were to find that some protected interest under the federal constitution were implicated so as to require a rational basis for the regulation we would still find the regulation to be constitutional. As acknowledged by the district court, the City has a legitimate interest in attempting to reduce health insurance costs and to increase productivity. On these facts, the City's policy cannot be deemed so irrational that it may be branded arbitrary. In fact, under the special circumstances supported by the record in this case, we would find that the City has established a compelling interest to support implementation of the regulation. As previously indicated, the record reflects that each smoking employee costs the City as much as $4,611 per year in 1981 dollars over what it incurs for non-smoking employees; that, of smokers who have adhered to the one year cessation requirement, a high percentage are unlikely to resume smoking; and that the City is a self-insurer who pays 100% of its employees' medical expenses. We find that the elimination of these costs, when considered in combination with the other special circumstances of this case, validates a compelling interest in the City's policy of gradually eliminating smokers from its work force. We also find that the City is using the least intrusive means in accomplishing this compelling interest because the regulation does not prevent current employees from smoking, it does not affect the present health care benefits of employees, and it gradually reduces the number of smokers through attrition. Thus, we find the regulation to be constitutional under both the federal and Florida constitutions.

For the reasons expressed, we answer the question in the negative, finding that Florida's constitutional privacy provision does not afford the applicant, Arlene Kurtz, protection because she has no reasonable expectation of privacy under the circumstances of this case.

JUDGE KOGAN wrote a dissenting opinion joined by JUDGE SHAW.

As the majority itself notes, job applicants are free to return to tobacco use once hired. I believe this concession reveals the anti-smoking policy to be rather more of a speculative pretense than a rational governmental policy. Therefore I would find it unconstitutional under the right of due process. The privacy issue is more troublesome, to my mind. There is a "slippery-slope" problem here because, if governmental employers can inquire too extensively into off-job-site behavior, a point eventually will be reached at which the right of privacy under article I, section 23 clearly will be breached. An obvious example would be an inquiry into the lawful sexual behavior of job applicants in an effort to identify those with the "most desirable" lifestyles. Such an effort easily could become the pretext for a constitutional violation. The time has not yet fully passed, for example, when women job applicants have been questioned about their plans for procreation in an effort to eliminate those who may be absent on family leave. I cannot conceive that such an act is anything other than a violation of the right of privacy when done by a governmental unit.

Health-based concerns like those expressed by the City also present a definite slippery slope to the courts. The time is fast approaching, for example, when human beings can be genetically tested so thoroughly that susceptibility to partic-ular diseases can be identified years in advance. To my mind, any governmental effort to identify those who might eventually suffer from cancer or heart disease, for instance, itself is a violation of bodily integrity guaranteed by article I, section 23. Moreover, I cannot help but note that any such effort comes perilously close to the discredited practice of eugenics.

The use of tobacco products is more troubling, however. While legal, tobacco use nevertheless is an activity increasingly regulated by the law. If the federal gov-ernment, for instance, chose to regulate tobacco as a controlled substance, I have no trouble saying that this act alone does not undermine anyone's privacy right. However, regulation is not the issue here because tobacco use today remains legal. The sole question is whether the government may inquire into off-job-site behavior that is legal, however unhealthy it might be. In light of the inherently poor fit between the governmental objective and the ends actually achieved, I am more inclined to agree with the district court that the right of privacy has been violated here. I might reach a different result if the objective were better served by the means chosen.

*****

Another issue that has been important is not really new: the challenge of attacking sexual harassment in the workplace. Harassment has been with us for many years, but there have been efforts since the 1980's to attack it more directly in court as sex discrimination under Title VII of the Civil Rights Act of 1964. In 1986, in *Meritor Savings Bank v. Vinson,* 477 U.S. 57 (1986), the Supreme Court agreed with the Equal Employment Opportunity Commission that sexual harassment is a violation of Title VII. It also agreed that harassment may be the result of a "quid pro quo" (this for that) demand for sexual favors or the creation of a "hostile environment" in which employees felt coerced to par-ticipate in sexual activities. The most recent effort by the Supreme Court to establish a standard for the responsibilities of employers in damages and the responsibilities of those who seek to obtain redress came about because of the behavior of two lifeguard supervisors in Boca Raton, Florida.

Faragher v. City of Boca Raton, 524 U.S. 775 (1998).

INTRODUCTION: Beth Ann Faragher took a job as a lifeguard for the City of Boca Raton. She was supervised by Bill Terry, David Silverman, and Robert Gordon. Faragher alleged that her supervisors maintained a "sexually hostile atmosphere" and subjected the female lifeguards to "uninvited and offensive touching," lewd language, and sexist comments. Although the lifeguards worked for the city parks and recreation department, they had virtually no contact with officials of that department or other city units. They were, in many respects, isolated from the other city offices. In fact, when in 1990 the city revised its sexual harassment policy, the lifeguards and their unit were not informed of it. Although the behavior of the two supervisors was extremely vulgar and demeaning, Faragher did not complain to superiors about their actions. At one point she spoke informally to the unit director, but made no formal complaint and took the matter no further. Gordon did nothing and did not report anything of the information Faragher had related to him. In the Spring of 1990, another lifeguard wrote to the city personnel director complaining about the harassment. The city found the complaints valid but the two men were given the choice of taking a leave without pay or forfeiting some of their accumulated leave time. Faragher quit shortly thereafter. She sued for violations of Title VII of the Civil Rights Act of 1964 and sought damages from the city for the behavior of her supervisors.

*****

JUSTICE SOUTER wrote the opinion for the Court.

This case calls for identification of the circumstances under which an employer may be held liable under Title VII of the Civil Rights Act of 1964, 42 U.S.C. §2000e et seq., for the acts of a supervisory employee whose sexual harassment of subordinates has created a hostile work environment amounting to employment discrimination. We hold that an employer is vicariously liable for actionable discrimination caused by a supervisor, but subject to an affirmative defense looking to the reasonableness of the employer's conduct as well as that of a plaintiff victim.

Since our decision in *Meritor* [*Savings Bank, FSB v. Vinson,* 477 U.S. 57 (1986)], Courts of Appeals have struggled to derive manageable standards to govern employer liability for hostile environment harassment perpetrated by supervisory employees. We now reverse the judgment of the Eleventh Circuit and remand for entry of judgment in Faragher's favor.

Under Title VII of the Civil Rights Act of 1964, "it shall be an unlawful employment practice for an employer . . . to fail or refuse to hire or to discharge any individual, or otherwise to discriminate against any individual with respect to his compensation, terms, conditions, or privileges of employment, because of such individual's race, color, religion, sex, or national origin." We have repeatedly made clear that although the statute mentions specific employment decisions with immediate consequences, the scope of the prohibition "'is not limited to "economic" or "tangible" discrimination,'" *Harris v. Forklift Systems, Inc.,* 510 U.S. 17, 21 (1993) and that it covers more than "'terms' and 'conditions' in the narrow contractual sense." Thus, in *Meritor* we held that sexual harassment so "severe or pervasive" as to "'alter the conditions of [the victim's] employment and create an abusive working environment'" violates Title VII.

[We have] explained that in order to be actionable under the statute, a sexually objectionable environment must be both objectively and subjectively offensive, one that a reasonable person would find hostile or abusive, and one that the victim in fact did perceive to be so. We directed courts to determine whether an environment is sufficiently hostile or abusive by "looking at all the circumstances," including the "frequency of the discriminatory conduct; its severity; whether it is physically threatening or humiliating, or a mere offensive utterance; and whether it unreasonably interferes with an employee's work performance." Most recently, we explained that Title VII does not prohibit "genuine but innocuous differences in the ways men and women routinely interact with members of the same sex and of the opposite sex." A recurring point in these opinions is that "simple teasing," offhand comments, and isolated incidents (unless extremely serious) will not amount to discriminatory changes in the "terms and conditions of employment."

These standards for judging hostility are sufficiently demanding to ensure that Title VII does not become a "general civility code." Properly applied, they will filter out complaints attacking "the ordinary tribulations of the workplace, such as the sporadic use of abusive language, gender-related jokes, and occasional teasing." We have made it clear that conduct must be extreme to amount to a change in the terms and conditions of employment, and the Courts of Appeals have heeded this view.

Meritor's statement of the law is the foundation on which we build today. Neither party before us has urged us to depart from our customary adherence to stare decisis in statutory interpretation. And the force of precedent here is enhanced by Congress's amendment to the liability provisions of Title VII since the *Meritor* decision, without providing any modification of our holding.

We agree with Faragher that in implementing Title VII it makes sense to hold an employer vicariously liable for some tortious conduct of a supervisor made possible by abuse of his supervisory authority. Several courts, indeed, have noted what Faragher has argued, that there is a sense in which a harassing supervisor is always assisted in his misconduct by the supervisory relationship. The agency relationship affords contact with an employee subjected to a supervisor's sexual harassment, and the victim may well be reluctant to accept the risks of blowing the whistle on a superior. When a person with supervisory authority discriminates in the terms and conditions of subordinates' employment, his actions necessarily draw upon his superior position over the people who report to him, or those under them, whereas an employee generally cannot check a supervisor's abusive conduct the same way that she might deal with abuse from a co-worker. When a fellow employee harasses, the victim can walk away or tell the offender where to go, but it may be difficult to offer such responses to a supervisor. Recognition of employer liability when discriminatory misuse of supervisory authority alters the terms and conditions of a victim's employment is underscored by the fact that the employer has a greater opportunity to guard against misconduct by supervisors than by common workers; employers have greater opportunity and incentive to screen them, train them, and monitor their performance.

In sum, there are good reasons for vicarious liability for misuse of supervisory authority. That rationale must, however, satisfy one more condition. We are not entitled to recognize this theory under Title VII unless we can square it with *Meritor's* holding that an employer is not "automatically" liable for harassment by a supervisor who creates the requisite degree of discrimination, and there is obviously some tension between that holding and the position that a supervisor's misconduct aided by supervisory authority subjects the employer to liability vicariously; if the "aid" may be the unspoken suggestion of retaliation by misuse of supervisory authority, the risk of automatic liability is high. To counter it, we think there are two basic alternatives, one being to require proof of some affirmative invocation of that authority by the harassing supervisor, the other to recognize an affirmative defense to liability in some circumstances, even when a supervisor has created the actionable environment.

As long ago as 1980, the Equal Employment Opportunity Commission (EEOC), charged with the enforcement of Title VII, adopted regulations advising employers to "take all steps necessary to prevent sexual harassment from occurring, such as . . . informing employees of their right to raise and how to raise the issue of harassment" and in 1990 the Commission issued a policy statement enjoining employers to establish a complaint procedure designed to encourage victims of harassment to come forward [without requiring] a victim to complain first to the offending supervisor." It would therefore implement clear statutory policy and complement the Government's Title VII enforcement efforts to recognize the employer's affirmative obligation to prevent violations and give credit here to employers who make reasonable efforts to discharge their duty. Indeed, a theory of vicarious liability for misuse of supervisory power would be at odds with the statutory policy if it failed to provide employers with some such incentive.

The requirement to show that the employee has failed in a coordinate duty to avoid or mitigate harm reflects an equally obvious policy imported from the general theory of damages, that a victim has a duty "to use such means as are reasonable under the circumstances to avoid or minimize the damages" that result from violations of the statute. An employer may, for example, have provided a proven, effective mechanism for reporting and resolving complaints of sexual harassment, available to the employee without undue risk or expense. If the plaintiff unreasonably failed to avail herself of the employer's preventive or remedial apparatus, she should not recover damages that could have been avoided if she had done so. If the victim could have avoided harm, no liability should be found against the employer who had taken reasonable care, and if damages could reasonably have been mitigated no award against a liable employer should reward a plaintiff for what her own efforts could have avoided.

In order to accommodate the principle of vicarious liability for harm caused by misuse of supervisory authority, as well as Title VII's equally basic policies of encouraging forethought by employers and saving action by objecting employees, we adopt the following holding in this case and in *Burlington Industries, Inc. v. Ellerth* also decided today. An employer is subject to vicarious liability to a victimized employee for an actionable hostile environment created by a supervisor with immediate (or successively higher) authority over the employee. When no tangible employment action is taken, a defending employer may raise an affirmative defense to liability or damages, subject to proof by a preponderance of the evidence. The defense comprises two necessary elements: (a) that the employer exercised reasonable care to prevent and correct promptly any sexually harassing behavior, and (b) that the plaintiff employee unreasonably failed to take advantage of any preventive or corrective opportunities provided by the employer or to avoid harm otherwise. While proof that an employer had promulgated an antiharassment policy with complaint procedure is not necessary in every instance as a matter of law, the need for a stated policy suitable to the employment circumstances may appropriately be addressed in any case when litigating the first element of the defense. And while proof that an employee failed to fulfill the corresponding obligation of reasonable care to avoid harm is not limited to showing an unreasonable failure to use any complaint procedure provided by the employer, a demonstration of such failure will normally suffice to satisfy the employer's burden under the second element of the defense. No affirmative defense is available, however, when the supervisor's harassment culminates in a tangible employment action, such as discharge, demotion, or undesirable reassignment.

Applying these rules here, we believe that the judgment of the Court of Appeals must be reversed. The District Court found that the degree of hostility in the work environment rose to the actionable level and was attributable to Silverman and Terry. It is undisputed that these supervisors "were granted virtually unchecked authority" over their subordinates, "directly controlling and supervising all aspects of [Faragher's] day-to-day activities." It is also clear that Faragher and her colleagues were "completely isolated from the City's higher management." The City did not seek review of these findings.

The Court of Appeals also rejected the possibility that it could hold the City liable for the reason that it knew of the harassment vicariously through the knowledge of its supervisors. We have no occasion to consider whether this was error, however. We are satisfied that liability on the ground of vicarious knowledge could not be determined without further factfinding on remand.

The judgment of the Court of Appeals for the Eleventh Circuit is reversed, and the case is remanded for reinstatement of the judgment of the District Court.

JUSTICE THOMAS wrote a dissent.

For the reasons given in my dissenting opinion in *Burlington Industries v. Ellerth,* absent an adverse employment consequence, an employer cannot be held vicariously liable if a supervisor creates a hostile work environment. Petitioner suffered no adverse employment consequence; thus the Court of Appeals was correct to hold that the City is not vicariously liable for the conduct of Chief Terry and Lieutenant Silverman. Because the Court reverses this judgment, I dissent.

I disagree with the Court's conclusion that merely because the City did not disseminate its sexual harassment policy, it should be liable as a matter of law. The

City should be allowed to show either that: (1) there was a reasonably available avenue through which petitioner could have complained to a City official who supervised both Chief Terry and Lieutenant Silverman or (2) it would not have learned of the harassment even if the policy had been distributed. Petitioner, as the plaintiff, would of course bear the burden of proving the City's negligence.

*****

ADDITIONAL READINGS

Carolyn Ban and Norma Riccucci, eds., *Public Personnel Management: Current Concerns, Future Challenges,* 2nd Ed. (New York: Longman, 1997).

Ivan E. Bodensteiner and Rosalie B. Levinson, "Litigating Age and Disability Claims against State and Local Government Employers in the New 'Federalism' Era," 22 *Berkeley J. Emp. & Lab. L.* 99 (2001).

Charles W. Hemingway, "A Closer Look at *Waters v. Churchill* and *United States v. National Treasury Employees Union*:

Constitutional Tensions Between the Government as Employer and the Citizen as Federal Employee," 44 *American University L. Rev.* 2231 (1995).

"Note: *City of North Miami v. Kurtz*: Is Sacrificing Employee Privacy Rights the Cost of Health Care Reform," 27 *University of Toledo L. Rev.* 545 (1996).

U.S. Merit System Protection Board, The Federal Workplace: Employee Perspectives (Washington, D.C.: Merit System Protection Board, 1998).

5

⚖️

Administrative
Responsibility*

O ne of the most dynamic and, in many respects, most complex areas of
public law and public administration is administrative responsibility. As
Public Law and Public Administration, Third Edition explains, it is a broad
topic with roots that reach well back into history. Even the modern debates
over responsibility trace back to the Friedrich/Finer debates of the 1930s.[1]
Even so, in the twenty-first century, the subject has become not only increasingly important but also more and more complex. That is true even if we limit
the discussion to external means of ensuring accountability and narrow it again
to the legal mechanisms of accountability. Not only are there new problems to
address, such as issues arising from increased contracting out of services, but the
United States Supreme Court has been dramatically reshaping longstanding
areas of the law, such as sovereign immunity. This chapter provides cases that
have considered the foundation issues, but it also emphasizes opinions that are
at the leading edge of major changes, including those topics about which we

---

* Related Material in *Public Law and Public Administration, Third Edition,* Chapter 13.

1. Herman Finer, "Better Government Personnel: America's Next Frontier," 51 *Political
Science Quarterly* 569 (1936); Carl Friedrich, "Public Policy and the Nature of
Administrative Responsibility," in C. J. Friedrich and E. S. Mason, eds., *Public Policy*
(Cambridge, Mass.: Harvard University Press, 1940); Herman Finer, "Administrative
Responsibility in Democratic Government," 1 *Public Administration Review* 335 (1941).

thought we had a well developed understanding but that are being reshaped today. It considers injunctions and related remedial orders, official liability and limited immunity, sovereign immunity and its recent dramatic expansions, and contract related concerns.

INJUNCTIONS AND
ENFORCEMENT ORDERS

Chapter 9 of *Public Law and Public Administration, Third Edition* discusses the nature and issues associated with the use of remedial orders to correct violations of law or issues of maladministration. It also explained that the Supreme Court has issued a string of opinions, dating back to the mid-1970s, warning federal district courts to limit the types of cases in which they become involved,[2] to constrain the scope of the remedies they impose when there is a need for injunctive relief,[3] and also to end their supervision of administrative operations as much as possible given the situation they face.[4] In the process, the Court encouraged the use of tort suits for damages instead of injunctions as a way to address abuses, fueling debates over rapidly multiplying tort suits.[5]

Notwithstanding all of that, however, judges continue to find themselves in situations that seem to require remedial orders. Consider the following two recent cases. In reading them, try as much as possible to sit in the judge's seat and see the problem from that point of view.

Maynor v. Morgan County, 147 F. Supp. 2d 1185 (NDAL 2001).

INTRODUCTION: The story of this case is revealed in the opinion. Though it is a particularly egregious example, it is in some respects reflective of problems that have emerged around the nation with burgeoning prison and jail populations and increasing stresses on state and local budgets. Ironically, the facts are reminiscent of some of the problems encountered in the early years of prison and jail conditions litigation. The problem is what to do about it. In that regard,

---

2. *Wilson v. Seiter,* 501 U.S. 294 (1991); *Rhodes v. Chapman,* 452 U.S. 337 (1981); *Rizzo v. Goode,* 423 U.S. 362 (1976).

3. See *Missouri v. Jenkins,* 515 U.S. 70 (1995); *Freeman v. Pitts,* 503 U.S. 467 (1992); *Board of Ed. of Oklahoma City v. Dowell,* 498 U.S. 237 (1991); *Milliken v. Bradley,* 418 U.S. 717 (1974).

4. *Board of Ed. of Oklahoma City v. Dowell, supra* note 3; *Pasadena City Bd. of Ed. v. Spangler,* 427 U. S. 424 (1976).

5. *Rizzo v. Goode, supra* note 2.

the frustration has not only been an issue for inmates, but also for the sheriffs and others responsible for correctional institutions. In fact, in the wake of state inaction to resolve the Morgan County and other cases, one sheriff took a busload of prisoners to a state facility and handcuffed them to the fence, telling the state officials that these people were their problem, and they should deal with it because the county refused to accept the situation any longer.

*****

JUDGE CLEMON wrote the opinion.

This case has been brought and certified as a class action by inmates of the Morgan County Jail. The Court has carefully considered the evidence adduced at the preliminary hearing of April 12, 2001, together (by agreement of the parties) with the evidence adduced at a similar hearing in the predecessor of this case. The Court makes the following preliminary Findings of Fact and Conclusions of Law.

I. To say that the Morgan County Jail is overcrowded is an understatement. The sardine-can appearance of its cell units more nearly resemble the holding units of slave ships during the Middle Passage of the eighteenth century than anything in the twenty-first century.

Inmates in the Morgan County Jail are required to sleep on the concrete floor space under bunks, on the concrete floor space between bunks within cells—sometimes within two feet of commodes or showers, on tables (on which meals are served) and between tables in the anterooms of the cell units. Sometimes, inmates are not provided with sleeping mats, blankets, or sheets.

The linen provided to inmates is not cleaned on a regular basis. When inmates send out their clothes for laundering, they must wait days or weeks (without clothes) until the laundry is returned.

The cell units are dirty and unkept. The Jail does not hire contract janitors, and the inmates are not provided with adequate cleaning supplies and equipment to clean the facilities themselves. The metal surfaces of the showers have in places been completely eroded by rust. Soiled clothes, papers, and other debris litter the floors.

The cell units are poorly ventilated. They are cold in the winter (the air-conditioning system runs on winter nights) and hot in the summer. The vents need cleaning.

Inmates unable to purchase towels, soap, and other items for personal hygiene are often not provided such items by Defendants.

Inmates are seldom (once or twice a month) allowed to leave their cells for exercise in the recreational area atop the jail.

The food is inadequate in amount and unsanitary in presentation.

The known medical needs of inmates go largely unattended: prescribed medications for serious illnesses are not made available for those inmates who cannot afford them; there is a dangerous delay between Defendants' awareness of the serious medical needs of inmates and the response, if any, to such needs. Defendants are largely indifferent to the needs of mentally ill inmates.

According to the State Fire Marshal, the Morgan County Jail is a fire hazard. Following a September 22, 2000, inspection of the Jail, he wrote:

> The occupant load of the jail is 96 inmates. The jail is occupied by 221 inmates and is over crowded. 70 or more inmates are sleeping on the floor. Stacked beds are jammed against each other in some cells.
>
> Building and fire code violations remain the same as reported in the original inspection in 1982. It appears that no attempt have been made to correct the building and fire code violations. There have been several fires in the jail, especially in the past year. Old fire damage was noted in several locations. . . .
>
> The fire alarm, smoke detector and manual fire alarm systems are not working. Reportedly, the system has not been operating for some time.
>
> Several sections were so over crowded that a person had to step around inmates to get around in the day room and cells. This created a dangerous situation as to the safety of the officers and inmates if an emergency occurred. . . .
>
> This building is a hazard to both life and property. It is recommended that this jail be immediately brought up to present day fire and building code requirements or the occupants removed and entrances to the building secured, until the unsafe conditions and overcrowding are abated. Plaintiffs' Exhibit ("PX") 24, p.1–2, Fire Marshal's Report.

Assuming the existence of an emergency evacuation procedure, the inmates have not been alerted to it.

II. The Alabama State Department of Corrections ("DOC")'s consistent failure to remove "state [prison] ready" inmates from the Morgan County Jail has been the principal cause of the jail's overcrowding. Under Alabama law, when an inmate has been convicted and sentenced in a circuit court and the court reporter's transcript has been filed with the circuit clerk, the DOC should "thereupon" transfer the inmate from the county jail to a state prison. But because of alleged overcrowding in the state prisons, the DOC has defaulted in its statutory obligation to remove state ready inmates from the Morgan County Jail.

Alabama's largest county, Jefferson, had 156 state ready inmates as of April 9, 2001; its next three larger counties, Mobile, Madison, and Morgan had 65, 0, and 57 state ready inmates, respectively. As of the same date, there were 104 state ready inmates in the Morgan County Jail. Tuscaloosa, Shelby, Baldwin, and Calhoun are larger than Morgan County, but the number of state ready inmates in each of these counties is significantly less than Morgan County.

As of January 2001, the DOC had the capacity for housing 23,506 inmates in its various penal facilities. Also on that date, the average inmate population in the state penal facilities was 22,738. Thus, despite the DOC's constant refrain that its prisons are filled to the brim and overflowing, the fact is that it is operating at 96.7% of its capacity—based on its own statistics. The Limestone facility—located in the adjacent county to Morgan—has a capacity for 2,388 inmates. Yet as of three months ago, it had only 2,041 state inmates—85.5% of its capacity. All of the inmates incarcerated in state prisons sleep in bunks or beds; not a single one of them sleeps on the floor!

Defendant Commissioner Michael Haley, before assuming his present position, swore under oath:

I cannot agree ... that nothing more can be done in each State prison facility to increase available bed space. It is noteworthy that Warden Ron Jones admits that the multi-purpose building in his prison, Draper Correctional Center, could be converted to bed space for approximately 220 additional inmates. ... If that is true for Draper, one of the older prisons, I would think it would be true for most, if not all, of the more modern prisons and on a larger scale. Modern prisons are designed with large opens spaces such as multi-purpose rooms, day rooms, gymnasiums, chapels, law libraries, meeting rooms, and what is termed "program areas"—all areas not originally designed as inmate housing. This space could be converted to additional bed space for the alleviation of most, if not all, of the backlogged state inmates currently housed in County jails. ...

Several counties have, on occasion and in times of over-capacity, used tents and trailers to house additional inmates and detainees. Further, this has been done without the addition of additional jail staff. Again, although this is not a preferable or desired alternative, it is what many counties have been forced to do in the face of over-crowding caused by State inmates. Such temporary facilities have passed Department of Corrections inspections and were therefore deemed reasonable by Department of Corrections officials. If the use of such temporary facilities is reasonable for use at the county level, they should be reasonable for use at the State level. Furthermore, State facilities, unlike most county jails, are surrounded by large open areas secured by perimeter fencing. These areas would be ideal locations for the use of such facilities. ...

Overcrowding in county jails presents more of a threat than it does to State prisons because of classification problems. The State system has the luxury of being able to designate portions of facilities as being set aside for special programs, e.g., substance abuse programs, sexual offender programs. The State system also has the luxury of setting aside portions of their prison system to house prisoners with extreme medical needs or extreme psychological needs.

Although the Commissioner's statements were made three years ago, he assured the Court in his testimony in this case that these statements are as true today as they were when they were made. The Court credits these statements.

The DOC pays nothing to Morgan County for its housing of state ready inmates who should be housed in state prisons. Morgan County is reimbursed by the Alabama State Comptroller the hefty sum of $1.75 per meal for the inmates fed in the Morgan County Jail. It costs the State of Alabama $26 daily to house a state prisoner. The DOC thus has a substantial financial incentive to leave its state prisoners on the barren concrete floors of the Morgan County Jail.

In sum, the Court is not convinced that there are insufficient beds in the state prisons to house the state ready inmates presently sleeping on the floors of the Morgan County Jail. It finds precisely to the contrary. Moreover, assuming *arguendo* a lack of capacity in the state prisons, as the Commissioner has forthrightly testified, the DOC is in a much better position than the Morgan County Defendants to arrange for temporary housing of the inmates for whom it bears legal responsibility.

Conclusion

The Court preliminarily concludes that Plaintiffs have carried their burden of showing that the conditions extant in the Morgan County Jail violate their rights to the minimal civilized measures of life's necessities and protection from a substantial risk of serious harm under the Eighth Amendment to the United States Constitution. Moreover, they have shown that Defendants have acted and failed to act with deliberate indifference to the uncivilized and hazardous conditions in the Morgan County Jail. Further, they have shown that Defendant Alabama State Department of Corrections, being primarily responsible for the overcrowding in the Morgan County Jail, has been deliberately indifferent to its capacity to correct that problem.

The preliminary injunctive relief to be ordered by this Court is narrowly tailored to remedy the established constitutional violations; and no less intrusive means is available to correct these serious constitutional violations.

By separate order, the requested Preliminary Injunction will be granted.

Done this 17th day of April, 2001.
U.W. Clemon
Chief United States District Judge

*****

In many ways, the Morgan County case is reminiscent of the early waves of institutional cases. In another respect, it is the result of the more contemporary effort to insulate governments from injunctive relief, making it tempting to ignore serious problems and return to the abuses of an earlier time.

Another dimension of the judge's challenge in this arena concerns the question of what to do when administrators fail to respond to clearly identified—even openly admitted—legal violations. This challenge has often been raised in discussions of state and local contexts. However, there are federal examples as well. The ongoing battle by Native Americans to make the U.S. Department of Interior honor its obligations demonstrates this problem in the federal government in the face of action that amounted, according to the judge, to "a fraud upon the court." Read this opinion with an effort to see it from the district court's point of view. Also, be clear about the facts and what the court actually ordered and avoid becoming caught up in the rhetoric.

Cobell v. Norton, 226 F. Supp. 2d 1 (D.D.C. 2002).

INTRODUCTION: Here again, the details are provided in the opinion and the challenge is how to respond. This one becomes complex for several reasons. The first is that after years of promising to fix the problem, the Department of the Interior has yet to figure out how much it owes, to whom, and where the money for which it had and has trustee responsibility has gone. Further, there is the problem of what to do when a federal agency behaves in the manner described in this opinion. This case focuses on events during both the Clinton and G.W. Bush administrations, though the facts of the case clearly reach much further back into history.

*****

The opinion was written by DISTRICT JUDGE ROYCE C. LAMBRETH.

MEMORANDUM OPINION

This matter comes before the Court after a twenty-nine day bench trial to determine whether defendants Gale Norton, Secretary of the Interior, and Neal McCaleb, Assistant Secretary of Interior for Indian Affairs, should be held in civil contempt of court. After carefully reviewing of all the evidence presented and representations made at trial, the record in this case, and the applicable law, the Court finds that these defendants are in civil contempt of court. The Court's findings of fact and conclusions of law are detailed below.

I. INTRODUCTION

The Department of Interior's administration of the Individual Indian Money (IIM) trust has served as the gold standard for mismanagement by the federal government for more than a century. As the trustee-delegate of the United States, the Secretary of Interior does not know the precise number of IIM trust accounts that she is to administer and protect, how much money is or should be in the trust, or even the proper balance for each individual account. Because of the Secretary's systemic failure as a trustee-delegate, the federal government regularly issues payments to beneficiaries—of their own money—in erroneous amounts. In fact, the Interior Department cannot provide an accurate accounting to the majority of the estimated 300,000 trust beneficiaries, despite a clear statutory mandate and the century-old obligation to do so. As the Court observed more than two years ago, "it is fiscal and governmental irresponsibility in its purest form."

Equally troubling is the manner in which the Department of Interior has conducted itself during the course of this litigation. In February of 1999, the Court held Bruce Babbitt, then-Secretary of the Interior, and Kevin Gover, then-Assistant

Secretary of Interior for Indian Affairs, in civil contempt for violating two of this Court's discovery orders.

Among other things, the Court found that almost immediately after proposing a clear and unambiguous order which the Court signed, "the defendants disobeyed that order and successfully covered up their disobedience through semantics and strained, unilateral, self-serving interpretations of their own duties." The defendants' misconduct did not end there. Since holding then-Secretary Babbitt and then-Assistant Secretary Gover in contempt, the Court has had to sanction the Department of Interior for filing frivolous motions, enter several temporary restraining orders to prevent the Department from taking potentially adverse actions, and appoint both a Special Master (to oversee discovery) and a Court Monitor (to review the defendants' trust related activities). Moreover, there are several motions currently pending before the Court regarding alleged misconduct by the Interior Department. In short, the Department of Interior has handled this litigation the same way that it has managed the IIM trust—disgracefully.

The issue now before the Court is whether the Secretary of the Interior and the Assistant Secretary of Interior for Indian Affairs should again be held in civil contempt of court. Specifically, the Court ordered these two government officials to show cause why they should not be held in civil contempt for: (1) failing to comply with the Court's Order of December 21, 1999, to initiate a Historical Accounting Project; (2) committing a fraud on the Court by concealing the Department's true actions regarding the Historical Accounting Project during the period from March 2000, until January 2001; (3) committing a fraud on the Court by failing to disclose the true status of the TAAMS project between September 1999 and December 21, 1999; (4) committing a fraud on the Court by filing false and misleading quarterly status reports starting in March 2000, regarding TAAMS and BIA Data Cleanup; and (5) committing a fraud on the Court by making false and misleading representations starting in March 2000, regarding computer security of IIM trust data. The Court will address each of these specifications below in turn.

II. BACKGROUND

A. FACTUAL BACKGROUND

During the early 1800s, the United States' policy towards Native Americans— which included entering into (and frequently violating) treaties as well as the use of force—led to the removal and relocation of many tribes from the East and Midwest to unsettled lands in the West. In the late 19th century, the United States' policy of relocation was replaced with a policy of assimilation. Under this new policy, the federal government allotted land that had been set aside for tribes to individual tribe members instead. The policy of assimilation was designed "to extinguish tribal sovereignty, erase reservation boundaries, and force assimilation of Indians into society at large." *Yakima v. Yakima Indian Nation,* 502 U.S. 251, 254 (1992).

The assimilationist policy, which began with individually negotiated treaties, became federal law when Congress passed the General Allotment Act of 1887, also known as the "Dawes Act." Under the Dawes Act, beneficial title of the allotted lands vested in the United States as trustee for individual Indians. The trust was to last for 25 years or more, at which point a fee patent would issue to the individual Indian allottee. During the trust period, individual accounts were to be set up for each Indian with a stake in the allotted lands, and the lands would be managed for the benefit of the individual allottees. Indians could not sell, lease, or otherwise burden their allotted lands without government approval. Where tribes resisted allotment, it could be imposed.

The United States' policy of assimilation and its allotment of tribal lands ended with the enactment of the Indian Reorganization Act of 1934 (IRA). Although the IRA provided that unallotted surplus Indian lands would be returned to tribal ownership, the statute did not disturb lands already allotted to individual Indians, and actually extended the trust period for allotted lands indefinitely. Thus, under the IRA the federal government maintained control of lands already allotted but not yet fee-patented, and accordingly retained its fiduciary obligations to administer the trust lands and funds arising therefrom for the benefit of individual Indian beneficiaries.[6] These lands form the basis of the IIM trust accounts that are at the core of this lawsuit.

There is no question that as a result of the allotments made from 1887–1934 and the IRA's indefinite extension of the trust period, the United States has assumed the fiduciary obligations of a trustee. Although the United States itself is the trustee of the IIM trust, under current law the Secretary of the Interior and the Secretary of the Treasury are the designated trustee-delegates. The failure of either Secretary to perform his or her particular fiduciary responsibilities results in the United States breaching its fiduciary obligations to the IIM trust beneficiaries.

The Department of Interior and its subagencies have utterly failed to manage the IIM trust in a manner consistent with the fiduciary obligations of a trustee-delegate.

> The federal government does not know the precise number of IIM trust accounts that it is to administer and protect. At present, the Interior Department's system contains over 300,000 accounts covering an estimated 11 million acres, but the Department is unsure whether this is the proper number of accounts. . . . [In fact,] not only does the Interior Department not know the proper number of accounts, it does not know the proper balances for each IIM account, nor does Interior have sufficient records to determine the value of IIM accounts. . . . Current account reconciliation procedures are insufficient to ensure that existing account records, reported account balances, or payments to IIM beneficiaries are accurate. . . . As a result, the government regularly issues payments to trust beneficiaries in erroneous amounts—from unreconciled accounts-some of which are known to have incorrect balances. [*Cobell v. Norton,* 240 F.3d 1081, 1089 (D.C. Cir. 2001)]

---

6. NOTE: A fiduciary obligation is a relationship of special trust in which the trustee is obliged to avoid conflicts of interest and emphasize the well-being of the principal over other considerations.

B. PROCEDURAL HISTORY

The plaintiffs filed the instant action against the Secretary of the Interior and other federal officials on June 10, 1996, "to compel performance of trust obligations." They alleged that the federal government's trustee-delegates, including the Secretary of Interior, breached (and continue to be in breach of) their fiduciary duty to plaintiffs by mismanaging IIM trust accounts. On February 22, 1999, after a two-week bench trial, the Court found Bruce Babbitt, then-Secretary of the Interior, Robert Rubin, then-Secretary of the Treasury, and Kevin Gover, then-Assistant Secretary of Interior for Indian Affairs, in civil contempt for violating two of this Court's discovery orders.

Notwithstanding "defendants' reckless disregard for this court's orders and their attorneys' mismanagement of this case," the Court limited "compensatory relief to monetary sanctions and coercive relief to the appointment of a special master." The Court noted, however, that "should it appear at any point that the defendants are not taking all reasonable steps to comply with the orders of this court, then harsher relief will be duly administered."

Having denied the government's motion to dismiss and its motions for summary judgment, the Court held a six-week bench trial during the summer of 1999 to address the plaintiffs' Phase I claims. The Court issued its Memorandum Opinion, which included extensive findings of fact and conclusions of law, on December 21, 1999. After determining that it had jurisdiction, the Court found that the federal government was in breach of certain fiduciary duties that it owed to plaintiffs. Specifically, the Court accepted a written stipulation filed by the defendants on the eve of trial in which they admitted that they were not in compliance with several obligations prescribed in the 1994 Act.

In order to allow the defendants the opportunity to come into compliance with its fiduciary obligations, the court remanded "the required actions to defendants for further proceedings not inconsistent with the court's Memorandum Opinion." In addition, the Court retained jurisdiction over the case for five years and ordered the defendants to submit "quarterly status reports setting forth and explaining the steps that [they] have taken to rectify the breaches of trust declared" by the Court and "to bring themselves into compliance with their statutory trust duties embodied in the" 1994 Act.

The defendants appealed this Court's decision, alleging that it improperly construed the nature and extent of the government's fiduciary duties to the IIM trust beneficiaries. The D.C. Circuit affirmed this Court's decision on February 23, 2001. Specifically, the D.C. Circuit found that: "The government's broad duty to provide a complete historical accounting to IIM beneficiaries necessarily imposes substantial subsidiary duties on those government officials with responsibility for ensuring that an accounting can and will take place. In particular, it imposes obligations on those who administer the IIM trust lands and funds to, among other things, maintain and complete existing records, recover missing records where possible, and develop plans and procedures sufficient to ensure that all aspects of the accounting process are carried out." [T]he D.C. Circuit remanded the case to this Court (stating that "while the district court may have mischaracterized some of the government's specific obligations, its broader conclusion that government officials breached their obligations to IIM beneficiaries is in accordance with the law and well supported by the evidentiary record. Therefore, we affirm the order of the district court and remand to that court for further proceedings.").

On November 28, 2001, the Court ordered Gale Norton, Secretary of the Interior, and Neal McCaleb, Assistant Secretary of the Interior for Indian Affairs, to show cause why they should not be held in civil contempt of court in their official capacities for the following:

1. Failing to comply with the Court's Order of December 21, 1999, to initiate a Historical Accounting Project.

2. Committing a fraud on the Court by concealing the Department's true actions regarding the Historical Accounting Project during the period from March 2000, until January 2001.

3. Committing a fraud on the Court by failing to disclose the true status of the TAAMS project between September 1999 and December 21, 1999.

4. Committing a fraud on the Court by filing false and misleading quarterly status reports starting in March 2000, regarding TAAMS and BIA Data Clean-up. *Cobell v. Norton,* 175 F.Supp.2d 24, 27 (D.D.C. 2001).

On December 6, 2001, the Court issued a supplemental order that required these defendants to show cause why they should not be held in civil contempt for:

5. Committing a fraud on the Court by making false and misleading representations starting in March, 2000, regarding computer security of IIM trust data.

V. CONCLUSIONS OF LAW

A. SPECIFICATION 1: FAILURE TO INITIATE A HISTORICAL ACCOUNTING PROJECT

The Court concludes that the defendants failed to initiate a historical accounting project as required by the Order of December 21, 1999. The findings of fact presented above clearly establish that the Department of Interior did not take any substantive measures (except publishing a sham notice in the Federal Register) during the eighteen month period following the Court's Phase I trial decision to provide the plaintiffs with the accounting that they are legally entitled to receive. The Court is both saddened and disgusted by the Department's intransigence in the face of the Phase I trial ruling.

Between December 21, 1999 and July 10, 2001, the Department of Interior failed to take any substantive steps towards completing the required historical accounting of the IIM trust accounts. Instead, for more than a year after the Court's Phase I trial ruling the Department engaged in a sham Federal Register process that greatly misled this Court. In particular, that process caused this Court to believe that the agency was utilizing a valid administrative approach to determine which accounting method it would use to perform the required historical accounting. In reality, the Department of Interior was using the Federal Register process to support its appeal of this Court's Phase I trial ruling. Irrespective of that deceitful process, for purposes of Specification 1 it is both sufficient and clear that as of July 10, 2001—more than a year and a half after the Court issued its Phase I trial ruling—the Department of Interior still had not started researching or analyzing the different accounting methods, or retrieving the missing documents that would be necessary to perform an accounting. Thus, as of July 2001 the Department had not even taken the preliminary steps that would enable it to select a particular method to perform the historical accounting.

Notwithstanding the above analysis and the extensive findings of fact regarding this specification, the Court will not issue a contempt citation at this time with respect to Specification 1. Instead, the Court finds that it is sufficient simply to hold that the defendants unreasonably delayed initiating the historical accounting project that they were required to perform in accordance with this Court's Order of December 21, 1999, and that such delay falls within the broad category of litigation misconduct that courts have the inherent power to redress.

B. SPECIFICATION 2: CONCEALING THE DEPARTMENT'S TRUE ACTIONS REGARDING THE HISTORICAL ACCOUNTING PROJECT FROM MARCH 2000 UNTIL JANUARY 2001

The Court concludes that the defendants committed a fraud on the Court by concealing the Department's true actions regarding the Historical Accounting Project during the period from March 2000, until January 2001. The evidence presented and representations made at this contempt trial with respect to this specification prove just how deceitful and disingenuous the defendants can be towards both the individual Indian trust beneficiaries and this Court. The Court's factual findings further demonstrate the lengths the Department will go to avoid having to provide the 300,000 plaintiffs in this action with an accounting of their money held in trust by the United States.

C. SPECIFICATION 3: FAILING TO DISCLOSE THE TRUE STATUS OF THE TAAMS PROJECT BETWEEN SEPTEMBER 1999 and DECEMBER 21, 1999

The Court concludes that the defendants committed a fraud on the Court by failing to disclose the true status of the TAAMS project between September 1999 and December 21, 1999. The Department of Interior (and its attorneys) knew, even before the Phase I trial ended, that many of the representations it had made during that trial with respect to TAAMS were inaccurate. Notwithstanding the fact that Interior was aware of these false statements and the need to correct them, the agency intentionally failed to inform the Court about the massive problems it was experiencing with the new land management system. Thus, the record upon which this Court based its Phase I trial decision was infected with numerous false statements and inaccurate documents put forth by the Interior defendants.

Our adversary system for the resolution of disputes rests on the unshakable foundation that truth is the object of the system's process which is designed for the purpose of dispensing justice. However, because no one has an exclusive insight into truth, the process depends on the adversarial presentation of evidence, precedent, and custom, and argument to reasoned conclusions—all directed with unwavering effort to what, in good faith, is believed to be true on matters material to the disposition. Even the slightest accommodation of deceit or lack of candor in any material respect quickly erodes the validity of the process. As soon as the process falters in that respect, the people are then justified in abandoning support for the system in favor of one where honesty is preeminent. . . . The system can provide no harbor for clever devices to divert the search, mislead opposing counsel or the court, or cover up that which is necessary for justice in the end. *Shaffer Equipment Company* [*United States v. Shaffer Equipment Company,* 11 F.3d 450, 458–59 (4th Cir. 1993)].

By intentionally failing to apprise the Court of the true status of TAAMS, the defendants plainly committed a fraud on this Court and are accordingly adjudged to be in civil contempt of court.

D. SPECIFICATION 4: FILING FALSE AND MISLEADING QUARTERLY STATUS REPORTS STARTING IN MARCH 2000, REGARDING TAAMS AND BIA DATA CLEANUP

The Court concludes that the defendants committed a fraud on the Court by filing false and misleading quarterly status reports starting in March 2000, regarding TAAMS and BIA Data Cleanup. The evidence presented and representations made during this contempt trial clearly demonstrate that the Interior defendants intentionally filed the false and misleading quarterly status reports to make this Court (and the plaintiffs) believe that significant headway had been made on these two critical subprojects. In reality, only minimal progress—if any at all—had been made during this time period, and presently neither the TAAMS nor the BIA Data Cleanup subproject are even remotely close to being completed. By filing false and misleading quarterly status reports the Department of Interior prevented both the Court and the plaintiffs from learning the true status of these two vital subprojects for more than eighteen months. In my fifteen years on the bench I have never seen a litigant make such a concerted effort to subvert the truth seeking function of the judicial process. I am immensely disappointed that I see such a litigant today and that the litigant is a Department of the United States government. The Department of Interior is truly an embarrassment to the federal government in general and the executive branch in particular. The 300,000 individual Indian beneficiaries deserve a better trustee-delegate than the Secretary of Interior.

The egregious nature of the Department's conduct in this regard is exacerbated by the fact that attorneys in the Solicitor's Office actively participated in the drafting of these false and misleading quarterly status reports.

Thus, the Court has no trouble finding that the Department of Interior committed a fraud on the Court by filing false and misleading quarterly status reports and that these defendants are in civil contempt of court for doing so. There is no question that the false and misleading information contained in these reports affected the Court's ability to adjudicate this matter fairly and that it all but destroyed the plaintiffs' ability to present their case. Moreover, the implication of attorneys in the Solicitor's Office clearly make this misconduct constitute fraud on the court. It is almost unfathomable that a federal agency would engage in such a pervasive scheme aimed at defrauding the Court and preventing the plaintiffs from learning the truth about the administration of their trust accounts.

E. SPECIFICATION 5: MAKING FALSE AND MISLEADING REPRESEN-TATIONS STARTING IN MARCH 2000, REGARDING COMPUTER SECURITY OF IIM TRUST DATA

[T]he defendants committed a fraud on the Court by making false and misleading representations starting in March 2000, regarding computer security of IIM trust data.

Beginning in March 2000, the plaintiffs started questioning the manner in which Interior secured the vast quantities of confidential trust information stored in its computer systems. In response to these motions, the Interior Department and its attorneys consistently represented to this Court that while there was a problem with data security, the agency was in the process of making the pertinent computer systems more physically and electronically secure. These representations were patently false, and the Department and its attorneys knew it.

By deliberately making these false and misleading representations, the defendants necessarily precluded this Court from fairly and promptly adjudicating this matter and undeniably hindered the plaintiffs' ability to present its case on this critical point.

[W]hile I agree that Courts must be mindful of the impact a contempt citation will have on a party, it does not stand to reason that once the necessary facts establishing contumacious conduct are proven the Court should simply decline to hold the wrongdoing party in contempt. To do so would make the contempt proceedings themselves a complete waste of time, which in this case would be quite substantial. Second, the extent of defendants' transgressions recounted above are so egregious that the Court has no difficulty concluding that the contempt citations levied today are warranted.

Finally, the defendants argue that "the Court is obliged to consider the prospective impact of a contempt finding upon the Secretary's ability to carry out the very reforms that all parties agree are essential to effective trust administration." During this contempt trial, Deputy Secretary Griles was not quite as diplomatic in the way he articulated this argument. Specifically, he testified that:

> I also know that . . . the inference around the Department is once that [contempt finding] was determined, people's efforts kind of—they went, well, he has already done the worst he can do to us; we are going to go on and do the other things. So I guess if we can find a way to move forward together, that is a lot better than the adversarial role, and that allows us to do it in a meaningful fashion without—I mean, this Secretary and us, if—the IIM accountholders and the tribal leaders and the people who we have to work with have to believe that we are going to do this if you give us a chance. If contempt is issued, I think that is going to put a big stigma on us, that, well, this Judge has already said they've already been in contempt.

The Court rejects this contention put forth by the defendants and Deputy Secretary Griles. The Department of Interior cannot engage in the type of despicable conduct detailed in this opinion and then argue that the Court should nevertheless not hold the Secretary and Assistant Secretary in civil contempt because it may affect their prospective ability to discharge their fiduciary obligations.

VI. RELIEF

The most taxing aspect of this case has been and continues to be fashioning appropriate relief for the plaintiffs. Each time it has been confronted with this difficult issue the Court has stuck to its constitutional roots by awarding only that relief which it finds to be absolutely necessary. For example, following the first contempt trial in this action, in which the Court held former-Secretary Babbitt and former-Assistant Secretary Gover in civil contempt of court after the plaintiffs proved by clear and convincing evidence that these defendants disobeyed two discovery orders and successfully covered up their disobedience through semantics and strained, unilateral, self-serving interpretations of their own duties, the Court took the moderate steps of appointing a special master to oversee the discovery process and awarding plaintiffs reasonable expenses and attorneys' fees incurred as a result of defendants' failure to obey the orders. *Cobell II*, 37 F.Supp.2d at 39.

Moreover, in its Order of December 21, 1999, after the plaintiffs proved that the defendants were in breach of the fiduciary obligations that they owe to the class of 300,000 IIM trust beneficiaries, the Court granted the most mild form of relief that it could fashion. Specifically, the Court declared that the defendants were in breach of certain fiduciary duties that they owe to the plaintiffs, and then remanded the matter back to the administrative agency to bring itself into compliance with those duties as well as the obligations found in the 1994 Act. *Cobell V*, 91 F.Supp.2d at 58-59. So as not to interfere unduly in the inner workings of the Interior Department, the Court further ordered the defendants to file quarterly status reports setting forth and explaining the steps that they have taken to rectify the breaches of trust declared by the Court and to bring themselves into compliance with their statutory trust duties embodied in the 1994. The Court thus explicitly declined at that time to issue a structural injunction or even to appoint a special master to monitor the defendants' progress towards bringing themselves into compliance with their trust duties.[7] The Court also rejected at that time the plaintiffs' request for the appointment of a receiver to manage the IIM trust accounts.[8]

A. THE APPOINTMENT OF A RECEIVER OVER THE IIM TRUST

The plaintiffs vigorously argue that the only adequate remedy to redress the defendants' egregious misconduct in this case is the appointment of a receiver over the IIM trust. Specifically, the plaintiffs contend that this Court should "be dissuaded no longer by any further misrepresentation or pettifoggery and promptly appoint a receiver so that trust reform may finally commence." In response, the defendants (arrogantly) fail to argue that the appointment of a

---

7. NOTE: A special master is an official appointed by a court to oversee implementation of a court order with some decision authority conferred by the court.

8. NOTE: The concept of a receiver comes from bankruptcy or default law in which the receiver is sent in by a court to take over the organization and bring it into compliance with the law.

receiver is not warranted in this case. Rather the defendants contend only that "the relief Plaintiffs seek is beyond this Court's authority to provide because the United States Constitution prohibits appointment of a receiver to assume the trust management and reform duties Congress has conferred on the Secretary [of Interior]." As the Court explains below, while it finds that the appointment of a receiver in this case would be consistent with both the 1994 Act and the United States Constitution, the Court will refrain from granting such relief at this time. Instead, the Court has determined that the more sound approach is to schedule and conduct further proceedings to determine what additional relief (other than a receiver) is warranted with respect to the fixing the system portion of the case, and approve an approach to conducting a historical accounting of the IIM trust accounts. The Court will discuss these future proceedings and what they will entail in the next section of this opinion.

B. FUTURE PROCEEDINGS—PHASE 1.5 TRIAL

It is now abundantly clear that the Phase II trial envisioned and described by the Court in the Memorandum Opinion issued on December 21, 1999, will not occur anytime in the foreseeable future. ([I]n general terms the Phase II trial "will involve the government bringing forward its proof on IIM trust balances and then plaintiffs making exceptions to that proof."). It is equally apparent to the Court that the defendants are no closer today to discharging their fiduciary responsibilities properly than they were during the Phase I trial back in the summer of 1999. At the conclusion of that trial, after the plaintiffs proved that the defendants were in breach of the fiduciary duties that they owe to the 300,000 individual Indian trust beneficiaries, the plaintiffs requested that this Court put the IIM trust under court supervision. The Court declined to grant such relief at that time because it felt that it was its constitutional duty to allow the defendants to correct the breaches declared by the Court and those found in the 1994 Act. Thus, by declaring the trust duties of the defendants and remanding the matter back to the agency, the Court granted the least intrusive form of relief that it could fashion.

In light of the current posture of this case, it is now obvious that this relief was and is insufficient. The recalcitrance exhibited by the Department of Interior in complying with the orders of this Court is only surpassed by the incompetence that the agency has shown in administering the IIM trust. Accordingly, the Court concludes that while its factual findings and legal conclusions in the Phase I trial ruling were correct (and will therefore not be disturbed), the relief granted by the Court at that time is no longer adequate. Consistent with this conclusion, the Court has determined that it must now consider granting further injunctive relief with respect to fixing the system portion of the case and the historical accounting project. To the extent plaintiffs believe that they are entitled to relief in addition to any injunction that may be entered by the Court, they may request such relief at the appropriate time.

In accordance with the foregoing analysis, the Court will schedule and conduct further proceedings (which shall hereinafter be referred to as the Phase 1.5 trial) to determine what additional relief is warranted in this matter. Specifically, the Phase 1.5 trial will encompass additional remedies with respect to the fixing

the system portion of the case, and approving an approach to conducting a historical accounting of the IIM trust accounts. In this regard, the Court will order the
Interior defendants to file with the Court and serve upon the plaintiffs a plan for
conducting a historical accounting of the IIM trust accounts. This plan shall be filed
and served upon completion but no later than January 6, 2003. In addition, the
Court will order the defendants to file with the Court and serve upon the plaintiffs
a plan for bringing themselves into compliance with the fiduciary obligations that
they owe to the IIM trust beneficiaries. As part of this plan, the defendants shall
describe, in detail, the standards by which they intend to administer the IIM trust
accounts, and how their proposed actions would bring them into compliance with
those standards. This plan should also be filed and served when completed but no
later than January 6, 2003. The Court will grant leave to the plaintiffs to file any
plan or plans of their own regarding the aforementioned matters. If the plaintiffs
wish to make such a filing, they should do so no later than January 6, 2003, and
should provide the defendants with a copy. The parties shall file any summary judgment motions with respect to the Phase 1.5 trial no later than January 31, 2003. The
parties shall also be afforded the opportunity to file a response to the plan or plans
of the other party. These responses shall be filed no later than January 31, 2003. The
Phase 1.5 trial shall begin on May 1, 2003, at 10:00 a.m. Dates for pretrial and
motions hearings will be set in subsequent orders.

There are two additional issues worth addressing before moving on to the
next section. First, since the Phase I trial ended, the Department of Interior has
annoyingly persisted in arguing that this Court lacks jurisdiction to review its
efforts to conduct a historical accounting of the IIM trust accounts because it has
not taken final agency action, as required by the APA. The Court finds the
Department's contention in this regard to be misplaced. Numerous courts have
recognized, and in fact the APA specifically provides, that where a federal court
has jurisdiction to hear challenges to an agency action it also has jurisdiction over
claims of unreasonable delay. In the instant matter, both this Court and the D.C.
Circuit have already concluded that the Department of Interior has unreasonably
delayed providing plaintiffs with an accurate accounting of their funds held in
trust by the United States, and in discharging their fiduciary duties properly. In
light of these findings, it is disingenuous for the defendants to continue to argue—
one-hundred years after the IIM trust was established, eight years after Congress
enacted the 1994 Act, and nearly three years after this Court issued its Phase I trial
decision—that the Court lacks jurisdiction to compel the agency to act when it
has unreasonably delayed in doing so.

The consequences of further agency delay are potentially quite severe. Documents necessary for a proper accounting and reconciliation have been lost or
destroyed, and the district court found little reason to believe that this would
change in the near future. The longer defendants delay in creating the plans necessary to render an accounting, the greater the chance that plaintiffs will never
receive an actual accounting of their own trust money. Given that many plaintiffs
rely upon their IIM trust accounts for their financial well-being, the injury from
delay could cause irreparable harm to plaintiffs' interests as IIM trust beneficiaries.
Thus, it seems that the interests at stake are not merely economic interests in an
administrative scheme, but personal interests in life and health.

C. PLAINTIFFS' REASONABLE EXPENSES & ATTORNEYS' FEES

There is no question that the defendants must be ordered to pay the reasonable expenses, including attorneys' fees, incurred by plaintiffs as a result of having to litigate this contempt trial. Courts have long recognized that such relief is appropriate to redress both contumacious and sanctionable conduct by a litigant. Awarding such relief is particularly appropriate in this case considering the severity of the defendants' transgressions and the fact that the conduct has undeniably exacerbated the already considerable harm that the plaintiffs have suffered as a result of the defendants' failure to discharge their fiduciary obligations properly.

[C]ourts have a duty to hold government officials responsible for their conduct when they infringe on the legitimate rights of others. These officials are responsible for seeing that the laws of the United States are faithfully executed. In this case, the laws—the orders of this court—were either ignored or thwarted at every turn by these officials and their subordinates. The court must hold such government officials accountable; otherwise, our citizens—as litigants—are reduced to mere supplicants of the government, taking whatever is dished out to them. That is not our system of government, as established by the Constitution. We have a government of law, and government officials must be held accountable under the law.

E. THE APPOINTMENT OF A SPECIAL MASTER-MONITOR

Although the Court declines at this juncture to place the IIM trust into receivership, the Court concludes that the appointment of a special master to monitor the status of trust reform is clearly warranted. The Court has decided to appoint another special master rather than expand the powers of Special Master Balaran in this regard because the scope of this lawsuit is such that it is not practical to have only one individual perform all of the required duties.

The special master-monitor shall ensure that the Court (and the plaintiffs) receive complete and accurate information regarding these matters by periodically filing status reports. In these reports, the special master-monitor may apprise the Court of any other matters that he deems pertinent to this litigation, but take no further action without prior approval of the Court, as well as provide the Court with any recommendations he may have regarding issues identified in the reports. The special master-monitor shall also oversee the discovery process and administer document production, except insofar as the issues raised by the parties relate to IT security, records preservation and retention, the Department of the Treasury, or Paragraph 19 documents.

F. FURTHER RELIEF—DISCOVERY

The defendants have amply demonstrated during the two and a half years since this Court's Phase I trial ruling that they cannot be trusted to report in a timely manner complete and accurate information regarding the status of trust reform and their efforts to discharge their fiduciary responsibilities properly. At the time the Court issued its Phase I trial decision, the Court found that it was sufficient for the defendants to file quarterly status reports and for plaintiffs to then "petition the court to order defendants to provide further information as needed if such information cannot be obtained through informal requests directly to defendants." The Court finds that this approach is no longer appropriate in light of the false and misleading quarterly status reports filed by the defendants since March 2000. Accordingly, the Court will permit plaintiffs full discovery on matters that they otherwise would not have been able to explore prior to this decision. While the Court will thus expand the scope of discovery for the plaintiffs, the Special Master-Monitor shall ensure that such discovery does not unreasonably interfere with the defendants' ability to develop their plans for submission to the Court. As noted above, the Court will also continue to require the defendants to file quarterly status reports pursuant to the December 21, 1999 Order.

G. IT SECURITY

Although the Court continues to be deeply concerned about the deplorable status of IT security and the fact that the defendants committed a fraud by making false and misleading representations regarding this matter, the Court has decided that further injunctive relief is not warranted at this time. Thus, the Court will not vacate or modify the consent order regarding information technology entered on December 17, 2001.[9] The Court reaches this conclusion in large part based on the representations made by the Special Master that Associate Deputy Secretary James Cason is working closely and cooperatively with him on these issues. If it appears in the future that further relief is warranted, however, the Court can and will take appropriate measures at that time.

I. CERTIFICATION OF ORDER FOR INTERLOCUTORY APPEAL

The Court certified its Order of December 21, 1999 for interlocutory appeal because it found that "an immediate appeal of the court's order may materially advance the ultimate termination of the litigation." In light of the extraordinary delay since that time caused by the defendants' unconscionable actions, the Court will not certify the order accompanying this Memorandum Opinion for inter-locutory appeal. Such an appeal by the defendants would undeniably delay even further this already protracted litigation, and compound the harm that plaintiffs suffer each day as a result of the defendants' inability to discharge properly their fiduciary duties. Moreover, the Court will not grant a motion for a stay pending appeal, should defendants seek to appeal today's decision. This Court will not authorize further delay by defendants.

VII. CONCLUSION

In February of 1999, at the end of the first contempt trial in this matter, I stated that "I have never seen more egregious misconduct by the federal govern-ment." Now, at the conclusion of the second contempt trial in this action, I stand corrected. The Department of Interior has truly outdone itself this time. The agency has indisputably proven to the Court, Congress, and the individual Indian

---

9. NOTE: A consent order is an agreement between the parties to a case that is entered as an order of the court and therefore is enforceable by the court using its powers of contempt.

beneficiaries that it is either unwilling or unable to administer competently the IIM trust. Worse yet, the Department has now undeniably shown that it can no longer be trusted to state accurately the status of its trust reform efforts. In short, there is no longer any doubt that the Secretary of Interior has been and continues to be an unfit trustee-delegate for the United States.

Over a two year period, the defendants successfully led this Court and the plaintiffs to believe that they were bringing themselves into compliance with the 1994 Act, and that they were taking steps that would one day provide the foundation for a historical accounting of the IIM trust accounts. In reality, as the Court chronicled in painstaking detail above, the Interior Department was experiencing so many difficulties in so many different aspects of its trust reform effort that the agency is still only at best marginally closer to discharging its fiduciary obligations properly than it was three years ago when the Court held the Phase I trial.

Congress has mandated, the Court has ordered, and the beneficiaries have pleaded for meaningful reform of the IIM trust. This Court need not sit supinely by waiting, hoping that the Department of Interior complies with the orders of this Court and the fiduciary obligations mandated by Congress in the 1994 Act. To do so would be futile. I may have life tenure, but at the rate the Department of Interior is progressing that is not a long enough appointment. Accordingly, the Court has ordered relief today that it views as being absolutely necessary to getting both this case and trust reform back on track. In the meantime, Secretary Norton and Assistant Secretary McCaleb can now rightfully take their place alongside former-Secretary Babbitt and former-Assistant Secretary Gover in the pantheon of unfit trustee-delegates.

✷✷✷✷✷

THE LIABILITY AND IMMUNITY
OF PUBLIC OFFICIALS

State and local officials have long been subject to suits for money damages for violation of the constitutional and statutory rights of citizens. As the *Public Law and Public Administration, Third Edition* explains, these suits have been brought in state courts under various state tort liability statutes and in federal courts, most often under 42 U.S.C. §1983.[10] Federal officials have also been subject to suit for their constitutional violations and have been called to answer in various ways in judicial proceedings, including actions brought against the president of the United States. In fact, it was such a suit against President Richard Nixon

---

10. "Every person who, under color of any statute, ordinance, regulation, custom, or usage . . . subjects, or causes to be subjected, any citizen of the United States or other person within the jurisdiction thereof to the deprivation of any rights, privileges, or immunities secured by the Constitution and laws, shall be liable to the party injured in an action at law, suit in equity, or other proper proceeding for redress. . . ."

and some of his aides that both tested the boundaries of executive immunity at the national level and established the basic rules about the obligations of public officials in tort suits at all levels.

Harlow v. Fitzgerald, 457 U.S. 800 (1982).

INTRODUCTION: A. Ernest Fitzgerald was the Deputy for Management Systems, working for the Secretary of the Air Force, when he was asked to testify before Senator William Proxmire's (D.,Wis.) Joint Economic Committee in 1968 and again in 1969. When asked direct questions about the C-5A cargo aircraft program, Fitzgerald indicated that it appeared likely that the program would run very large cost overruns, perhaps as much as $2 billion (a very large sum in those days). Shortly after he testified for the second time, his job was eliminated. Fitzgerald fought for over a decade to win reinstatement, despite the fact that it had long since been discovered that there was a memorandum prepared by the Air Force early as 1969 targeting him for punishment and explaining how he could be terminated.[11] Congress eventually enacted the Whistleblower Protection Act in no small part because of this disgraceful story.

But there was another part to the story that reached into the White House. While the Air Force moved against Fitzgerald during the waning weeks of President Johnson's term, he was not actually terminated until nearly a year into the Nixon administration. There was an immediate outcry from Congress and others that Fitzgerald's punishment was the clearest possible case of retribution for having done the right thing. Nixon responded to press inquiries by promising further consideration of the situation. Later events indicated that the president had asked H.R. Haldeman, then White House Chief of Staff, to find Fitzgerald another position.

However, the Nixon administration demanded absolute loyalty and would not tolerate perceived disloyalty. It was on that basis that some Nixon staffers resisted efforts to keep Fitzgerald in government. The Supreme Court observed that: "White House aide Alexander Butterfield reported to Haldeman that 'Fitzgerald is no doubt a top-notch cost expert, but he must be given very low marks in loyalty; and after all, loyalty is the name of the game.' Butterfield therefore recommended that '[we] should let him bleed, for a while at least.' There is no evidence of White House efforts to reemploy Fitzgerald subsequent to the Butterfield memorandum."[12] During the litigation that followed

---

11. Memorandum of John Lang to Harold Brown, January 6, 1969, *Nixon v. Fitzgerald,* 457 U.S. 731, 733 n1 (1982). See also Monte E. Crane, Air Force Central Labor Law Office AFLSA/JACL, *Office of Special Counsel and Whistleblower Protection Primer* (http://www .bop.gov/hrmpg/lmr/hrmlmryy.pdf), September 7, 2002.

12. *Nixon v. Fitzgerald,* 457 U.S. 731, 735–736 (1982).

his termination, Secretary of the Air Force Seamans denied Fitzgerald's charges but also admitted that he had received "'some advice' from the White House before Fitzgerald's job was abolished. But the Secretary declined to be more specific. . . , invoking 'executive privilege.'"[13]

President Nixon did a double reverse on his own position when he asserted in a news conference that it was not Secretary Seamans who made the decision to fire Fitzgerald, but his own action. That statement was retracted the next day by the White House. However, the record showed that Nixon had told Charles Colson and John Ehrlichman on the day of the news conference that he was the one responsible for Fitzgerald's ouster.[14]

Ultimately, Fitzgerald's case alleged that Butterfield and Bryce Harlow, a long-time White House advisor, had acted in conspiracy with the president to destroy his career. At that time Harlow was responsible for congressional relations for the president and was alleged to have had a number of discussions with the Secretary of the Air Force about Fitzgerald's termination when the Secretary contacted him to assess likely congressional reaction. Secretary Seamans later testified, however, that Harlow had recommended against the Air Force plans. There was also a Nixon tape recording that recalled that "Harlow was 'all for canning' Fitzgerald" as well as information concerning a conversation with John Erlichman in which Nixon indicated that Harlow favored the firing.[15]

The case against the president came to the Supreme Court as a separate matter because of a claim of absolute immunity from suits against a president for actions taken while in office.

The *Harlow* case raised a different issue as to whether and what type of immunity could be used by White House officials to shield them from liability.

$$\ast\ast\ast\ast\ast$$

JUSTICE POWELL wrote the opinion for the Court.

The issue in this case is the scope of the immunity available to the senior aides and advisers of the President of the United States in a suit for damages based upon their official acts.

I. Harlow argues that exhaustive discovery has adduced no direct evidence of his involvement in any wrongful activity. He asserts he had no reason to believe that a conspiracy existed. He contends that he took all his actions in good faith. For his part, Butterfield denies that he was involved in any decision concerning Fitzgerald's employment status until Haldeman sought his advice in December

---

13. Id., at 736–737.

14. Id., at 737.

15. *Harlow v. Fitzgerald,* 457 U.S. 800, 803 (1982).

1969—more than a month after Fitzgerald's termination had been scheduled and announced publicly by the Air Force.

[T]he District Court upheld the legal sufficiency of Fitzgerald's *Bivens* (*Bivens v. Six Unknown Fed. Narcotics Agents,* 403 U.S. 388 (1971)) claim under the First Amendment and his "inferred" statutory causes of action. The court found that genuine issues of disputed fact remained for resolution at trial. It also ruled that petitioners were not entitled to absolute immunity.

Independently of former President Nixon, petitioners appealed the denial of their immunity defense to the Court of Appeals for the District of Columbia Circuit. The Court of Appeals dismissed the appeal without opinion. Never having determined the immunity available to the senior aides and advisers of the President of the United States, we granted *certiorari*.

II. [O]ur decisions consistently have held that government officials are entitled to some form of immunity from suits for damages. As recognized at common law, public officers require this protection to shield them from undue interference with their duties and from potentially disabling threats of liability.

Our decisions have recognized immunity defenses of two kinds. For officials whose special functions or constitutional status requires complete protection from suit, we have recognized the defense of "absolute immunity." The absolute immunity of legislators, in their legislative functions, see, e.g., *Eastland v. United States Servicemen's Fund,* 421 U.S. 491 (1975), and of judges, in their judicial functions, see, e.g., *Stump v. Sparkman,* 435 U.S. 349 (1978), now is well settled. Our decisions also have extended absolute immunity to certain officials of the Executive Branch. These include prosecutors and similar officials, see *Butz v. Economou,* 438 U.S. 478, 508–512 (1978), executive officers engaged in adjudicative functions, and the President of the United States, see *Nixon v. Fitzgerald,* [457 U.S. 731 (1982)].

For executive officials in general, however, our cases make plain that qualified immunity represents the norm. In *Scheuer v. Rhodes,* 416 U.S. 232 (1974), we acknowledged that high officials require greater protection than those with less complex discretionary responsibilities. Nonetheless, we held that a governor and his aides could receive the requisite protection from qualified or good-faith immunity. In *Butz v. Economou, supra,* we extended the approach of *Scheuer* to high federal officials of the Executive Branch. [W]e explained that the recognition of a qualified immunity defense for high executives reflected an attempt to balance competing values: not only the importance of a damages remedy to protect the rights of citizens, but also "the need to protect officials who are required to exercise their discretion and the related public interest in encouraging the vigorous exercise of official authority." Without discounting the adverse consequences of denying high officials an absolute immunity from private lawsuits alleging constitutional violations we emphasized our expectation that insubstantial suits need not proceed to trial: "Insubstantial lawsuits can be quickly terminated by federal courts alert to the possibilities of artful pleading. Unless the complaint states a compensable claim for relief . . . , it should not survive a motion to dismiss. Moreover, the Court recognized in *Scheuer* that damages suits concerning constitutional violations need not proceed to trial, but can be terminated on a properly supported motion for summary judgment based on the defense of immunity. . . . In responding to such a motion, plaintiffs may not play dog in the manger; and firm application of the Federal Rules of Civil Procedure will ensure that federal officials are not harassed by frivolous lawsuits."

Butz continued to acknowledge that the special functions of some officials might require absolute immunity. But the Court held that "federal officials who seek absolute exemption from personal liability for unconstitutional conduct must bear the burden of showing that public policy requires an exemption of that scope." This we reaffirmed today in *Nixon v. Fitzgerald.*

III. A. Petitioners argue that they are entitled to a blanket protection of absolute immunity as an incident of their offices as Presidential aides. In deciding this claim we do not write on an empty page. In *Butz v. Economou,* [w]e rejected [a sitting cabinet member's claim of absolute immunity as a cabinet member]. In so doing we did not question the power or the importance of the Secretary's office. Nor did we doubt the importance to the President of loyal and efficient subordinates in executing his duties of office. Yet we found these factors, alone, to be insufficient to justify absolute immunity. "[The] greater power of [high] officials," we reasoned, "affords a greater potential for a regime of lawless conduct." Damages actions against high officials were therefore "an important means of vindicating constitutional guarantees." Moreover, we concluded that it would be "untenable to draw a distinction for purposes of immunity law between suits brought against state officials under [42 U. S. C.] §1983 and suits brought directly under the Constitution against federal officials."

Having decided in *Butz* that Members of the Cabinet ordinarily enjoy only qualified immunity from suit, we conclude today that it would be equally untenable to hold absolute immunity an incident of the office of every Presidential subordinate based in the White House. Members of the Cabinet are direct subordinates of the President, frequently with greater responsibilities, both to the President and to the Nation, than White House staff. The considerations that supported our decision in *Butz* apply with equal force to this case. It is no disparagement of the offices held by petitioners to hold that Presidential aides, like Members of the Cabinet, generally are entitled only to a qualified immunity.

B. Petitioners also assert an entitlement to immunity based on the "special functions" of White House aides. For aides entrusted with discretionary authority in such sensitive areas as national security or foreign policy, absolute immunity might well be justified to protect the unhesitating performance of functions vital to the national interest. But a "special functions" rationale does not warrant a blanket recognition of absolute immunity for all Presidential aides in the performance of all their duties.

The burden of justifying absolute immunity rests on the official asserting the claim. In order to establish entitlement to absolute immunity a Presidential aide first must show that the responsibilities of his office embraced a function so sensitive as to require a total shield from liability. He then must demonstrate that he was discharging the protected function when performing the act for which liability is asserted.

Applying these standards to the claims advanced by petitioners Harlow and Butterfield, we cannot conclude on the record before us that either has shown that "public policy requires [for any of the functions of his office] an exemption of [absolute] scope." Nor, assuming that petitioners did have functions for which absolute immunity would be warranted, could we now conclude that the acts charged in this lawsuit would lie within the protected area. We do not, however, foreclose the possibility that petitioners, on remand, could satisfy the standards properly applicable to their claims.

IV. Even if they cannot establish that their official functions require absolute immunity, petitioners assert that public policy at least mandates an application of the qualified immunity standard that would permit the defeat of insubstantial claims without resort to trial. We agree.

A. The resolution of immunity questions inherently requires a balance between the evils inevitable in any available alternative. In situations of abuse of office, an action for damages may offer the only realistic avenue for vindication of constitutional guarantees. It is this recognition that has required the denial of absolute immunity to most public officers. At the same time, however, it cannot be disputed seriously that claims frequently run against the innocent as well as the guilty—at a cost not only to the defendant officials, but to society as a whole. These social costs include the expenses of litigation, the diversion of official energy from pressing public issues, and the deterrence of able citizens from acceptance of public office. Finally, there is the danger that fear of being sued will "dampen the ardor of all but the most resolute, or the most irresponsible [public officials], in the unflinching discharge of their duties."

In identifying qualified immunity as the best attainable accommodation of competing values, we [have] relied on the assumption that this standard would permit "[insubstantial] lawsuits [to] be quickly terminated." Yet petitioners advance persuasive arguments that the dismissal of insubstantial lawsuits without trial requires an adjustment of the "good faith" standard established by our decisions.

B. Qualified or "good faith" immunity is an affirmative defense that must be pleaded by a defendant official. Decisions of this Court have established that the "good faith" defense has both an "objective" and a "subjective" aspect. The objective element involves a presumptive knowledge of and respect for "basic, unquestioned constitutional rights." *Wood v. Strickland,* 420 U.S. 308, 322 (1975). The subjective component refers to "permissible intentions." Referring both to the objective and subjective elements, we have held that qualified immunity would be defeated if an official "knew or reasonably should have known that the action he took within his sphere of official responsibility would violate the constitutional rights of the [plaintiff], or if he took the action with the malicious intention to cause a deprivation of constitutional rights or other injury. . . ."

The subjective element of the good-faith defense frequently has proved incompatible with our admonition that insubstantial claims should not proceed to trial. Rule 56 of the Federal Rules of Civil Procedure provides that disputed questions of fact ordinarily may not be decided on motions for summary judgment.

And an official's subjective good faith has been considered to be a question of fact that some courts have regarded as inherently requiring resolution by a jury.

[I]t now is clear that substantial costs attend the litigation of the subjective good faith of government officials. Not only are there the general costs of subjecting officials to the risks of trial—distraction of officials from their governmental duties, inhibition of discretionary action, and deterrence of able people from public service. There are special costs to "subjective" inquiries of this kind. Immunity generally is available only to officials performing discretionary functions. In contrast with the thought processes accompanying "ministerial" tasks, the judgments surrounding discretionary action almost inevitably are influenced by the decision-maker's experiences, values, and emotions. These variables explain in part why questions of subjective intent so rarely can be decided by summary judgment. Yet they also frame a background in which there often is no clear end to the relevant evidence. Judicial inquiry into subjective motivation therefore may entail broad-ranging discovery and the deposing of numerous persons, including an official's professional colleagues. Inquiries of this kind can be peculiarly disruptive of effective government.

Consistently with the balance at which we aimed in *Butz,* we conclude today that bare allegations of malice should not suffice to subject government officials either to the costs of trial or to the burdens of broad-reaching discovery. We therefore hold that government officials performing discretionary functions generally are shielded from liability for civil damages insofar as their conduct does not violate clearly established statutory or constitutional rights of which a reasonable person would have known.

Reliance on the objective reasonableness of an official's conduct, as measured by reference to clearly established law, should avoid excessive disruption of government and permit the resolution of many insubstantial claims on summary judgment. On summary judgment, the judge appropriately may determine, not only the currently applicable law, but whether that law was clearly established at the time an action occurred. If the law at that time was not clearly established, an official could not reasonably be expected to anticipate subsequent legal developments, nor could he fairly be said to "know" that the law forbade conduct not previously identified as unlawful. Until this threshold immunity question is resolved, discovery should not be allowed. If the law was clearly established, the immunity defense ordinarily should fail, since a reasonably competent public official should know the law governing his conduct. Nevertheless, if the official pleading the defense claims extraordinary circumstances and can prove that he neither knew nor should have known of the relevant legal standard, the defense should be sustained. But again, the defense would turn primarily on objective factors.

By defining the limits of qualified immunity essentially in objective terms, we provide no license to lawless conduct. The public interest in deterrence of unlawful conduct and in compensation of victims remains protected by a test that focuses on the objective legal reasonableness of an official's acts. Where an official could be expected to know that certain conduct would violate statutory or constitutional rights, he should be made to hesitate; and a person who suffers injury caused by such conduct may have a cause of action. But where an official's duties legitimately require action in which clearly established rights are not implicated, the public interest may be better served by action taken "with independence and without fear of consequences."

V. The judgment of the Court of Appeals is vacated, and the case is remanded for further action consistent with this opinion. So ordered.

JUSTICE BRENNAN wrote a concurring opinion joined by JUSTICES MARSHALL and BLACKMUN.

I agree with the substantive standard announced by the Court today, imposing liability when a public-official defendant "knew or should have known" of the constitutionally violative effect of his actions. This standard would not allow the official who actually knows that he was violating the law to escape liability for his actions, even if he could not "reasonably have been expected" to know what he actually did know. Thus the clever and unusually well-informed violator of constitutional rights will not evade just punishment for his crimes. I also agree that this standard applies "across the board," to all "government officials performing discretionary functions." I write separately only to note that given this standard, it seems inescapable to me that some measure of discovery may sometimes be required to determine exactly what a public-official defendant did "know" at the time of his actions. Of course, summary judgment will be readily available to public-official defendants whenever the state of the law was so ambiguous at the time of the alleged violation that it could not have been "known" then, and thus liability could not ensue. In my view, summary judgment will also be readily available whenever the plaintiff cannot prove, as a threshold matter, that a violation of his constitutional rights actually occurred. I see no reason why discovery of defendants' "knowledge" should not be deferred by the trial judge pending decision of any motion of defendants for summary judgment on grounds such as these.

JUSTICES BRENNAN, WHITE, MARSHALL, and BLACKMUN authored a joint concurring opinion.

We join the Court's opinion but, having dissented in *Nixon v. Fitzgerald,* we disassociate ourselves from any implication in the Court's opinion in the present case that *Nixon v. Fitzgerald* was correctly decided.

JUSTICE REHNQUIST wrote a concurring opinion.

At such time as a majority of the Court is willing to reexamine our holding in *Butz v. Economou,* I shall join in that undertaking with alacrity. But until that time comes, I agree that the Court's opinion in this case properly disposes of the issues presented, and I therefore join it.

CHIEF JUSTICE BURGER wrote a dissenting opinion.

The Court today decides in *Nixon v. Fitzgerald* what has been taken for granted for 190 years, that it is implicit in the Constitution that a President of the United States has absolute immunity from civil suits arising out of official acts as

Chief Executive. I agree fully that absolute immunity for official acts of the President is, like executive privilege, "fundamental to the operation of Government and inextricably rooted in the separation of powers under the Constitution."

In this case the Court decides that senior aides of the President do not have derivative immunity from the President. I am at a loss, however, to reconcile this conclusion with our holding in *Gravel v. United States,* 408 U.S. 606 (1972). The Court reads *Butz v. Economou* as resolving that question; I do not. *Butz* is clearly distinguishable.

In *Gravel* we held that it is implicit in the Constitution that aides of Members of Congress have absolute immunity for acts performed for Members in relation to their legislative function. We viewed the aides' immunity as deriving from the Speech or Debate Clause, which provides that "for any Speech or Debate in either House, [Senators and Representatives] shall not be questioned in any other Place." Art. I, §6, cl. 1. Read literally, the Clause would, of course, limit absolute immunity only to the Member and only to speech and debate within the Chamber. But we have read much more into this plain language. The Clause says nothing about "legislative acts" outside the Chambers, but we concluded that the Constitution grants absolute immunity for legislative acts not only "in either House" but in committees and conferences and in reports on legislative activities.

Nor does the Clause mention immunity for congressional aides. Yet, going far beyond any words found in the Constitution itself, we held that a Member's aides who implement policies and decisions of the Member are entitled to the same absolute immunity as a Member.

We very properly recognized in *Gravel* that the central purpose of a Member's absolute immunity would be "diminished and frustrated" if the legislative aides were not also protected by the same broad immunity. I joined in that analysis and continue to agree with it, for without absolute immunity for these "elbow aides," who are indeed "alter egos," a Member could not effectively discharge all of the assigned constitutional functions of a modern legislator.

The Court has made this reality a matter of our constitutional jurisprudence. How can we conceivably hold that a President of the United States, who represents a vastly larger constituency than does any Member of Congress, should not have "alter egos" with comparable immunity? To perform the constitutional duties assigned to the Executive would be "literally impossible, in view of the complexities of the modern [Executive] process, . . . without the help of aides and assistants." These words reflect the precise analysis of *Gravel,* and this analysis applies with at least as much force to a President.

✹✹✹✹✹

Nixon v. Fitzgerald, 457 U.S. 731 (1982).

INTRODUCTION: The other half of this battle is related but quite different. It addresses the issues of the president's immunity from suit. The facts were, of course, discussed in the introduction to the *Harlow* decision.

*****

JUSTICE POWELL wrote the opinion for the Court.

The plaintiff in this lawsuit seeks relief in civil damages from a former President of the United States. The claim rests on actions allegedly taken in the former President's official capacity during his tenure in office. The issue before us is the scope of the immunity possessed by the President of the United States.

III. A. This Court consistently has recognized that government officials are entitled to some form of immunity from suits for civil damages. In *Spalding v. Vilas,* 161 U.S. 483 (1896), the Court considered the immunity available to the Postmaster General in a suit for damages based upon his official acts. Drawing upon principles of immunity developed in English cases at common law, the Court concluded that "[the] interests of the people" required a grant of absolute immunity to public officers. In the absence of immunity, the Court reasoned, executive officials would hesitate to exercise their discretion in a way "injuriously [affecting] the claims of particular individuals," even when the public interest required bold and unhesitating action.

Decisions subsequent to *Spalding* have extended the defense of immunity to actions besides those at common law. In *Tenney v. Brandhove,* 341 U.S. 367 (1951), the Court held that the passage of 42 U. S. C. §1983 had not abrogated the privilege accorded to state legislators at common law. Similarly, the decision in *Pierson v. Ray,* 386 U.S. 547 (1967), involving a §1983 suit against a state judge, recognized the continued validity of the absolute immunity of judges for acts within the judicial role. The Court in *Pierson* also held that police officers are entitled to a qualified immunity protecting them from suit when their official acts are performed in "good faith."

In *Scheuer v. Rhodes,* 416 U.S. 232 (1974), we rejected [state executive] officials' claim to absolute immunity, finding instead that state executive officials possessed a "good faith" immunity from §1983 suits alleging constitutional violations. Balancing the purposes of §1983 against the imperatives of public policy, the Court held that "in varying scope, a qualified immunity is available to officers of the executive branch of government, the variation being dependent upon the scope of discretion and responsibilities of the office and all the circumstances as they reasonably appeared at the time of the action on which liability is sought to be based."

Scheuer established a two-tiered division of immunity defenses in §1983 suits. To most executive officers *Scheuer* accorded qualified immunity. For them the scope of the defense varied in proportion to the nature of their official functions and the range of decisions that conceivably might be taken in "good faith." This "functional" approach also defined a second tier, however, at which the especially sensitive duties of certain officials—notably judges and prosecutors—required the continued recognition of absolute immunity.

In *Butz v. Economou,* 438 U.S. 478 (1978), we considered for the first time the kind of immunity possessed by federal executive officials sued for constitutional violations. Concluding that a blanket recognition of absolute immunity would be anomalous in light of the qualified immunity standard applied to state executive officials, we held that federal officials generally have the same qualified immunity possessed by state officials in cases under §1983. [However], in *Butz* itself we upheld a claim of absolute immunity for administrative officials engaged in functions analogous to those of judges and prosecutors.

B. Our decisions concerning the immunity of government officials from civil damages liability have been guided by the Constitution, federal statutes, and history. Additionally, at least in the absence of explicit constitutional or congressional guidance, our immunity decisions have been informed by the common law. This Court necessarily also has weighed concerns of public policy, especially as illuminated by our history and the structure of our government.

This case now presents the claim that the President of the United States is shielded by absolute immunity from civil damages liability. In the case of the President the inquiries into history and policy, though mandated independently by our cases, tend to coverage. Because the Presidency did not exist through most of the development of common law, any historical analysis must draw its evidence primarily from our constitutional heritage and structure. This inquiry involves policies and principles that may be considered implicit in the nature of the President's office in a system structured to achieve effective government under a constitutionally mandated separation of powers.

IV. Applying the principles of our cases, we hold that petitioner, as a former President of the United States, is entitled to absolute immunity from damages liability predicated on his official acts. We consider this immunity a functionally mandated incident of the President's unique office, rooted in the constitutional tradition of the separation of powers and supported by our history.

A. The President occupies a unique position in the constitutional scheme. Article II, §1, of the Constitution provides that "[the] executive Power shall be vested in a President of the United States. . . ." This grant of authority establishes the President as the chief constitutional officer of the Executive Branch, entrusted with supervisory and policy responsibilities of utmost discretion and sensitivity. These include the enforcement of federal law—it is the President who is charged constitutionally to "take Care that the Laws be faithfully executed"; the conduct of foreign affairs—a realm in which the Court has recognized that "[it] would be intolerable that courts, without the relevant information, should review and perhaps nullify actions of the Executive taken on information properly held secret"; and management of the Executive Branch—a task for which "imperative reasons [require] an unrestricted power [in the President] to remove the most important of his subordinates in their most important duties."

Because of the singular importance of the President's duties, diversion of his energies by concern with private lawsuits would raise unique risks to the effective functioning of government. As is the case with prosecutors and judges—for whom absolute immunity now is established—a President must concern himself with matters likely to "arouse the most intense feelings." Yet, as our decisions have recognized, it is in precisely such cases that there exists the greatest public interest in providing an official "the maximum ability to deal fearlessly and impartially with" the duties of his office. This concern is compelling where the officeholder must make the most sensitive and far-reaching decisions entrusted to any official under our constitutional system. Nor can the sheer prominence of the President's office be ignored. In view of the visibility of his office and the effect of his actions on countless people, the President would be an easily identifiable target for suits for civil damages. Cognizance of this personal vulnerability frequently could distract a President from his public duties, to the detriment of not only the President and his office but also the Nation that the Presidency was designed to serve.

B. It is settled law that the separation-of-powers doctrine does not bar every exercise of jurisdiction over the President of the United States. But our cases also have established that a court, before exercising jurisdiction, must balance the constitutional weight of the interest to be served against the dangers of intrusion on the authority and functions of the Executive Branch. When judicial action is needed to serve broad public interests—as when the Court acts, not in derogation of the separation of powers, but to maintain their proper balance or to vindicate the public interest in an ongoing criminal prosecution the exercise of jurisdiction has been held warranted. In the case of this merely private suit for damages based on a President's official acts, we hold it is not.

C. In defining the scope of an official's absolute privilege, this Court has recognized that the sphere of protected action must be related closely to the immunity's justifying purposes. Frequently our decisions have held that an official's absolute immunity should extend only to acts in performance of particular functions of his office. But the Court also has refused to draw functional lines finer than history and reason would support. In view of the special nature of the President's constitutional office and functions, we think it appropriate to recognize absolute Presidential immunity from damages liability for acts within the "outer perimeter" of his official responsibility.

Here respondent argues that petitioner Nixon would have acted outside the outer perimeter of his duties by ordering the discharge of an employee who was lawfully entitled to retain his job in the absence of "such cause as will promote the efficiency of the service." Because Congress has granted this legislative protection, respondent argues, no federal official could, within the outer perimeter of his duties of office, cause Fitzgerald to be dismissed without satisfying this standard in prescribed statutory proceedings.

This construction would subject the President to trial on virtually every allegation that an action was unlawful, or was taken for a forbidden purpose. Adoption of this construction thus would deprive absolute immunity of its intended effect. It clearly is within the President's constitutional and statutory authority to prescribe the manner in which the Secretary will conduct the business of the Air Force. Because this mandate of office must include the authority to prescribe reorganizations and reductions in force, we conclude that petitioner's alleged wrongful acts lay well within the outer perimeter of his authority.

V. A rule of absolute immunity for the President will not leave the Nation without sufficient protection against misconduct on the part of the Chief Executive. There remains the constitutional remedy of impeachment. In addition, there are formal and informal checks on Presidential action that do not apply with equal force to other executive officials. The President is subjected to constant scrutiny by the press. Vigilant oversight by Congress also may serve to deter Presidential abuses of office, as well as to make credible the threat of impeachment. Other incentives to avoid misconduct may include a desire to earn reelection, the need to maintain prestige as an element of Presidential influence, and a President's traditional concern for his historical stature.

The existence of alternative remedies and deterrents establishes that absolute immunity will not place the President "above the law." For the President, as for judges and prosecutors, absolute immunity merely precludes a particular private remedy for alleged misconduct in order to advance compelling public ends.

VI. For the reasons stated in this opinion, the decision of the Court of Appeals is reversed, and the case is remanded for action consistent with this opinion.

CHIEF JUSTICE BURGER wrote a concurring opinion.

I join the Court's opinion, but I write separately to underscore that the Presidential immunity derives from and is mandated by the constitutional doctrine of separation of powers. Indeed, it has been taken for granted for nearly two centuries. In reaching this conclusion we do well to bear in mind that the focus must not be simply on the matter of judging individual conduct in a fact-bound setting; rather, in those familiar terms of John Marshall, it is a Constitution we are expounding. Constitutional adjudication often bears unpalatable fruit. But the needs of a system of government sometimes must outweigh the right of individuals to collect damages.

The immunity of a President from civil suits is not simply a doctrine derived from this Court's interpretation of common law or public policy. Absolute immunity for a President for acts within the official duties of the Chief Executive is either to be found in the constitutional separation of powers or it does not exist. The Court today holds that the Constitution mandates such immunity and I agree.

JUSTICE WHITE wrote a dissenting opinion joined by JUSTICES BRENNAN, MARSHALL, and BLACKMUN.

The four dissenting members of the Court in *Butz v. Economou* argued that all federal officials are entitled to absolute immunity from suit for any action they take in connection with their official duties. That immunity would extend even to actions taken with express knowledge that the conduct was clearly contrary to the controlling statute or clearly violative of the Constitution. Fortunately, the majority of the Court rejected that approach: We held that although public officials perform certain functions that entitle them to absolute immunity, the immunity attaches to particular functions—not to particular offices. Officials performing functions for which immunity is not absolute enjoy qualified immunity; they are liable in damages only if their conduct violated well-established law and if they should have realized that their conduct was illegal.

The Court now applies the dissenting view in *Butz* to the Office of the President: A President, acting within the outer boundaries of what Presidents normally do, may, without liability, deliberately cause serious injury to any number of citizens even though he knows his conduct violates a statute or tramples on the constitutional rights of those who are injured. Even if the President in this case ordered Fitzgerald fired by means of a trumped-up reduction in force, knowing that such a discharge was contrary to the civil service laws, he would be absolutely immune from suit. By the same token, if a President, without following the statutory procedures which he knows apply to himself as well as to other federal officials, orders his subordinates to wiretap or break into a home for the purpose of installing a listening device, and the officers comply with his request, the President would be absolutely immune from suit. He would be immune regardless of the damage he inflicts, regardless of how violative of the statute and of the Constitution he knew his conduct to be, and regardless of his purpose.[16]

The Court intimates that its decision is grounded in the Constitution. If that is the case, Congress cannot provide a remedy against Presidential misconduct and the criminal laws of the United States are wholly inapplicable to the President. I find this approach completely unacceptable. I do not agree that if the Office of President is to operate effectively, the holder of that Office must be permitted, without fear of liability and regardless of the function he is performing, deliberately to inflict injury on others by conduct that he knows violates the law.

We have not taken such a scatter-gun approach in other cases. *Butz* held that absolute immunity did not attach to the office held by a member of the President's Cabinet but only to those specific functions performed by that officer for which absolute immunity is clearly essential. Members of Congress are absolutely immune under the Speech or Debate Clause of the Constitution, but the immunity extends only to their legislative acts. We have never held that in order for legislative work to be done, it is necessary to immunize all of the tasks that legislators must perform. Constitutional immunity does not extend to those many things that Senators and Representatives regularly and necessarily do that are not legislative acts. Members of Congress, for example, repeatedly importune the executive branch and administrative agencies outside hearing rooms and legislative halls, but they are not immune if in connection with such activity they deliberately violate the law. Neither is a Member of Congress or his aide immune from damages suits if in order to secure information deemed relevant to a legislative investigation, he breaks into a house and carries away records. Judges are absolutely immune from liability for damages, but only when performing a judicial function, and even then they are subject to criminal liability. The absolute immunity of prosecutors is likewise limited to the prosecutorial function. A prosecutor who directs that an investigation be carried out in a way that is patently illegal is not immune.

---

16. This, of course, is not simply a hypothetical example. See *Halperin v. Kissinger*, 606 F.2d 1192 (1979), aff'd by an equally divided Court, 452 U.S. 713 (1981).

Attaching absolute immunity to the Office of the President, rather than to particular activities that the President might perform, places the President above the law. It is a reversion to the old notion that the King can do no wrong. Until now, this concept had survived in this country only in the form of sovereign immunity. That doctrine forecloses suit against the Government itself and against Government officials, but only when the suit against the latter actually seeks relief against the sovereign. Suit against an officer, however, may be maintained where it seeks specific relief against him for conduct contrary to his statutory authority or to the Constitution. Now, however, the Court clothes the Office of the President with sovereign immunity, placing it beyond the law.

In *Marbury v. Madison,* the Chief Justice, speaking for the Court, observed: "The Government of the United States has been emphatically termed a government of laws, and not of men. It will certainly cease to deserve this high appellation, if the laws furnish no remedy for the violation of a vested legal right." Until now, the Court has consistently adhered to this proposition.

[Today], [t]he Court casually, but candidly, abandons the functional approach to immunity that has run through all of our decisions. Indeed, the majority turns this rule on its head by declaring that because the functions of the President's office are so varied and diverse and some of them so profoundly important, the office is unique and must be clothed with officewide, absolute immunity. This is policy, not law, and in my view, very poor policy.

I. The petitioner and the United States rely principally on two arguments to support the claim of absolute immunity for the President from civil liability: absolute immunity is an "incidental power" of the Presidency, historically recognized as implicit in the Constitution, and absolute immunity is required by the separation-of-powers doctrine.

A. [N]owhere does the Constitution directly address the issue of Presidential immunity. Petitioner nevertheless argues that the debates at the Constitutional Convention and the early history of constitutional interpretation demonstrate an implicit assumption of absolute Presidential immunity. In support of this position, petitioner relies primarily on three separate items: First, preratification remarks made during the discussion of Presidential impeachment at the Convention and in The Federalist; second, remarks made during the meeting of the first Senate; and third, the views of Justice Story.

The debate at the Convention on whether or not the President should be impeachable did touch on the potential dangers of subjecting the President to the control of another branch, the Legislature. Whatever the fear of subjecting the President to the power of another branch, it was not sufficient, or at least not sufficiently shared, to insulate the President from political liability in the impeachment process.

Moreover, the Convention debate did not focus on wrongs the President might commit against individuals, but rather on whether there should be a method of holding him accountable for what might be termed wrongs against the state. The only conclusions that can be drawn from this debate are that the independence of the Executive was not understood to require a total lack of accountability to the other branches and that there was no general desire to insulate the President from the consequences of his improper acts.

In the North Carolina ratifying convention, for example, there was a discussion of the adequacy of the impeachment mechanism for holding executive officers accountable for their misdeeds. Governor Johnson defended the constitutional plan by distinguishing three legal mechanisms of accountability: "If an officer commits an offence against an individual, he is amenable to the courts of law. If he commits crimes against the state, he may be indicted and punished. Impeachment only extends to high crimes and misdemeanors in a public office. It is a mode of trial pointed out for great misdemeanors against the public."

A similar distinction between different possible forms of Presidential accountability was drawn by Mr. Wilson at the Pennsylvania ratifying convention: "[The President] is placed high, and is possessed of power far from being contemptible; yet not a single privilege is annexed to his character; far from being above the laws, he is amenable to them in his private character as a citizen, and in his public character by impeachment."

To the extent that historical inquiry is appropriate in this context, it is constitutional history, not common law, that is relevant. From the history discussed above, however, all that can be concluded is that absolute immunity from civil liability for the President finds no support in constitutional text or history, or in the explanations of the earliest commentators. This is too weak a ground to support a declaration by this Court that the President is absolutely immune from civil liability, regardless of the source of liability or the injury for which redress is sought.

B. No bright line can be drawn between arguments for absolute immunity based on the constitutional principle of separation of powers and arguments based on what the Court refers to as "public policy." The difference is only one of degree. While absolute immunity might maximize executive efficiency and therefore be a worthwhile policy, lack of such immunity may not so disrupt the functioning of the Presidency as to violate the separation-of-powers doctrine. Insofar as liability in this case is of congressional origin, petitioner must demonstrate that subjecting the President to a private damages action will prevent him from "accomplishing [his] constitutionally assigned functions."

Taken at face value, the Court's position that as a matter of constitutional law the President is absolutely immune should mean that he is immune not only from damages actions but also from suits for injunctive relief, criminal prosecutions and, indeed, from any kind of judicial process. But there is no contention that the President is immune from criminal prosecution in the courts under the criminal laws enacted by Congress or by the States for that matter. Nor would such a claim be credible. The Constitution itself provides that impeachment shall not bar "Indictment, Trial, Judgment and Punishment, according to Law." Art. I, §3, cl. 7. Similarly, our cases indicate that immunity from damages actions carries no protection from criminal prosecution.

Neither can there be a serious claim that the separation-of-powers doctrine insulates Presidential action from judicial review or insulates the President from judicial process. No argument is made here that the President, whatever his liability for money damages, is not subject to the courts' injunctive powers. See,

e. g., *Youngstown Sheet & Tube Co., supra; Korematsu v. United States,* 323 U.S. 214
(1944); *Panama Refining Co. v. Ryan,* 293 U.S. 388 (1935). Indeed, it is the rule, not
the exception, that executive actions—including those taken at the immediate
direction of the President—are subject to judicial review. Regardless of the possibility of money damages against the President, then, the constitutionality of the
President's actions or their legality under the applicable statutes can and will be
subject to review.

Nor can private damages actions be distinguished on the ground that such
claims would involve the President personally in the litigation in a way not necessitated by suits seeking declaratory or injunctive relief against certain Presidential
actions. The President has been held to be subject to judicial process at least since
1807. *United States v. Burr,* 25 F. Cas. 30 (No. 14, 692d) (CC Va. 1807) (Marshall,
C. J., sitting as Circuit Justice). Chief Justice Marshall flatly rejected any suggestion
that all judicial process, in and of itself, constitutes an unwarranted interference in
the Presidency. This position was recently rearticulated by the Court in *United
States v. Nixon,* "[Neither] the doctrine of separation of powers, nor the need for
confidentiality . . . without more, can sustain an absolute, unqualified Presidential
privilege of immunity from judicial process under all circumstances."

The principle that should guide the Court in deciding this question was stated
long ago by Chief Justice Marshall: "The very essence of civil liberty certainly
consists in the right of every individual to claim the protection of the laws, whenever he receives an injury." *Marbury v. Madison,* 1 Cranch, at 163. To the extent that
the Court denies an otherwise appropriate remedy, it denies the victim the right
to be made whole and, therefore, denies him "the protection of the laws."

The possibility of liability may, in some circumstances, distract officials from
the performance of their duties and influence the performance of those duties in
ways adverse to the public interest. The Court's response, until today, to this problem has been to apply the argument to individual functions, not offices, and to
evaluate the effect of liability on governmental decision-making within that function, in light of the substantive ends that are to be encouraged or discouraged.

The majority suggests that the separation-of-powers doctrine permits exercising jurisdiction over the President only in those instances where "judicial action is
needed to serve broad public interests—as when the Court acts, not in derogation
of the separation of powers, but to maintain their proper balance." Without explanation, the majority contends that a "merely private suit for damages" does not
serve this function.

The suggestion that enforcement of the rule of law does not further the separation of powers, but rather is in derogation of this purpose, is bizarre. Regardless
of what the Court might think of the merits of Mr. Fitzgerald's claim, the idea
that pursuit of legal redress offends the doctrine of separation of powers is a frivolous contention passing as legal argument. It cannot be seriously argued that the
President must be placed beyond the law and beyond judicial enforcement of
constitutional restraints upon executive officers in order to implement the principle of separation of powers.

JUSTICE BLACKMUN wrote a dissent joined by JUSTICES BRENNAN and MARSHALL.

I join Justice White's dissent. For me, the Court leaves unanswered his unanswerable argument that no man, not even the President of the United States, is absolutely and fully above the law. Until today, I had thought this principle was the foundation of our national jurisprudence. It now appears that it is not.

Nor can I understand the Court's holding that the absolute immunity of the President is compelled by separation-of-powers concerns, when the Court at the same time expressly leaves open the possibility that the President nevertheless may be fully subject to congressionally created forms of liability. These two concepts, it seems to me, cannot coexist.

*****

Clinton v. Jones, **520 U.S. 681 (1997).**

INTRODUCTION: This case arose in a complex political context and had a variety of elements. It began as a case brought by Paula Corbin Jones based on allegations that then-Governor Bill Clinton made sexual advances toward her in his hotel room in the Excelsior Hotel in Little Rock, Arkansas in 1991. At the time, Jones was an Arkansas state employee. She claimed that she suffered retribution on the job for having rejected Clinton's advances and that he later defamed her in statements he made as president. Clinton responded to the case with a motion to dismiss the Jones suit on grounds of presidential immunity, relying on *Nixon v. Fitzgerald*.

*****

JUSTICE STEVENS wrote the opinion for the Court.

This case raises a constitutional and a prudential question concerning the Office of the President of the United States. Respondent, a private citizen, seeks to recover damages from the current occupant of that office based on actions allegedly taken before his term began. The President submits that in all but the most exceptional cases the Constitution requires federal courts to defer such litigation until his term ends and that, in any event, respect for the office warrants such a stay. Despite the force of the arguments supporting the President's submissions, we conclude that they must be rejected.

The District Judge denied the motion to dismiss on immunity grounds and ruled that discovery in the case could go forward, but ordered any trial stayed until the end of petitioner's Presidency. Although she recognized that a "thin majority" in *Nixon v. Fitzgerald*, had held that "the President has absolute immunity from civil damage actions arising out of the execution of official duties of office," she was not convinced that "a President has absolute immunity from civil causes of action arising prior to assuming the office." She was, however, persuaded by some of the reasoning in our opinion in *Fitzgerald* that deferring the trial if one were required would be appropriate. Relying in part on the fact that respondent had failed to bring her complaint until two days before the 3-year period of limitations expired, she concluded that the public interest in avoiding litigation that might hamper the President in conducting the duties of his office outweighed any demonstrated need for an immediate trial.

Petitioner's principal submission—that "in all but the most exceptional cases," the Constitution affords the President temporary immunity from civil damages litigation arising out of events that occurred before he took office—cannot be sustained on the basis of precedent.

Only three sitting Presidents have been defendants in civil litigation involving their actions prior to taking office. Complaints against Theodore Roosevelt and Harry Truman had been dismissed before they took office; the dismissals were affirmed after their respective inaugurations. Two companion cases arising out of an automobile accident were filed against John F. Kennedy in 1960 during the Presidential campaign. After taking office, he unsuccessfully argued that his status as Commander in Chief gave him a right to a stay under the Soldiers' and Sailors' Civil Relief Act of 1940. The motion for a stay was denied by the District Court, and the matter was settled out of court. Thus, none of those cases sheds any light on the constitutional issue before us.

The principal rationale for affording certain public servants immunity from suits for money damages arising out of their official acts is inapplicable to unofficial conduct. In cases involving prosecutors, legislators, and judges we have repeatedly explained that the immunity serves the public interest in enabling such officials to perform their designated functions effectively without fear that a particular decision may give rise to personal liability. "The point of immunity for such officials is to forestall an atmosphere of intimidation that would conflict with their resolve to perform their designated functions in a principled fashion."

That rationale provided the principal basis for our holding that a former President of the United States was "entitled to absolute immunity from damages liability predicated on his official acts." Our central concern was to avoid rendering the President "unduly cautious in the discharge of his official duties."

This reasoning provides no support for an immunity for unofficial conduct. As we explained in *Fitzgerald,* "the sphere of protected action must be related closely to the immunity's justifying purposes." Because of the President's broad responsibilities, we recognized in that case an immunity from damages claims arising out of official acts extending to the "outer perimeter of his authority." But we have never suggested that the President, or any other official, has an immunity that extends beyond the scope of any action taken in an official capacity.

Moreover, when defining the scope of an immunity for acts clearly taken within an official capacity, we have applied a functional approach. "Frequently our decisions have held that an official's absolute immunity should extend only to acts in performance of particular functions of his office." Hence, for example, a judge's absolute immunity does not extend to actions performed in a purely administrative capacity. As our opinions have made clear, immunities are grounded in "the nature of the function performed, not the identity of the actor who performed it."

Petitioner's effort to construct an immunity from suit for unofficial acts grounded purely in the identity of his office is unsupported by precedent.

V. We are also unpersuaded by the evidence from the historical record to which petitioner has called our attention. He points to a comment by Thomas Jefferson protesting the subpoena duces tecum Chief Justice Marshall directed to him in the Burr trial, a statement in the diaries kept by Senator William Maclay of the first Senate debates, in which then Vice-President John Adams and Senator Oliver Ellsworth are recorded as having said that "the President personally [is] not . . . subject to any process whatever," lest it be "put . . . in the power of a common Justice to exercise any Authority over him and Stop the Whole Machine of Government," and to a quotation from Justice Story's Commentaries on the Constitution. None of these sources sheds much light on the question at hand.[17]

Respondent, in turn, has called our attention to conflicting historical evidence. Speaking in favor of the Constitution's adoption at the Pennsylvania Convention, James Wilson—who had participated in the Philadelphia Convention at which the document was drafted—explained that, although the President "is placed [on] high," "not a single privilege is annexed to his character; far from being above the laws, he is amenable to them in his private character as a citizen, and in his public character by impeachment." 2 J. Elliot, *Debates on the Federal Constitution* 480 (2d ed. 1863) (emphasis omitted).[18] This description is consistent with both the doctrine of presidential immunity as set forth in *Fitzgerald*, and rejection of the immunity claim in this case. With respect to acts taken in his "public character"—that is official acts—the President may be disciplined principally by impeachment, not by private lawsuits for damages. But he is otherwise subject to the laws for his purely private acts.

In the end, as applied to the particular question before us, we reach the same conclusion about these historical materials that Justice Jackson described when confronted with an issue concerning the dimensions of the President's power. "Just what our forefathers did envision, or would have envisioned had they foreseen modern conditions, must be divined from materials almost as enigmatic as the dreams Joseph was called upon to interpret for Pharoah [sic]. A century and a half of partisan debate and scholarly speculation yields no net result but only supplies more or less apt quotations from respected sources on each side. . . . They largely cancel each other." *Youngstown Sheet & Tube Co. v. Sawyer*, 343 U.S. 579, 634–635 (1952) (concurring opinion).

VI. Petitioner's strongest argument supporting his immunity claim is based on the text and structure of the Constitution. He does not contend that the occupant of the Office of the President is "above the law," in the sense that his conduct is entirely immune from judicial scrutiny. The President argues merely for a

---

17. NOTE: This is ironic in light of the fact that Clinton's counsel was relying on many of the same historical sources that majority cited in *Nixon v. Fitzgerald, ante*.

18. NOTE: Jones' attorneys, not surprisingly, relied on the sources cited by the dissenters in *Fitzgerald*.

postponement of the judicial proceedings that will determine whether he violated any law. His argument is grounded in the character of the office that was created by Article II of the Constitution, and relies on separation of powers principles that have structured our constitutional arrangement since the founding.

As a starting premise, petitioner contends that he occupies a unique office with powers and responsibilities so vast and important that the public interest demands that he devote his undivided time and attention to his public duties. He submits that—given the nature of the office—the doctrine of separation of powers places limits on the authority of the Federal Judiciary to interfere with the Executive Branch that would be transgressed by allowing this action to proceed.

We have no dispute with the initial premise of the argument. Former presidents, from George Washington to George Bush, have consistently endorsed petitioner's characterization of the office. In 1967, the Twenty-fifth Amendment to the Constitution was adopted to ensure continuity in the performance of the powers and duties of the office; one of the sponsors of that Amendment stressed the importance of providing that "at all times" there be a President "who has complete control and will be able to perform" those duties. As Justice Jackson has pointed out, the Presidency concentrates executive authority "in a single head in whose choice the whole Nation has a part, making him the focus of public hopes and expectations. In drama, magnitude and finality his decisions so far overshadow any others that almost alone he fills the public eye and ear." We have, in short, long recognized the "unique position in the constitutional scheme" that this office occupies. Thus, we accept the initial premise of the Executive's argument.

It does not follow, however, that separation of powers principles would be violated by allowing this action to proceed. The doctrine of separation of powers is concerned with the allocation of official power among the three co-equal branches of our Government. The Framers "built into the tripartite Federal Government . . . a self-executing safeguard against the encroachment or aggrandizement of one branch at the expense of the other." Thus, for example, the Congress may not exercise the judicial power to revise final judgments or the executive power to manage an airport. And, the judicial power to decide cases and controversies does not include the provision of purely advisory opinions to the Executive, or permit the federal courts to resolve nonjusticiable questions.

Of course the lines between the powers of the three branches are not always neatly defined. But in this case there is no suggestion that the Federal Judiciary is being asked to perform any function that might in some way be described as "executive." Respondent is merely asking the courts to exercise their core Article III jurisdiction to decide cases and controversies. Whatever the outcome of this case, there is no possibility that the decision will curtail the scope of the official powers of the Executive Branch. The litigation of questions that relate entirely to the unofficial conduct of the individual who happens to be the President poses no perceptible risk of misallocation of either judicial power or executive power.

Rather than arguing that the decision of the case will produce either an aggrandizement of judicial power or a narrowing of executive power, petitioner contends that—as a by-product of an otherwise traditional exercise of judicial power—burdens will be placed on the President that will hamper the performance of his official duties. We have recognized that "even when a branch does not arrogate power to itself . . . the separation-of-powers doctrine requires that a branch not impair another in the performance of its constitutional duties." As a factual matter, petitioner contends that this particular case—as well as the potential additional litigation that an affirmance of the Court of Appeals judgment might spawn—may impose an unacceptable burden on the President's time and energy, and thereby impair the effective performance of his office.

If the past is any indicator, it seems unlikely that a deluge of such litigation will ever engulf the Presidency. As for the case at hand, if properly managed by the District Court, it appears to us highly unlikely to occupy any substantial amount of petitioner's time.

Of greater significance, petitioner errs by presuming that interactions between the Judicial Branch and the Executive, even quite burdensome interactions, necessarily rise to the level of constitutionally forbidden impairment of the Executive's ability to perform its constitutionally mandated functions. "Our . . . system imposes upon the Branches a degree of overlapping responsibility, a duty of interdependence as well as independence the absence of which 'would preclude the establishment of a Nation capable of governing itself effectively.'" As Madison explained, separation of powers does not mean that the branches "ought to have no partial agency in, or no control over the acts of each other." The fact that a federal court's exercise of its traditional Article III jurisdiction may significantly burden the time and attention of the Chief Executive is not sufficient to establish a violation of the Constitution. Two long-settled propositions, first announced by Chief Justice Marshall, support that conclusion.

First, we have long held that when the President takes official action, the Court has the authority to determine whether he has acted within the law. Perhaps the most dramatic example of such a case is our holding that President Truman exceeded his constitutional authority when he issued an order directing the Secretary of Commerce to take possession of and operate most of the Nation's steel mills in order to avert a national catastrophe. Despite the serious impact of that decision on the ability of the Executive Branch to accomplish its assigned mission, and the substantial time that the President must necessarily have devoted to the matter as a result of judicial involvement, we exercised our Article III jurisdiction to decide whether his official conduct conformed to the law. Our holding was an application of the principle established in *Marbury v. Madison,* 5 U.S. 137 (1803), that "it is emphatically the province and duty of the judicial department to say what the law is."

Second, it is also settled that the President is subject to judicial process in appropriate circumstances. Although Thomas Jefferson apparently thought otherwise, Chief Justice Marshall, when presiding in the treason trial of Aaron Burr, ruled that a subpoena *duces tecum* could be directed to the President. We unequivocally and emphatically endorsed Marshall's position when we held that President Nixon was obligated to comply with a subpoena commanding him to produce certain tape recordings of his conversations with his aides. As we explained, "neither the doctrine of separation of powers, nor the need for confidentiality of high-level communications, without more, can sustain an absolute, unqualified Presidential privilege of immunity from judicial process under all circumstances."

Sitting Presidents have responded to court orders to provide testimony and other information with sufficient frequency that such interactions between the Judicial and Executive Branches can scarcely be thought a novelty. Moreover, sitting Presidents have also voluntarily complied with judicial requests for testimony.

In sum, "it is settled law that the separation-of-powers doctrine does not bar every exercise of jurisdiction over the President of the United States." If the Judiciary may severely burden the Executive Branch by reviewing the legality of the President's official conduct, and if it may direct appropriate process to the President himself, it must follow that the federal courts have power to determine the legality of his unofficial conduct. The burden on the President's time and energy that is a mere by-product of such review surely cannot be considered as onerous as the direct burden imposed by judicial review and the occasional invalidation of his official actions. We therefore hold that the doctrine of separation of powers does not require federal courts to stay all private actions against the President until he leaves office.

VII. The Court of Appeals described the District Court's discretionary decision to stay the trial as the "functional equivalent" of a grant of temporary immunity. Strictly speaking the stay was not the functional equivalent of the constitutional immunity that petitioner claimed, because the District Court ordered discovery to proceed. Moreover, a stay of either the trial or discovery might be justified by considerations that do not require the recognition of any constitutional immunity. Although we have rejected the argument that the potential burdens on the President violate separation of powers principles, those burdens are appropriate matters for the District Court to evaluate in its management of the case. The high respect that is owed to the office of the Chief Executive, though not justifying a rule of categorical immunity, is a matter that should inform the conduct of the entire proceeding, including the timing and scope of discovery.

Nevertheless, we are persuaded that it was an abuse of discretion for the District Court to defer the trial until after the President leaves office. Such a lengthy and categorical stay takes no account whatever of the respondent's interest in bringing the case to trial. The complaint was filed within the statutory limitations period—albeit near the end of that period—and delaying trial would increase the danger of prejudice resulting from the loss of evidence, including the inability of witnesses to recall specific facts, or the possible death of a party.

VIII. We add a final comment on two matters that are discussed at length in the briefs: the risk that our decision will generate a large volume of politically motivated harassing and frivolous litigation, and the danger that national security concerns might prevent the President from explaining a legitimate need for a continuance.

We are not persuaded that either of these risks is serious. Most frivolous and vexatious litigation is terminated at the pleading stage or on summary judgment, with little if any personal involvement by the defendant. Moreover, the availability of sanctions provides a significant deterrent to litigation directed at the President in his unofficial capacity for purposes of political gain or harassment. History indicates that the likelihood that a significant number of such cases will be filed is remote. Although scheduling problems may arise, there is no reason to assume that the District Courts will be either unable to accommodate the President's needs or unfaithful to the tradition—especially in matters involving national security—of giving "the utmost deference to Presidential responsibilities." Several Presidents, including petitioner, have given testimony without jeopardizing the Nation's security. In short, we have confidence in the ability of our federal judges to deal with both of these concerns.

If Congress deems it appropriate to afford the President stronger protection, it may respond with appropriate legislation. As petitioner notes in his brief, Congress has enacted more than one statute providing for the deferral of civil litigation to accommodate important public interests. If the Constitution embodied the rule that the President advocates, Congress, of course, could not repeal it. But our holding today raises no barrier to a statutory response to these concerns.

The Federal District Court has jurisdiction to decide this case. Like every other citizen who properly invokes that jurisdiction, respondent has a right to an orderly disposition of her claims. Accordingly, the judgment of the Court of Appeals is affirmed.

JUSTICE BREYER wrote an opinion concurring in the judgment.

I agree with the majority that the Constitution does not automatically grant the President an immunity from civil lawsuits based upon his private conduct. In my view, however, once the President sets forth and explains a conflict between judicial proceeding and public duties, the matter changes. At that point, the Constitution permits a judge to schedule a trial in an ordinary civil damages action only within the constraints of a constitutional principle—a principle that forbids a federal judge in such a case to interfere with the President's discharge of his public duties. I have no doubt that the Constitution contains such a principle applicable to civil suits, based upon Article II's vesting of the entire "executive Power" in a single individual, implemented through the Constitution's structural separation of powers, and revealed both by history and case precedent.

I fear that to disregard [this principle] now may appear to deny it. I also fear that the majority's description of the relevant precedents de-emphasizes the extent to which they support a principle of the President's independent authority to control his own time and energy. Further, if the majority is wrong in predicting the future infrequency of private civil litigation against sitting Presidents, acknowledgement and future delineation of the constitutional principle will prove a practically necessary institutional safeguard.

The Constitution states that the "executive Power shall be vested in a President." Article II makes a single President responsible for the actions of the Executive Branch in much the same way that the entire Congress is responsible for the actions of the Legislative Branch, or the entire Judiciary for those of the Judicial Branch. It thereby creates a constitutional equivalence between a single President, on the one hand, and many legislators, or judges, on the other.

Precedent that suggests that the Constitution does not offer a sitting President significant protections from potentially distracting civil litigation—consists of the following: (1) In several instances sitting Presidents have given depositions or testified at criminal trials, and (2) this Court has twice authorized the enforcement of subpoenas seeking documents from a sitting President for use in a criminal case.

The first set of precedents amount to voluntary actions on the part of a sitting President. The second set of precedents amounts to a search for documents, rather than a direct call upon Presidential time. More important, both sets of precedents involve criminal proceedings in which the President participated as a witness. [T]hey are not normally subject to postponement, and ordinarily they put at risk, not a private citizen's hope for monetary compensation, but a private citizen's freedom from enforced confinement.

The remaining precedent concerns official action. And any Presidential time spent dealing with, or action taken in response to, that kind of case is part of a Presidents official duties. Hence court review in such circumstances could not interfere with, or distract from, official duties.

Case law, particularly, *Nixon v. Fitzgerald,* strongly supports the principle that judges hearing a private civil damages action against a sitting President may not issue orders that could significantly distract a President from his official duties. It is not surprising that the Court's immunity-related case law should rely on both distraction and distortion, for the ultimate rationale underlying those cases embodies both concerns. If the latter concern can justify an "absolute" immunity in the case of a President no longer in office, where distraction is no longer a consideration, so can the former justify, not immunity, but a postponement, in the case of a sitting President.

I concede the possibility that district courts, supervised by the Courts of Appeals and perhaps this Court, might prove able to manage private civil damage actions against sitting Presidents without significantly interfering with the discharge of Presidential duties—at least if they manage those actions with the constitutional problem in mind. Nonetheless, predicting the future is difficult, and I am skeptical. Should the majority's optimism turn out to be misplaced, then, in my view, courts will have to develop administrative rules applicable to such cases (including postponement rules of the sort at issue in this case) in order to implement the basic constitutional directive.

✱✱✱✱✱

The question still remains concerning the liability of other public officials for violations of constitutionally protected rights; and the types of immunity, if any, available to shield those officers.

Bivens v. Six Unknown Named Agents of Federal Bureau of Narcotics, **403 U.S. 388 (1971).**

INTRODUCTION: Mr. Bivens was at home with his family the morning of November 26, 1965 when, he charged, six federal narcotics agents, acting without a warrant, arrested him, searched the house, and threatened his family with arrest. His wife and children were not only threatened themselves but were witnesses to the humiliation of Mr. Bivens. He was taken to a federal facility, strip searched, booked, and interrogated. He challenged the search and the arrest and added charges of unreasonable force and infliction of mental suffering, including the fact that this treatment was carried out in the view of Bivens' wife and children. The district court dismissed Bivens' claim and the court of appeals affirmed.

*****

JUSTICE BRENNAN wrote the opinion for the Court.

The Fourth Amendment provides that: "The right of the people to be secure in their persons, houses, papers, and effects, against unreasonable searches and seizures, shall not be violated. . . ." In *Bell v. Hood,* 327 U.S. 678 (1946), we reserved the question whether violation of that command by a federal agent acting under color of his authority gives rise to a cause of action for damages consequent upon his unconstitutional conduct. Today we hold that it does.

I. Respondents do not argue that petitioner should be entirely without remedy for an unconstitutional invasion of his rights by federal agents. In respondents' view, however, the rights that petitioner asserts—primarily rights of privacy—are creations of state and not of federal law. Accordingly, they argue, petitioner may obtain money damages to redress invasion of these rights only by an action in tort, under state law, in the state courts. In this scheme the Fourth Amendment would serve merely to limit the extent to which the agents could defend the state law tort suit by asserting that their actions were a valid exercise of federal power: if the agents were shown to have violated the Fourth Amendment, such a defense would be lost to them and they would stand before the state law merely as private individuals. Candidly admitting that it is the policy of the Department of Justice to remove all such suits from the state to the federal courts for decision, respondents nevertheless urge that we uphold dismissal of petitioner's complaint in federal court, and remit him to filing an action in the state courts in order that the case may properly be removed to the federal court for decision on the basis of state law.

We think that respondents' thesis rests upon an unduly restrictive view of the Fourth Amendment's protection against unreasonable searches and seizures by federal agents, a view that has consistently been rejected by this Court. Respondents seek to treat the relationship between a citizen and a federal agent unconstitutionally exercising his authority as no different from the relationship between two private citizens. In so doing, they ignore the fact that power, once granted, does not disappear like a magic gift when it is wrongfully used. An agent acting—albeit unconstitutionally—in the name of the United States possesses a far greater capacity for harm than an individual trespasser exercising no authority other than his own. Accordingly, as our cases make clear, the Fourth Amendment operates as a limitation upon the exercise of federal power regardless of whether the State in whose jurisdiction that power is exercised would prohibit or penalize the identical act if engaged in by a private citizen. It guarantees to citizens of the United States the absolute right to be free from unreasonable searches and seizures carried out by virtue of federal authority. And "where federally protected rights have been invaded, it has been the rule from the beginning that courts will be alert to adjust their remedies so as to grant the necessary relief."

First. Our cases have long since rejected the notion that the Fourth Amendment proscribes only such conduct as would, if engaged in by private persons, be condemned by state law. And our recent decisions regarding electronic surveillance have made it clear beyond peradventure that the Fourth Amendment is not tied to the niceties of local trespass laws. *Katz v. United States,* 389 U.S. 347 (1967); *Berger v. New York,* 388 U.S. 41 (1967). In light of these cases, respondents' argument that the Fourth Amendment serves only as a limitation on federal defenses to a state law claim, and not as an independent limitation upon the exercise of federal power, must be rejected.

Second. The interests protected by state laws regulating trespass and the invasion of privacy, and those protected by the Fourth Amendment's guarantee against unreasonable searches and seizures, may be inconsistent or even hostile. Thus, we may bar the door against an unwelcome private intruder, or call the police if he persists in seeking entrance. The availability of such alternative means for the protection of privacy may lead the State to restrict imposition of liability for any consequent trespass. The mere invocation of federal power by a federal law enforcement official will normally render futile any attempt to resist an unlawful entry or arrest by resort to the local police; and a claim of authority to enter is likely to unlock the door as well. "In such cases there is no safety for the citizen, except in the protection of the judicial tribunals, for rights which have been invaded by the officers of the government, professing to act in its name. There remains to him but the alternative of resistance, which may amount to crime." *United States v. Lee,* 106 U.S. 196, 219 (1882).

Third. That damages may be obtained for injuries consequent upon a violation of the Fourth Amendment by federal officials should hardly seem a surprising proposition. Historically, damages have been regarded as the ordinary remedy for an invasion of personal interests in liberty. Of course, the Fourth Amendment does not in so many words provide for its enforcement by an award of money damages for the consequences of its violation. But "it is . . . well settled that where legal rights have been invaded, and a federal statute provides for a general right to sue for such invasion, federal courts may use any available remedy to make good the wrong done." The present case involves no special factors counseling hesitation in the absence of affirmative action by Congress. Finally, we cannot accept respondents' formulation of the question as whether the availability of money damages is necessary to enforce the Fourth Amendment. The question is merely whether petitioner, if he can demonstrate an injury consequent upon the violation by federal agents of his Fourth Amendment rights, is entitled to redress his injury through a particular remedial mechanism normally available in the federal courts. "The very essence of civil liberty certainly consists in the right of every individual to claim the protection of the laws, whenever he receives an injury." *Marbury v.*

Madison, 1 Cranch 137, 163 (1803). Having concluded that petitioner's complaint states a cause of action under the Fourth Amendment, we hold that petitioner is entitled to recover money damages for any injuries he has suffered as a result of the agents' violation of the Amendment.

JUSTICE HARLAN wrote an opinion concurring in the judgment.

My initial view of this case was that the Court of Appeals was correct in dismissing the complaint, but for reasons stated in this opinion I am now persuaded to the contrary.

The major thrust of the Government's position is that, where Congress has not expressly authorized a particular remedy, a federal court should exercise its power to accord a traditional form of judicial relief at the behest of a litigant, who claims a constitutionally protected interest has been invaded, only where the remedy is "essential," or "indispensable for vindicating constitutional rights." It is argued that historically the Court has rarely exercised the power to accord such relief in the absence of an express congressional authorization and that "if Congress had thought that federal officers should be subject to a law different than state law, it would have had no difficulty in saying so, as it did with respect to state officers. . . ."

To be sure, "it must be remembered that legislatures are ultimate guardians of the liberties and welfare of the people in quite as great a degree as the courts." But it must also be recognized that the Bill of Rights is particularly intended to vindicate the interests of the individual in the face of the popular will as expressed in legislative majorities; at the very least, it strikes me as no more appropriate to await express congressional authorization of traditional judicial relief with regard to these legal interests than with respect to interests protected by federal statutes.

The question then, is, as I see it, whether compensatory relief is "necessary" or "appropriate" to the vindication of the interest asserted. In resolving that question, it seems to me that the range of policy considerations we may take into account is at least as broad as the range of those a legislature would consider with respect to an express statutory authorization of a traditional remedy. In this regard I agree with the Court that the appropriateness of according Bivens compensatory relief does not turn simply on the deterrent effect liability will have on federal official conduct. Damages as a traditional form of compensation for invasion of a legally protected interest may be entirely appropriate even if no substantial deterrent effects on future official lawlessness might be thought to result. Bivens, after all, has invoked judicial processes claiming entitlement to compensation for injuries resulting from allegedly lawless official behavior, if those injuries are properly compensable in money damages. I do not think a court of law—vested with the power to accord a remedy—should deny him his relief simply because he cannot show that future lawless conduct will thereby be deterred.

The only substantial policy consideration advanced against recognition of a federal cause of action for violation of Fourth Amendment rights by federal officials is the incremental expenditure of judicial resources that will be necessitated by this class of litigation. There is, however, something ultimately self-defeating about this argument. For if, as the Government contends, damages will rarely be realized by plaintiffs in these cases because of jury hostility, the limited resources of the official concerned, etc., then I am not ready to assume that there will be a significant increase in the expenditure of judicial resources on these claims. Few responsible lawyers and plaintiffs are likely to choose the course of litigation if the statistical chances of success are truly *de minimis*. And I simply cannot agree with my Brother Black that the possibility of "frivolous" claims—if defined simply as claims with no legal merit—warrants closing the courthouse doors to people in Bivens' situation. There are other ways, short of that, of coping with frivolous lawsuits.

JUSTICE BLACK dissented.[19]

In my opinion for the Court in *Bell v. Hood,* we reserve[d] the question whether an unreasonable search made by a federal officer in violation of the Fourth Amendment gives the subject of the search a federal cause of action for damages against the officers making the search. There can be no doubt that Congress could create a federal cause of action for damages for an unreasonable search in violation of the Fourth Amendment. Although Congress has created such a federal cause of action against state officials acting under color of state law, it has never created such a cause of action against federal officials. If it wanted to do so, Congress could, of course, create a remedy against federal officials who violate the Fourth Amendment in the performance of their duties. But the point of this case and the fatal weakness in the Court's judgment is that neither Congress nor the State of New York has enacted legislation creating such a right of action. For us to do so is, in my judgment, an exercise of power that the Constitution does not give us.

Even if we had the legislative power to create a remedy, there are many reasons why we should decline to create a cause of action where none has existed since the formation of our Government. The courts of the United States as well as those of the States are choked with lawsuits. The number of cases on the docket of this Court have reached an unprecedented volume in recent years. A majority of these cases are brought by citizens with substantial complaints—persons who are physically or economically injured by torts or frauds or governmental infringement of their rights; persons who have been unjustly deprived of their liberty or their property; and persons who have not yet received the equal opportunity in education, employment, and pursuit of happiness that was the dream of our forefathers. Unfortunately, there have also been a growing number of frivolous lawsuits, particularly actions for damages against law enforcement officers whose conduct has been judicially sanctioned by state trial and appellate courts and in many instances even by this Court. My fellow Justices on this Court and our brethren throughout the federal judiciary know only too well the time-consuming task of conscientiously poring over hundreds of thousands of pages of factual allegations of misconduct by police, judicial, and corrections officials. Of course, there are instances of legitimate grievances, but legislators might well desire to devote judicial resources to other problems of a more serious nature.

---

19. Chief Justice Burger also wrote a dissent, but his opinion was primarily focused on his dissatisfaction with the exclusionary rule as a remedy for Fourth Amendment violations.

We sit at the top of a judicial system accused by some of nearing the point of collapse. Many criminal defendants do not receive speedy trials and neither society nor the accused are assured of justice when inordinate delays occur. Citizens must wait years to litigate their private civil suits. Substantial changes in correctional and parole systems demand the attention of the lawmakers and the judiciary. If I were a legislator I might well find these and other needs so pressing as to make me believe that the resources of lawyers and judges should be devoted to them rather than to civil damage actions against officers who generally strive to perform within constitutional bounds. There is also a real danger that such suits might deter officials from the proper and honest performance of their duties.[20]

All of these considerations make imperative careful study and weighing of the arguments both for and against the creation of such a remedy under the Fourth Amendment. I would have great difficulty for myself in resolving the competing policies, goals, and priorities in the use of resources, if I thought it were my job to resolve those questions. But that is not my task. The task of evaluating the pros and cons of creating judicial remedies for particular wrongs is a matter for Congress and the legislatures of the States. Congress has not provided that any federal court can entertain a suit against a federal officer for violations of Fourth Amendment rights occurring in the performance of his duties. A strong inference can be drawn from creation of such actions against state officials that Congress does not desire to permit such suits against federal officials. Should the time come when Congress desires such lawsuits, it has before it a model of valid legislation, 42 U. S. C. §1983, to create a damage remedy against federal officers. Cases could be cited to support the legal proposition which I assert, but it seems to me to be a matter of common understanding that the business of the judiciary is to interpret the laws and not to make them.

✳✳✳✳✳

Then there is the question of the relationship between individual officers and governments, specifically local governments. The important question is whether cities are persons within the meaning of civil rights laws, and therefore subject to suit. This is an important issue for a number of reasons. In the first place, while juries may be disinclined to impose damages on an individual employee, such as a police officer, they are quite willing to make local governments pay. Beyond that, however, what is really at issue in many cases is not alone the conduct of particular officials, but the policies that formed the basis for their actions.

Owen v. City of Independence, 445 U.S. 622 (1980).

INTRODUCTION: This case began with the discovery by the Kansas City police that a felon had a handgun that records indicated had supposedly been

---

20. NOTE: Justice Blackmun also filed a separate dissent, but largely on the same grounds as set forth by Justice Black in this paragraph.

destroyed by the Independence, Missouri Police Department. At that point, the Independence city manager launched an investigation into the operation of the property room. The manager explained the results of the investigation to the city council and promised corrective action. He also issued a public statement to the mayor and council that promised to correct the problems uncovered by the investigation.

Although there were no actual violations of law disclosed by the investigation, the manager decided to remove the chief, though he was offered another position in the department. The chief refused to step down voluntarily. The city charter authorized the city manager to hire and fire department heads. The chief submitted a letter to the office of the city manager while he was away on vacation demanding specification of charges against him and due process in the form of a public adjudicative hearing.

One member of the city council obtained a copy of the investigative report while the city manager was away on vacation. At the next meeting of the city council he made strong charges against the management of the police department property room, including indications that the chief had personally benefited from the mismanagement. The council member obtained passage of a resolution that would make the council's findings about the department available to the media. The city manager terminated the chief the following day. The full results of the investigation were not released to the press; however, the information was turned over to the prosecutor's office. While the material was presented to a grand jury, no indictment was issued and no charges were ultimately filed. Not surprisingly, the whole affair, including the firing and the council statements received dramatic publicity in news outlets, both print and broadcast.

✱✱✱✱✱

JUSTICE BRENNAN wrote the opinion for the Court.

Monell v. New York City Dept. of Social Services, 436 U.S. 658 (1978), overruled *Monroe v. Pape,* 365 U.S. 167 (1961), insofar as *Monroe* held that local governments were not among the "persons" to whom 42 U. S. C. §1983 applies and were therefore wholly immune from suit under the statute.[21] *Monell* reserved decision, however, on the question whether local governments, although not entitled to an absolute immunity, should be afforded some form of official immunity in §1983

---

21. Title 42 U. S. C. §1983 provides: "Every person who, under color of any statute, ordinance, regulation, custom, or usage, of any State or Territory, subjects, or causes to be subjected, any citizen of the United States or other person within the jurisdiction thereof to the deprivation of any rights, privileges, or immunities secured by the Constitution and laws, shall be liable to the party injured in an action at law, suit in equity, or other proper proceeding for redress."

suits. In this action brought by petitioner in the District Court for the Western District of Missouri, the Court of Appeals for the Eighth Circuit held that respondent city of Independence, Mo., "is entitled to qualified immunity from liability" based on the good faith of its officials: "We extend the limited immunity the district court applied to the individual defendants to cover the City as well, because its officials acted in good faith and without malice." 589 F.2d 335, 337–338 (1978). We granted certiorari. We reverse.

II. The Court of Appeals concluded that the city's allegedly false public accusations had blackened petitioner's name and reputation, thus depriving him of liberty without due process of law. That the stigmatizing charges did not come from the City Manager and were not included in the official discharge notice was, in the court's view, immaterial. What was important, the court explained, was that "the official actions of the city council released charges against [petitioner] contemporaneous and, in the eyes of the public, connected with that discharge." The Court of Appeals on the remand [from this Court] reaffirmed its original determination that the city had violated petitioner's rights under the Fourteenth Amendment, but held that all respondents, including the city, were entitled to qualified immunity from liability.

Monell held that "a local government may not be sued under §1983 for an injury inflicted solely by its employees or agents. Instead, it is when execution of a government's policy or custom, whether made by its lawmakers or by those whose edicts or acts may fairly be said to represent official policy, inflicts the injury that the government as an entity is responsible under §1983." The Court of Appeals held in the instant case that the municipality's official policy was responsible for the deprivation of petitioner's constitutional rights: "[The] stigma attached to [petitioner] in connection with his discharge was caused by the official conduct of the City's lawmakers, or by those whose acts may fairly be said to represent official policy. Such conduct amounted to official policy causing the infringement of [petitioner's] constitutional rights, in violation of section 1983."

Nevertheless, the Court of Appeals affirmed the judgment of the District Court denying petitioner any relief against the respondent city, stating: "The Supreme Court's decisions in *Board of Regents v. Roth* [and] *Perry v. Sindermann,* crystallized the rule establishing the right to a name-clearing hearing for a government employee allegedly stigmatized in the course of his discharge. The Court decided those two cases two months after the discharge in the instant case. Thus, officials of the City of Independence could not have been aware of [petitioner's] right to a name-clearing hearing in connection with the discharge. The City of Independence should not be charged with predicting the future course of constitutional law. We extend the limited immunity the district court applied to the individual defendants to cover the City as well, because its officials acted in good faith and without malice. We hold the City not liable for actions it could not reasonably have known violated [petitioner's] constitutional rights."

III. Because the question of the scope of a municipality's immunity from liability under §1983 is essentially one of statutory construction, the starting point in our analysis must be the language of the statute itself. By its terms, §1983 "creates a species of tort liability that on its face admits of no immunities." Its language is absolute and unqualified; no mention is made of any privileges, immunities, or defenses that may be asserted. Rather, the Act imposes liability upon "every person" who, under color of state law or custom, "subjects, or causes to be subjected, any citizen of the United States ... to the deprivation of any rights, privileges, or immunities secured by the Constitution and laws." And *Monell* held that these words were intended to encompass municipal corporations as well as natural "persons."

Moreover, the congressional debates surrounding the passage of §1 of the Civil Rights Act of 1871, 17 Stat. 13—the forerunner of §1983—confirm the expansive sweep of the statutory language. Representative Shellabarger, the author and manager of the bill in the House, explained in his introductory remarks the breadth of construction that the Act was to receive: "I have a single remark to make in regard to the rule of interpretation of those provisions of the Constitution under which all the sections of the bill are framed. This act is remedial, and in aid of the preservation of human liberty and human rights. All statutes and constitutional provisions authorizing such statutes are liberally and beneficently construed. It would be most strange and, in civilized law, monstrous were this not the rule of interpretation. As has been again and again decided by your own Supreme Court of the United States, and everywhere else where there is wise judicial interpretation, the largest latitude consistent with the words employed is uniformly given in construing such statutes and constitutional provisions as are meant to protect and defend and give remedies for their wrongs to all the people."

Similar views of the Act's broad remedy for violations of federally protected rights were voiced by its supporters in both Houses of Congress.

However, notwithstanding §1983's expansive language and the absence of any express incorporation of common-law immunities, we have, on several occasions, found that a tradition of immunity was so firmly rooted in the common law and was supported by such strong policy reasons that "Congress would have specifically so provided had it wished to abolish the doctrine."

Subsequent cases have required that we consider the personal liability of various other types of government officials. In each of these cases, our finding of §1983 immunity "was predicated upon a considered inquiry into the immunity historically accorded the relevant official at common law and the interests behind it." Where the immunity claimed by the defendant was well established at common law at the time §1983 was enacted, and where its rationale was compatible with the purposes of the Civil Rights Act, we have construed the statute to incorporate that immunity. But there is no tradition of immunity for municipal corporations, and neither history nor policy supports a construction of §1983 that would justify the qualified immunity accorded the city of Independence by the Court of Appeals. We hold, therefore, that the municipality may not assert the good faith of its officers or agents as a defense to liability under §1983.

A. Since colonial times, a distinct feature of our Nation's system of governance has been the conferral of political power upon public and municipal corporations for the management of matters of local concern. As *Monell* recounted, by 1871, municipalities—like private corporations—were treated as natural persons for virtually all purposes of constitutional and statutory analysis. In particular, they were routinely sued in both federal and state courts. Local governmental units were regularly held to answer in damages for a wide range of statutory and constitutional violations, as well as for common-law actions for breach of contract. And although, as we discuss below, a municipality was not subject to suit for all manner of tortious conduct, it is clear that at the time §1983 was enacted, local governmental bodies did not enjoy the sort of "good-faith" qualified immunity extended to them by the Court of Appeals.

As a general rule, it was understood that a municipality's tort liability in damages was identical to that of private corporations and individuals. Under this general theory of liability, a municipality was deemed responsible for any private losses generated through a wide variety of its operations and functions, from personal injuries due to its defective sewers, thoroughfares, and public utilities, to property damage caused by its trespasses and uncompensated takings. Yet in the hundreds of cases from that era awarding damages against municipal governments for wrongs committed by them, one searches in vain for much mention of a qualified immunity based on the good faith of municipal officers. Indeed, where the issue was discussed at all, the courts had rejected the proposition that a municipality should be privileged where it reasonably believed its actions to be lawful.

To be sure, there were two doctrines that afforded municipal corporations some measure of protection from tort liability. The first sought to distinguish between a municipality's "governmental" and "proprietary" functions; as to the former, the city was held immune, whereas in its exercise of the latter, the city was held to the same standards of liability as any private corporation. The second doctrine immunized a municipality for its "discretionary" or "legislative" activities, but not for those which were "ministerial" in nature. A brief examination of the application and the rationale underlying each of these doctrines demonstrates that Congress could not have intended them to limit a municipality's liability under §1983.

The governmental-proprietary distinction owed its existence to the dual nature of the municipal corporation. On the one hand, the municipality was a corporate body, capable of performing the same "proprietary" functions as any private corporation, and liable for its torts in the same manner and to the same extent, as well. On the other hand, the municipality was an arm of the State, and when acting in that "governmental" or "public" capacity, it shared the immunity traditionally accorded the sovereign. But the principle of sovereign immunity—itself a somewhat arid fountainhead for municipal immunity—is necessarily nullified when the State expressly or impliedly allows itself, or its creation, to be sued. Municipalities were therefore liable not only for their "proprietary" acts, but also for those "governmental" functions as to which the State had withdrawn their immunity. And, by the end of the 19th century, courts regularly held that in imposing a specific duty on the municipality either in its charter or by statute, the State had impliedly withdrawn the city's immunity from liability for the nonperformance or misperformance of its obligation. Thus, despite the nominal existence of an immunity for "governmental" functions, municipalities were found liable in damages in a multitude of cases involving such activities.

That the municipality's common-law immunity for "governmental" functions derives from the principle of sovereign immunity also explains why that doctrine could not have served as the basis for the qualified privilege respondent city claims under §1983. First, because sovereign immunity insulates the municipality from unconsented suits altogether, the presence or absence of good faith is simply irrelevant. The critical issue is whether injury occurred while the city was exercising governmental, as opposed to proprietary, powers or obligations—not whether its agents reasonably believed they were acting lawfully in so conducting themselves. More fundamentally, however, the municipality's "governmental" immunity is obviously abrogated by the sovereign's enactment of a statute making it amenable to suit. Section 1983 was just such a statute. By including municipalities within the class of "persons" subject to liability for violations of the Federal Constitution and laws, Congress—the supreme sovereign on matters of federal law—abolished whatever vestige of the State's sovereign immunity the municipality possessed.

The second common-law distinction between municipal functions—that protecting the city from suits challenging "discretionary" decisions—was grounded not on the principle of sovereign immunity, but on a concern for separation of powers. A large part of the municipality's responsibilities involved broad discretionary decisions on issues of public policy—decisions that affected large numbers of persons and called for a delicate balancing of competing considerations. For a court or jury, in the guise of a tort suit, to review the reasonableness of the city's judgment on these matters would be an infringement upon the powers properly vested in a coordinate and coequal branch of government. In order to ensure against any invasion into the legitimate sphere of the municipality's policymaking processes, courts therefore refused to entertain suits against the city "either for the non-exercise of, or for the manner in which in good faith it exercises, discretionary powers of a public or legislative character."

Although many, if not all, of a municipality's activities would seem to involve at least some measure of discretion, the influence of this doctrine on the city's liability was not as significant as might be expected. For just as the courts implied an exception to the municipality's immunity for its "governmental" functions, here, too, a distinction was made that had the effect of subjecting the city to liability for much of its tortious conduct. While the city retained its immunity for decisions as to whether the public interest required acting in one manner or another, once any particular decision was made, the city was fully liable for any injuries incurred in the execution of its judgment. Thus municipalities remained liable in damages for a broad range of conduct implementing their discretionary decisions.

Once again, an understanding of the rationale underlying the common-law immunity for "discretionary" functions explains why that doctrine cannot serve as the foundation for a good-faith immunity under §1983. That common-law doctrine merely prevented courts from substituting their own judgment on matters within the lawful discretion of the municipality. But a municipality has no "discretion" to violate the Federal Constitution; its dictates are absolute and imperative. And when a court passes judgment on the municipality's conduct in a §1983 action, it does not seek to second-guess the "reasonableness" of the city's decision nor to interfere with the local government's resolution of competing policy considerations. Rather, it looks only to whether the municipality has conformed to the requirements of the Federal Constitution and statutes.

In sum, we can discern no "tradition so well grounded in history and reason" that would warrant the conclusion that in enacting §1 of the Civil Rights Act, the 42d Congress *sub silentio* [without clear statement or explanation] extended to municipalities a qualified immunity based on the good faith of their officers. Absent any clearer indication that Congress intended so to limit the reach of a statute expressly designed to provide a "broad remedy for violations of federally protected civil rights," we are unwilling to suppose that injuries occasioned by a municipality's unconstitutional conduct were not also meant to be fully redressable through its sweep.

B. Our rejection of a construction of §1983 that would accord municipalities a qualified immunity for their good-faith constitutional violations is compelled both by the legislative purpose in enacting the statute and by considerations of public policy. The central aim of the Civil Rights Act was to provide protection to those persons wronged by the "[misuse] of power, possessed by virtue of state law and made possible only because the wrongdoer is clothed with the authority of state law." By creating an express federal remedy, Congress sought to "enforce provisions of the Fourteenth Amendment against those who carry a badge of authority of a State and represent it in some capacity, whether they act in accordance with their authority or misuse it."

How "uniquely amiss" it would be, therefore, if the government itself—"the social organ to which all in our society look for the promotion of liberty, justice, fair and equal treatment, and the setting of worthy norms and goals for social conduct"—were permitted to disavow liability for the injury it has begotten. A damages remedy against the offending party is a vital component of any scheme for vindicating cherished constitutional guarantees, and the importance of assuring its efficacy is only accentuated when the wrongdoer is the institution that has been established to protect the very rights it has transgressed. Yet owing to the qualified immunity enjoyed by most government officials, many victims of municipal malfeasance would be left remediless if the city were also allowed to assert a good-faith defense. Unless countervailing considerations counsel otherwise, the injustice of such a result should not be tolerated.

Moreover, §1983 was intended not only to provide compensation to the victims of past abuses, but to serve as a deterrent against future constitutional deprivations, as well. The knowledge that a municipality will be liable for all of its injurious conduct, whether committed in good faith or not, should create an incentive for officials who may harbor doubts about the lawfulness of their intended actions to err on the side of protecting citizens' constitutional rights. Furthermore, the threat that damages might be levied against the city may encourage those in a policymaking position to institute internal rules and programs designed to minimize the likelihood of unintentional infringements on constitutional rights. Such procedures are particularly beneficial in preventing those "systemic" injuries that result not so much from the conduct of any single individual, but from the interactive behavior of several government officials, each of whom may be acting in good faith.

Our previous decisions conferring qualified immunities on various government officials, are not to be read as derogating the significance of the societal interest in compensating the innocent victims of governmental misconduct. Rather, in each case we concluded that overriding considerations of public policy nonetheless demanded that the official be given a measure of protection from personal liability. The concerns that justified those decisions, however, are less compelling, if not wholly inapplicable, when the liability of the municipal entity is at issue.

In *Scheuer v. Rhodes,* the Chief Justice identified the two "mutually dependent rationales" on which the doctrine of official immunity rested: "(1) the injustice, particularly in the absence of bad faith, of subjecting to liability an officer who is required, by the legal obligations of his position, to exercise discretion; (2) the danger that the threat of such liability would deter his willingness to execute his office with the decisiveness and the judgment required by the public good."

The first consideration is simply not implicated when the damages award comes not from the official's pocket, but from the public treasury. It hardly seems unjust to require a municipal defendant which has violated a citizen's constitutional rights to compensate him for the injury suffered thereby. Indeed, Congress enacted §1983 precisely to provide a remedy for such abuses of official power. Elemental notions of fairness dictate that one who causes a loss should bear the loss.

The second rationale also loses its force when it is the municipality, in contrast to the official, whose liability is at issue. At the heart of this justification for a qualified immunity for the individual official is the concern that the threat of personal monetary liability will introduce an unwarranted and unconscionable consideration into the decisionmaking process, thus paralyzing the governing official's decisiveness and distorting his judgment on matters of public policy. The inhibiting effect is significantly reduced, if not eliminated, however, when the threat of personal liability is removed. First, as an empirical matter, it is questionable whether the hazard of municipal loss will deter a public officer from the conscientious exercise of his duties; city officials routinely make decisions that either require a large expenditure of municipal funds or involve a substantial risk of depleting the public fisc. More important, though, is the realization that consideration of the municipality's liability for constitutional violations is quite properly the concern of its elected or appointed officials. Indeed, a decisionmaker would be derelict in his duties if, at some point, he did not consider whether his decision comports with constitutional mandates and did not weigh the risk that a violation might result in an award of damages from the public treasury. As one commentator aptly put it: "Whatever other concerns should shape a particular official's actions, certainly one of them should be the constitutional rights of individuals who will be affected by his actions. To criticize section 1983 liability because it leads decisionmakers to avoid the infringement of constitutional rights is to criticize one of the statute's raisons d'etre."

IV. In sum, our decision holding that municipalities have no immunity from damages liability flowing from their constitutional violations harmonizes well with developments in the common law and our own pronouncements on official immunities under §1983. Doctrines of tort law have changed significantly over the past century, and our notions of governmental responsibility should properly reflect that evolution. No longer is individual "blameworthiness" the acid test of liability; the principle of equitable loss-spreading has joined fault as a factor in distributing the costs of official misconduct.

We believe that today's decision, together with prior precedents in this area, properly allocates these costs among the three principals in the scenario of the §1983 cause of action: the victim of the constitutional deprivation; the officer whose conduct caused the injury; and the public, as represented by the municipal entity. The innocent individual who is harmed by an abuse of governmental authority is assured that he will be compensated for his injury. The offending official, so long as he conducts himself in good faith, may go about his business secure in the knowledge that a qualified immunity will protect him from personal liability for damages that are more appropriately chargeable to the populace as a whole. And the public will be forced to bear only the costs of injury inflicted by the "execution of a government's policy or custom, whether made by its lawmakers or by those whose edicts or acts may fairly be said to represent official policy."

JUSTICE POWELL wrote a dissenting opinion joined by the CHIEF JUSTICE, JUSTICE STEWART, and JUSTICE REHNQUIST.

The [police chief's] dismissal involved only the proper exercise of discretionary powers according to prevailing constitutional doctrine. The city imposed no stigma on petitioner that would require a "name clearing" hearing under the Due Process Clause. [Because I disagree with the Court's interpretation of the statute and precedent] and because this decision will hamper local governments unnecessarily, I dissent.

Due process requires a hearing on the discharge of a government employee "if the employer creates and disseminates a false and defamatory impression about the employee in connection with his termination. . . ." This principle was first announced in *Board of Regents v. Roth,* which was decided in June 1972, 10 weeks after Owen was discharged. The pivotal question after *Roth* is whether the circumstances of the discharge so blackened the employee's name as to impair his liberty interest in his professional reputation.

[A] "name clearing" hearing is not necessary unless the employer makes a public statement that "might seriously damage [the employee's] standing and associations in his community." No hearing is required after the "discharge of a public employee whose position is terminable at the will of the employer when there is no public disclosure of the reasons for the discharge."

The Court does not address directly the question whether any stigma was imposed by the discharge. Even if the Council resolution is viewed as part of the discharge process, Owen has demonstrated no denial of his liberty. Neither the City Manager nor the Council cast any aspersions on Owen's character. [N]othing in the actions of the City Manager or the City Council triggered a constitutional right to a name-clearing hearing.

The statements by Councilman Roberts were neither measured nor benign, but they provide no basis for this action against the city of Independence. Under *Monell,* the city cannot be held liable for Roberts' statements on a theory of *respondeat superior.* That case held that §1983 makes municipalities liable for constitutional deprivations only if the challenged action was taken "pursuant to official municipal policy of some nature. . . ." As the Court noted, "a municipality cannot be held liable solely because it employs a tortfeasor. . . ." The statements of a single councilman scarcely rise to the level of municipal policy.

After today's decision, municipalities will have gone in two short years from absolute immunity under §1983 to strict liability. As a policy matter, I believe that strict municipal liability unreasonably subjects local governments to damages judgments for actions that were reasonable when performed. It converts municipal governance into a hazardous slalom through constitutional obstacles that often are unknown and unknowable.

The Court today abandons any attempt to harmonize §1983 with traditional tort law. It points out that municipal immunity may be abrogated by legislation. Thus, according to the Court, Congress "abolished" municipal immunity when it included municipalities "within the class of 'persons' subject to liability" under §1983. This reasoning flies in the face of our prior decisions under this statute.

In addition, basic fairness requires a qualified immunity for municipalities. The good-faith defense recognized under §1983 authorizes liability only when officials acted with malicious intent or when they "knew or should have known that their conduct violated the constitutional norm." The standard incorporates the idea that liability should not attach unless there was notice that a constitutional right was at risk. This idea applies to governmental entities and individual officials alike. Constitutional law is what the courts say it is, and—as demonstrated by today's decision and its precursor, *Monell*—even the most prescient lawyer would hesitate to give a firm opinion on matters not plainly settled. Municipalities, often acting in the utmost good faith, may not know or anticipate when their action or inaction will be deemed a constitutional violation.

*****

THE CONTEMPORARY DEVELOPMENT
OF ELEVENTH AMENDMENT IMMUNITY

Until 1996, there was little question that states could be made subject to suit under federal statutes by abrogating their sovereign immunity. With the ruling by the Court in the *Seminole* case, all of that changed.

Seminole Tribe of Florida v. Florida, 517 U.S. 44 (1996).

INTRODUCTION: As the popularity of gambling and casino construction on tribal lands grew, so did controversies within the states about the role of state governments in decisions about gambling in the state, albeit on tribal lands.

Congress sought to address the problem with the passage of the Indian Gaming Regulatory Act of 1988. The statute, adopted under the so-called "Indian Commerce Clause," Art. I, §8, cl. 3 of the Constitution, required states to enter into good faith negotiations with tribes to create a compact to government gaming. It also plainly provided for suits by tribes against states that refused to do so. In the process, Congress very specifically indicated that it was abrogating the immunity of a state from suit to facilitate the tribal legal actions.

This case grew out of demands by the Seminole Tribe of Florida that the state of Florida enter into negotiations under the Indian Gaming Act. Florida rejected that demand and challenged the legitimacy of the Act and its authorization of suits against the state.

*****

CHIEF JUSTICE REHNQUIST wrote the opinion for the Court.

[W]e granted *certiorari* in order to [decide the question]: Does the Eleventh Amendment prevent Congress from authorizing suits by Indian tribes against States for prospective injunctive relief to enforce legislation enacted pursuant to the Indian Commerce Clause? We answer the question in the affirmative and we therefore affirm the Eleventh Circuit's dismissal of petitioner's suit. We hold that notwithstanding Congress' clear intent to abrogate the States' sovereign immunity, the Indian Commerce Clause does not grant Congress that power, and therefore cannot grant jurisdiction over a State that does not consent to be sued.

The Eleventh Amendment provides: "The Judicial power of the United States shall not be construed to extend to any suit in law or equity, commenced or prosecuted against one of the United States by Citizens of another State, or by Citizens or Subjects of any Foreign State." Although the text of the Amendment would appear to restrict only the Article III diversity jurisdiction of the federal courts, "we have understood the Eleventh Amendment to stand not so much for what it says, but for the presupposition . . . which it confirms." That presupposition, first observed over a century ago in *Hans v. Louisiana,* 134 U.S. 1 (1890), has two parts: first, that each State is a sovereign entity in our federal system; and second, that "'it is inherent in the nature of sovereignty not to be amenable to the suit of an individual without its consent.'"

II. Petitioner argues that Congress through the Act abrogated the States' immunity from suit. In order to determine whether Congress has abrogated the States' sovereign immunity, we ask two questions: first, whether Congress has "unequivocally expressed its intent to abrogate the immunity;" and second, whether Congress has acted "pursuant to a valid exercise of power."

B. [O]ur inquiry into whether Congress has the power to abrogate unilaterally the States' immunity from suit is narrowly focused on one question: Was the Act in question passed pursuant to a constitutional provision granting Congress the power to abrogate? Previously, in conducting that inquiry, we have found authority to abrogate under only two provisions of the Constitution. In *Fitzpatrick v. Bitzer,* 427 U.S. 445 (1976), we recognized that the Fourteenth Amendment, by expanding federal power at the expense of state autonomy, had fundamentally altered the balance of state and federal power struck by the Constitution. We noted that §1 of the Fourteenth Amendment contained prohibitions expressly directed at the States and that §5 of the Amendment expressly provided that "The Congress shall have power to enforce, by appropriate legislation, the provisions of this article." We held that through the Fourteenth Amendment, federal power extended to intrude upon the province of the Eleventh Amendment and therefore that §5 of the Fourteenth Amendment allowed Congress to abrogate the immunity from suit guaranteed by that Amendment.

In only one other case has congressional abrogation of the States' Eleventh Amendment immunity been upheld. In *Pennsylvania v. Union Gas Co.,* 491 U.S. 1 (1989), a plurality of the Court found that the Interstate Commerce Clause, Art. I, §8, cl. 3, granted Congress the power to abrogate state sovereign immunity, stating that the power to regulate interstate commerce would be "incomplete without the authority to render States liable in damages."

Both parties make their arguments from the plurality decision in *Union Gas,* and we, too, begin there. We think it clear that Justice Brennan's opinion finds Congress' power to abrogate under the Interstate Commerce Clause from the States' cession of their sovereignty when they gave Congress plenary power to regulate interstate commerce. While the plurality decision states that Congress' power under the Interstate Commerce Clause would be incomplete without the power to abrogate, that statement is made solely in order to emphasize the broad scope of Congress' authority over interstate commerce.

Following the rationale of the *Union Gas* plurality, our inquiry is limited to determining whether the Indian Commerce Clause, like the Interstate Commerce Clause, is a grant of authority to the Federal Government at the expense of the States. The answer to that question is obvious. If anything, the Indian Commerce Clause accomplishes a greater transfer of power from the States to the Federal Government than does the Interstate Commerce Clause. This is clear enough from the fact that the States still exercise some authority over interstate trade but have been divested of virtually all authority over Indian commerce and Indian tribes. Under the rationale of *Union Gas,* if the States' partial cession of authority over a particular area includes cession of the immunity from suit, then their virtually total cession of authority over a different area must also include cession of the immunity from suit. We agree with petitioner that the plurality opinion in *Union Gas* allows no principled distinction in favor of the States to be drawn between the Indian Commerce Clause and the Interstate Commerce Clause.

Respondents argue, however, that we need not conclude that the Indian Commerce Clause grants the power to abrogate the States' sovereign immunity. Instead, they contend that if we find the rationale of the Union Gas plurality to extend to the Indian Commerce Clause, then "*Union Gas* should be reconsidered and overruled." Generally, the principle of *stare decisis,* and the interests that it serves, counsel strongly against reconsideration of our precedent. Nevertheless, we always have treated stare decisis as a "principle of policy," and not as an "inexorable command."'"When governing decisions are unworkable or are badly reasoned,'this Court has never felt constrained to follow precedent.'" Our willingness to reconsider our earlier decisions has been "particularly true in constitutional cases, because in such cases 'correction through legislative action is practically impossible.'"

The plurality's rationale [in *Union Gas*] also deviated sharply from our established federalism jurisprudence and essentially eviscerated our decision in *Hans*. In the five years since it was decided, *Union Gas* has proved to be a solitary departure from established law. [B]oth the result in *Union Gas* and the plurality's rationale depart from our established understanding of the Eleventh Amendment and undermine the accepted function of Article III. We feel bound to conclude that *Union Gas* was wrongly decided and that it should be, and now is, overruled.

In overruling *Union Gas* today, we reconfirm that the background principle of state sovereign immunity embodied in the Eleventh Amendment is not so ephemeral as to dissipate when the subject of the suit is an area, like the regulation of Indian commerce, that is under the exclusive control of the Federal Government. Even when the Constitution vests in Congress complete law-making authority over a particular area, the Eleventh Amendment prevents congressional authorization of suits by private parties against unconsenting States. The Eleventh Amend-ment restricts the judicial power under Article III, and Article I cannot be used to circumvent the constitutional limitations placed upon federal jurisdiction. Petitioner's suit against the State of Florida must be dismissed for a lack of jurisdiction.

JUSTICE STEVENS wrote a dissent.

This case is about power—the power of the Congress of the United States to create a private federal cause of action against a State, or its Governor, for the violation of a federal right. In *Chisholm v. Georgia,* the entire Court assumed that Congress had such power. In *Hans v. Louisiana*—a case the Court purports to follow today—the Court again assumed that Congress had such power. In *Fitzpatrick v. Bitzer* and *Pennsylvania v. Union Gas Co.,* the Court squarely held that Congress has such power. In a series of cases beginning with *Atascadero State Hospital v. Scanlon,* 473 U.S. 234, 238–239 (1985), the Court formulated a special "clear statement rule" to determine whether specific Acts of Congress contained an effective exercise of that power. Nevertheless, in a sharp break with the past, today the Court holds that with the narrow and illogical exception of statutes enacted pursuant to the Enforcement Clause of the Fourteenth Amendment, Congress has no such power.

The importance of the majority's decision to overrule the Court's holding in *Pennsylvania v. Union Gas Co.* cannot be overstated. The majority's opinion does not simply preclude Congress from establishing the rather curious statutory scheme under which Indian tribes may seek the aid of a federal court to secure a State's good-faith negotiations over gaming regulations. Rather, it prevents Congress from providing a federal forum for a broad range of actions against States, from those sounding in copyright and patent law, to those concerning bankruptcy, environmental law, and the regulation of our vast national economy.

There may be room for debate over whether, in light of the Eleventh Amendment, Congress has the power to ensure that such a cause of action may be enforced in federal court by a citizen of another State or a foreign citizen. There can be no serious debate, however, over whether Congress has the power to ensure that such a cause of action may be brought by a citizen of the State being sued.

[T]he Court's contrary conclusion is profoundly misguided. [T]he shocking character of the majority's affront to a coequal branch of our Government merits additional comment.

I. For the purpose of deciding this case, I can readily assume that Justice Iredell's dissent in *Chisholm* and the Court's opinion in *Hans,* correctly stated the law that should govern our decision today. As I shall explain, both of those opinions relied on an interpretation of an Act of Congress rather than a want of congressional power to authorize a suit against the State.

The precise holding in *Chisholm* is difficult to state because each of the Justices in the majority wrote his own opinion. They seem to have held, however, that Article III of the Constitution itself required the Supreme Court to entertain original actions against unconsenting States. I agree with Justice Iredell that such a construction of Article III is incorrect; that Article should not then have been construed, and should not now be construed, to prevent Congress from granting States a sovereign immunity defense in such cases. That reading of Article III, however, explains why the majority's holding in *Chisholm* could not have been reversed by a simple statutory amendment adopting Justice Iredell's interpretation of the Judiciary Act of 1789. There is a special irony in the fact that the error committed by the *Chisholm* majority was its decision that this Court, rather than Congress, should define the scope of the sovereign immunity defense. That, of course, is precisely the same error the Court commits today.

As it was, the plain text of the Eleventh Amendment would seem to limit the judicial power itself in a certain class of cases. In doing so, however, the Amendment's quite explicit text establishes only a partial bar to a federal court's power to entertain a suit against a State. Justice Brennan has persuasively explained that the Eleventh Amendment's jurisdictional restriction is best understood to apply only to suits premised on diversity jurisdiction, see *Atascadero State Hospital v. Scanlon,* (dissenting opinion), and Justice Scalia has agreed that the plain text of the Amendment cannot be read to apply to federal-question cases. Whatever the precise dimensions of the Amendment, its express terms plainly do not apply to all suits brought against unconsenting States.

II. The majority appears to acknowledge that one cannot deduce from either the text of Article III or the plain terms of the Eleventh Amendment that the judicial power does not extend to a congressionally created cause of action against a State brought by one of that State's citizens. Nevertheless, the majority asserts that precedent compels that same conclusion. I disagree. The majority relies first on our decision in *Hans v. Louisiana. Hans* does not hold, however, that the Eleventh Amendment, or any other constitutional provision, precludes federal courts from entertaining actions brought by citizens against their own States in the face of contrary congressional direction. *Hans* instead reflects, at the most, this Court's conclusion that, as a matter of federal common law, federal courts should decline to entertain suits against unconsenting States. Because *Hans,* like these other cases, involved a suit that attempted to make a State honor its debt, its holding need not be read to stand even for the relatively limited proposition that there is a presumption in favor of sovereign immunity in all federal-question cases.

III. In reaching my conclusion that the Constitution does not prevent Congress from making the State of Florida suable in federal court for violating one of its statutes, I emphasize that I agree with the majority that in all cases to which the judicial power does not extend—either because they are not within any category defined in Article III or because they are within the category withdrawn from Article III by the Eleventh Amendment—Congress lacks the power to confer jurisdiction on the federal courts.

In confronting the question whether a federal grant of jurisdiction is within the scope of Article III, as limited by the Eleventh Amendment, I see no reason to distinguish among statutes enacted pursuant to the power granted to Congress to regulate commerce among the several States, and with the Indian tribes, Art. I, §8, cl. 3, the power to establish uniform laws on the subject of bankruptcy, Art. I, §8, cl. 4, the power to promote the progress of science and the arts by granting exclusive rights to authors and inventors, Art. I, §8, cl. 8, the power to enforce the provisions of the Fourteenth Amendment, §5, or indeed any other provision of the Constitution. There is no language anywhere in the constitutional text that authorizes Congress to expand the borders of Article III jurisdiction or to limit the coverage of the Eleventh Amendment.

The fundamental error that continues to lead the Court astray is its failure to acknowledge that its modern embodiment of the ancient doctrine of sovereign immunity "has absolutely nothing to do with the limit on judicial power contained in the Eleventh Amendment." It rests rather on concerns of federalism and comity that merit respect but are nevertheless, in cases such as the one before us, subordinate to the plenary power of Congress.

IV. Except insofar as it has been incorporated into the text of the Eleventh Amendment, the doctrine [of sovereign immunity] is entirely the product of judge-made law. Three features of its English ancestry make it particularly unsuitable for incorporation into the law of this democratic Nation. First, the assumption that it could be supported by a belief that "the King can do no wrong" has always been absurd. Second, centuries ago the belief that the monarch served by divine right made it appropriate to assume that redress for wrongs committed by the sovereign should be the exclusive province of still higher authority. Third, in a society where noble birth can justify preferential treatment, it might have been unseemly to allow a commoner to hale the monarch into court.

In this country the sovereignty of the individual States is subordinate both to the citizenry of each State and to the supreme law of the federal sovereign. In my view, neither the majority's opinion today, nor any earlier opinion by any Member of the Court, has identified any acceptable reason for concluding that the absence of a State's consent to be sued in federal court should affect the power of Congress to authorize federal courts to remedy violations of federal law by States or their officials in actions not covered by the Eleventh Amendment's explicit text.

Justice Souter wrote a dissent joined by Justices Ginsburg and Breyer.

In holding the State of Florida immune to suit under the Indian Gaming Regulatory Act, the Court today holds for the first time since the founding of the Republic that Congress has no authority to subject a State to the jurisdiction of a federal court at the behest of an individual asserting a federal right. Although the Court invokes the Eleventh Amendment as authority for this proposition, the only sense in which that amendment might be claimed as pertinent here was tolerantly phrased by Justice Stevens in his concurring opinion in *Union Gas.* There, he explained how it has come about that we have two Eleventh Amendments, the one ratified in 1795, the other invented by the Court nearly a century later in *Hans v. Louisiana.* Justice Stevens saw in that second Eleventh Amendment no bar to the exercise of congressional authority under the Commerce Clause in providing for suits on a federal question by individuals against a State, and I can only say that after my own canvass of the matter I believe he was entirely correct in that view, for reasons given below. His position, of course, was also the holding in *Union Gas,* which the Court now overrules and repudiates.

The fault I find with the majority today is not in its decision to reexamine *Union Gas.* Instead, I part company from the Court because I am convinced that its decision is fundamentally mistaken.

I. It is useful to separate three questions: (1) whether the States enjoyed sovereign immunity if sued in their own courts in the period prior to ratification of the National Constitution; (2) if so, whether after ratification the States were entitled to claim some such immunity when sued in a federal court exercising jurisdiction either because the suit was between a State and a nonstate litigant who was not its citizen, or because the issue in the case raised a federal question; and (3) whether any state sovereign immunity recognized in federal court may be abrogated by Congress.

The answer to the first question is not clear. The second question was not debated at the time of ratification, except as to citizen-state diversity jurisdiction, but in due course the Court in *Chisholm* answered that a state defendant enjoyed no such immunity. As to federal-question jurisdiction, state sovereign immunity seems not to have been debated prior to ratification, [suggesting] a general understanding at the time that the States would have no immunity in such cases. The adoption of the Eleventh Amendment soon changed the result in *Chisholm,* not by mentioning sovereign immunity, but by eliminating citizen-state diversity jurisdiction over cases with state defendants.

The Court's answer today to the third question is likewise at odds with the Founders' view that common law, when it was received into the new American legal system, was always subject to legislative amendment. In ignoring the reasons for this pervasive understanding at the time of the ratification, and in holding that a nontextual common-law rule limits a clear grant of congressional power under

Article I, the Court follows a course that has brought it to grief before in our history, and promises to do so again.

A. The doctrine of sovereign immunity comprises two distinct rules, which are not always separately recognized. The one rule holds that the King or the Crown, as the font of law, is not bound by the law's provisions; the other provides that the King or Crown, as the font of justice, is not subject to suit in its own courts. The one rule limits the reach of substantive law; the other, the jurisdiction of the courts. We are concerned here only with the latter rule.

Whatever the scope of sovereign immunity might have been in the Colonies, however, or during the period of Confederation, the proposal to establish a National Government under the Constitution drafted in 1787 presented a prospect unknown to the common law prior to the American experience: the States would become parts of a system in which sovereignty over even domestic matters would be divided or parceled out between the States and the Nation, the latter to be invested with its own judicial power and the right to prevail against the States whenever their respective substantive laws might be in conflict. With this prospect in mind, the 1787 Constitution might have addressed state sovereign immunity by eliminating whatever sovereign immunity the States previously had, as to any matter subject to federal law or jurisdiction; by recognizing an analogue to the old immunity in the new context of federal jurisdiction, but subject to abrogation as to any matter within that jurisdiction; or by enshrining a doctrine of inviolable state sovereign immunity in the text, thereby giving it constitutional protection in the new federal jurisdiction.

The 1787 draft in fact said nothing on the subject, and it was this very silence that occasioned some, though apparently not widespread, dispute among the Framers and others over whether ratification of the Constitution would preclude a State sued in federal court from asserting sovereign immunity as it could have done on any matter of nonfederal law litigated in its own courts. [T]hen, as now, there was no textual support for contending that Article III or any other provision would "constitutionalize" state sovereign immunity, and no one uttered any such contention.

B. The argument among the Framers and their friends about sovereign immunity in federal citizen-state diversity cases, in any event, was short lived and ended when this Court, in *Chisholm,* chose between the constitutional alternatives of abrogation and recognition of the immunity enjoyed at common law. The 4-to-1 majority adopted the reasonable interpretation that the first of the two Citizen-State Diversity Clauses abrogated for purposes of federal jurisdiction any immunity the States might have enjoyed in their own courts, and Georgia was accordingly held subject to the judicial power in a[n] action by a South Carolina citizen suing to collect a debt.

C. The Eleventh Amendment, of course, repudiated *Chisholm* and clearly divested federal courts of some jurisdiction as to cases against state parties. There are two plausible readings of this provision's text. Under the first, it simply repeals the

Citizen-State Diversity Clauses of Article III for all cases in which the State appears as a defendant. Under the second, it strips the federal courts of jurisdiction in any case in which a state defendant is sued by a citizen not its own, even if jurisdiction might otherwise rest on the existence of a federal question in the suit. Neither reading of the Amendment, of course, furnishes authority for the Court's view in today's case.

The history and structure of the Eleventh Amendment convincingly show that it reaches only to suits subject to federal jurisdiction exclusively under the Citizen-State Diversity Clauses. If the Framers had meant the Amendment to bar federal-question suits as well, they could not only have made their intentions clearer very easily, but could simply have adopted the first post-*Chisholm* proposal, introduced in the House of Representatives by Theodore Sedgwick of Massachusetts on instructions from the Legislature of that Commonwealth.

It should accordingly come as no surprise that the weightiest commentary following the Amendment's adoption described it simply as constricting the scope of the Citizen-State Diversity Clauses. In *Cohens v. Virginia,* 19 U.S. (6 Wheat.) 264 (1821), Chief Justice Marshall, writing for the Court, emphasized that the Amendment had no effect on federal courts' jurisdiction grounded on the "arising under" provision of Article III and concluded that "a case arising under the constitution or laws of the United States, is cognizable in the Courts of the Union, whoever may be the parties to that case."

The good sense of this early construction of the Amendment as affecting the diversity jurisdiction and no more has the further virtue of making sense of this Court's repeated exercise of appellate jurisdiction in federal-question suits brought against States in their own courts by out-of-staters. Exercising appellate jurisdiction in these cases would have been patent error if the Eleventh Amendment limited federal-question jurisdiction, for the Amendment's unconditional language ("shall not be construed") makes no distinction between trial and appellate jurisdiction. The best explanation for our practice belongs to Chief Justice Marshall: the Eleventh Amendment bars only those suits in which the sole basis for federal jurisdiction is diversity of citizenship.

Thus, regardless of which of the two plausible readings one adopts, the further point to note here is that there is no possible argument that the Eleventh Amendment, by its terms, deprives federal courts of jurisdiction over all citizen law-suits against the States. Because the plaintiffs in today's case are citizens of the State that they are suing, [w]e must therefore look elsewhere for the source of that immunity by which the Court says their suit is barred from a federal court.

II. The obvious place to look elsewhere, of course, is *Hans v. Louisiana,* and *Hans* was indeed a leap in the direction of today's holding. The parties in *Hans* raised, and the Court in that case answered, only what I have called the second question, that is, whether the Constitution, without more, permits a State to plead sovereign immunity to bar the exercise of federal-question jurisdiction. [T]he *Hans* Court had no occasion to consider whether Congress could abrogate that background immunity by statute. Indeed (except in the special circumstance of Congress's power to enforce the Civil War Amendments), this question never came before our Court until *Union Gas.* In *Union Gas* the Court held that the immunity recognized in *Hans* had no constitutional status and was subject to congressional abrogation. Today the Court overrules *Union Gas* and holds just the opposite. In deciding how to choose between these two positions, the place to begin is with *Hans's* holding that a principle of sovereign immunity derived from the common law insulates a State from federal-question jurisdiction at the suit of its own citizen. A critical examination of that case will show that it was wrongly decided, as virtually every recent commentator has concluded. It follows that the Court's further step today of constitutionalizing *Hans's* rule against abrogation by Congress compounds and immensely magnifies the century-old mistake of *Hans* itself and takes its place with other historic examples of textually untethered elevations of judicially derived rules to the status of inviolable constitutional law.

A. The Louisiana plaintiff in *Hans* held bonds issued by that State, which, like virtually all of the Southern States, had issued them in substantial amounts during the Reconstruction era. [H]owever, the post-Reconstruction regimes sought to repudiate these debts, and the *Hans* litigation arose out of Louisiana's attempt to renege on its bond obligations.

Hans sued the State in federal court, asserting that the State's default amounted to an impairment of the obligation of its contracts in violation of the Contract Clause. This Court affirmed the dismissal of the suit, despite the fact that the case fell within the federal court's "arising under," or federal-question, jurisdiction.

Taking *Hans* only as far as its holding, its vulnerability is apparent. The Court rested its opinion on avoiding the supposed anomaly of recognizing jurisdiction to entertain a citizen's federal question suit, but not one brought by a noncitizen. There was, however, no such anomaly at all. As already explained, federal-question cases are not touched by the Eleventh Amendment, which leaves a State open to federal-question suits by citizens and noncitizens alike.

Although there was thus no anomaly to be cured by *Hans,* the case certainly created its own anomaly in leaving federal courts entirely without jurisdiction to enforce paramount federal law at the behest of a citizen against a State that broke it. It destroyed the congruence of the judicial power under Article III with the substantive guarantees of the Constitution, and with the provisions of statutes passed by Congress in the exercise of its power under Article I: when a State injured an individual in violation of federal law no federal forum could provide direct relief. Absent an alternative process to vindicate federal law John Marshall saw just what the consequences of this anomaly would be in the early Republic, and he took that consequence as good evidence that the Framers could never have intended such a scheme. [See] *Cohens v. Virginia,* 6 Wheat. at 386–387.

[H]istory explains, but does not honor, *Hans.* The ultimate demerit of the case centers, however, not on its politics but on the legal errors on which it rested.

B. The *Hans* Court held the suit barred by a non-constitutional common-law immunity. The Court's broad theory of immunity runs doubly afoul of the appellate jurisdiction problem that I noted earlier in rejecting an interpretation of the Eleventh Amendment's text that would bar federal-question suits. If "the whole sum of the judicial power granted by the Constitution to the United States does not embrace the authority to entertain a suit brought by a citizen against his own State without its consent," and if consent to suit in state court is not sufficient to show consent in federal court, then Article III would hardly permit this Court to exercise appellate jurisdiction over issues of federal law arising in lawsuits brought against the States in their own courts. We have, however, quite rightly ignored any post-*Hans* dicta in that sort of case and exercised the jurisdiction that the plain text of Article III provides.

If these examples were not enough, one would need only to consider a final set of cases: those in which we have assumed, without deciding, that congressional power to abrogate state sovereign immunity exists even when §5 of the Fourteenth Amendment has no application. A majority of this Court was willing to make that assumption in *Hoffman v. Connecticut Dept. of Income Maintenance,* 492 U.S. 96, 101 (1989), in *Welch v. Texas Dept. of Highways and Public Transp.,* 483 U.S. 468, 475 (1987), and in *County of Oneida v. Oneida Indian Nation of N.Y.,* 470 U.S. 226, 252 (1985). Although the Court in each of these cases failed to find abrogation for lack of a clear statement of congressional intent, the assumption that such power was available would hardly have been permissible if, at that time, today's majority's view of the law had been firmly established.

III. Three critical errors in *Hans* weigh against constitutionalizing its holding as the majority does today. The first we have already seen: the *Hans* Court misread the Eleventh Amendment. It also misunderstood the conditions under which common-law doctrines were received or rejected at the time of the founding, and it fundamentally mistook the very nature of sovereignty in the young Republic that was supposed to entail a State's immunity to federal-question jurisdiction in a federal court. [T]he Court today simply compounds already serious error in taking *Hans* the further step of investing its rule with constitutional inviolability against the considered judgment of Congress to abrogate it.

A. There is and could be no dispute that the doctrine of sovereign immunity that *Hans* purported to apply had its origins in the "familiar doctrine of the common law," "derived from the laws and practices of our English ancestors." This fact of the doctrine's common-law status in the period covering the founding and the later adoption of the Eleventh Amendment should have raised a warning flag to the *Hans* Court and it should do the same for the Court today. It is not that the Framers failed to see themselves to be children of the common law. But still it is clear that the adoption of English common law in America was not taken for granted, and that the exact manner and extent of the common law's reception were subject to careful consideration by courts and legislatures in each of the new States. An examination of the States' experience with common-law reception will shed light on subsequent theory and practice at the national level, and demonstrate that our history is entirely at odds with *Hans*'s resort to a common-law principle to limit the Constitution's contrary text.

While the States had limited their reception of English common law to principles appropriate to American conditions, the 1787 draft Constitution contained no provision for adopting the common law at all. This omission stood in sharp contrast to the state constitutions then extant, virtually all of which contained explicit provisions dealing with common-law reception. Since the experience in the States set the stage for thinking at the national level, this failure to address the notion of common-law reception could not have been inadvertent. Instead, the Framers chose to recognize only particular common-law concepts, such as the writ of *habeas corpus* and the distinction between law and equity.

Records of the ratification debates support Marshall's understanding that everyone had to know that the new Constitution would not draw the common law in its train. The Framers also recognized that the diverse development of the common law in the several States made a general federal reception impossible. There was not, then, any unified "Common Law" in America that the Federal Constitution could adopt.

Rejecting the idea of any federal reception, Madison insisted that "the consequence of admitting the common law as the law of the United States, on the authority of the individual States, is as obvious as it would be fatal. As this law relates to every subject of legislation, and would be paramount to the Constitutions and laws of the States, the admission of it would overwhelm the residuary sovereignty of the States, and by one constructive operation new model the whole political fabric of the country." Madison concluded that "it is . . . distressing to reflect that it ever should have been made a question, whether the Constitution, on the whole face of which is seen so much labor to enumerate and define the several objects of Federal power, could intend to introduce in the lump, in an indirect manner, and by a forced construction of a few phrases, the vast and multifarious jurisdiction involved in the common law—a law filling so many ample volumes; a law overspreading the entire field of legislation; and a law that would sap the foundation of the Constitution as a system of limited and specified powers."

B. Given the refusal to entertain any wholesale reception of common law, given the failure of the new Constitution to make any provision for adoption of common law as such, and given the protests already quoted that no general reception had occurred, the *Hans* Court and the Court today cannot reasonably argue that something like the old immunity doctrine somehow slipped in as a tacit but enforceable background principle.

The Court's attempt to convert isolated statements by the Framers into answers to questions not before them is fundamentally misguided. The Court's difficulty is far more fundamental, however, for the Court's position runs afoul of the general theory of sovereignty that gave shape to the Framers' enterprise. An enquiry into the development of that concept demonstrates that American political thought had so revolutionized the concept of sovereignty itself that calling for the immunity of a State as against the jurisdiction of the national courts would have been sheer illogic.

2. While there is no need here to calculate exactly how close the American States came to sovereignty in the classic sense prior to ratification of the Constitution, it is clear that the act of ratification affected their sovereignty in a way different from

any previous political event in America or anywhere else. For the adoption of the Constitution made them members of a novel federal system that sought to balance the States' exercise of some sovereign prerogatives delegated from their own people with the principle of a limited but centralizing federal supremacy.

The American development of divided sovereign powers, which "shattered . . . the categories of government that had dominated Western thinking for centuries" was made possible only by a recognition that the ultimate sovereignty rests in the people themselves. The people possessing this plenary bundle of specific powers were free to parcel them out to different governments and different branches of the same government as they saw fit. Chief Justice Marshall's descri[bed the situation] of the National and State Governments as [one in which] "each sovereign, with respect to the objects committed to it, and neither sovereign with respect to the objects committed to the other." *McCulloch v. Maryland,* 17 U.S. (4 Wheat.) 316 (1819).

[T]he ratification demonstrated that state governments were subject to a superior regime of law in a judicial system established, not by the State, but by the people through a specific delegation of their sovereign power to a National Government that was paramount within its delegated sphere. When individuals sued States to enforce federal rights, the Government that corresponded to the "sovereign" in the traditional common-law sense was not the State but the National Government, and any state immunity from the jurisdiction of the Nation's courts would have required a grant from the true sovereign, the people, in their Constitution, or from the Congress that the Constitution had empowered.

State immunity to federal-question jurisdiction would, moreover, have run up against the common understanding of the practical necessity for the new federal relationship. According to Madison, the "multiplicity," "mutability," and "injustice" of then-extant state laws were prime factors requiring the formation of a new government. These concerns ultimately found concrete expression in a number of specific limitations on state power, including provisions barring the States from enacting bills of attainder or ex post facto laws, coining money or emitting bills of credit, denying the privileges and immunities of out-of-staters, or impairing the obligation of contracts. But the proposed Constitution also dealt with the old problems affirmatively by granting the powers to Congress enumerated in Article I, §8, and by providing through the Supremacy Clause that Congress could pre-empt state action in areas of concurrent state and federal authority.

Given the Framers' general concern with curbing abuses by state governments, it would be amazing if the scheme of delegated powers embodied in the Constitution had left the National Government powerless to render the States judicially accountable for violations of federal rights. And of course the Framers did not understand the scheme to leave the Government powerless.

The very idea of a federal question depended on the rejection of the simple concept of sovereignty from which the immunity doctrine had developed; under the English common law, the question of immunity in a system of layered sovereignty simply could not have arisen. Today's majority discounts this concern. Without citing a single source to the contrary, the Court dismisses the historical evidence regarding the Framers' vision of the relationship between national and state sovereignty. In the end, is it plausible to contend that the plan of the convention was meant to leave the National Government without any way to render individuals capable of enforcing their federal rights directly against an intransigent State?

C. The Framers feared judicial power over substantive policy and the ossification of law that would result from transforming common law into constitutional law, and their fears have been borne out every time the Court has ignored Madison's counsel on subjects that we generally group under economic and social policy. It is, in fact, remarkable that as we near the end of this century the Court should choose to open a new constitutional chapter in confining legislative judgments on these matters by resort to textually unwarranted common-law rules, for it was just this practice in the century's early decades that brought this Court to the nadir of competence that we identify with *Lochner v. New York,* 198 U.S. 45 (1905). It was the defining characteristic of the *Lochner* era, and its characteristic vice, that the Court treated the common-law background as paramount, while regarding congressional legislation to abrogate the common law on these economic matters as constitutionally suspect.

The majority today, indeed, seems to be going *Lochner* one better. Today the Court is not struggling to fulfill a responsibility to reconcile two arguably conflicting and Delphic constitutional provisions, nor is it struggling with any Delphic text at all. For even the Court concedes that the Constitution's grant to Congress of plenary power over relations with Indian tribes at the expense of any state claim to the contrary is unmistakably clear, and this case does not even arguably implicate a textual trump to the grant of federal-question jurisdiction.

John Marshall recognized it over a century and a half ago in the very context of state sovereign immunity in federal-question cases: "The jurisdiction of the court, then, being extended by the letter of the constitution to all cases arising under it, or under the laws of the United States, it follows that those who would withdraw any case of this description from that jurisdiction, must sustain the exemption they claim on the spirit and true meaning of the constitution, which spirit and true meaning must be so apparent as to overrule the words which its framers have employed." *Cohens v. Virginia,* 6 Wheat. at 379–380.

*****

The Court has taken the *Seminole* doctrine much further. One of the clearest illustrations of that is its ruling striking down the Americans with Disabilities Act as it applies to states and the ability of those affected to sue for redress.

Board of Trustees of the University of Alabama v. Garrett, 531 U.S. 356 (2001).

INTRODUCTION: Two employees of the State of Alabama encountered difficulties on the job which ultimately led to the litigation. Patricia Garrett was the head OB/GYN/Neonatal nurse at the University of Alabama Birmingham Hospital when she learned that she had breast cancer. She took a leave from her position and received a lumpectomy as well as radiation and chemotherapy. When she returned from her leave of absence, she was told that she could no longer be the Director and then was transferred to a lower level position. She filed suit against the state under the Americans with Disabilities Act (ADA).

The other employee was Milton Ash, who was employed by the Alabama Department of Youth Services. Mr. Ash indicated that he had several medical problems that required accommodations on the job, including asthma and sleep apnea. The employer did not respond to these requests. He filed a discrimination complaint but then concluded that his performance evaluations showed retribution for his complaint. He later sued in federal district court under the ADA.

✱✱✱✱✱

CHIEF JUSTICE REHNQUIST wrote the opinion for the Court.

We decide here whether employees of the State of Alabama may recover money damages by reason of the State's failure to comply with the provisions of Title I of the Americans with Disabilities Act of 1990. We hold that such suits are barred by the Eleventh Amendment.

The ADA prohibits certain employers, including the States, from "discriminating against a qualified individual with a disability because of the disability of such individual in regard to job application procedures, the hiring, advancement, or discharge of employees, employee compensation, job training, and other terms, conditions, and privileges of employment." To this end, the Act requires employers to "make reasonable accommodations to the known physical or mental limitations of an otherwise qualified individual with a disability who is an applicant or employee, unless [the employer] can demonstrate that the accommodation would impose an undue hardship on the operation of the [employer's] business." The Act also prohibits employers from "utilizing standards, criteria, or methods of administration . . . that have the effect of discrimination on the basis of disability." The Act defines "disability" to include "(A) a physical or mental impairment that substantially limits one or more of the major life activities of such individual; (B) a record of such an impairment; or (C) being regarded as having such an impairment."

I. The Eleventh Amendment provides: "The Judicial power of the United States shall not be construed to extend to any suit in law or equity, commenced or prosecuted against one of the United States by Citizens of another State, or by Citizens or Subjects of any Foreign State."

Although by its terms the Amendment applies only to suits against a State by citizens of another State, our cases have extended the Amendment's applicability to suits by citizens against their own States. See *Kimel v. Florida Bd. of Regents,* 528 U.S. 62, 72–73 (2000); *Seminole Tribe of Fla. v. Florida,* 517 U.S. 44, 54 (1996); *Hans v. Louisiana,* 134 U.S. 1 (1890). The ultimate guarantee of the Eleventh Amendment is that nonconsenting States may not be sued by private individuals in federal court.

We have recognized, however, that Congress may abrogate the States' Eleventh Amendment immunity when it both unequivocally intends to do so and "acts pursuant to a valid grant of constitutional authority." The first of these requirements is not in dispute here. The question [in this case] is whether Congress acted within its constitutional authority by subjecting the States to suits in federal court for money damages under the ADA.

Congress may not, of course, base its abrogation of the States' Eleventh Amendment immunity upon the powers enumerated in Article I. See *Kimel, supra,* at 79; *Seminole Tribe, supra,* at 72–73. In *Fitzpatrick v. Bitzer,* 427 U.S. 445 (1976), however, we concluded, Congress may subject nonconsenting States to suit in federal court when it does so pursuant to a valid exercise of its §5 power. Accordingly, the ADA can apply to the States only to the extent that the statute is appropriate §5 legislation.

Section 1 of the Fourteenth Amendment provides, in relevant part: "No State shall make or enforce any law which shall abridge the privileges or immunities of citizens of the United States; nor shall any State deprive any person of life, liberty, or property, without due process of law; nor deny to any person within its jurisdiction the equal protection of the laws." Section 5 of the Fourteenth Amendment grants Congress the power to enforce the substantive guarantees contained in §1 by enacting "appropriate legislation." Congress is not limited to mere legislative repetition of this Court's constitutional jurisprudence. "Rather, Congress' power 'to enforce' the Amendment includes the authority both to remedy and to deter violation of rights guaranteed thereunder by prohibiting a somewhat broader swath of conduct, including that which is not itself forbidden by the Amendment's text."

City of Boerne v. Flores, 521 U.S. 507, 536 (1997), also confirmed, however, the long-settled principle that it is the responsibility of this Court, not Congress, to define the substance of constitutional guarantees. Accordingly, §5 legislation reaching beyond the scope of §1's actual guarantees must exhibit "congruence and proportionality between the injury to be prevented or remedied and the means adopted to that end."

II. The first step in applying these now familiar principles is to identify with some precision the scope of the constitutional right at issue. Here, that inquiry requires us to examine the limitations §1 of the Fourteenth Amendment places upon States' treatment of the disabled.

In *Cleburne v. Cleburne Living Center, Inc.,* 473 U.S. 432 (1985), [t]he specific question before us was whether the Court of Appeals had erred by holding that mental retardation qualified as a "quasi-suspect" classification under our equal protection jurisprudence. We answered that question in the affirmative, concluding instead that such legislation incurs only the minimum "rational-basis" review applicable to general social and economic legislation.[22]

Under rational-basis review, where a group possesses "distinguishing characteristics relevant to interests the State has the authority to implement," a State's

---

22. Applying the basic principles of rationality review, *Cleburne* struck down the city ordinance in question.

decision to act on the basis of those differences does not give rise to a constitutional violation. "Such a classification cannot run afoul of the Equal Protection Clause if there is a rational relationship between the disparity of treatment and some legitimate governmental purpose." Moreover, the State need not articulate its reasoning at the moment a particular decision is made. Rather, the burden is upon the challenging party to negative "any reasonably conceivable state of facts that could provide a rational basis for the classification."

Thus, the result of *Cleburne* is that States are not required by the Fourteenth Amendment to make special accommodations for the disabled, so long as their actions towards such individuals are rational. They could quite hardheadedly—and perhaps hardheartedly—hold to job-qualification requirements which do not make allowance for the disabled. If special accommodations for the disabled are to be required, they have to come from positive law and not through the Equal Protection Clause.

III. Once we have determined the metes and bounds of the constitutional right in question, we examine whether Congress identified a history and pattern of unconstitutional employment discrimination by the States against the disabled. Just as §1 of the Fourteenth Amendment applies only to actions committed "under color of state law," Congress' §5 authority is appropriately exercised only in response to state transgressions. The legislative record of the ADA, however, simply fails to show that Congress did in fact identify a pattern of irrational state discrimination in employment against the disabled.[23]

Respondents contend that the inquiry as to unconstitutional discrimination should extend not only to States themselves, but to units of local governments, such as cities and counties. All of these, they say, are "state actors" for purposes of the Fourteenth Amendment. This is quite true, but the Eleventh Amendment does not extend its immunity to units of local government. See *Lincoln County v. Luning,* 133 U.S. 529, 530 (1890). These entities are subject to private claims for damages under the ADA without Congress' ever having to rely on §5 of the Fourteenth Amendment to render them so.[24] It would make no sense to consider constitutional violations on their part, as well as by the States themselves, when only the States are the beneficiaries of the Eleventh Amendment.

Congress made a general finding in the ADA that "historically, society has tended to isolate and segregate individuals with disabilities, and, despite some improvements, such forms of discrimination against individuals with disabilities continue to be a serious and pervasive social problem." The record assembled by Congress includes many instances to support such a finding. But the great majority of these incidents do not deal with the activities of States.

Several of these incidents [cited in the Respondents' brief] undoubtedly evidence an unwillingness on the part of state officials to make the sort of accommo-

---

23. NOTE: While one may agree or disagree with many aspects of Rehnquist's opinion, this statement is patently false and the dissent provided state-by-state evidence in an appendix that filled many pages in the U.S. Reports not reproduced in this excerpt.

24. NOTE: The fact is that virtually all such cases are brought under 42 U.S.C. §1983, which is in fact based upon Congress' authority under Section 5 of the Fourteenth Amendment.

dations for the disabled required by the ADA. Whether they were irrational under our decision in *Cleburne* is more debatable, particularly when the incident is described out of context. But even if it were to be determined that each incident upon fuller examination showed unconstitutional action on the part of the State, these incidents taken together fall far short of even suggesting the pattern of unconstitutional discrimination on which §5 legislation must be based. Congress, in enacting the ADA, found that "some 43,000,000 Americans have one or more physical or mental disabilities." In 1990, the States alone employed more than 4.5 million people. It is telling, we think, that given these large numbers, Congress assembled only such minimal evidence of unconstitutional state discrimination in employment against the disabled.

Even were it possible to squeeze out of these examples a pattern of unconstitutional discrimination by the States, the rights and remedies created by the ADA against the States would raise the same sort of concerns as to congruence and proportionality as were found in *City of Boerne*. For example, whereas it would be entirely rational (and therefore constitutional) for a state employer to conserve scarce financial resources by hiring employees who are able to use existing facilities, the ADA requires employers to "make existing facilities used by employees readily accessible to and usable by individuals with disabilities." The ADA does except employers from the "reasonable accommodation" requirement where the employer "can demonstrate that the accommodation would impose an undue hardship on the operation of the business of such covered entity." However, even with this exception, the accommodation duty far exceeds what is constitutionally required in that it makes unlawful a range of alternate responses that would be reasonable but would fall short of imposing an "undue burden" upon the employer. The Act also makes it the employer's duty to prove that it would suffer such a burden, instead of requiring (as the Constitution does) that the complaining party negate reasonable bases for the employer's decision.

Congressional enactment of the ADA represents its judgment that there should be a "comprehensive national mandate for the elimination of discrimination against individuals with disabilities." Congress is the final authority as to desirable public policy, but in order to authorize private individuals to recover money damages against the States, there must be a pattern of discrimination by the States which violates the Fourteenth Amendment, and the remedy imposed by Congress must be congruent and proportional to the targeted violation. Those requirements are not met here.

JUSTICE KENNEDY wrote a concurring opinion.

There can be little doubt that persons with mental or physical impairments are confronted with prejudice which can stem from indifference or insecurity as well as from malicious ill will. It is a question of quite a different order, however, to say that the States in their official capacities, the States as governmental entities, must be held in violation of the Constitution on the assumption that they embody the misconceived or malicious perceptions of some of their citizens. For the reasons explained by the Court, an equal protection violation has not been shown with respect to the several States in this case.

It must be noted, moreover, that what is in question is not whether the Congress, acting pursuant to a power granted to it by the Constitution, can compel the States to act. What is involved is only the question whether the States can be subjected to liability in suits brought not by the Federal Government (to which the States have consented) but by private persons seeking to collect moneys from the state treasury without the consent of the State.

JUSTICE BREYER dissented joined by JUSTICES STEVENS, SOUTER, and GINSBURG.

Reviewing the congressional record as if it were an administrative agency record, the Court holds the statutory provision before us unconstitutional. The Court concludes that Congress assembled insufficient evidence of unconstitutional discrimination. Section 5, however, grants Congress the "power to enforce, by appropriate legislation" the Fourteenth Amendment's equal protection guarantee. [S]tate discrimination in employment against persons with disabilities might "'run afoul of the Equal Protection Clause'" where there is no "'rational relationship between the disparity of treatment and some legitimate governmental purpose.'" In my view, Congress reasonably could have concluded that the remedy before us constitutes an "appropriate" way to enforce this basic equal protection requirement. And that is all the Constitution requires.

I. The Court says that its primary problem with this statutory provision is one of legislative evidence. It says that "Congress assembled only . . . minimal evidence of unconstitutional state discrimination in employment." In fact, Congress compiled a vast legislative record documenting "'massive, society-wide discrimination'" against persons with disabilities. In addition to the information presented at 13 congressional hearings (see Appendix A, infra), and its own prior experience gathered over 40 years during which it contemplated and enacted considerable similar legislation (see Appendix B, infra), Congress created a special task force to assess the need for comprehensive legislation. Congress' own hearings, and an analysis of "census data, national polls, and other studies" led Congress to conclude that "people with disabilities, as a group, occupy an inferior status in our society, and are severely disadvantaged socially, vocationally, economically, and educationally." As to employment, Congress found that "two-thirds of all disabled Americans between the age of 16 and 64 [were] not working at all," even though a large majority wanted to, and were able to, work productively. And Congress found that this discrimination flowed in significant part from "stereotypic assumptions" as well as "purposeful unequal treatment."

The powerful evidence of discriminatory treatment throughout society in general, including discrimination by private persons and local governments, implicates state governments as well, for state agencies form part of that same larger society. The Court claims that it "makes no sense" to take into consideration constitutional violations committed by local governments. But the substantive obligation that the Equal Protection Clause creates applies to state and local governmental entities alike. Local governments often work closely with, and under the supervision of, state officials, and in general, state and local government employers are similarly situated.

In any event, there is no need to rest solely upon evidence of discrimination by local governments or general societal discrimination. There are roughly 300 examples of discrimination by state governments themselves in the legislative record. See, e.g., Appendix C, infra. I fail to see how this evidence "falls far short of even suggesting the pattern of unconstitutional discrimination on which §5 legislation must be based." They reveal, not what the Court describes as "half a dozen" instances of discrimination, but hundreds of instances of adverse treatment at the hands of state officials.

[A] legislature is not a court of law. And Congress, unlike courts, must, and does, routinely draw general conclusions from anecdotal and opinion-based evidence of this kind, particularly when the evidence lacks strong refutation. In reviewing §5 legislation, we have never required the sort of extensive investigation of each piece of evidence that the Court appears to contemplate. Nor has the Court traditionally required Congress to make findings as to state discrimination, or to break down the record evidence, category by category.

II. The Court's failure to find sufficient evidentiary support may well rest upon its decision to hold Congress to a strict, judicially created evidentiary standard, particularly in respect to lack of justification. And the Court itself points out that, when economic or social legislation is challenged in court as irrational, hence unconstitutional, the "burden is upon the challenging party to negative any reasonably conceivable state of facts that could provide a rational basis for the classification." Imposing this special "burden" upon Congress, the Court fails to find in the legislative record sufficient indication that Congress has "negatived" the presumption that state action is rationally related to a legitimate objective.

The problem with the Court's approach is that neither the "burden of proof" that favors States nor any other rule of restraint applicable to judges applies to Congress when it exercises its §5 power. Rational-basis review—with its presumptions favoring constitutionality—is "a paradigm of judicial restraint." And the Congress of the United States is not a lower court.

Moreover, unlike judges, Members of Congress are elected. When the Court has applied the majority's burden of proof rule, it has explained that we, i.e., the courts, do not "sit as a superlegislature to judge the wisdom or desirability of legislative policy determinations."

III. The Court argues in the alternative that the statute's damage remedy is not "congruent" with and "proportional" to the equal protection problem that Congress found. The Court suggests that the Act's "reasonable accommodation" requirement and disparate impact standard "far exceed what is constitutionally required." But we have upheld disparate impact standards in contexts where they were not "constitutionally required."

And what is wrong with a remedy that, in response to unreasonable employer behavior, requires an employer to make accommodations that are reasonable? Of course, what is "reasonable" in the statutory sense and what is "unreasonable" in the constitutional sense might differ. In other words, the requirement may exceed what is necessary to avoid a constitutional violation. But it is just that power—the power to require more than the minimum—that §5 grants to Congress, as this Court has repeatedly confirmed. *Ex parte Virginia,* 100 U.S. 339, 346 (1880).

In keeping with these principles, the Court has said that "it is not for us to review the congressional resolution of 'the various conflicting considerations—the risk or pervasiveness of the discrimination in governmental services . . . , the adequacy or availability of alternative remedies, and the nature and significance of the state interests that would be affected.' It is enough that we be able to perceive a basis upon which the Congress might resolve the conflict as it did."

The Court's more recent cases have professed to follow the longstanding principle of deference to Congress. And even today, the Court purports to apply, not to depart from, these standards. But the Court's analysis and ultimate conclusion deprive its declarations of practical significance. The Court "sounds the word of promise to the ear but breaks it to the hope."

IV. The Court's harsh review of Congress' use of its §5 power is reminiscent of the similar (now-discredited) limitation that it once imposed upon Congress' Commerce Clause power. I could understand the legal basis for such review were we judging a statute that discriminated against those of a particular race or gender, or a statute that threatened a basic constitutionally protected liberty such as free speech. The legislation before us, however, does not discriminate against anyone, nor does it pose any threat to basic liberty. And it is difficult to understand why the Court, which applies "minimum 'rational-basis' review" to statutes that burden persons with disabilities, subjects to far stricter scrutiny a statute that seeks to help those same individuals.

The Court, through its evidentiary demands, its non-deferential review, and its failure to distinguish between judicial and legislative constitutional competencies, improperly invades a power that the Constitution assigns to Congress. Its decision saps §5 of independent force, effectively "confining the legislative power . . . to the insignificant role of abrogating only those state laws that the judicial branch [is] prepared to adjudge unconstitutional."

*****

CONTRACTORS AND ADMINISTRATIVE RESPONSIBILITY

As in many areas of public law and public administration these days, the status of contractors in terms of liability is very much up in the air. That said, the pressure to contract out more and more government activities makes this lack of clarity one of the most serious problems of modern governance. This is an issue developed in greater detail in *Governing by Contract* (Washington, D.C.: CQ Press, 2003).

Richardson v. McKnight, **521 U.S. 399 (1997).**

INTRODUCTION: Tennessee contracted with the Corrections Corporation of America for the operation of a number of its correctional facilities. As part of its operations, the firm hired correctional officers to staff the facilities. A prisoner at the South Central Correctional Center brought suit against two of those guards on grounds that they placed on him excessively tight restraints, allegedly subjecting him to a violation of his constitutional rights. These suits were brought under 42 U.S.C. §1983, the same provision that would be the basis for a suit against a state-employed prison guard. The guards asserted that they were entitled to the same kind of qualified immunity that would be available to a civil servant working in the same kind of position. The lower courts rejected that argument. However, since this case was brought up as an interlocutory appeal (in the midst of litigation), the record in the case was very limited.

*****

JUSTICE BREYER wrote the opinion for the Court.

The issue before us is whether prison guards who are employees of a private prison management firm are entitled to a qualified immunity from suit by prisoners charging a violation of 42 U.S.C. §1983. We hold that they are not.

I. The District Court noted that Tennessee had "privatized" the management of a number of its correctional facilities, and that consequently a private firm, not the state government, employed the guards. The court held that, because they worked for a private company rather than the government, the law did not grant the guards immunity from suit. It therefore denied the guards' motion to dismiss. The Court of Appeals concluded, primarily for reasons of "public policy," that the privately employed prison guards were not entitled to the immunity provided their governmental counterparts. We granted *certiorari* to review this holding. We now affirm.

II. [Our recent ruling in *Wyatt v. Cole,* 504 U.S. 158 (1992)] did not answer the legal question before us. It does tell us, however, to look both to history and to the purposes that underlie government employee immunity in order to find the answer. History does not reveal a "firmly rooted" tradition of immunity applicable to privately employed prison guards. Correctional services in the United States have undergone various transformations. Government-employed prison guards may have enjoyed a kind of immunity defense arising out of their status as public employees at common law. But correctional functions have never been exclusively public and private contractors were heavily involved in prison management during the 19th century.

During that time, some states, including southern states like Tennessee, leased their entire prison systems to private individuals or companies which frequently took complete control over prison management, including inmate labor and discipline. [W]e have found evidence that the common law provided mistreated prisoners in prison leasing States with remedies against mistreatment by those private lessors. Yet, we have found no evidence that the law gave purely private companies or their employees any special immunity from such suits.

The common law [long ago] forbade those jailers to subject "their prisoners to any pain or torment," whether through harsh confinement in leg irons, or otherwise. See *In re Birdsong,* 39 F. 599, 601 (SD Ga. 1889); 1 E. Coke, *Institutes,* 315, 316, 381 (1797). Apparently the law did provide a kind of immunity for certain private defendants, such as doctors or lawyers who performed services at the behest of the sovereign. But we have found no indication of any more general immunity that might have applied to private individuals working for profit. History therefore does not provide significant support for the immunity claim.

C. Whether the immunity doctrine's purposes warrant immunity for private prison guards presents a closer question. [We have] described the doctrine's purposes as protecting "government's ability to perform its traditional functions" by providing immunity where "necessary to preserve" the ability of government officials "to serve the public good or to ensure that talented candidates were not deterred by the threat of damages suits from entering public service." Earlier precedent described immunity as protecting the public from unwarranted timidity on the part of public officials by, for example, "encouraging the vigorous exercise of official authority," by contributing to "principled and fearless decision-making," and by responding to the concern that threatened liability would "dampen the ardour of all but the most resolute, or the most irresponsible" public officials.

The guards argue that those purposes support immunity whether their employer is private or public. Since private prison guards perform the same work as state prison guards, they say, they must require immunity to a similar degree. To say this, however, is to misread this Court's precedents. The Court has sometimes applied a functional approach in immunity cases, but only to decide which type of immunity—absolute or qualified—a public officer should receive. And it never has held that the mere performance of a governmental function could make the difference between unlimited §1983 liability and qualified immunity, especially for a private person who performs a job without government supervision or direction. Indeed a purely functional approach bristles with difficulty, particularly since, in many areas, government and private industry may engage in fundamentally similar activities, ranging from electricity production, to waste disposal, to even mail delivery.

Petitioners' argument [sic.] also overlook certain important differences that, from an immunity perspective, are critical. First, the most important special government immunity-producing concern—unwarranted timidity—is less likely present, or at least is not special, when a private company subject to competitive market pressures operates a prison. Competitive pressures mean not only that a firm whose guards are too aggressive will face damages that raise costs, thereby threatening its replacement, but also that a firm whose guards are too timid will face threats of replacement by other firms with records that demonstrate their ability to do both a safer and a more effective job.

These ordinary marketplace pressures are present here. The private prison guards before us work for a large, multistate private prison management firm. The firm is systematically organized to perform a major administrative task for profit. It performs that task independently, with relatively less ongoing direct state supervision. It must buy insurance sufficient to compensate victims of civil rights torts. And, since the firm's first contract expires after three years, its performance is disciplined, not only by state review, but also by pressure from potentially competing firms who can try to take its place.

In other words, marketplace pressures provide the private firm with strong incentives to avoid overly timid, insufficiently vigorous, unduly fearful, or "nonarduous" employee job performance. And the contract's provisions—including those that might permit employee indemnification and avoid many civil-service restrictions—grant this private firm freedom to respond to those market pressures through rewards and penalties that operate directly upon its employees. To this extent, the employees before us resemble those of other private firms and differ from government employees.

This is not to say that government employees, in their efforts to act within constitutional limits, will always, or often, sacrifice the otherwise effective performance of their duties. Rather, it is to say that government employees typically act within a different system. They work within a system that is responsible through elected officials to voters who, when they vote, rarely consider the performance of individual subdepartments or civil servants specifically and in detail. And that system is often characterized by multidepartment civil service rules that, while providing employee security, may limit the incentives or the ability of individual departments or supervisors flexibly to reward, or to punish, individual employees. Hence a judicial determination that "effectiveness" concerns warrant special immunity-type protection in respect to this latter (governmental) system does not prove its need in respect to the former. Consequently, we can find no special immunity-related need to encourage vigorous performance.

Second, "privatization" helps to meet the immunity-related need "to ensure that talented candidates" are "not deterred by the threat of damages suits from entering public service." It does so in part because of the comprehensive insurance-coverage requirements just mentioned. The insurance increases the likelihood of employee indemnification and to that extent reduces the employment-discouraging fear of unwarranted liability potential applicants face. Because privatization law also frees the private prison-management firm from many civil service law restraints, it permits the private firm, unlike a government department, to offset any increased employee liability risk with higher pay or extra benefits.

In respect to this second government-immunity-related purpose then, it is difficult to find a special need for immunity, for the guards' employer can operate like other private firms; it need not operate like a typical government department.

Third, lawsuits may well "distract" these employees "from their . . . duties," but the risk of "distraction" alone cannot be sufficient grounds for an immunity. Our qualified immunity cases do not contemplate the complete elimination of lawsuit-based distractions. And it is significant that, here, Tennessee law reserves certain important discretionary tasks—those related to prison discipline, to parole, and to good time—for state officials. Given a continual and conceded need for deterring constitutional violations and our sense that the firm's tasks are not enormously different in respect to their importance from various other publicly important tasks carried out by private firms, we are not persuaded that the threat of distracting workers from their duties is enough virtually by itself to justify providing an immunity.

D. Our examination of history and purpose thus reveals nothing special enough about the job or about its organizational structure that would warrant providing these private prison guards with a governmental immunity. The job is one that private industry might, or might not, perform; and which history shows private firms did sometimes perform without relevant immunities. The organizational structure is one subject to the ordinary competitive pressures that normally help private firms adjust their behavior in response to the incentives that tort suits provide—pressures not necessarily present in government departments. Since there are no special reasons significantly favoring an extension of governmental immunity, and since *Wyatt* makes clear that private actors are not automatically immune, we must conclude that private prison guards, unlike those who work directly for the government, do not enjoy immunity from suit in a §1983 case.

III. We have answered the immunity question narrowly, in the context in which it arose. That context is one in which a private firm, systematically organized to assume a major lengthy administrative task (managing an institution) with limited direct supervision by the government, undertakes that task for profit and potentially in competition with other firms. The case does not involve a private individual briefly associated with a government body, serving as an adjunct to government in an essential governmental activity, or acting under close official supervision.

　　[Further], *Wyatt* explicitly stated that it did not decide whether or not the private defendants before it might assert, not immunity, but a special "good faith" defense. The Court said that it "did not foreclose the possibility that private defendants faced with §1983 liability could be entitled to an affirmative defense based on good faith and/or probable cause or that §1983 suits against private, rather than governmental, parties could require plaintiffs to carry additional burdens." Like the Court in *Wyatt,* and the Court of Appeals in this case, we do not express a view on this last-mentioned question.

JUSTICE SCALIA wrote a dissent joined by CHIEF JUSTICE REHNQUIST, and JUSTICES KENNEDY and THOMAS.

　　Today the Court declares that [qualified immunity] is unavailable to employees of private prison management firms, who perform the same duties as state-employed correctional officials, who exercise the most palpable form of state police power, and who may be sued for acting "under color of state law." This holding is supported neither by common-law tradition nor public policy, and contradicts our settled practice of determining §1983 immunity on the basis of the public function being performed.

I. I do not agree with the Court that the petitioners' claim to immunity is defeated if they cannot provide an actual case, antedating or contemporaneous with the enactment of §1983, in which immunity was successfully asserted by a private prison guard. It is only the absence of such a case, and not any explicit rejection of immunity by any common-law court, that the Court relies upon. The opinion observes that private jailers existed in the 19th century, and that they were successfully sued by prisoners. [A]s far as my research has disclosed, there may be more case-law support for immunity in the private-jailer context than in the government-jailer context. The only pre-§1983 jailer-immunity case of any sort that I am aware of is *Williams v. Adams,* 85 Mass. 171 (1861), decided only 10 years before §1983 became law. And that case, which explicitly acknowledged that the issue of jailer immunity was "novel," appears to have conferred immunity upon an independent contractor.

[T]he historical principles on which common-law immunity was based, and which are reflected in our jurisprudence, plainly cover the private prison guard if they cover the nonprivate. Those principles are two: (1) immunity is determined by function, not status, and (2) even more specifically, private status is not disqualifying. Private individuals have regularly been accorded immunity when they perform a governmental function that qualifies. We have long recognized the absolute immunity of grand jurors, noting that like prosecutors and judges they must "exercise a discretionary judgment on the basis of evidence presented to them." "The common law," we have observed, "provided absolute immunity from subsequent damages liability for all persons—governmental or otherwise—who were integral parts of the judicial process." There is no more reason for treating private prison guards differently.

II. Later in its opinion, the Court seeks to establish that there are policy reasons for denying to private prison guards the immunity accorded to public ones. As I have indicated above, I believe that history and not judicially analyzed policy governs this matter—but even on its own terms the Court's attempted policy distinction is unconvincing. The Court suggests two differences between civil-service prison guards and those employed by private prison firms which preclude any "special" need to give the latter immunity. First, the Court says that "unwarranted timidity" on the part of private guards is less likely to be a concern, since their companies are subject to market pressures that encourage them to be effective in the performance of their duties. If a private firm does not maintain a proper level of order, the Court reasons, it will be replaced by another one—so there is no need for qualified immunity to facilitate the maintenance of order.

This is wrong for several reasons. First of all, it is fanciful to speak of the consequences of "market" pressures in a regime where public officials are the only purchaser, and other people's money the medium of payment. Ultimately, one prison-management firm will be selected to replace another prison-management firm only if a decision is made by some political official not to renew the contract. This is a government decision, not a market choice. The process can come to resemble a market choice only to the extent that political actors (1) are willing to pay attention to the issue of prison services, among the many issues vying for their attention, and (2) are willing to place considerations of cost and quality of service ahead of such political considerations as personal friendship, political alliances, in-state ownership of the contractor, etc.

Secondly and more importantly, however, if one assumes a political regime that is bent on emulating the market in its purchase of prison services, it is almost certainly the case that, short of mismanagement so severe as to provoke a prison riot, price (not discipline) will be the predominating factor in such a regime's selection of a contractor. A contractor's price must depend upon its costs; lawsuits increase costs; and "fearless" maintenance of discipline increases lawsuits. The incentive to down-play discipline will exist, moreover, even in those states where the politicians' zeal for market-emulation and budget-cutting has waned, and where prison-management contract renewal is virtually automatic: the more cautious the prison guards, the fewer the lawsuits, the higher the profits. In sum, it seems that "market-competitive" private prison managers have even greater need than civil-service prison managers for immunity as an incentive to discipline.

The Court's second distinction between state and private prisons is that privatization "helps to meet the immunity-related need to ensure that talented candidates are not deterred by the threat of damages suits from entering public service" as prison guards. This is so because privatization brings with it (1) a statutory requirement for insurance coverage against civil-rights claims, which assertedly "increases the likelihood of employee indemnification," and (2) a liberation "from many civil service law restraints" which prevent increased employee risk from being "offset . . . with higher pay or extra benefits." As for the former (civil-rights liability insurance): surely it is the availability of that protection, rather than its actual presence in the case at hand, which decreases (if it does decrease, which I doubt) the need for immunity protection. But the second factor—liberation from civil-service limitations—is the more interesting one. First of all, simply as a philosophical matter it is fascinating to learn that one of the prime justifications for §1983 immunity should be a phenomenon (civil-service laws) that did not even exist when §1983 was enacted and the immunity created. Also as a philosophical matter, it is poetic justice (or poetic revenge) that the Court should use one of the principal economic benefits of "prison outsourcing"—namely, the avoidance of civil-service salary and tenure encrustations—as the justification for a legal rule rendering out-sourcing more expensive. [G]overnments need not have civil-service salary encrustations (or can exempt prisons from them); and hence governments, no more than private prison employers, have any need for §1983 immunity.

In concluding, I must observe that since there is no apparent reason for making immunity hinge upon the Court's distinction between public and private guards, the precise nature of that distinction must also remain obscure. Is it privity of contract that separates the two categories—so that guards paid directly by the State are "public" prison guards and immune, but those paid by a prison-management company "private" prison guards and not immune? Or is it rather "employee" versus "independent contractor" status—so that even guards whose compensation is paid directly by the State are not immune if they are not also supervised by a state official? Or is perhaps state supervision alone (without direct payment) enough to confer immunity? Or is it the formal designation of the guards, or perhaps of the guards' employer, as a "state instrumentality" that makes the difference? Since, as I say, I see no sense in the public-private distinction, neither do I see what precisely it consists of.

The only sure effect of today's decision—and the only purpose, as far as I can tell—is that it will artificially raise the cost of privatizing prisons. Whether this will cause privatization to be prohibitively expensive, or instead simply divert state funds that could have been saved or spent on additional prison services, it is likely that taxpayers and prisoners will suffer as a consequence.

*****

However, if anyone thought the situation involving contractor liability was clear after the *McKnight* ruling, they were mistaken. The Court took a very different case in a federal corrections contractor case not long thereafter.

Correctional Services Corporation v. Malesko, 534 U.S. 61 (2001).

INTRODUCTION: This case involved an inmate with a heart condition and other ailments. When the facility management changed the rules and prohibited the residents from using the elevator, Malesko was injured. He sued the contractor.

*****

CHIEF JUSTICE REHNQUIST wrote the opinion for the Court.

We decide here whether the implied damages action first recognized in *Bivens v. Six Unknown Fed. Narcotics Agents,* should be extended to allow recovery against a private corporation operating a halfway house under contract with the Bureau of Prisons. We decline to so extend *Bivens.*

In *Bivens,* we recognized for the first time an implied private action for damages against federal officers alleged to have violated a citizen's constitutional rights. Respondent now asks that we extend this limited holding to confer a right of action for damages against private entities acting under color of federal law. We decline to do so.

Our authority to imply a new constitutional tort, not expressly authorized by statute, is anchored in our general jurisdiction to decide all cases "arising under the Constitution, laws, or treaties of the United States." We first exercised this authority in *Bivens,* where we held that a victim of a Fourth Amendment violation by federal officers may bring suit for money damages against the officers in federal court. [R]elying largely on earlier decisions implying private damages actions into federal statutes, and finding "no special factors counseling hesitation in the absence of affirmative action by Congress," we found an implied damages remedy available under the Fourth Amendment.

In the decade following *Bivens,* we recognized an implied damages remedy under the Due Process Clause of the Fifth Amendment, *Davis v. Passman,* 442 U.S. 228 (1979), and the Cruel and Unusual Punishment Clause of the Eighth Amendment, *Carlson v. Green,* 446 U.S. 14 (1980). In both *Davis* and *Carlson,* we applied the core holding of *Bivens,* recognizing in limited circumstances a claim for money damages against federal officers who abuse their constitutional authority. In *Davis,* we inferred a new right of action chiefly because the plaintiff lacked any other remedy for the alleged constitutional deprivation. In *Carlson,* we inferred a right of action against individual prison officials where the plaintiff's only alternative was a Federal Tort Claims Act (FTCA) claim against the United States. We reasoned that the threat of suit against the United States was insufficient to deter the unconstitutional acts of individuals. We also found it "crystal clear" that Congress intended the FTCA and Bivens to serve as "parallel" and "complementary" sources of liability.

Since *Carlson* we have consistently refused to extend *Bivens* liability to any new context or new category of defendants. In *Bush v. Lucas,* 462 U.S. 367 (1983), we declined to create a *Bivens* remedy against individual Government officials for a First Amendment violation arising in the context of federal employment. In *Schweiker v. Chilicky,* 487 U.S. 412 (1988), we declined to infer a damages action against individual government employees alleged to have violated due process in their handling of Social Security applications.

Most recently, in *FDIC v. Meyer,* we unanimously declined an invitation to extend Bivens to permit suit against a federal agency, even though the agency—because Congress had waived sovereign immunity—was otherwise amenable to suit. Our opinion emphasized that "the purpose of *Bivens* is to deter the officer," not the agency. We reasoned that if given the choice, plaintiffs would sue a federal agency instead of an individual who could assert qualified immunity as an affirmative defense. To the extent aggrieved parties had less incentive to bring a damages claim against individuals, "the deterrent effects of the *Bivens* remedy would be lost." We noted further that "special factors" counseled hesitation in light of the "potentially enormous financial burden" that agency liability would entail.

The purpose of *Bivens* is to deter individual federal officers from committing constitutional violations. *Meyer* made clear that the threat of litigation and liability will adequately deter federal officers for *Bivens* purposes no matter that they may enjoy qualified immunity, are indemnified by the employing agency or entity or are acting pursuant to an entity's policy. *Meyer* also made clear that the threat of suit against an individual's employer was not the kind of deterrence contemplated by *Bivens.* This case is, in every meaningful sense, the same. For if a corporate defendant is available for suit, claimants will focus their collection efforts on it, and not the individual directly responsible for the alleged injury. On the logic of *Meyer,* inferring a constitutional tort remedy against a private entity like CSC is therefore foreclosed.

Respondent claims that even under *Meyer's* deterrence rationale, implying a suit against private corporations acting under color of federal law is still necessary to advance the core deterrence purpose of *Bivens.* He argues that because corporations respond to market pressures and make decisions without regard to constitutional obligations, requiring payment for the constitutional harms they commit is the best way to discourage future harms. That may be so, but it has no relevance to *Bivens,* which is concerned solely with deterring the unconstitutional acts of individual officers.

There is no reason for us to consider extending *Bivens* beyond this core premise here. To begin with, no federal prisoners enjoy respondent's contemplated remedy. If a federal prisoner in a BOP facility alleges a constitutional deprivation, he may bring a *Bivens* claim against the offending individual officer, subject to the defense of qualified immunity. The prisoner may not bring a *Bivens* claim against the officer's employer, the United States or the BOP. With respect to the alleged constitutional deprivation, his only remedy lies against the individual; a remedy *Meyer* found sufficient, and which respondent did not timely pursue. Whether it makes sense to impose asymmetrical liability costs on private prison facilities alone is a question for Congress, not us, to decide.

Inmates in respondent's position also have full access to remedial mechanisms established by the BOP, including suits in federal court for injunctive relief and grievances filed through the BOP's Administrative Remedy Program (ARP). This program provides yet another means through which allegedly unconstitutional actions and policies can be brought to the attention of the BOP and prevented from recurring. And unlike the *Bivens* remedy, which we have never considered a proper vehicle for altering an entity's policy, injunctive relief has long been recognized as the proper means for preventing entities from acting unconstitutionally.

In sum, respondent is not a plaintiff in search of a remedy as in *Bivens* and *Davis.* Nor does he seek a cause of action against an individual officer, otherwise lacking, as in *Carlson.* Respondent instead seeks a marked extension of *Bivens,* to contexts that would not advance *Bivens'* core purpose of deterring individual officers from engaging in unconstitutional wrongdoing. The caution toward extending *Bivens* remedies into any new context, a caution consistently and repeatedly recognized for three decades, forecloses such an extension here.

JUSTICE SCALIA wrote a concurring opinion joined by JUSTICE THOMAS.

In joining the Court's opinion, however, I do not mean to imply that, if the narrowest rationale of *Bivens* did apply to a new context, I would extend its holding. I would not. *Bivens* is a relic of the heady days in which this Court assumed common-law powers to create causes of action—decreeing them to be "implied" by the mere existence of a statutory or constitutional prohibition. [W]e have abandoned that power to invent "implications" in the statutory field. There is even greater reason to abandon it in the constitutional field, since an "implication" imagined in the Constitution can presumably not even be repudiated by Congress. I would limit *Bivens* and its two follow-on cases (*Davis v. Passman* and *Carlson v. Green*) to the precise circumstances that they involved.

JUSTICE STEVENS wrote a dissenting opinion joined by JUSTICE SOUTER, GINSBURG, and BREYER.

In *Bivens,* the Court affirmatively answered the question that it had reserved in *Bell v. Hood:* whether a violation of the Fourth Amendment "by a federal agent acting under color of his authority gives rise to a cause of action for damages consequent upon his unconstitutional conduct." Nearly a decade later, in *Carlson v. Green,* we held that a violation of the Eighth Amendment by federal prison officials gave rise to a *Bivens* remedy despite the fact that the plaintiffs also had a remedy against the United States under the Federal Tort Claims Act (FTCA). We stated: "*Bivens* established that the victims of a constitutional violation by a federal agent have a right to recover damages against the official in federal court despite the absence of any statute conferring such a right."

In subsequent cases, we have decided that a *Bivens* remedy is not available for every conceivable constitutional violation. We have never, however, qualified our holding that Eighth Amendment violations are actionable under *Bivens.* Nor have we ever suggested that a category of federal agents can commit Eighth Amendment violations with impunity.

The parties before us have assumed that respondent's complaint has alleged a violation of the Eighth Amendment. The violation was committed by a federal agent—a private corporation employed by the Bureau of Prisons to perform functions that would otherwise be performed by individual employees of the Federal Government. Thus, the question presented by this case is whether the Court should create an exception to the straightforward application of *Bivens* and *Carlson,* not whether it should extend our cases beyond their "core premise." This point is evident from the fact that prior to our recent decision in *FDIC v. Meyer,* the Courts of Appeals had consistently and correctly held that corporate agents performing federal functions, like human agents doing so, were proper defendants in *Bivens* actions.

Meyer, which concluded that federal agencies are not suable under *Bivens,* does not lead to the outcome reached by the Court today.

*****

ADDITIONAL READINGS

Herman Finer, "Better Government Personnel: America's Next Frontier," 51 *Political Science Quarterly* 569 (1936).

Herman Finer, "Administrative Responsibility in Democratic Government," 1 *Public Administration Rev.* 335 (1941).

Carl Friedrich, "Public Policy and the Nature of Administrative Responsibility," in C. J. Friedrich and E. S. Mason, eds., *Public Policy* (Cambridge, Mass.: Harvard, 1940).

Jeffrey G. Homrig, "*Alden v. Maine*: A New Genre of Federalism Shifts the Balance of Power," 89 *Calif. L. Rev.* 183 (2001).

Herman Schwartz, "The Supreme Court's Federalism: Fig Leaf for Conservatives," 574 *Annals* 119 (2001).

Charles R. Wise, "The Supreme Court's New Constitutional Federalism: Implications for Public Administration," 61 *Public Administration Review* 343 (2001).

6

⚖️

Classic Cases*

hapter 4 of *Public Law and Public Administration, Third Edition* traces the history of public law and administrative law in particular. Of course, that history is filled with many landmark cases rendered over the more than two centuries of American constitutional and administrative development. However, reviewers of this casebook noted that many students come to the study with little or no awareness of some of the most fundamental historical opinions that have shaped the field. This chapter seeks to provide a small set of such cases that take the reader through the basics of judicial review, discussions of federalism, a consideration of the basic congressional authority under the commerce clause, taxing and spending, necessary and proper clauses of Article I of the Constitution, early arguments about sovereign immunity and official liability, and fundamental approaches to the evaluation of executive powers. Readers with more background in this field may find it useful to reread these old cases with an eye toward comparison and contrast with contemporary trends. For example, comparing *Cohens v. Virginia* and *McCulloch v. Maryland* with the *Seminole* opinion in Chapter 5 is an interesting study.

These opinions were edited to highlight the elements of the rulings that have been taken as the foundation for later public law development. Most

---

* Related Material in *Public Law and Public Administration, Third Edition*, Chapter 4.

separate opinions have been eliminated, except where they have come to play a significant role later in history.

JUDICIAL REVIEW, SEPARATION OF POWERS, AND JUDICIAL FEDERALISM

The classic case that established the place of judicial review in American constitutional law was *Marbury v. Madison*. It was followed by rulings in which the Court established its authority to strike down state actions in violation of the U.S. Constitution, *Fletcher v. Peck,* 10 U.S. (6 Cranch) 87 (1810), and to decide appeals from state courts in civil cases, *Martin v. Hunter's Lessee,* 14 U.S. (1 Wheat.) 304 (1816), as well as criminal cases, *Cohens v. Virginia,* 19 U.S. (6 Wheat.) 264 (1821), where federal questions were involved (those presenting U.S. constitutional or national statutory issues). What follows are opinions from *Marbury* and *Cohens.* Beyond the basic judicial review issues, it is important to be alert in reading these cases to the other messages that Marshall was sending about his (and the Court's) view of the Constitution and the nation it created.

NOTE: The citations to these early cases may seem confusing because they contain an extra component. The number and name in parenthesis such as (1 Cranch) refer to the fact that these opinions were originally published by private publishers whose names and volume numbers are still usually provided along with the U.S. reference to the *United States Reports,* which is now the official reporter of U.S. Supreme Court opinions.

Marbury v. Madison, 5 U.S. (1 Cranch) 137 (1803).

INTRODUCTION: This is probably the most famous opinion ever rendered by the United States Supreme Court, and by Chief Justice John Marshall in particular. When the Jeffersonian Republicans ousted the Federalists, led by John Adams, from control of the Congress and the presidency, the battle for the judiciary was obviously an important next front in American politics, and it was hotly contested. The Federalists passed legislation known as the Judiciary Act of 1801, creating a variety of new judgeships, and sought to fill them with partisans as quickly as possible—certainly before Jefferson's administration took office. However, some of the appointments that had been made were not delivered for reasons that were purely accidental. When Secretary of State James Madison took office, he found the undelivered appointments and the Jefferson administration decided not to deliver them.

William Marbury sought an order that Madison be required to turn over his commission as a Justice of the Peace in Washington, D.C. This kind of order is known as a *mandamus* and commands an official to carry out the legal requirements of his or her office. What became more important than the substantive argument about whether Marbury was or was not entitled to the office was the way that the case was litigated. It was brought on original jurisdiction in the U.S. Supreme Court under §13 of the Judiciary Act of 1789, the legislation that created most of what we have since come to know as the federal courts. Unlike the vast majority of cases that come to the Supreme Court on appeal from lower courts, Marbury sought to have the Supreme Court itself consider his plea directly and to issue the order.

In reading the case, it is useful to be aware that John Marshall knew how weak an institution the U.S. Supreme Court had been to that point in the early history of the nation. He also knew that Jefferson and his allies would likely resist a direct order to them, thus suggesting an even further weakening of the Court and its effectiveness.

*****

CHIEF JUSTICE JOHN MARSHALL wrote the opinion for the Court.

The following questions have been considered and decided.

1st Has the applicant a right to the commission he demands?

2nd If he has a right, and that right has been violated, do the laws of his country afford him a remedy?

3rd If they do afford him a remedy, is it a mandamus issuing from this court?

Has the applicant a right to the commission he demands? His right originates in an act of congress passed in February, 1801, concerning the district of Columbia. It appears, from the affidavits, that in compliance with this law, a commission for William Marbury as a justice of peace for the county of Washington, was signed by John Adams, then president of the United States; after which the seal of the United States was affixed to it; but the commission has never reached the person for whom it was made out.[1]

In order to determine whether he is entitled to this commission, it becomes necessary to enquire whether he has been appointed to the office.

The 2d section of the 2d article of the constitution, declares, that "the president shall nominate, and, by and with the advice and consent of the senate, shall appoint ambassadors, other public ministers and consuls, and all other officers of the United States, whose appointments are not otherwise provided for."

This is an appointment by the President, by and with the advice and consent of the senate, and is evidenced by no act but the commission itself. The last act to be

---

1. NOTE: Marshall was fully aware of this fact, since he had been the Secretary of State who had processed the commission.

done by the President is the signature of the commission. The time for deliberations has then passed. He has decided. His judgment, on the advice and consent of the senate concurring with his nomination, has been made, and the officer is appointed.

The commission being signed, the subsequent duty of the secretary of state is prescribed by law, and not to be guided by the will of the President. He is to affix the seal of the United States to the commission, and is to record it. It is a ministerial act which the law enjoins on a particular officer for a particular purpose.[2]

Mr. Marbury, then, since his commission was signed by the President, and sealed by the secretary of state, was appointed; and as the law creating the office, gave the officer a right to hold for five years, independent of the executive, the appointment was not revocable; but vested in the officer legal rights, which are protected by the laws of his country.

To withhold his commission, therefore, is an act deemed by the court not warranted by law, but violative of a vested legal right.

This brings us to the second enquiry; which is, [i]f he has a right, and that right has been violated, do the laws of his country afford him a remedy?

The very essence of civil liberty certainly consists in the right of every individual to claim the protection of the laws, whenever he receives an injury. One of the first duties of government is to afford that protection.

The government of the United States has been emphatically termed a government of laws, and not of men. It will certainly cease to deserve this high appellation, if the laws furnish no remedy for the violation of a vested legal right.

It is then the opinion of the court, 1st That by signing the commission of Mr. Marbury, the president of the United States appointed him a justice of peace, for the county of Washington in the district of Columbia; and that the seal of the United States, affixed thereto by the secretary of state, is conclusive testimony of the verity of the signature, and of the completion of the appointment; and that the appointment conferred on him a legal right to the office for the space of five years. 2nd That, having this legal title to the office, he has a consequent right to the commission; a refusal to deliver which, is a plain violation of that right, for which the laws of his country afford him a remedy.

[I]t only remains to be enquired [w]hether it can issue from this court. The act to establish the judicial courts of the United States authorizes the supreme court "to issue writs of mandamus, in cases warranted by the principles and usages of law, to any courts appointed, or persons holding office, under the authority of the United States."

The secretary of state, being a person holding an office under the authority of the United States, is precisely within the letter of the description; and if this court is not authorized to issue a writ of mandamus to such an officer, it must be because the law is unconstitutional, and therefore absolutely incapable of conferring the authority, and assigning the duties which its words purport to confer and assign.

---

2. NOTE: A ministerial act is one that is mandatory and in which the official involved has no discretion. Thus, the argument here is that once the commission was signed, the Secretary of State was obliged to ensure that the commission was delivered.

The constitution vests the whole judicial power of the United States in one supreme court, and such inferior courts as congress shall, from time to time, ordain and establish. This power is expressly extended to all cases arising under the laws of the United States; and consequently, in some form, may be exercised over the present case; because the right claimed is given by a law of the United States.

In the distribution of this power it is declared that "the supreme court shall have original jurisdiction in all cases affecting ambassadors, other public ministers and consuls, and those in which a state shall be a party. In all other cases, the supreme court shall have appellate jurisdiction."

If it had been intended to leave it to the discretion of the legislature to apportion the judicial power between the supreme and inferior courts according to the will of that body, it would certainly have been useless to have proceeded further than to have defined the judicial powers, and the tribunals in which it should be vested. The subsequent part of the section is mere surplusage, is entirely without meaning, if such is to be the construction. If congress remains at liberty to give this court appellate jurisdiction, where the constitution has declared their jurisdiction shall be original; and original jurisdiction where the constitution has declared it shall be appellate; the distribution of jurisdiction, made in the constitution, is form without substance. It cannot be presumed that any clause in the constitution is intended to be without effect; and therefore such a construction is inadmissible, unless the words require it.

To enable this court then to issue a mandamus, it must be shown to be an exercise of appellate jurisdiction, or to be necessary to enable them to exercise appellate jurisdiction.

It has been stated at the bar that the appellate jurisdiction may be exercised in a variety of forms, and that if it be the will of the legislature that a mandamus should be used for that purpose, that will must be obeyed. This is true, yet the jurisdiction must be appellate, not original.

It is the essential criterion of appellate jurisdiction, that it revises and corrects the proceedings in a cause already instituted, and does not create that cause. Although, therefore, a mandamus may be directed to courts, yet to issue such a writ to an officer for the delivery of a paper, is in effect the same as to sustain an original action for that paper, and therefore seems not to belong to appellate, but to original jurisdiction.

The authority, therefore, given to the supreme court, by the act establishing the judicial courts of the United States, to issue writs of mandamus to public officers, appears not to be warranted by the constitution; and it becomes necessary to enquire whether a jurisdiction, so conferred, can be exercised.

The question, whether an act, repugnant to the constitution, can become the law of the land, is a question deeply interesting to the United States; but, happily, not of an intricacy proportioned to its interest. It seems only necessary to recognize certain principles, supposed to have been long and well established, to decide it.

That the people have an original right to establish, for their future government, such principles as, in their opinion, shall most conduce to their own happiness, is the basis, on which the whole American fabric has been erected. The exercise of this original right is a very great exertion; nor can it, nor ought it to be frequently repeated. The principles, therefore, so established, are deemed fundamental. And as the authority, from which they proceed, is supreme, and can seldom act, they are designed to be permanent.

This original and supreme will organizes the government, and assigns to different departments, their respective powers. It may either stop here; or establish certain limits not to be transcended by those departments.

The government of the United States is of the latter description. The powers of the legislature are defined, and limited; and that those limits may not be mistaken, or forgotten, the constitution is written. The distinction, between a government with limited and unlimited powers, is abolished, if those limits do not confine the persons on whom they are imposed, and if acts prohibited and acts allowed, are of equal obligation. It is a proposition too plain to be contested, that the constitution controls any legislative act repugnant to it; or, that the legislature may alter the constitution by an ordinary act.

Between these alternatives there is no middle ground. The constitution is either a superior, paramount law, unchangeable by ordinary means, or it is on a level with ordinary legislative acts, and like other acts, is alterable when the legislature shall please to alter it.

If the former part of the alternative be true, then a legislative act contrary to the constitution is not law: if the latter part be true, then written constitutions are absurd attempts, on the part of the people, to limit a power, in its own nature illimitable.

Certainly all those who have framed written constitutions contemplate them as forming the fundamental and paramount law of the nation, and consequently the theory of every such government must be, that an act of the legislature, repugnant to the constitution, is void.

If an act of the legislature, repugnant to the constitution, is void, does it, notwithstanding its invalidity, bind the courts, and oblige them to give it effect? Or, in other words, though it be not law, does it constitute a rule as operative as if it was a law?

It is emphatically the province and duty of the judicial department to say what the law is. Those who apply the rule to particular cases, must of necessity expound and interpret that rule. If two laws conflict with each other, the courts must decide on the operation of each.

So if a law be in opposition to the constitution; if both the law and the constitution apply to a particular case, so that the court must either decide that case conformably to the law, disregarding the constitution; or conformably to the constitution, disregarding the law; the court must determine which of these conflicting rules governs the case. This is of the very essence of judicial duty.

If then the courts are to regard the constitution; and the constitution is superior to any ordinary act of the legislature; the constitution, and not such ordinary act, must govern the case to which they both apply.

The judicial power of the United States is extended to all cases arising under the constitution. Could it be the intention of those who gave this power, to say that, in using it, the constitution should not be looked into? That a case arising under the constitution should be decided without examining the instrument under which it arises? This is too extravagant to be maintained.

[I]t is apparent, that the framers of the constitution contemplated that instrument, as a rule for the government of courts, as well as of the legislature. Why otherwise does it direct the judges to take an oath to support it? This oath certainly applies, in an especial manner, to their conduct in their official character. How immoral to impose it on them, if they were to be used as the instruments, and the knowing instruments, for violating what they swear to support!

Why does a judge swear to discharge his duties agreeably to the constitution of the United States, if that constitution forms no rule for his government? if it is closed upon him, and cannot be inspected by him? If such be the real state of things, this is worse than solemn mockery. To prescribe, or to take this oath, becomes equally a crime.

[T]he particular phraseology of the constitution of the United States confirms and strengthens the principle, supposed to be essential to all written constitutions, that a law repugnant to the constitution is void; and that courts, as well as other departments, are bound by that instrument.

*****

Notice that Marshall managed to issue a ruling that provided a strong foundation for an independent judicial, coequal with the executive and legislative branches. He used a strategy that seemed to give his opponents a victory. Marbury did not receive his order from the Supreme Court directing Madison to deliver his commission. In refusing to issue an order Marshall knew would be ignored, the Court left Jefferson with essentially no effective way to win a victory against the Supreme Court. Marshall used the same strategy when Virginia challenged the authority of the U.S. Supreme Court to hear an appeal in a criminal case.

Cohens v. Virginia, 19 U.S. (6 Wheat.) 264 (1821).

INTRODUCTION: Congress adopted legislation delegating authority to govern the District of Columbia on a day-to-day basis to the city government, though, of course, the power to control the District belongs to Congress under the Constitution. The legislation authorized the city as a corporate entity to operate lotteries. The Virginia legislature outlawed the sale of these lottery tickets in the state and the Cohen brothers were arrested and tried for violation of the state law. However, they appealed to the U.S. Supreme Court, claiming that the congressional legislation superceded the state law and the basis for their prosecution was therefore invalid.

Virginia insisted that the U.S. Supreme Court had no jurisdiction to hear an appeal from a state criminal conviction. Chief Justice Marshall and his colleagues, however, were quite prepared to address this issue.

*****

CHIEF JUSTICE MARSHALL wrote the opinion for the Court.

The questions presented to the Court by the two first points made at the bar are of great magnitude, and may be truly said vitally to affect the Union. [Virginia] maintain[s] that the nation does not possess a department capable of restraining peaceably, and by authority of law, any attempts which may be made, by a part, against the legitimate powers of the whole; and that the government is reduced to the alternative of submitting to such attempts, or of resisting them by force. They maintain that the constitution of the United States has provided no tribunal for the final construction of itself, or of the laws or treaties of the nation; but that this power may be exercised in the last resort by the Courts of every State in the Union. That the constitution, laws, and treaties, may receive as many constructions as there are States; and that this is not a mischief, or, if a mischief, is irremediable.

If such be the constitution, it is the duty of the Court to bow with respectful submission to its provisions. If such be not the constitution, it is equally the duty of this Court to say so; and to perform that task which the American people have assigned to the judicial department.

The first question to be considered is, whether the jurisdiction of this Court is excluded by the character of the parties, one of them being a State, and the other a citizen of that State?

The second section of the third article of the constitution defines the extent of the judicial power of the United States. Jurisdiction is given to the Courts of the Union in two classes of cases. In the first, their jurisdiction depends on the character of the cause, whoever may be the parties. This class comprehends "all cases in law and equity arising under this constitution, the laws of the United States, and treaties made, or which shall be made, under their authority." This clause extends the jurisdiction of the Court to all the cases described, without making in its terms any exception whatever, and without any regard to the condition of the party. If there be any exception, it is to be implied against the express words of the article.

In the second class, the jurisdiction depends entirely on the character of the parties. In this are comprehended "controversies between two or more States, between a State and citizens of another State," "and between a State and foreign States, citizens or subjects." If these be the parties, it is entirely unimportant what may be the subject of controversy. Be it what it may, these parties have a constitutional right to come into the Courts of the Union.

The jurisdiction of the Court, then, being extended by the letter of the constitution to all cases arising under it, or under the laws of the United States, it follows that those who would withdraw any case of this description from that jurisdiction, must sustain the exemption they claim on the spirit and true meaning of the constitution, which spirit and true meaning must be so apparent as to overrule the words which its framers have employed.

The American States, as well as the American people, have believed a close and firm Union to be essential to their liberty and to their happiness. They have been taught by experience, that this Union cannot exist without a government for the whole; and they have been taught by the same experience that this government would be a mere shadow, that must disappoint all their hopes, unless invested with portions of that sovereignty which belongs to independent States.

If it could be doubted, whether from its nature, it were not supreme in all cases where it is empowered to act, that doubt would be removed by the declaration, that "this constitution, and the laws of the United States, which shall be made in pursuance thereof, and all treaties made, or which shall be made, under the authority of the United States, shall be the supreme law of the land; and the judges in every State shall be bound thereby; any thing in the constitution or laws of any State to the contrary notwithstanding."

This is the authoritative language of the American people; and, if gentlemen please, of the American States. It marks, with lines too strong to be mistaken, the characteristic distinction between the government of the Union, and those of the States. The general government, though limited as to its objects, is supreme with respect to those objects.

To this supreme government ample powers are confided; and if it were possible to doubt the great purposes for which they were so confided, the people of the United States have declared, that they are given "in order to form a more perfect union, establish justice, ensure domestic tranquillity, provide for the common defence, promote the general welfare, and secure the blessings of liberty to themselves and their posterity."

With the ample powers confided to this supreme government, for these interesting purposes, are connected many express and important limitations on the sovereignty of the States, which are made for the same purposes. [T]he judicial department is authorized to decide all cases of every description, arising under the constitution or laws of the United States. From this general grant of jurisdiction, no exception is made of those cases in which a State may be a party. When we consider the situation of the government of the Union and of a State, in relation to each other; the nature of our constitution; the subordination of the State governments to that constitution; the great purpose for which jurisdiction over all cases arising under the constitution and laws of the United States, is confided to the judicial department; are we at liberty to insert in this general grant, an exception of those cases in which a State may be a party? Will the spirit of the constitution justify this attempt to control its words? We think it will not. We think a case arising under the constitution or laws of the United States, is cognizable in the Courts of the Union, whoever may be the parties to that case.

Had any doubt existed with respect to the just construction of this part of the section, that doubt would have been removed by the enumeration of those cases to which the jurisdiction of the federal Courts is extended, in consequence of the character of the parties. In that enumeration, we find "controversies between two or more States, between a State and citizens of another State," "and between a State and foreign States, citizens, or subjects."

One of the express objects, then, for which the judicial department was established, is the decision of controversies between States, and between a State and individuals. The mere circumstance, that a State is a party, gives jurisdiction to the Court. The constitution gave to every person having a claim upon a State, a right to submit his case to the Court of the nation. However unimportant his claim might be, however little the community might be interested in its decision, the framers of our constitution thought it necessary for the purposes of justice, to provide a tribunal as superior to influence as possible, in which that claim might be decided. Can it be imagined, that the same persons considered a case involving the constitution of our country and the majesty of the laws, questions in which every American citizen must be deeply interested, as withdrawn from this tribunal, because a State is a party?

[T]he judicial power of every well constituted government must be co-extensive with the legislative, and must be capable of deciding every judicial question which grows out of the constitution and laws.

The mischievous consequences of the construction contended for on the part of Virginia would prostrate, it has been said, the government and its laws at the feet of every State in the Union. What power of the government could be executed by its own means, in any State disposed to resist its execution by a course of legislation? The laws must be executed by individuals acting within the several States. If these individuals may be exposed to penalties, and if the Courts of the Union cannot correct the judgments by which these penalties may be enforced, the course of the government may be, at any time, arrested by the will of one of its members. Each member will possess a veto on the will of the whole.

Different States may entertain different opinions on the true construction of the constitutional powers of Congress. We have no assurance that we shall be less divided than we have been. States may legislate in conformity to their opinions, and may enforce those opinions by penalties. It would be hazarding too much to assert, that the judicatures of the States will be exempt from the prejudices by which the legislatures and people are influenced, and will constitute perfectly impartial tribunals. In many States the judges are dependent for office and for salary on the will of the legislature. When we observe the importance which that constitution attaches to the independence of judges, we are the less inclined to suppose that it can have intended to leave these constitutional questions to tribunals where this independence may not exist, in all cases where a State shall prosecute an individual who claims the protection of an act of Congress. How extensive may be the mischief if the first decisions in such cases should be final!

[A] constitution is framed for ages to come, and is designed to approach immortality as nearly as human institutions can approach it. Its course cannot always be tranquil. It is exposed to storms and tempests, and its framers must be unwise statesmen indeed, if they have not provided it with the means of self-preservation from the perils it may be destined to encounter. No government ought to be so defective in its organization, as not to contain within itself the means of securing the execution of its own laws against other dangers than those which occur every day. Courts of justice are the means most usually employed; and it is reasonable to expect that a government should repose on its own Courts, rather than on others. There is certainly nothing in the circumstances under which our constitution was formed; nothing in the history of the times, which would justify the opinion that the confidence reposed in the States was so implicit as to leave in them and their tribunals the power of resisting or defeating, in the form of law, the legitimate measures of the Union.

After bestowing on this subject the most attentive consideration, the Court can perceive no reason founded on the character of the parties for introducing an exception which the constitution has not made; and we think that the judicial power, as originally given, extends to all cases arising under the constitution or a law of the United States, whoever may be the parties.

It has been also contended, that this jurisdiction, if given, is original, and cannot be exercised in the appellate form.

[I]n every case to which the judicial power extends, and in which original jurisdiction is not expressly given, that judicial power shall be exercised in the appellate, and only in the appellate form. The original jurisdiction of this Court cannot be enlarged, but its appellate jurisdiction may be exercised in every case cognizable under the third article of the constitution.

It is most true that this Court will not take jurisdiction if it should not: but it is equally true, that it must take jurisdiction if it should. The judiciary cannot, as the legislature may, avoid a measure because it approaches the confines of the constitution. We cannot pass it by because it is doubtful. We have no more right to decline the exercise of jurisdiction which is given, than to usurp that which is not given. The one or the other would be treason to the constitution. Questions may occur which we would gladly avoid; but we cannot avoid them. All we can do is, to exercise our best judgment, and conscientiously to perform our duty. In doing this, on the present occasion, we find this tribunal invested with appellate jurisdiction in all cases arising under the constitution and laws of the United States. We find no exception to this grant, and we cannot insert one.

We think, then, that, as the constitution originally stood, the appellate jurisdiction of this Court, in all cases arising under the constitution, laws, or treaties of the United States, was not arrested by the circumstance that a State was a party.

2d. The second objection to the jurisdiction of the Court is, that its appellate power cannot be exercised, in any case, over the judgment of a State Court.

This objection is sustained chiefly by arguments drawn from the supposed total separation of the judiciary of a State from that of the Union, and their entire independence of each other. The argument considers the federal judiciary as completely foreign to that of a State; and as being no more connected with it in any respect whatever, than the Court of a foreign State.

That the United States form, for many, and for most important purposes, a single nation, has not yet been denied. In war, we are one people. In making peace, we are one people. In all commercial regulations, we are one and the same people. In many other respects, the American people are one, and the government which is alone capable of controling and managing their interests in all these respects, is the government of the Union. It is their government, and in that character they have no other. American has chosen to be, in many respects, and to many purposes, a nation; and for all these purposes, her government is complete; to all these objects, it is competent. The people have declared, that in the exercise of all powers given for these objects, it is supreme. It can, then, in effecting these objects, legitimately control all individuals or governments within the American territory. The constitution and laws of a State, so far as they are repugnant to the constitution and laws of the United States, are absolutely void. These States are constituent parts of the United States. They are members of one great empire— for some purposes sovereign, for some purposes subordinate.

In a government so constituted, is it unreasonable that the judicial power should be competent to give efficacy to the constitutional laws of the legislature? That department can decide on the validity of the constitution or law of a State, if it be repugnant to the constitution or to a law of the United States. Is it unreasonable that it should also be empowered to decide on the judgment of a State tribunal enforcing such unconstitutional law? Is it so very unreasonable as to furnish a justification for controling the words of the constitution?

We think it is not. We think that in a government acknowledgedly supreme, with respect to objects of vital interest to the nation, there is nothing inconsistent with sound reason, nothing incompatible with the nature of government, in making all its departments supreme, so far as respects those objects, and so far as is necessary to their attainment. The exercise of the appellate power over those judgments of the State tribunals which may contravene the constitution or laws of the United States, is, we believe, essential to the attainment of those objects.

The propriety of entrusting the construction of the constitution, and laws made in pursuance thereof, to the judiciary of the Union, has not, we believe, as yet, been drawn into question. It seems to be a corollary from this political axiom, that the federal Courts should either possess exclusive jurisdiction in such cases, or a power to revise the judgment rendered in them, by the State tribunals. If the federal and State Courts have concurrent jurisdiction in all cases arising under the constitution, laws, and treaties of the United States; and if a case of this description brought in a State Court cannot be removed before judgment, nor revised after judgment, then the construction of the constitution, laws, and treaties of the United States, is not confided particularly to their judicial department, but is confided equally to that department and to the State Courts, however they may be constituted. "Thirteen independent Courts," says a very celebrated statesman, (and we have now more than twenty such Courts,) "of final jurisdiction over the same causes, arising upon the same laws, is a hydra in government, from which nothing but contradiction and confusion can proceed." [Alexander Hamilton, in *The Federalist,* No. 80]

The framers of the constitution would naturally examine the state of things existing at the time; and their work sufficiently attests that they did so. All acknowledge that they were convened for the purpose of strengthening the confederation by enlarging the powers of the government, and by giving efficacy to those which it before possessed, but could not exercise. They inform us themselves, in the instrument they presented to the American public, that one of its objects was to form a more perfect union.

The Convention which framed the constitution, on turning their attention to the judicial power, found it limited to a few objects, but exercised, with respect to some of those objects, in its appellate form, over the judgments of the State Courts. They extend it, among other objects, to all cases arising under the constitution, laws, and treaties of the United States; and in a subsequent clause declare, that in such cases, the Supreme Court shall exercise appellate jurisdiction. Nothing seems to be given which would justify the withdrawal of a judgment rendered in a State Court, on the constitution, laws, or treaties of the United States, from this appellate jurisdiction.

Let the nature and objects of our Union be considered; let the great fundamental principles, on which the fabric stands, be examined; and we think the result must be, that there is nothing so extravagantly absurd in giving to the Court of the nation the power of revising the decisions of local tribunals on questions which affect the nation, as to require that words which import this power should be restricted by a forced construction.

*****

From this excerpt of the opinion, it would appear that the Cohen brothers prevailed in the case. Not true. Once again, the Court made its point about its own authority but did it in a manner that avoided a head-on confrontation with the states. After having established, in no uncertain terms, the authority of the federal courts to hear an appeal in a criminal case, Marshall promptly concluded that Virginia had been well within its authority to prosecute the Cohens. He reasoned that while the Congress had authorized the District of Columbia to hold a lottery, it had said nothing at all about sales of lottery tickets outside the District. "The Corporation was merely empowered to authorize the drawing of lotteries; and the mind of Congress was not directed to any provision for the sale of the tickets beyond the limits of the Corporation." Thus, there was no protection afforded by the congressional statute outside the city.

CONGRESS AND THE STATES

To be sure, the powers of the judiciary were not the only issues argued by the states against the branches of the federal government in the nation's formative period. Even today, most of the federal agencies, policies, and programs are based upon the power to regulate interstate commerce, the taxing and spending powers, and the so-called necessary and proper clause of Article I of the Constitution. The *McCulloch v. Maryland* and *Gibbons v. Ogden* cases provided next were two of the most important statements by the Supreme Court of the breadth and character of the national legislative powers. At the same time, these cases, which consider the nature and scope of the national government, by necessity also speak to the nature and limits of the powers of the states under the American system of federalism.

McCulloch v. Maryland, 17 U.S. (4 Wheat.) 316 (1819).

INTRODUCTION: Article I of the Constitution provided Congress with a host of powers so that it could create and maintain the economic infrastructure of

the nation. What it did not contain was any reference to a central financial institution that could facilitate these efforts at building an economy, as well as a
physical infrastructure such as post roads. Congress created a Bank of the
United States which was ultimately dismantled. However, despite pitched political battles, it seemed clear that such an institution was necessary and the
Second Bank of the United States was created. However, states sought to assert
control over the bank and its officials while simultaneously attacking the
authority of Congress to create it in the first place. One such state was
Maryland.

✳✳✳✳✳

CHIEF JUSTICE JOHN MARSHALL wrote the opinion for the Court.

The first question made in the cause is, has Congress power to incorporate a
bank?

The power now contested was exercised by the first Congress elected under
the present constitution. The original act was permitted to expire; but a short
experience of the embarrassments to which the refusal to revive it exposed the
government, convinced those who were most prejudiced against the measure of
its necessity, and induced the passage of the present law.

In discussing this question, the counsel for the State of Maryland have deemed
it of some importance, in the construction of the constitution, to consider that
instrument not as emanating from the people, but as the act of sovereign and
independent States. The powers of the general government, it has been said, are
delegated by the States, who alone are truly sovereign; and must be exercised in
subordination to the States, who alone possess supreme dominion.

It would be difficult to sustain this proposition. The Convention which
framed the constitution was indeed elected by the State legislatures. But the
instrument, when it came from their hands, was a mere proposal, without obligation, or pretensions to it. It was reported to the then existing Congress of the
United States, with a request that it might "be submitted to a Convention of
Delegates, chosen in each State by the people thereof, under the recommendation
of its Legislature, for their assent and ratification." This mode of proceeding was
adopted; and by the Convention, by Congress, and by the State Legislatures, the
instrument was submitted to the people. They acted upon it in the only manner in
which they can act safely, effectively, and wisely, on such a subject, by assembling
in Convention. It is true, they assembled in their several States—and where else
should they have assembled? But the measures they adopt do not, on that account,
cease to be the measures of the people themselves, or become the measures of the
State governments.

From these Conventions the constitution derives its whole authority. The government proceeds directly from the people; is "ordained and established" in the
name of the people; and is declared to be ordained, "in order to form a more perfect union, establish justice, ensure domestic tranquillity, and secure the blessings of

liberty to themselves and to their posterity." The assent of the States, in their sovereign capacity, is implied in calling a Convention, and thus submitting that instrument to the people. But the people were at perfect liberty to accept or reject it; and their act was final. It required not the affirmance, and could not be negatived, by the State governments. The constitution, when thus adopted, was of complete obligation, and bound the State sovereignties.

The government of the Union, then, is, emphatically, and truly, a government of the people. In form and in substance it emanates from them. Its powers are granted by them, and are to be exercised directly on them, and for their benefit.

This government is acknowledged by all to be one of enumerated powers. The principle, that it can exercise only the powers granted to it, would seem too apparent to have required to be enforced by all those arguments which it enlightened friends, while it was depending before the people, found it necessary to urge. That principle is now universally admitted. But the question respecting the extent of the powers actually granted, is perpetually arising, and will probably continue to arise, as long as our system shall exist.

If any one proposition could command the universal assent of mankind, we might expect it would be this—that the government of the Union, though limited in its powers, is supreme within its sphere of action. It is the government of all; its powers are delegated by all; it represents all, and acts for all. Though any one State may be willing to control its operations, no State is willing to allow others to control them. The nation, on those subjects on which it can act, must necessarily bind its component parts. But this question is not left to mere reason: the people have, in express terms, decided it, by saying, "this constitution, and the laws of the United States, which shall be made in pursuance thereof," "shall be the supreme law of the land," and by requiring that the members of the State legislatures, and the officers of the executive and judicial departments of the States, shall take the oath of fidelity to it.

The government of the United States, then, though limited in its powers, is supreme; and its laws, when made in pursuance of the constitution, form the supreme law of the land, "any thing in the constitution or laws of any State to the contrary notwithstanding."

Among the enumerated powers, we do not find that of establishing a bank or creating a corporation. But there is no phrase in the instrument which, like the articles of confederation, excludes incidental or implied powers; and which requires that every thing granted shall be expressly and minutely described. Even the 10th amendment, which was framed for the purpose of quieting the excessive jealousies which had been excited, omits the word "expressly," and declares only that the powers "not delegated to the United States, nor prohibited to the States, are reserved to the States or to the people;" thus leaving the question, whether the particular power which may become the subject of contest has been delegated to the one government, or prohibited to the other, to depend on a fair construction of the whole instrument. The men who drew and adopted this amendment had experienced the embarrassments resulting from the insertion of this word in the articles of confederation, and probably omitted it to avoid those embarrassments. A constitution, to contain an accurate detail of all the subdivisions of which its great powers will admit, and of all the means by which they may be carried into execution, would partake of the prolixity of a legal code, and could scarcely be embraced by the human mind. Its nature, therefore, requires, that only its great outlines should be marked, its important objects designated, and the minor ingredients which compose those objects be deduced from the nature of the objects themselves. In considering this question, then, we must never forget, that it is a constitution we are expounding.

Although, among the enumerated powers of government, we do not find the word "bank" or "incorporation," we find the great powers to lay and collect taxes; to borrow money; to regulate commerce; to declare and conduct a war; and to raise and support armies and navies. The sword and the purse, all the external relations, and no inconsiderable portion of the industry of the nation, are entrusted to its government. It can never be pretended that these vast powers draw after them others of inferior importance, merely because they are inferior. Such an idea can never be advanced. But it may with great reason be contended, that a government, entrusted with such ample powers, on the due execution of which the happiness and prosperity of the nation so vitally depends, must also be entrusted with ample means for their execution. The power being given, it is the interest of the nation to facilitate its execution. It can never be their interest, and cannot be presumed to have been their intention, to clog and embarrass its execution by withholding the most appropriate means.

It is not denied, that the powers given to the government imply the ordinary means of execution. That, for example, of raising revenue, and applying it to national purposes, is admitted to imply the power of conveying money from place to place, as the exigencies of the nation may require, and of employing the usual means of conveyance.

[T]he constitution of the United States has not left the right of Congress to employ the necessary means, for the execution of the powers conferred on the government, to general reasoning. To its enumeration of powers is added that of making "all laws which shall be necessary and proper, for carrying into execution the foregoing powers, and all other powers vested by this constitution, in the government of the United States, or in any department thereof."

The subject is the execution of those great powers on which the welfare of a nation essentially depends. To have prescribed the means by which government should, in all future time, execute its powers, would have been to change, entirely, the character of the instrument, and give it the properties of a legal code. It would have been an unwise attempt to provide, by immutable rules, for exigencies which, if foreseen at all, must have been seen dimly, and which can be best provided for as they occur.

In ascertaining the sense in which the word "necessary" is used in this clause of the constitution, we may derive some aid from that with which it is associated. Congress shall have power "to make all laws which shall be necessary and proper to carry into execution" the powers of the government. This clause, as construed by the State of Maryland, would abridge, and almost annihilate this useful and necessary right of the legislature to select its means. That this could not be intended, is, we should think, had it not been already controverted, too apparent for controversy. We think so for the following reasons:

1st. The clause is placed among the powers of Congress, not among the limitations on those powers.

2nd. Its terms purport to enlarge, not to diminish the powers vested in the government. It purports to be an additional power, not a restriction on those already granted.

We admit, as all must admit, that the powers of the government are limited, and that its limits are not to be transcended. But we think the sound construction of the constitution must allow to the national legislature that discretion, with respect to the means by which the powers it confers are to be carried into execution, which will enable that body to perform the high duties assigned to it, in the manner most beneficial to the people. Let the end be legitimate, let it be within the scope of the constitution, and all means which are appropriate, which are plainly adapted to that end, which are not prohibited, but consist with the letter and spirit of the constitution, are constitutional.

After the most deliberate consideration, it is the unanimous and decided opinion of this Court, that the act to incorporate the Bank of the United States is a law made in pursuance of the constitution, and is a part of the supreme law of the land.

It being the opinion of the Court, that the act incorporating the bank is constitutional; and that the power of establishing a branch in the State of Maryland might be properly exercised by the bank itself, we proceed to inquire—Whether the State of Maryland may, without violating the constitution, tax that branch?

[T]he constitution and the laws made in pursuance thereof are supreme; they control the constitution and laws of the respective States, and cannot be controlled by them. From this, other propositions are deduced, on the truth or error of which the cause has been supposed to depend. These are, 1st that a power to create implies a power to preserve. 2nd That a power to destroy, if wielded by a different hand, is hostile to, and incompatible with these powers to create and to preserve. 3rd That where this repugnancy exists, that authority which is supreme must control, not yield to that over which it is supreme.

The power of Congress to create, and of course to continue, the bank, was the subject of the preceding part of this opinion; and is no longer to be considered as questionable.

That the power of taxing it by the States may be exercised so as to destroy it, is too obvious to be denied. But taxation is said to be an absolute power, which acknowledges no other limits than those expressly prescribed in the constitution, and like sovereign power of every other description, is trusted to the discretion of those who use it. But the very terms of this argument admit that the sovereignty of the State, in the article of taxation itself, is subordinate to, and may be controlled by the constitution of the United States.

The argument on the part of the State of Maryland, is, not that the States may directly resist a law of Congress, but that they may exercise their acknowledged powers upon it, and that the constitution leaves them this right in the confidence that they will not abuse it.

The people of a State give to their government a right of taxing themselves and their property, and as the exigencies of government cannot be limited, they prescribe no limits to the exercise of this right, resting confidently on the interest of the legislator, and on the influence of the constituents over their representative, to guard then against its abuse. But the means employed by the government of the Union have no such security, nor is the right of a State to tax them sustained by the same theory. Those means are not given by the people of a particular State, not given by the constituents of the legislature, which claim the right to tax them, but by the people of all the States. They are given by all, for the benefit of all—and upon [this] theory, should be subjected to that government only which belongs to all.

It may be objected to this definition, that the power of taxation is not confined to the people and property of a State. It may be exercised upon every object brought within its jurisdiction.

This is true. The sovereignty of a State extends to every thing which exists by its own authority, or is introduced by its permission; but does it extend to those means which are employed by Congress to carry into execution powers conferred on that body by the people of the United States? We think it demonstrable that it does not. Those powers are not given by the people of a single State. They are given by the people of the United States, to a government whose laws, made in pursuance of the constitution, are declared to be supreme. Consequently, the people of a single State cannot confer a sovereignty which will extend over them.

That the power to tax involves the power to destroy; that the power to destroy may defeat and render useless the power to create; that there is a plain repugnance, in conferring on one government a power to control the constitutional measures of another, which other, with respect to those very measures, is declared to be supreme over that which exerts the control, are propositions not to be denied. But all inconsistencies are to be reconciled by the magic of the word CONFIDENCE. Taxation, it is said, does not necessarily and unavoidably destroy. To carry it to the excess of destruction would be an abuse, to presume which, would banish that confidence which is essential to all government.

But is this a case of confidence? Would the people of any one State trust those of another with a power to control the most insignificant operations of their State government?

We know they would not. Why, then, should we suppose that the people of any one State should be willing to trust those of another with a power to control the operations of a government to which they have confided their most important and most valuable interests? In the legislature of the Union alone, are all represented. The legislature of the Union alone, therefore, can be trusted by the people with the power of controlling measures which concern all, in the confidence that it will not be abused.

If we apply the principle for which the State of Maryland contends, to the constitution generally, we shall find it capable of changing totally the character of that instrument. We shall find it capable of arresting all the measures of the government, and of prostrating it at the foot of the States. The American people have declared their constitution, and the laws made in pursuance thereof, to be supreme; but this principle would transfer the supremacy, in fact, to the States.

If the controling power of the States be established; if their supremacy as to taxation be acknowledged; what is to restrain their exercising this control in any shape they may please to give it? Their sovereignty is not confined to taxation.

That is not the only mode in which it might be displayed. The question is, in truth, a question of supremacy; and if the right of the States to tax the means employed by the general government be conceded, the declaration that the constitution, and the laws made in pursuance thereof, shall be the supreme law of the land, is empty and unmeaning declamation.

We are unanimously of opinion, that the law passed by the legislature of Maryland, imposing a tax on the Bank of the United States, is unconstitutional and void.

*****

Gibbons v. Ogden, 22 **U.S. (9 Wheat.) 1 (1824).**

INTRODUCTION: The New York legislature granted exclusive rights to operate steamships in the waters of the state to Robert Livingston and Robert Fulton. These rights were eventually assigned to Aaron Ogden. However, Thomas Gibbons operated a ferry line with two boats, the *Stoudinger* and the *Bellona,* between New Jersey and New York. Gibbons was licensed to operate in the coasting trade under congressional legislation adopted in 1793. Ogden sued Gibbons in New York courts, seeking an injunction to block Gibbons' operations and protect his state-granted rights. The Chancery Court upheld the New York legislation and Ogden's claims under it, and that ruling was affirmed on appeal in the state courts.

*****

CHIEF JUSTICE JOHN MARSHALL wrote the opinion for the Court.

The appellant contends [that] the laws which purport to give the exclusive privilege [held by Ogden], are repugnant to the constitution and laws of the United States. [Specifically, t]hey are said to be repugnant [t]o that clause in the constitution which authorizes Congress to regulate commerce. The State of New York maintains the constitutionality of these laws; and their Legislature, their Council of Revision, and their Judges, have repeatedly concurred in this opinion.

[R]eference has been made to the political situation of these States [before the Constitution]. It has been said, that they were sovereign, were completely independent, and were connected with each other only by a league. This is true. But, when these allied sovereigns converted their league into a government, when they converted their Congress of Ambassadors, deputed to deliberate on their common concerns, and to recommend measures of general utility, into a Legislature, empowered to enact laws on the most interesting subjects, the whole character in which the States appear, underwent a change, the extent of which must be determined by a fair consideration of the instrument by which that change was effected.

This instrument contains an enumeration of powers expressly granted by the people to their government. It has been said, that these powers ought to be construed strictly. But why ought they to be so construed? Is there one sentence in the constitution which gives countenance to this rule? What do gentlemen mean, by a strict construction? If they contend for that narrow construction which, in support of some theory not to be found in the constitution, would deny to the government those powers which the words of the grant import, and which are consistent with the general views and objects of the instrument, then we cannot perceive the propriety of this strict construction, nor adopt it as the rule by which the constitution is to be expounded. We know of no rule for construing the extent of such powers, other than is given by the language of the instrument which confers them, taken in connection with the purposes for which they were conferred.

The words are, "Congress shall have power to regulate commerce with foreign nations, and among the several States, and with the Indian tribes." The subject to be regulated is commerce; and our constitution being, as was aptly said at the bar, one of enumeration, and not of definition, to ascertain the extent of the power, it becomes necessary to settle the meaning of the word. Commerce, undoubtedly, is traffic, but it is something more: it is intercourse. It describes the commercial intercourse between nations, and parts of nations, in all its branches, and is regulated by prescribing rules for carrying on that intercourse.

The word used in the constitution comprehends, and has been always understood to comprehend, navigation within its meaning; and a power to regulate navigation, is as expressly granted, as if that term had been added to the word "commerce."

To what commerce does this power extend? The constitution informs us, to commerce "with foreign nations, and among the several States, and with the Indian tribes." It has, we believe, been universally admitted, that these words comprehend every species of commercial intercourse between the United States and foreign nations. No sort of trade can be carried on between this country and any other, to which this power does not extend. It has been truly said, that commerce, as the word is used in the constitution, is a unit, every part of which is indicated by the term.

The subject to which the power is next applied, is to commerce "among the several States." The word "among" means intermingled with. Commerce among the States, cannot stop at the external boundary line of each State, but may be introduced into the interior.

Comprehensive as the word "among" is, it may very properly be restricted to that commerce which concerns more States than one. The genius and character of the whole government seem to be, that its action is to be applied to all the external concerns of the nation, and to those internal concerns which affect the States generally; but not to those which are completely within a particular State, which do not affect other States, and with which it is not necessary to interfere, for the purpose of executing some of the general powers of the government. The completely internal commerce of a State, then, may be considered as reserved for the State itself.

[T]he power of Congress does not stop at the jurisdictional lines of the several States. It would be a very useless power, if it could not pass those lines. The commerce of the United States with foreign nations, is that of the whole United States. Every district has a right to participate in it. The deep streams which penetrate our country in every direction, pass through the interior of almost every State in the Union, and furnish the means of exercising this right. If Congress has the power to regulate it, that power must be exercised whenever the subject exists. If it exists within the States, if a foreign voyage may commence or terminate at a port within a State, then the power of Congress may be exercised within a State.

We are now arrived at the inquiry—What is this power? It is the power to regulate; that is, to prescribe the rule by which commerce is to be governed. This power, like all others vested in Congress, is complete in itself, may be exercised to its utmost extent, and acknowledges no limitations, other than are prescribed in the constitution.

[I]t has been contended, that if a law passed by a State, in the exercise of its acknowledged sovereignty, comes into conflict with a law passed by Congress in pursuance of the constitution, they affect the subject, and each other, like equal opposing powers.

But the framers of our constitution foresaw this state of things, and provided for it, by declaring the supremacy not only of itself, but of the laws made in pursuance of it. The nullity of any act, inconsistent with the constitution, is produced by the declaration, that the constitution is the supreme law. In every such case, the act of Congress, or the treaty, is supreme; and the law of the State, though enacted in the exercise of powers not controverted, must yield to it.

*****

"NO MAN IS SO HIGH THAT HE IS ABOVE THE LAW": OFFICIAL RESPONSIBILITY AND SOVEREIGN IMMUNITY

The other side of the creation of a powerful national government, as well as the increasingly wide and varied authority asserted by state officials, is the challenge of ensuring responsibility. Chapter 13 of *Public Law and Public Administration, Third Edition* discusses this subject at length (see also Chapter 5 of this book). However, there is one historic opinion that few people have read but that is actually the source of the famous assertion that all are subject to law. In it, the Court provides more than a ruling on immunity and liability. It provides an exploration of the challenges of administrative responsibility.

United States v. Lee, 106 U.S. 196 (1882).

INTRODUCTION: This case, which is the source in American constitutional law of the famous quote that "no man is so high that he is above the law," actually concerned a battle over the right to the land on which Arlington National

Cemetery is located. That land, among other holdings, belonged to George Washington Parke Curtis who left it to his daughter. It is an interesting side note that this daughter was the wife of General Robert E. Lee. The will provided that the land would go to Mrs. Lee but that in the event of her death it would pass to George W.P.C. Lee. However, the U.S. government took possession of the land, known as the Arlington estate, for use as a cemetery and for other purposes. The government acquired the land after it was put up for tax sale following enactment of legislation, passed in 1863, concerned with "collection of direct taxes in the insurrectionary districts within the United States."

Mr. Lee brought suit against Frederick Kaufman and Richard Strong, commissioners in charge of the property for the federal government. While the case was originally filed in a Virginia court, it was promptly removed to the federal circuit court.[3] The U.S. government was not named as a party but the government contested the action against its officials in the case, hence the case was styled *United States v. Lee.*

In this opinion, Justice Miller provided a strong statement distinguishing concepts of sovereign and official immunity in England and those in the United States under the Constitution.

✳✳✳✳✳

JUSTICE MILLER wrote the opinion for the Court.

The counsel for plaintiffs in error and in behalf of the United States assert the proposition, that though it has been ascertained by the verdict of the jury that the plaintiff has the title to the land in controversy, and that what is set up in behalf of the United States is no title at all, the court can render no judgment in favor of the plaintiff against the defendants in the action, because the latter hold the property as officers and agents of the United States, and it is appropriated to lawful public uses.

This proposition rests on the principle that the United States cannot be lawfully sued without its consent in any case, and that no action can be maintained against any individual without such consent, where the judgment must depend on the right of the United States to property held by such persons as officers or agents for the government.

The first branch of this proposition is conceded to be the established law of this country and of this court at the present day; the second, as a necessary or proper deduction from the first, is denied.

There is in this country no such thing as the petition of right, as there is no such thing as a kingly head to the nation, or to any of the States which compose

---

3. NOTE: This is in the days before creation of the United States Circuit Courts of Appeals which established a distinction between U.S. District Courts and Circuit Courts of Appeals.

it.[4] There is vested in no officer or body the authority to consent that the State shall be sued except in the law-making power, which may give such consent on the terms it may choose to impose. Congress has created a court [of claims] in which it has authorized suits to be brought against the United States, but has limited such suits to those arising on contract, with a few unimportant exceptions.

What were the reasons which forbid that the King should be sued in his own court, and how do they apply to the political body corporate which we call the United States of America? As regards the King, one reason given by the old judges was the absurdity of the King's sending a writ to himself to command the King to appear in the King's court. No such reason exists in our government, as process runs in the name of the President, and may be served on the Attorney General. Nor can it be said that the government is degraded by appearing as a defendant in the courts of its own creation, because it is constantly appearing as a party in such courts, and submitting its rights as against the citizen to their judgment.

Under our system the people, who are there called subjects, are the sovereign. Their rights, whether collective or individual, are not bound to give way to a sentiment of loyalty to the person of a monarch. The citizen here knows no person, however near to those in power, or however powerful himself, to whom he need yield the rights which the law secures to him when it is well administered. When he, in one of the courts of competent jurisdiction, has established his right to property, there is no reason why deference to any person, natural artificial, not even the United States, should prevent him from using the means which the law gives him for the protection and enforcement of that right.

What is that right as established by the verdict of the jury in this case? It is the right to the possession of the homestead of plaintiff. A right to recover that which has been taken from him by force and violence, and detained by the strong hand. This right being clearly established, we are told that the court can proceed no further, because it appears that certain military officers, acting under the orders of the President, have seized this estate, and converted one part of it into a military fort and another into a cemetery.

It is not pretended, as the case now stands, that the President had any lawful authority to do this, or that the legislative body could give him any such authority except upon payment of just compensation. The defence stands here solely upon the absolute immunity from judicial inquiry of every one who asserts authority from the executive branch of the government, however clear it may be made that the executive possessed no such power. Not only no such power is given, but it is absolutely prohibited, both to the executive and the legislative, to deprive any one of life, liberty, or property without due process of law, or to take private property without just compensation.

These provisions for the security of the rights of the citizen stand in the Constitution in the same connection and upon the same ground, as they regard

---

4. NOTE: Justice Miller explained that in England the tradition was for those with claims against the government to seek a petition of right that would usually be granted by the king's government allowing the suit to proceed.

his liberty and his property. It cannot be denied that both were intended to be enforced by the judiciary as one of the departments of the government established by that Constitution. As we have already said, the writ of *habeas corpus* has been often used to defend the liberty of the citizen, and even his life, against the assertion of unlawful authority on the part of the executive and the legislative branches of the government.

No man in this country is so high that he is above the law. No officer of the law may set that law at defiance with impunity. All the officers of the government, from the highest to the lowest, are creatures of the law, and are bound to obey it.

It is the only supreme power in our system of government, and every man who by accepting office participates in its functions is only the more strongly bound to submit to that supremacy, and to observe the limitations which it imposes upon the exercise of the authority which it gives.

Courts of justice are established, not only to decide upon the controverted rights of the citizens as against each other, but also upon rights in controversy between them and the government; and the docket of this court is crowded with controversies of the latter class.

Shall it be said, in the face of all this, and of the acknowledged right of the judiciary to decide in proper cases, statutes which have been passed by both branches of Congress and approved by the President to be unconstitutional, that the courts cannot give a remedy when the citizen has been deprived of his property by force, his estate seized and converted to the use of the government without lawful authority, without process of law, and without compensation, because the President has ordered it and his officers are in possession?

If such be the law of this country, it sanctions a tyranny which has no existence in the monarchies of Europe, nor in any other government which has a just claim to well-regulated liberty and the protection of personal rights.

The evils supposed to grow out of the possible interference of judicial action with the exercise of powers of the government essential to some of its most important operations, will be seen to be small indeed compared to this evil, and much diminished, if they do not wholly disappear, upon a recurrence to a few considerations.

One of these, of no little significance, is, that during the existence of the government for now nearly a century under the present Constitution, with this principle and the practice under it well established, no injury from it has come to that government. During this time at least two wars, so serious as to call into exercise all the powers and all the resources of the government, have been conducted to a successful issue. One of these was a great civil war, such as the world has seldom known, which strained the powers of the national government to their utmost tension. In the course of this war persons hostile to the Union did not hesitate to invoke the powers of the courts for their protection as citizens, in order to cripple the exercise of the authority necessary to put down the rebellion; yet no improper interference with the exercise of that authority was permitted or attempted by the courts.

Another consideration is, that since the United States cannot be made a defendant to a suit concerning its property, and no judgment in any suit against an individual who has possession or control of such property can bind or conclude the government already referred to, the government is always at liberty to avail itself of all the remedies which the law allows to every person, natural or artificial, for the vindication and assertion of its rights. Hence, taking the present case as an illustration, the United States may proceed by a bill in chancery to quiet its title [o]r it may bring an action of ejectment, in which the title of the United States could be judicially determined. Or, if satisfied that its title has been shown to be invalid, and it still desires to use the property, or any part of it, for the purposes to which it is now devoted, it may purchase such property by fair negotiation, or condemn it by a judicial proceeding, in which a just compensation shall be ascertained and paid according to the Constitution.

If it be said that the proposition here established may subject the property, the officers of the United States, and the performance of their indispensable functions to hostile proceedings in the State courts, the answer is, that no case can arise in a State court, where the interests, the property, the rights, or the authority of the Federal government may come in question, which cannot be removed into a court of the United States under existing laws. In all cases, therefore, where such questions can arise, they are to be decided, at the option of the parties representing the United States, in courts which are the creation of the Federal government.

The slightest consideration of the nature, the character, the organization, and the powers of these courts will dispel any fear of serious injury to the government at their hands.

While by the Constitution the judicial department is recognized as one of the three great branches among which all the powers and functions of the government are distributed, it is inherently the weakest of them all.

Dependent as its courts are for the enforcement of their judgments upon officers appointed by the executive and removable at his pleasure, with no patronage and no control of the purse or the sword, their power and influence rest solely upon the public sense of the necessity for the existence of a tribunal to which all may appeal for the assertion and protection of rights guaranteed by the Constitution and by the laws of the land, and on the confidence reposed in the soundness of their decisions and the purity of their motives.

From such a tribunal no well-founded fear can be entertained of injustice to the government, or of a purpose to obstruct or diminish its just authority.

The Circuit Court was competent to decide the issues in this case between the parties that were before it; in the principles on which these issues were decided no error has been found; and its judgment is affirmed.[5]

*****

---

5. NOTE: Justice Gray wrote a dissent, joined by Justices Waite, Bradley, and Woods, in which he simply asserted a broad based conception of sovereign immunity to bar any such suit.

THE DELEGATION OF AUTHORITY
UNDER THE CONSTITUTION

Chapter 1 discussed issues of the authority and jurisdiction of federal agencies based upon delegations of authority provided by Congress, or in the states by state legislatures. The two leading historic cases in which the Supreme Court explained the outer limits of permissible delegations are *Panama Refining Co. v. Ryan* and *A.L.A. Schechter Poultry v. United States.*

Panama Refining Co. v. Ryan, 293 U.S. 388 (1935).

INTRODUCTION: When Franklin Delano Roosevelt took office in 1933, the Great Depression had wreaked havoc on the national economy. Businesses demanded that the government do something to stabilize prices and regulate destructive practices in the marketplace in order to restore confidence and provided a foundation for an economic recovery. One of the key administration initiatives in pursuit of these goals was passed by Congress as the National Industrial Recovery Act (NIRA). Among other things, the act allowed industry groups to come together to develop codes of fair competition which were then submitted to the White House. Once the president issued an executive order sanctioning the code, it came to have the force of law under the NIRA. It also allowed the president to take similar action to render state practices, in this case oil quotas, legally binding under federal law, using executive orders as the vehicle of action. Oil sold in excess of these limits was known as "hot oil." Thus, this case is sometimes referred to in constitutional history as the Hot Oil Case.

The facts in this case are complex and even somewhat bizarre. Although the case began when the government took action against an oil company for violating the relevant order, that order was actually changed while the litigation was in progress. Even the government attorneys were confused as to exactly what the state of the law was at various points in the case. In fact, it was this debacle that was instrumental in the passage of the Federal Register Act so that there would be a readily available and properly organized record of official pronouncements by the executive branch.

This opinion, along with the *Schechter Poultry* ruling (which follows this case) are historic examples in which the U.S. Supreme Court struck down administrative authority under the so-called delegation doctrine.

*****

CHIEF JUSTICE CHARLES EVANS HUGHES wrote the opinion for the Court.

On July 11, 1933, the President, by Executive Order, prohibited "the transportation in interstate and foreign commerce of petroleum and the products thereof produced or withdrawn from storage in excess of the amount permitted to be produced or withdrawn from storage by any State law or valid regulation or order prescribed thereunder, by any board, commission, officer, or other duly authorized agency of a State." This action was based on § 9 (c) of Title I of the National Industrial Recovery Act of June 16, 1933. That section provides "(c) The President is authorized to prohibit the transportation in interstate and foreign commerce of petroleum and the products thereof produced or withdrawn from storage in excess of the amount permitted to be produced or withdrawn from storage by any state law or valid regulation or order prescribed thereunder, by any board, commission, officer, or other duly authorized agency of a State. Any violation of any order of the President issued under the provisions of this subsection shall be punishable by fine of not to exceed $1,000, or imprisonment for not to exceed six months, or both."

Section 9 (c) is assailed upon the ground that it is an unconstitutional delegation of legislative power. The section purports to authorize the President to pass a prohibitory law. Assuming for the present purpose, that the Congress has power to interdict the transportation of that excess in interstate and foreign commerce, the question whether that transportation shall be prohibited by law is obviously one of legislative policy. Accordingly, we look to the statute to see whether the Congress has declared a policy with respect to that subject; whether the Congress has set up a standard for the President's action; whether the Congress has required any finding by the President in the exercise of the authority to enact the prohibition.

Section 9 (c) leaves to the States the determination of what production shall be permitted. It does not qualify the President's authority by reference to the basis, or extent, of the State's limitation of production. Section 9 (c) does not state whether, or in what circumstances or under what conditions, the President is to prohibit the transportation of the amount of petroleum or petroleum products produced in excess of the State's permission. It establishes no criterion to govern the President's course. It does not require any finding by the President as a condition of his action. The Congress in §9(c) thus declares no policy as to the transportation of the excess production. So far as this section is concerned, it gives to the President an unlimited authority to determine the policy and to lay down the prohibition, or not to lay it down, as he may see fit. And disobedience to his order is made a crime punishable by fine and imprisonment.

T[he statute's] general outline of policy contains nothing as to the circumstances or conditions in which transportation of petroleum or petroleum products should be prohibited,—nothing as to the policy of prohibiting, or not prohibiting, the transportation of production exceeding what the States allow. The general policy declared is "to remove obstructions to the free flow of interstate and foreign commerce." As to production, the section lays down no policy of limitation. It favors the fullest possible utilization of the present productive capacity of industries. It speaks, parenthetically, of a possible temporary restriction of production, but of what, or in what circumstances, it gives no suggestion. The section also speaks in general terms of the conservation of natural resources, but it prescribes no policy for the achievement of that end.

It is no answer to insist that deleterious consequences follow the transportation of "hot oil,"—oil exceeding state allowances. The Congress did not prohibit that transportation. The Congress did not undertake to say that the transportation of "hot oil" was injurious. The Congress did not say that transportation of that oil was "unfair competition." The Congress did not declare in what circumstances that transportation should be forbidden, or require the President to make any determination as to any facts or circumstances. Among the numerous and diverse objectives broadly stated, the President was not required to choose. The President was not required to ascertain and proclaim the conditions prevailing in the industry which made the prohibition necessary. The Congress left the matter to the President without standard or rule, to be dealt with as he pleased. The [act] permits such a breadth of authorized action as essentially to commit to the President the functions of a legislature rather than those of an executive or administrative officer executing a declared legislative policy. We find nothing in §1 which limits or controls the authority conferred by §9(c).

We pass to the other sections of the Act. Section 2 relates to administrative agencies which may be constituted. Section 3 provides for the approval by the President of "codes" for trades or industries. These are to be codes of "fair competition" and the authority is based upon certain express conditions which require findings by the President. Action under §9(c) is not made to depend on the formulation of a code under §3. In fact, the President's action under §9(c) was taken more than a month before a petroleum code was approved. None of these provisions can be deemed to prescribe any limitation of the grant of authority in §9(c).

The question whether such a delegation of legislative power is permitted by the Constitution is not answered by the argument that it should be assumed that the President has acted, and will act, for what he believes to be the public good. The point is not one of motives but of constitutional authority, for which the best of motives is not a substitute. While the present controversy relates to a delegation to the President, the basic question has a much wider application. If the Congress can make a grant of legislative authority of the sort attempted by §9(c), we find nothing in the Constitution which restricts the Congress to the selection of the President as grantee. The Congress may vest the power in the officer of its choice or in a board or commission such as it may select or create for the purpose. Nor, with respect to such a delegation, is the question concerned merely with the transportation of oil, or of oil produced in excess of what the State may allow. If legislative power may thus be vested in the President, or other grantee, as to that excess of production, we see no reason to doubt that it may similarly be vested with respect to the transportation of oil without reference to the State's requirements. And if that legislative power may be given to the President or other grantee, it would seem to follow that such power may similarly be conferred with respect to the transportation of other commodities in interstate commerce with or without reference to state action, thus giving to the grantee of the power the determination of what is a wise policy as to that transportation, and authority to permit or prohibit it, as the person, or board or commission, so chosen, may think desirable. In that view, there would appear to be no ground for denying a similar prerogative of delegation with respect to other subjects of legislation.

The Constitution provides that "All legislative powers herein granted shall be vested in a Congress of the United States, which shall consist of a Senate and

House of Representatives." Art. I, §1. And the Congress is empowered "To make all laws which shall be necessary and proper for carrying into execution" its general powers. The Congress manifestly is not permitted to abdicate, or to transfer to others, the essential legislative functions with which it is thus vested. Undoubtedly legislation must often be adapted to complex conditions involving a host of details with which the national legislature cannot deal directly. The Constitution has never been regarded as denying to the Congress the necessary resources of flexibility and practicality, which will enable it to perform its function in laying down policies and establishing standards, while leaving to selected instrumentalities the making of subordinate rules within prescribed limits and the determination of facts to which the policy as declared by the legislature is to apply. Without capacity to give authorizations of that sort we should have the anomaly of a legislative power which in many circumstances calling for its exertion would be but a futility. But the constant recognition of the necessity and validity of such provisions, and the wide range of administrative authority which has been developed by means of them, cannot be allowed to obscure the limitations of the authority to delegate, if our constitutional system is to be maintained.

In *Field v. Clark,* [143 U.S. 649 (1892)] the Court emphatically declared that the principle that "Congress cannot delegate legislative power to the President" is "universally recognized as vital to the integrity and maintenance of the system of government ordained by the Constitution."

[A]uthorizations given by Congress to selected instrumentalities for the purpose of ascertaining the existence of facts to which legislation is directed, have constantly been sustained. Moreover, the Congress may not only give such authorizations to determine specific facts but may establish primary standards, devolving upon others the duty to carry out the declared legislative policy, that is, as Chief Justice Marshall expressed it, "to fill up the details" under the general provisions made by the legislature.

So, also, from the beginning of the Government, the Congress has conferred upon executive officers the power to make regulations,—"not for the government of their departments, but for administering the laws which did govern." *United States v. Grimaud,* 220 U.S. 506, 517 (1911). Such regulations become, indeed, binding rules of conduct, but they are valid only as subordinate rules and when found to be within the framework of the policy which the legislature has sufficiently defined. In *Grimaud,* [t]he Court observed that "it was impracticable for Congress to provide general regulations for these various and varying details of management," and that, in authorizing the Secretary of Agriculture to meet local conditions, Congress "was merely conferring administrative functions upon an agent, and not delegating to him legislative power."

[I]n *Hampton & Co. v. United States,* 276 U.S. 394 (1928), the Court said, "If Congress shall lay down by legislative act an intelligible principle to which the person or body authorized to fix such rates is directed to conform, such legislative action is not a forbidden delegation of legislative power."

Thus, in every case in which the question has been raised, the Court has recognized that there are limits of delegation which there is no constitutional authority to transcend. We think that §9(c) goes beyond those limits. [T]he Congress has declared no policy, has established no standard, has laid down no rule. There is no requirement, no definition of circumstances and conditions in which the transportation is to be allowed or prohibited.

If §9(c) were held valid, it would be idle to pretend that anything would be left of limitations upon the power of the Congress to delegate its law-making function. The reasoning of the many decisions we have reviewed would be made vacuous and their distinctions nugatory. Instead of performing its law-making function, the Congress could at will and as to such subjects as it chose transfer that function to the President or other officer or to an administrative body. The question is not of the intrinsic importance of the particular statute before us, but of the constitutional processes of legislation which are an essential part of our system of government.

There is another objection to the validity of the prohibition laid down by the Executive Order under §9(c). The Executive Order contains no finding, no statement of the grounds of the President's action in enacting the prohibition. To hold that he is free to select as he chooses from the many and various objects generally described in the [statute], and then to act without making any finding with respect to any object that he does select, and the circumstances properly related to that object, would be in effect to make the conditions inoperative and to invest him with an uncontrolled legislative power.

We see no escape from the conclusion that the Executive Orders of July 11, 1933, and July 14, 1933, and the Regulations issued by the Secretary of the Interior thereunder, are without constitutional authority.

✻✻✻✻✻

A.L.A. Schechter Poultry v. United States, 295 U.S. 995 (1935).

INTRODUCTION: There were two issues in this classic case. The first involved whether the poultry business that the federal government sought to regulate was in interstate commerce and therefore within the Article I powers of Congress. The second asked whether the delegation of power provided in the National Industrial Recovery Act (NIRA) violated Article I. The excerpt that follows focuses on that second question.

✻✻✻✻✻

CHIEF JUSTICE CHARLES EVANS HUGHES wrote the opinion for the Court.

The question of the delegation of legislative power. We recently had occasion to review the pertinent decisions and the general principles which govern the determination of this question. *Panama Refining Co. v. Ryan.* The Constitution provides that "All legislative powers herein granted shall be vested in a Congress of the United States, which shall consist of a Senate and House of Representatives." And the Congress is authorized "To make all laws which shall be necessary and proper for carrying into execution" its general powers. The Congress is not permitted to abdicate or to transfer to others the essential legislative functions with which it is thus vested. We have repeatedly recognized the necessity of adapting legislation to complex conditions involving a host of details with which the national legislature cannot deal directly. We pointed out in the *Panama Company* case that the Constitution has never been regarded as denying to Congress the necessary resources of flexibility and practicality, which will enable it to perform its function in laying down policies and establishing standards, while leaving to selected instrumentalities the making of subordinate rules within prescribed limits and the determination of facts to which the policy as declared by the legislature is to apply. But we said that the constant recognition of the necessity and validity of such provisions, and the wide range of administrative authority which has been developed by means of them, cannot be allowed to obscure the limitations of the authority to delegate, if our constitutional system is to be maintained.

Accordingly, we look to the statute to see whether Congress has overstepped these limitations—whether Congress in authorizing "codes of fair competition" has itself established the standards of legal obligation, thus performing its essential legislative function, or, by the failure to enact such standards, has attempted to transfer that function to others.

The aspect in which the question is now presented is distinct from that which was before us in the case of the *Panama Company*. There, the subject of the statutory prohibition was defined. National Industrial Recovery Act, §9 (c). That subject was the transportation in interstate and foreign commerce of petroleum and petroleum products which are produced or withdrawn from storage in excess of the amount permitted by state authority. The question was with respect to the range of discretion given to the President in prohibiting that transportation. As to the "codes of fair competition," under §3 of the Act, the question is more fundamental. It is whether there is any adequate definition of the subject to which the codes are to be addressed.

What is meant by "fair competition" as the term is used in [§3 of the] Act? Does it refer to a category established in the law, and is the authority to make codes limited accordingly? Or is it used as a convenient designation for whatever set of laws the formulators of a code for a particular trade or industry may propose and the President may approve (subject to certain restrictions), or the President may himself prescribe, as being wise and beneficent provisions for the government of the trade or industry in order to accomplish the broad purposes of rehabilitation, correction and expansion which are stated in the first section of Title I?

We think the conclusion is inescapable that the authority sought to be conferred by §3 was not merely to deal with "unfair competitive practices" or to create administrative machinery for the application of established principles of law to particular instances of violation. Rather, the purpose is clearly disclosed to authorize new and controlling prohibitions through codes of laws which would embrace what the formulators would propose, and what the President would approve, or prescribe, as wise and beneficent measures for the government of trades and industries in order to bring about their rehabilitation, correction and development, according to the general declaration of policy in section one. Codes of laws of this sort are styled "codes of fair competition."

The Government urges that the codes will "consist of rules of competition deemed fair for each industry by representative members of that industry—by the persons most vitally concerned and most familiar with its problems." But would it be seriously contended that Congress could delegate its legislative authority to trade or industrial associations or groups so as to empower them to enact the laws they deem to be wise and beneficent for the rehabilitation and expansion of their trade or industries? The answer is obvious. Such a delegation of legislative power is unknown to our law and is utterly inconsistent with the constitutional prerogatives and duties of Congress.

The question, then, turns upon the authority which §3 of the Recovery Act vests in the President to approve or prescribe. If the codes have standing as penal statutes, this must be due to the effect of the executive action. But Congress cannot delegate legislative power to the President to exercise an unfettered discretion to make whatever laws he thinks may be needed or advisable for the rehabilitation and expansion of trade or industry.

Such a sweeping delegation of legislative power finds no support in the decisions upon which the Government especially relies. By the Interstate Commerce Act, Congress has itself provided a code of laws regulating the activities of the common carriers subject to the Act, in order to assure the performance of their services upon just and reasonable terms, with adequate facilities and without unjust discrimination. Congress from time to time has elaborated its requirements, as needs have been disclosed. To facilitate the application of the standards prescribed by the Act, Congress has provided an expert body. That administrative agency, in dealing with particular cases, is required to act upon notice and hearing, and its orders must be supported by findings of fact which in turn are sustained by evidence. When the Commission is authorized to issue, for the construction, extension or abandonment of lines, a certificate of "public convenience and necessity," or to permit the acquisition by one carrier of the control of another, if that is found to be "in the public interest," we have pointed out that these provisions are not left without standards to guide determination. The authority conferred has direct relation to the standards prescribed for the service of common carriers and can be exercised only upon findings, based upon evidence, with respect to particular conditions of transportation.

Similarly, we have held that the Radio Act of 1927 established standards to govern radio communications and, in view of the limited number of available broadcasting frequencies, Congress authorized allocation and licenses. The Federal Radio Commission was created as the licensing authority, in order to secure a reasonable equality of opportunity in radio transmission and reception. The authority of the Commission to grant licenses "as public convenience, interest or necessity requires" was limited by the nature of radio communications, and by the scope, character and quality of the services to be rendered and the relative advantages to be derived through distribution of facilities. These standards established by Congress were to be enforced upon hearing, and evidence, by an administrative body acting under statutory restrictions adapted to the particular activity.

To summarize and conclude upon this point: Section 3 of the Recovery Act is without precedent. It supplies no standards for any trade, industry or activity. It does not undertake to prescribe rules of conduct to be applied to particular states of fact determined by appropriate administrative procedure. Section 3 sets up no standards, aside from the statement of the general aims of rehabilitation, correction and expansion described in section one. In view of the scope of that broad declaration, and of the nature of the few restrictions that are imposed, the discretion of the President in approving or prescribing codes, and thus enacting laws for the government of trade and industry throughout the country, is virtually unfettered. We think that the code-making authority thus conferred is an unconstitutional delegation of legislative power.

JUSTICE CARDOZO wrote a concurring opinion that is remembered to this day as some of the strongest language about delegation expressed by a member of the Court.

The delegated power of legislation which has found expression in this code is not canalized within banks that keep it from overflowing. It is unconfined and vagrant. Here in effect is a roving commission to inquire into evils and upon discovery correct them.

[T]here is no unlawful delegation of legislative functions when the President is directed to inquire into such practices and denounce them when discovered. For many years a like power has been committed to the Federal Trade Commission with the approval of this court in a long series of decisions.

But there is another conception of codes of fair competition, their significance and function, which leads to very different consequences, though it is one that is struggling now for recognition and acceptance. By this other conception a code is not to be restricted to the elimination of business practices that would be characterized by general acceptance as oppressive or unfair. It is to include whatever ordinances may be desirable or helpful for the well-being or prosperity of the industry affected. If that conception shall prevail, anything that Congress may do within the limits of the commerce clause for the betterment of business may be done by the President upon the recommendation of a trade association by calling it a code. This is delegation running riot.

✶✶✶✶✶

THE EVALUATION OF EXECUTIVE
CLAIMS TO POWER

The final case for this chapter is one that was, and continues to be, important in terms of the question of how courts are to evaluate the executive branch, specifically presidential claims to power. The approach taken by Justice Black commanded a majority of the Court and resulted in a defeat for President Truman's assertion of authority to seize steel mills during a labor dispute. Although Justice Jackson concurred, his quite different approach is the one that prevails today.

Youngstown Sheet & Tube v. Sawyer, 343 U.S. 579 (1952).

INTRODUCTION: In the years following World War II, President Truman sought to guide the nation through economic recovery. However, unlike the war years, neither labor nor management was in a mood to sacrifice or to wait any longer to receive what it demanded. Management contended that its profits had been kept artificially low and unions answered that they had sacrificed their wage needs to the war efforts.

As if all of that were not complex enough, there were three other complicating factors. The country was committed to assisting in the rebuilding of Europe and redevelopment in Japan. Later, the nation found itself once again at war, this time in Korea. Finally, in enacting critical labor legislation known as the Taft-Hartley Act, Congress had refused to authorize the president to seize facilities during labor disputes to keep them running, though the statute did not contain a specific prohibition.

When labor and management in the steel industry came to an impasse, the stage was set for a strike. The union voluntarily delayed, pending a study by the Federal Wage Stabilization Board. Management refused recommendations for pay increases and requests that it limit price increases, given inflation dangers and government obligations. President Truman issued an executive order, directing the Secretary of Commerce to seize the mills and keep them operating. The companies challenged the president's authority.

Justice Black wrote for the Court, setting forth what was, for many years, the controlling standard for evaluating the exercise of executive power. The concurring opinion by Justice Jackson provided what has since become the controlling standard, at least since the Court's ruling in *Dames & Moore v. Regan,* 453 U.S. 654 (1981), the case growing out of the settlement of the Iran Hostage crisis in which both Carter and Reagan participated.

*****

JUSTICE BLACK wrote the opinion for the Court.

We are asked to decide whether the President was acting within his constitutional power when he issued an order directing the Secretary of Commerce to take possession of and operate most of the Nation's steel mills.

The President's power, if any, to issue the order must stem either from an act of Congress or from the Constitution itself. There is no statute that expressly authorizes the President to take possession of property as he did here. Nor is there any act of Congress to which our attention has been directed from which such a power can fairly be implied. Indeed, we do not understand the Government to rely on statutory authorization for this seizure.

Moreover, the use of the seizure technique to solve labor disputes in order to prevent work stoppages was not only unauthorized by any congressional enactment; prior to this controversy, Congress had refused to adopt that method of settling labor disputes. When the Taft-Hartley Act was under consideration in 1947, Congress rejected an amendment which would have authorized such governmental seizures in cases of emergency. Instead, the plan sought to bring about settlements by use of the customary devices of mediation, conciliation, investigation by boards of inquiry, and public reports. In some instances temporary injunctions were authorized to provide cooling-off periods. All this failing, unions were left free to strike after a secret vote by employees as to whether they wished to accept their employers' final settlement offer.

It is clear that if the President had authority to issue the order he did, it must be found in some provision of the Constitution. And it is not claimed that express constitutional language grants this power to the President. The contention is that presidential power should be implied from the aggregate of his powers under the Constitution. Particular reliance is placed on provisions in Article II which say that "The executive Power shall be vested in a President . . ."; that "he shall take Care that the Laws be faithfully executed"; and that he "shall be Commander in Chief of the Army and Navy of the United States."

The order cannot properly be sustained as an exercise of the President's military power as Commander in Chief of the Armed Forces. The Government attempts to do so by citing a number of cases upholding broad powers in military commanders engaged in day-to-day fighting in a theater of war. Such cases need not concern us here. Even though "theater of war" be an expanding concept, we cannot with faithfulness to our constitutional system hold that the Commander in Chief of the Armed Forces has the ultimate power as such to take possession of private property in order to keep labor disputes from stopping production. This is a job for the Nation's lawmakers, not for its military authorities.

Nor can the seizure order be sustained because of the several constitutional provisions that grant executive power to the President. In the framework of our Constitution, the President's power to see that the laws are faithfully executed refutes the idea that he is to be a lawmaker. The Constitution limits his functions in the lawmaking process to the recommending of laws he thinks wise and the vetoing of laws he thinks bad. And the Constitution is neither silent nor equivocal about who shall make laws which the President is to execute. The first section of the first article says that "All legislative Powers herein granted shall be vested in a Congress of the United States. . . ."

The President's order does not direct that a congressional policy be executed in a manner prescribed by Congress—it directs that a presidential policy be executed in a manner prescribed by the President. The power of Congress to adopt such public policies as those proclaimed by the order is beyond question. It can authorize the taking of private property for public use. It can make laws regulating the relationships between employers and employees, prescribing rules designed to settle labor disputes, and fixing wages and working conditions in certain fields of our economy. The Constitution does not subject this lawmaking power of Congress to presidential or military supervision or control.

It is said that other Presidents without congressional authority have taken possession of private business enterprises in order to settle labor disputes. But even if this be true, Congress has not thereby lost its exclusive constitutional authority to make laws necessary and proper to carry out the powers vested by the Constitution "in the Government of the United States, or any Department or Officer thereof."

The Founders of this Nation entrusted the lawmaking power to the Congress alone in both good and bad times. It would do no good to recall the historical events, the fears of power and the hopes for freedom that lay behind their choice. Such a review would but confirm our holding that this seizure order cannot stand.

JUSTICE JACKSON wrote a concurring opinion.[6]

That comprehensive and undefined presidential powers hold both practical advantages and grave dangers for the country will impress anyone who has served as legal adviser to a President in time of transition and public anxiety. The opinions of judges, no less than executives and publicists, often suffer the infirmity of confusing the issue of a power's validity with the cause it is invoked to promote, of confounding the permanent executive office with its temporary occupant. The tendency is strong to emphasize transient results upon policies—such as wages or stabilization—and lose sight of enduring consequences upon the balanced power structure of our Republic.

The actual art of governing under our Constitution does not and cannot conform to judicial definitions of the power of any of its branches based on isolated clauses or even single Articles torn from context. While the Constitution diffuses power the better to secure liberty, it also contemplates that practice will integrate the dispersed powers into a workable government. It enjoins upon its branches separateness but interdependence, autonomy but reciprocity. Presidential powers are not fixed but fluctuate, depending upon their disjunction or conjunction with those of Congress. We may well begin by a somewhat over-simplified grouping of practical situations in which a President may doubt, or others may challenge, his powers, and by distinguishing roughly the legal consequences of this factor of relativity.

1. When the President acts pursuant to an express or implied authorization of Congress, his authority is at its maximum, for it includes all that he possesses in his own right plus all that Congress can delegate. A seizure executed by the President pursuant to an Act of Congress would be supported by the strongest of presumptions and the widest latitude of judicial interpretation, and the burden of persuasion would rest heavily upon any who might attack it.

2. When the President acts in absence of either a congressional grant or denial of authority, he can only rely upon his own independent powers, but there is a zone

---

6. NOTE: Justices Frankfurter, Douglas, and Clark all filed concurring opinions. Chief Justice Vinson wrote a dissenting opinion joined by Justices Reed and Minton. The truly important separate opinion is the concurring opinion prepared by Justice Jackson which provides an alternative framework for the analysis of executive power and one that has since been adopted by the Court. See *Dames & Moore v. Regan,* 453 U.S. 654 (1981).